AN
INTRODUCTION
TO
EDUCATIONAL
RESEARCH

AN INTRODUCTION TO EDUCATIONAL RESEARCH

FOURTH EDITION

ROBERT M. W. TRAVERS

Western Michigan University

MACMILLAN PUBLISHING CO., INC.
New York

COLLIER MACMILLAN PUBLISHERS
London

Copyright © 1978, Macmillan Publishing Co., Inc.

Printed in the United States of America

All rights reserved. No part of this book may be reproduced or transmitted in any form or by any means, electronic or mechanical, including photocopying, recording, or any information storage and retrieval system, without permission in writing from the Publisher.

Earlier editions © 1958 and 1964 by Macmillan Publishing Co., Inc., and copyright © 1969 by Robert M. W. Travers.

Macmillan Publishing Co., Inc.
866 Third Avenue, New York, New York 10022

Collier Macmillan Canada, Ltd.

Library of Congress Cataloging in Publication Data

Travers, Robert Morris William, (date)
    An introduction to educational research.

    Bibliography: p.
    Includes indexes.
    1. Educational research.   I. Title.
LB1028.T7   1978   370'.78   77-4234
ISBN 0-02-421370-5

Printing: 1 2 3 4 5 6 7 8   Year: 8 9 0 1 2 3 4

PREFACE

Educational research is approaching a stage in its development at which its accomplishments can be seen in historical perspective. Educational research is a relatively new enterprise compared with research in other areas and is, indeed, so new that a picture is only now slowly emerging of what it can or cannot accomplish. When I wrote the first edition of this book twenty years ago, the central message had to be one of hope Educational research, I believed, could accomplish much if only it were given a chance. The message of a large portion of this edition is that research has had substantial impact on education, although much research has had little or no impact. Since the first edition of this book was written, the pattern of influence of research on education has become sufficiently evident to provide a general picture of the kind of research enterprise that is likely to influence the schools in the future. Twenty years is a major part of the total historical time during which research has played a role in education.

The educational research worker of today comes to his work with a rich knowledge of the successes and failures of previous generations of researchers. He cannot disregard the work that was done in the past, for previous work may tell him what can be successful and what cannot. For this reason, much of the discussion of educational research in this volume is presented in historical context. One cannot discuss the techniques of educational research in a vacuum, so a sizable part of this book discusses the achievements and failures of research in areas related to education and how these achievements and failures have had an impact on educational practice over the last fifty years.

Research has influenced education in three major ways. The main impact has been through the influence research has had on the development of materials. For this reason large sections of the book are concerned with this impact, which will continue into the future. A second source of influence of research has been in providing conceptions of the nature of the human learner that have been incorporated into philosophies of education. For example, during the past twenty-five years the influence of an operant type of behaviorism, for good or for bad, has been particularly marked. At the present time the assumptions of Jean Piaget are beginning to influence the way in which education is viewed, and may well dominate education as the influence of operant psychology wanes.

A third way in which research can influence education is by providing means of solving persistent educational problems. Teachers have long hoped that research would provide them with a repertoire of simple techniques that would enable them to cope with daily problems. No simple set of problem-solving techniques has ever emerged, nor is one likely to emerge. Although research cannot provide specific remedies, it can provide broad general principles that will help the teacher cope effectively with many problems and aid the curriculum developer to produce more useful materials.

In addition to the different impacts of research on education that have been mentioned, the technology of research has had an impact on administrative practices. For example, modern actuarial methods permit the prediction of future school enrollments with far greater accuracy than was possible with the crude methods of the past. Survey techniques permit fact finding in relation to policymaking at a much higher level of sophistication than was previously possible. Such applications of research techniques do not produce educational revolutions, as some aspects of scientific research may well do, but they do provide some assistance to school administrators. Probably most of those who say that they are engaged in educational research are occupied with such fact-finding tasks. Although the focus of this book is on scientific research related to education that really makes a sweeping difference, research at lower levels cannot be ignored for it too plays an important part in educational administration. Many courses in educational research give the student a glimpse only of the application of research techniques to the handling of administrative matters. My hope is that this book will give the student a broader view of what scientific research can accomplish in relation to education.

I hope that the message of this book is that research has had a vital impact on education. Those who cannot see this impact are generally looking for cookbook solutions to problems and cookbook solutions do not emerge from research in most fields. Although the primary message is a positive one, there is also the secondary message that research has also been misapplied in education. All those who claim that they have scientific knowledge of value to education do not necessarily have such knowledge. Psychology, as a discipline, has had a history of overgeneralizing from too little data. History has taught us little, for the tendency is as apparent today as it was during the wave of enthusiasm for Watson's behaviorism of the 1920s. I hope that a sufficient number of examples of the misuse of research are cited in this book to make the student wary of researchers who claim to have answers to some of the most pressing educational problems.

The discussion of techniques of educational research has been reserved for the last section of the book, because techniques cannot be discussed profitably until the reader has acquired an understanding of the aspects of education that can be influenced by research. The review of educational research in the second part of the book provides a sample of the accomplishments and failures of research workers. This review of educational research is not intended to be a comprehensive one, but it does present what I consider to be some of the highlights. Many worthwhile contributions have been made that receive no mention, but only so much can be presented in a book of this kind and the knowledge of the author is also limited. Omission of a particular line of research does not necessarily mean that it was judged as being unworthy of mention.

R. M. W. T.

CONTENTS

PART II
THE ACHIEVEMENTS AND LIMITATIONS OF EDUCATIONAL RESEARCH

5
Research as It Relates to the Design and Use of Classroom Materials

6
Research as It Relates to Development and Learning and Its Impact on Education

13

14

PART I
EDUCATIONAL RESEARCH AS A SCIENCE OF BEHAVIOR

CHAPTER 1
The History of Educational Research

During the last century the use of the term *research* has expanded to cover an ever increasing range of activities. Although the term originally referred to activities related to the acquisition of basic knowledge in the sciences, humanities, and arts, its contemporary usage permits it to be applied to the acquisition of any form of information however trivial that information may be. There has been a further expansion of the usage of the term, as when it is used to denote an organization whose activity is only remotely related to inquiry. Thus, during the earlier part of this century, colleges of education, throughout the country, developed research bureaus. These were not bureaus that undertook research in any classical sense of the term and, indeed, one may have difficulty in finding out what these bureaus ever did. They left behind no publications or scholarly works. They did not develop young students who developed into great research workers, as Rutherford did in the history of atomic physics. Nor did they have any impact on the development of educational practice. Some of their enterprises were not far short of being intellectual disasters. They were quite unable to attract the research workers that were to have some impact on education. The names of their directors do not even find a place in the footnotes of books on the history of education, which makes one wonder what these individuals actually did.

The bureaus of educational research, founded in the early part of the century, seem to have been bases from which professors performed many service functions to schools. They conducted surveys of school facilities. They provided consultative services to schools on such matters as curriculum development. They helped school systems make projections of future enrollments and future building and staff needs. They performed most of the functions that school consultative services provide today. To some degree they were concessions for business, and organizations through which faculty could make extra pay, often amounting to small fortunes. Indeed, these bureaus were, more than anything else, business enterprises to which the term *research* had been applied to give the organization prestige and to justify its existence before the board of trustees or state legislature.

These bureaus not only undertook no research but also gave educational research a bad name. Eventually inquiring minds began to ask whether

3

these bureaus had produced any findings of importance. Of course, they had not, and the conclusion was likely to have been drawn that educational research workers either did not know what they were doing or that educational research was not the way to improve education. Bureaus of educational research did much to give educational research a bad name before extensive educational research had even started. In addition, all too often the doctoral dissertations, sponsored by such enterprises, were nothing short of disgraces.

Although bureaus of educational research up until about 1950 had made virtually no worthwhile contributions to the development of knowledge about education, important knowledge was being produced elsewhere. Institutionalized educational research had been a failure, but there were a few individuals whose work was to become almost a model of how scientific research can influence education. In the first quarter of the century, no single person had more influence in this respect than Edward L. Thorndike.

The young Thorndike had been a student at Harvard where he had come under the spell of William James. A close relationship grew between James and Thorndike, perhaps because James realized that he was no experimentalist and he must have seen in the young Thorndike someone who had the qualities he lacked. Thorndike could find no place on the Harvard campus where he could keep his experimental animals, so James permitted him to keep his animals in the James' basement, much to the delight of James' children. Thorndike's doctoral dissertation became a classic study of learning and is still cited. It was, indeed, one of the first American systematic experimental studies of animal learning, and created a whole new line of research that is still flourishing today.

Fortunately for education, the young Thorndike's interest in the study of learning came to the attention of perhaps the most influential psychologist of that age, James McKeen Cattell. As the main promoter of the behavioral sciences in his day, Cattell had no rival. He had the vision to see that behavioral sciences would have an important part to play in education in the future, and he was able to persuade Teachers College of Columbia University to employ the young Thorndike as a person who might develop a science of learning within an educational context. Thorndike was given an attic at Teachers College where he kept his animals, but he soon turned his attention to human learning.

Thorndike, like some of his contemporaries who sought to change edution through research, pursued the traditional role of the laboratory scientist. Thorndike did not visit schools and his contacts with teachers were minimal. He saw himself as a scientist, working in a laboratory, and able to undertake research that would have implications for education. Occasionally, he did have his assistants collect data from schools, but that was unusual. He believed that his work was like that of the chemist who works in his laboratory, learns how to produce particular effects, and then expects the results to be applied, but not necessarily by himself.

One of the most lasting contributions of Thorndike's laboratory research to schools was the emphasis it placed on providing the learner with knowledge of how he was doing, or what Thorndike called rewards and later psychologists called reinforcements. The related law, which Thorndike referred to as the *law of effect,* was later rewritten by Skinner in slightly different language and given the name of the law of reinforcement. Thorndike's emphasis on the law of effect had impact, because all too often children in schools were given little information about how they were doing and what they were doing right and what they were doing wrong. Thorndike did not emphasize any need for rapid reinforcement in human learning, as Skinner erroneously did many years later.

Thorndike's influence on education came mainly through the impact he had on educational materials, though some of the ideas he derived from research had widespread impact. An example of the latter is the finding, derived from his early research, that what a pupil learned in one situation was not easily generalized to other situations. This finding struck a blow at the age-old doctrine that a few difficult school subjects, such as Latin and mathematics, could provide general training for the mind. The results of Thorndike's famous research on transfer of training was taken by educators to imply that one could not generally expect much transfer, and that whatever was to be learned should be learned directly. Thus, there was little point in learning Latin in the hope that it would help build English vocabulary by sensitizing the pupil to the roots of words. English vocabulary could be more efficiently built by giving the pupil the opportunity to expand his vocabulary by reading and by being exposed to teachers who would slowly introduce new words. Thorndike's work produced radical changes in the school curriculum because they showed that there were no school subjects that had any magical powers for training the mind.

Thorndike's work on word counts had some of the most important consequences for education of any of his accomplishments. The most direct outcome of this work was that it provided a new way for developing dictionaries. Earlier lexicographers had not thought of producing dictionaries for particular groups, and the only basis they had for including one word rather than another in a dictionary was their personal judgment. Thorndike found out how frequently words occurred in printed matter, and used these frequencies for deciding whether a word should, or should not, be included in a dictionary designed for elementary school children. On this basis Thorndike produced his *Junior Dictionary,* which became an immediate publishing success and made Thorndike a wealthy man.

Word counts were used to determine how difficult each word was in a particular textbook designed for children, and the vocabulary level could be adjusted by taking out the more difficult words. Thorndike did this in an attempt to make literature more readable for children, and he revised many of the classics of literature in a special series for the elementary school. This led Thorndike to realize that the level of reading difficulty of a piece of prose was much more than a matter of the vocabulary that was included in it. More comprehensive measures of reading difficulty were needed and Thorndike, in cooperation with Lorge, developed such measures (Lorge and Thorndike, 1940).

Thorndike also wrote books that provided teachers with a theoretical framework for the teaching of arithmetic and algebra, and certain aspects of English, such as the teaching of suffixes. However, these books did not have the lasting impact that his work in other areas had. Thorndike also brought from his experiences on army testing during World War I enthusiasm for the development of measures of intelligence. But this work did not have lasting impact, perhaps because it was so much colored by the prejudices of his generation that held that certain classes were genetically superior to other classes and that certain groups of immigrants were superior to other groups. One might here note that Congress passed a series of acts, beginning with the Emergency Quota Act of 1921, which had the effect of reducing the immigration to the United States of groups who were considered to be inferior, and that these acts were based on the testimony of psychologists. Thorndike was convinced that the measures of intelligence that he had developed measured mainly an innate characteristic and that such tests could be used to identify genetically superior individuals at an early age. Even great men may misapply their research, often with grave social consequences.

Nevertheless, the age of Thorndike did produce some worthwhile contributions to education that were derived from the use of tests. For example, Lewis Terman (1931) undertook his classic studies of gifted children, which provided many findings of the greatest importance to teachers. Terman was able to show that gifted children were not odd, peculiar, or neurotic. Indeed, these children seemed to adjust as well, if not better, in social situations as did average children. Teachers had long held the prejudice that the gifted children were queer, unreliable, and unable to relate well to others. Terman improved the relationship between the teacher and the gifted children by showing that one might expect such a relationship to be a comfortable and easy one. Not all of the contributions of Terman were on the same solid ground. Indeed, his sponsorship of the English version of Binet's famous intelligence tests has remained controversial.

Long before Thorndike had finished making his classic contributions to education, a new generation had begun to provide ideas that were to have an impact on education. This new generation, although it is now beyond retirement age, is perhaps still too close to us, in time, for us to be able to fully evaluate the lasting contribution it made to the progress of education. The generation that followed Thorndike and Terman includes such names as Sidney Pressey, B. Frederick Skinner, and Jean Piaget. If one places aside the issue of whether their contributions will be transitory or lasting, one can see that all three of these individuals have had an impact on education. Their histories bear clear testimony to the fact that the research worker does have an impact on education. Pressey will go down in the history of education as the individual who first promoted the idea of developing mechanical devices for teaching. The earliest devices of this kind were designed to be gadgets that would test as well as teach, and would also provide immediate feedback concerning the correctness of the answers. Pressey first built these devices for the U.S. Navy, but he saw that they had potential for use in the nation's schools. Pressey did not want to see education as a mechanized form of activity. In fact, Pressey had been a strong supporter of the Progressive Education Movement of the 1930s, and was one of the first to write a textbook on educational psychology that attempted to provide support for the movement from psychological research related to education. He saw his machines as contributing to a program for self-teaching, perhaps as a device that pupils might turn to, from time to time, for mastering some of the more routine aspects of their studies.

Skinner's impact on education is by far the most difficult to appraise at this time. Of all contributions mentioned in this chapter, his is the most controversial. Skinner's grand entrée into the field of education came with his reinvention of Pressey's teaching machines. When Skinner proposed to use teaching machines, he was quite unaware that Pressey had already attempted to use them. Oddly enough, Skinner seems to have reinvented teaching machines for the wrong reason. Skinner visited classrooms and was appalled at the lack of immediate reinforcements for the students. He was appalled because he believed, as had Thorndike before him, that frequent positive reinforcement of learning was essential for efficiency. Skinner also believed, erroneously, that in human verbal learning, immediacy of reinforcement was also crucial. We now know that immediacy of reinforcement is not only not crucial but that delayed reinforcements are often more effective than immediate reinforcements. Nevertheless, even at this late date, twenty years later, Skinner and his followers do not seem to have modified their position with respect to this issue.

In many ways Skinner's operant psychology was a close relative of Thorndike's connectionist psychology. Both Skinner and Thorndike emphasized the need for feedback in school learning. Both saw that the nature of the materials was crucial in determining the efficiency of learning. Thorndike emphasized the control of the language factor. He recognized, in the case of mathematics, that skills had to be learned in a particular order. Skinner revived a notion, dear to the scholastics of 1,000 years ago, that all learning involved a hierarchy of knowledge and skill. For the teacher of the Middle Ages, this had been a matter of crucial importance. The catechism was an attempt to order subject matter in some "best" order. Skinner revived this issue and proposed producing modern versions of the school catechism, which he called learning programs. These materials were first developed as materials to be used with teaching machines, but later the programmed text made it possible to use materials of the same format, without the use of machines.

At the present time, the use of the programmed text and the teaching machine does not seem to have established itself as a part of the school materials. No convincing evidence has come forward to show that such materials are particularly effective and, since they cost more than other forms of materials, their use has declined since 1960. Certainly, these machines have not produced the manyfold increase in rate of learning that their original promoters claimed they would produce. A part of the lack of promise of these materials may well be that those who write them seem to be devoid of any literary talent whatsoever. The resulting product is, then, drab, pedantic, and humorless. The human primate likes to learn in a playful way, but programmed materials are as dull as their ancestors, the catechism. Perhaps a new generation of writers of such materials may sometime emerge who will understand that materials for children have to have artistic and literary qualities. The materials that are at present available in the programmed format are as thrilling to read as the sets of instructions that accompany manufactured articles that have to be assembled by consumers.

The operant psychology of Skinner seems to have made an easy, though probably transitory, impact on education because his position with respect to behavior is closely tied to the American culture. Although Skinner interprets human culture as following the same laws that he believes characterize animal behavior, another way of looking at operant psychology is possible. Some of the less kind critics of Skinner think that he looked at his experimental rats and pigeons and saw them as behaving in terms of the laws of behavior that characterize individuals living in a capitalist society. Such individuals are believed by the owners of industry to be controlled by the reward system, or by reinforcements, as Skinner would say. Thus, by manipulating the reward system, it is possible to move individuals from one industry to another, from one location to another, and so forth. Whoever controls the reward system is believed to control behavior in a free capitalist system. Skinner sees himself as exercising the same kind of control over his pigeons and rats as the influential capitalist exercises over those who work for him. Rats, of course, do not bargain collectively with experimenters, but collective bargaining is simply a complex way of maximizing reinforcements. Just as influential capitalists are coming to realize that there is more to a worker's life than wages, psychologists who are critical of Skinner, emphasize that there is more to learning than merely the manipulation of reinforcements.

Operant psychologists found an ally in their program to change education in a movement started by Ralph Tyler in the 1930s at Ohio State University. Tyler had been given an appointment at Ohio State for the purpose of introducing effective ways of evaluating new trends in education that were under investigation at the university. Tyler saw that what had been accomplished up to the time of his appointment had been almost worthless for a very simple reason. The newer trends in education had such vague goals that one could not determine, by any means, whether these goals were or were not achieved. For example, all school programs that claimed to be a part of what was called progressive education in the 1930s, took the position that "critical thinking" was an outcome of crucial importance. There was little argument on that point. However, there was argument concerning what was meant by critical thinking. One vague definition after another was proposed, but these definitions were wholly inadequate for establishing evaluation procedures that might discover whether the objective was, or was not, achieved. The young Tyler saw that the first step that had to be undertaken was to define what was meant by critical thinking. He saw that this had to be done by identifying the particular forms of behavior that an effective critical thinker would manifest. Tyler introduced into education the idea that objectives should be defined in terms of specific behaviors, a doctrine that has continued to have an impact ever since it was introduced. Undoubtedly, Tyler had come under the influence of the work of Percy Bridgman, the authority on the physics of high pressure, who had written a much publicized book saying that the vagueness of thought in the social sciences and politics and education was because of the fact that individuals would not bother to define the words they used in terms of specific events. Much philosophical thought of the same period assumed the same position.

Operant psychology was influenced, almost from the beginning, by the same trend. Skinner took the strong stand that only terms that could be defined in terms of observable events should be included in scientific discourse. Thus, terms such as *reinforcement* and *extinction* were always carefully defined in terms of laboratory situations. A reinforcement was a particular event, such as the delivery of a food pellet, which influenced behavior in an equally well-defined way. When the operant psychologists turned their attention to education, they sought to define the outcomes of education with the same precision with which they had defined the basic terms of their scientific language. In education, they found that many educators were already interested in achieving a similar precision in the use of terms.

As a result of this trend, major efforts were made during the early 1960s and early 1970s to define educational objectives with an increasing precision. Objectives became defined in enormous detail. An elementary mathematics curriculum might be defined in terms of as many as 10,000 specific items of behavior that might characterize the child in whom the objectives had been achieved. Although this seemed to be a reasonable way of getting rid of much of the vagueness that has so often characterized educational thought, it did not seem to lead to any great advances either in education or in the thoughts behind it. Neither did it seem to provide a basis for useful or provocative educational research.

The difficulty with Skinner's operant psychology, as well as with Tyler's attempt to reduce complex educational objectives to simple components, was that it never proved to be a useful way of describing human intellectual performance. Jean Piaget had long taken the position that this form of reductionism, that is to say, reducing the complex to the simple, could never lead to a satisfactory understanding of the nature of human intellectual performance. The impact of Piaget's research on American education is relatively recent, coming nearly fifty years after Piaget began to make his classic contributions to the behavioral sciences. His impact was slow, partly because he writes in a ponderous, academic style that draws its vocabulary heavily from logic and biology, and partly because his theory of the nature of the human intellect is complex. Piaget is difficult to read, and he does not provide any simple formula for understanding human behavior as Skinner does. Also Piaget and his associates have not been much interested in promoting the practical application of their work. They want only to pursue their research and to slowly clarify their concept of the nature of the human intellect.

Piaget's basic premise is that complex forms of human behavior cannot be reduced to simple forms. There is no way, according to his viewpoint, whereby complex problem-solving behavior can be reduced to a set of conditioned operants, as Skinner would have us believe, or a set of classically conditioned responses, as Pavlov envisioned. Complex phenomena have to be studied in all of their complexity and there are laws of complex forms of behavior, just as there are laws of simple forms of behavior, but they are different laws.

Piaget does not deny the existence of either operant or classical conditioning as phenomena, but he views them as referring to trivial aspects of behavior. Thus, he understands that behavior is influenced by what operant psychologists call reinforcements, and others call incentives, but he does not see these as having any relevance to human intellectual performance.

Piaget's program of research has been a grand, lifetime effort. Its purpose has been to develop a model of the human intellect and a description of how that intellect develops and the conditions that facilitate this development. His basic assumption is that the mature intellect has been well defined by logicians. Indeed, his position is that logicians did not discover logic, but in writing their treatises on the subject they were merely describing the behavior of mature intellects that solve problems effectively. Mature intellects are necessarily logical.

Piaget's view of the mature intellect is that it is not only logical but also mathematical, for he views mathematics as being a form of logic. Piaget has strong support for his position in that individuals obviously do solve problems daily by the application of logical principles of which they may not be explicitly aware. Piaget also has a theory that explains how the human came to have such an intellect. The answer is that the human lives in a mathematical-logical universe that can be understood only by a mathematical-logical brain. The human brain evolved in a form that could undertake mathematical-logical operations because only such a brain would be fully effective in coping with the surrounding universe. The brain is an instrument of human adaptation and is in tune with the laws of the universe. The argument is quite persuasive.

Once Piaget had identified the nature of the mature intellect and the kinds of operations through which such an intellect solves problems, his next problem was to identify the kinds of behaviors that were prerequisites for mature logical behavior. Thus, Piaget has identified a logic of classes that is a prerequisite for mature logic and has explored, experimentally, the development of classificatory behavior in children. These studies help to define a whole number of tasks and logical operations that children have to master if they are to become mature intellects. The logic of classification also has prerequisites that are defined in terms of the behavior of children in the two- to five-year age range. These too have prerequisites, and Piaget defines them as the development of understandings of the fundamental characteristics of the universe, such as space, time, causation, and the permanence of objects. The later understandings are slowly developed during infancy, but more mature aspects of them continue to develop throughout childhood. Piaget's studies of the intellectual development of the infant, though conducted only on his own three children, have had an enormous impact on subsequent research in the area.

Piaget provided educators with a plausible model of intellectual development and a description of the conditions that would promote this development. This model has become a basis for developing school materials, particularly in the area of mathematics and science. The most notable of these materials are the Nuffield Science Program and the Nuffield Mathematics Program, which are widely used in England, as well as in North America by many teachers who conduct open classrooms. Some American science materials have also been developed along the lines suggested by Piaget's work. Piaget's model has been extensively used for such a purpose, not because it is believed to be unquestionably valid, but because there is no competing model at this time. Operant psychologists have virtually nothing of consequence to say about high-level intellectual processes, and associationistic psychologists have even less. The model has been attacked for being, in many respects, vague (see Ennis, 1975), and there have also been extensive efforts to clarify the model. Russian psychologists have been particularly critical of the model because it has many features that they reject because they seem to conflict with Marxian views concerning human nature. For example, Piaget has held that the child starts out with what he calls an egocentric viewpoint and an inability to comprehend the viewpoint of the other person, and that this egocentricism persists throughout the preschool years and, to some degree, even into adult life. Russian psychologists claim that this egocentricism is a result of the bourgeois Western culture in which the children have been raised. Thus, Piaget's model can be seen as controversial.

One merit of the Piaget model is that it is limited in scope. The behavioral sciences are probably not yet sufficiently advanced, at this time, to develop comprehensive models of behavior, though Skinner claims he has one. Piaget's model has little to say about social development, personality development, emotional development, aesthetic experience, and numerous other important aspects of living. In addition, the development of logic is only one aspect of intellectual development, but another aspect is the development of a body of knowledge that can be used for interpreting the world around us and for solving specific problems. Piaget has also little to say about what knowledge should be included in the curriculum. Of course, Skinner and his followers have also nothing novel to say about these matters, tending to accept currently existing curricula.

Before leaving Piaget, mention must be made of his attitude toward educational research in the United States. He sees much of this research focused on the problem of how to speed up education so that more is learned in the same or less time than previously. Piaget, who refers to this as the "American problem," views it as a trivial problem. He can see no point in rushing through childhood, which he views as a beautiful experience and much too beautiful to be rushed through. Piaget has absolutely no interest in that problem. He does believe that childhood should be a time of exciting discovery and the invention of ideas that will be of value to the individual throughout his entire life. One suspects that Piaget found the process of growing up to be exciting and that he would like to see all other children derive the same intellectual enjoyments that meant so much to him.

The individuals who have been mentioned thus far have had widespread influence, but many other behavioral scientists have also had an impact on narrower aspects of education. J. P. Guilford (1967) has provided educators with a model of the intellect in which educators became interested because of the distinction it made between divergent and convergent thinking. Training in divergent thinking was believed to be related to the development of creative ability, but this has remained a controversial issue. Guilford's model had some influence on the development of aptitude tests, and has stimulated thought concerning the dimensions of the human intellect that should be considered for training. Lawrence Kohlberg (1958) wrote a doctoral dissertation on moral development and then continued to pursue a program of research related to the same topic. His theory of moral development builds on that developed by Piaget nearly forty years previously. The pattern of moral development described by Kohlberg is claimed to be universal, and has stimulated research to verify that view in numerous different cultures around the world. Kohlberg also has a theory concerning the conditions that result in the individual moving from one stage to another, and this theory has been embraced by educators. Although Kohlberg's theory has been extensively criticized, it still holds a strong position in the field of education related to values and the development of ethical behavior, because no plausible alternative has been advanced at this time. This is a good place to make the point that a scientific theory will continue to dominate a field, despite evidence to the contrary, until a better alternative theory is advanced. Thus, practically all psychological theories, as well as most theories in physics, are contradicted by many pieces of evidence, but still hold their position for lack of a plausible alternative.

Mention must also be made of the work undertaken by Eleanor Gibson (1967) on perception in relation to reading. Gibson's work on perception has provided a basis for understanding reading as a perceptual task, though reading is much more than a perceptual task. The work of Kurt Lewin also merits mention here for its lasting impact on our concept of the leadership role of the teacher as well as for his research related to that leadership role.

One could extend this list to great length. Many psychologists and sociologists have made important contributions to our understanding of attitudes and values and the conditions under which these are learned and change. Some progress has been made on the development of a theory of motivation, and particularly achievement motivation. And so the list of names can be extended through numerous different areas of psychological research.

The reader should not be left with the impression that the main source of educational change in the world is educational research, for it obviously is not. Thinkers who take an analytical approach to the problems of education have probably had far more impact than have educational research workers. In the present century no man has had a greater impact on education than has John Dewey. The impact of Maria Montessori, in the last century, is still felt a hundred years later. Lesser luminaries have also had an impact in particular fields, as, for example, Victor Lowenfeld in art education. Educational research still has a long way to go before it can claim to be the major source of educational innovation, but as a minor source, it can be of great importance.

Direct Attacks on Educational Problems

The research considered up to this point has consisted of programs that were designed to extend knowledge of basic behavioral phenomena. These studies were not conducted for the purpose of solving particular practical problems. Nevertheless they represent the main impact that research has had on education. Educators have shown little interest in supporting this type of basic research, because they have believed that its progress is too slow. Educators have wanted research that would solve the immediate and pressing problems of education with speed. For this reason, strong support has developed over the years for research that would be oriented toward the solution of specific educational problems. The argument for this kind of research is persuasive. Why wait for years for the basic knowledge to solve problems, when solutions may be discovered by a direct attack on these problems?

History provides many examples of how problems may be solved through a direct attack on them, and without the development of basic knowledge. A frequently cited example of such an approach is the discovery by William Jenner that smallpox could be prevented by inoculation with cowpox. Of course, Jenner did not know that smallpox was caused by a virus, and he had absolutely no knowledge of the immunity mechanism of the body. The story is told that he overheard a milkmaid say, "I cannot get smallpox because I have had cowpox." Jenner's research on the subject was limited to showing that a boy, who had cowpox, did not develop smallpox after he had been inoculated with the contents of the pustule of a smallpox victim. The disease was virtually eliminated from the world less than 200 years after Jenner's work, yet the mechanism of immunity still remains obscure.

A better example of a practical solution to a problem that came about through direct research was the development of salvarsan, an arsenical compound that was used for fifty years for the treatment of syphilis. Paul Ehrlich developed the compound and treatment after years of research in which hundreds of compounds were tried with varying degrees of success. Salvarsan also became known as 606 because it was the six hundred and sixth compound that Ehrlich used in his attempt to find a cure for syphilis. Here again, one must point out that the procedures of Ehrlich did not resemble too closely those that have been traditionally used by scientists. Ehrlich's experiments had much of a hit-or-miss character about them, but his hits were characterized by brilliant intuition.

One has difficulty in finding cases in which problems have been solved through direct research, except where there already existed a solid body of scientific knowledge on which the research could be built. Neither Jenner nor Ehrlich had such a solid body, and each of their works represents very exceptional cases of important problems being solved through a direct attack. The development of the atomic bomb was certainly not in the same character, for the entire technology of the atomic bomb rested on a solid scientific foundation that began with J. J. Thompson's discovery of the electron over a century ago and culminated in the work of Einstein's relating mass to energy. Without such a highly organized body of scientific knowledge, the atomic bomb and later civilian uses of atomic energy could never have happened.

Most psychologists would doubt that there is a corresponding body of knowledge in the behavioral sciences that would permit a direct and successful assault on practical problems of education, in much the same way that the Manhattan Project of World War II developed the atomic bomb. Most educators and government officials concerned with education take the opposite position. They believe that educational problems can be solved by a direct research attack on them. Since some effort has been made to attack educational problems in this way, we would do well at this time to consider what success has been achieved.

In the early part of the century, educators and educational administrators had a brief period of enthusiasm for research directed toward the solution of what appeared to be the crucial educational problems of the day. This enthusiasm was, no doubt, sparked by the success that Lillian and Frank Gilbreth and Frederick Taylor had had in improving the efficiency of industrial work through the application of time-and-motion study. Certainly, the Gilbreths and Taylor were able to show dramatic improvements in worker output, through the careful planning of worker behavior, and their contemporaries in education argued that simple improvements in the efficiency of education could surely be produced through systematic studies of pupils and teachers. The arguments were plausible and so persuasive that many administrators believed that, within a few years, all of the major problems of education would be solved. Administrators and professors of education alike were quite unaware of the enormous difficulty of developing knowledge that might help to reform education. They were also unaware of the fact that the industrial model of time-and-motion study, although it might produce immediate increases in efficiency, would, over the long haul, produce a deep alienation on the part of workers toward the entire industrial enterprise, with a resulting disruption of industry. The alienation of pupils toward schools was to come much later.

The enthusiasm for educational research of the early part of the century was short-lived. Research did not, and could not, produce the basis for educational reform that influential people in education thought it could. Research came to be seen as a painfully slow, and expensive, way of producing educational change. Many administrators thought they could produce more rapid and effective change merely by imposing their ideas on the schools or by obtaining acceptance of their innovative ideas. Of course, much could be accomplished by administrative fiat. The ideas of John Dewey were beginning to impress themselves on the educational community, largely through the activity of the faculty of Teachers College, Columbia University, which had come to play a major role in the training of educational administrators. Though Dewey was not affiliated with Teachers College; he was chairman of the department of philosophy at Columbia University, across the street from Teachers College, and thus had many devoted disciples in Teachers College who brought his message to the educational establishment. All over the country, school programs began to blossom that were based on the ideas of John Dewey or, more often, on corruptions of those ideas.

The decline in support for research from those in public education left graduate schools, and particularly graduate students, as the main producers of research designed to make frontal attacks on educational problems. The thousands of students who have to do such research each year, in order to complete their degrees, have produced an enormous volume of studies over the last seventy-five years. Much of this research was inevitably quite primitive, because very difficult problems were attacked by very simplistic means. Consider, for example, the problem of discovering what makes a teacher effective, a very old problem for study. Large numbers of studies of this problem were undertaken during the period 1910–1945. Although no one has ever bothered to make a complete count of such studies, annotated bibliographies published a quarter of a century ago listed hundreds of them. The number is certainly now in the thousands. Enormous amounts of energy have been devoted to research in this area, but the fact remains that all methods that have ever been proposed for measuring teacher effectiveness remain extremely controversial. The early studies in the area were virtually worthless because investigators had not yet discovered that the problem is a difficult one and that two teachers may be equally effective for quite different reasons. Many of the early studies sought to find out quite specific acts that might characterize an effective teacher. Then research workers began to find some evidence that a teacher who was effective with one method might be ineffective with another. Later came the suggestion that teachers who were effective with particular categories of pupils might be less effective with other categories of pupils. A problem that educational researchers at the beginning of the century thought would be a simple one turned out to be overwhelmingly complex.

The vast volume of research that was undertaken on problems related to measuring teacher effectiveness, or exploring the characteristics of the teacher related to effectiveness, seemed to have a bleak future by mid-century. Indeed, by that time research workers had become so discouraged with the area that relatively few studies appeared during the following two decades. Nevertheless, the work that had been undertaken had some redeeming features that had to be distilled out of it by later workers. Credit for doing this must go to Barak Rosenshine and later to his associate Norma Furst. Rosenshine was interested in the studies that attempted to relate the characteristics of teachers to measures of teacher effectiveness, but he realized that, for such a study to be useful, there had to be a measure of pupil achievement. He was able to find a limited number of studies in which there was an objective measure of pupil achievement and, hence an objective measure of how well the pupils had been taught (assuming that the objective measure of achievement was related to what the teacher believed to be the purposes of instruction). After Rosenshine had assembled such studies, he was able to show some consistent relationships between characteristics of teacher behavior and pupil achievement. One article that summarizes the findings in that area is Rosenshine and Furst (1973).

Two points should be noted. One is that almost seventy-five years of research had to be pursued before any consequential results were achieved. This is not the kind of rapid progress that advocates of practical problem-oriented research expected. Some would argue that the slowness with which the results appeared reflected the incompetence of the research workers, and that perhaps a better trained group of research workers may, today, produce results more rapidly. They may. The second point is that studies often have to be repeated many times before one can be sure that the results are genuinely replicable. Most studies in the behavioral sciences, when they are repeated, do not produce the same results twice. For this reason, an accumulation of studies with consistent results is necessary in educational research before one can draw conclusions. Anyone who thinks he can just undertake a single study, and come out with a solution to a problem, does not know how hard it is to solve educational problems through research.

There is probably no very quick way of solving educational problems through educational research. Over the long haul, research will have an impact as it has had in the past, but quick direct attacks are unlikely to be effective. The kind of slow accumulation of knowledge that has taken place in the area of teacher effectiveness has taken place in other areas. For example, our ways of helping the retarded and the handicapped have slowly been improved through extensive research over many decades. We are slowly coming to understand the problems of the disadvantaged learner. There has also been some accumulation of knowledge in the area of reading. Research is a slow but sure instrument for educational progress.

The Federal Government Becomes Involved

The federal government did little to support research until after World War II. The success of the Manhattan Project in developing the atomic bomb and other successful excursions of government into the area of research during the war raised high hopes that major problems in our society could be solved through government-sponsored research. The establishment of the National Science Foundation was one step in this direction, but the foundation did not support any direct attacks on educational problems, though it did support research in the behavioral sciences that might have implications for educational practice. The National Science Foundation operated some projects that were related to curriculum development in the science areas, but these tended to be dominated by subject-matter specialists and tended to neglect what psychologists and educators had to say about the nature of children's learning. The foundation also sponsored workshops designed to help teachers use the new materials that had been developed. Some of these materials would have been rejected by almost anyone familiar with what is known about learning. For example, hundreds of films were produced providing lectures and demonstrations on almost every phase of elementary physics, but the sponsors of the films failed to recognize that children might learn far more, and learn it more effectively, by doing the experiments themselves rather than watching an adult perform the experiments. Ultimately, the federal government came to recognize that special provision had to be made for supporting research related to education and for the development of educational research workers.

The breakthrough in federal sponsorship of research came in 1954 when Congress passed the Cooperative Research Act. This act made provisions for grants to be given to institutions to provide support for educational research. The act was not funded until 1957 when a million dollars was appropriated for research purposes with the bulk of it being earmarked for research related to the education of the mentally retarded. The appropriations in the years that followed continued to be quite small but they had a considerable impact. Most of the money went to academicians who developed some worthwhile lines of research but, even more important, the money was used to help graduate students who became apprentices in the field of research. The field may have needed, more than anything else, a new generation of well-trained young men and women, who could bring to educational research a sophistication that many believed it has generally lacked. Although the program of research sponsored by the Cooperative Research Act was small in scope, it still managed to sponsor some research that has had a lasting impact. For example, Eleanor Gibson's research on the perceptual aspects of reading was sponsored by the program, and so too were many of Ned Flanders' researches on classroom interaction and some of E. Paul Torrance's work on creativity, among other enterprises that are still cited in the research literature. The emphasis of the program was on helping promising research workers develop their ideas.

Although academicians were generally pleased with what the Cooperative Research Program was achieving, the federal bureaucracy was not. The United States Office of Education that administered the program wanted to sponsor research that would have a quick impact on education. Some congressmen were even more impatient, wanting to change the program so that it might produce evidence of worthwhile change before the next election. Pressure for quick results is inherent in the entire system of federal government. Unfortunately, modern governments cannot do what governments often did during the Middle Ages and draw up plans that would take 200 years to consummate. The federal bureaucracy was correct in saying that the few million dollars spent on the program of the Cooperative Research Act had not changed education in the few years in which the program had existed. What was not recognized was that the program had hardly even had a chance to develop, and the money appropriated for it by Congress was less than a private corporation might budget for the development of a simple camera or a new form of photographic film. The Cooperative Research Program was terminated less than ten years after it was started. It was replaced by an ambitious new program that had implicit in it the vision of changing education within a few years. Those who formulated the new program took the position that the only way to produce educational progress through research was to have it focus on specific educational problems that would have to be attacked directly. Educational problems could be solved in much the same way that the problem of producing an atomic bomb could be solved through a targeted program of research. It did not seem to occur to anyone involved in the planning that the way to produce an atomic bomb might not be the way to produce a revolution in education. The two problems might not be comparable at all.

The new approach to educational research was included in Title IV of the Elementary and Secondary Education Act of 1965. This act specifically abolished the Cooperative Research Program. In its place there were to be a series of research and development centers and regional laboratories that were to undertake research and disseminate and apply the results. The legislation did not say how many there were to be, but twenty regional laboratories and nine research and development centers were initially funded. In establishing the regional laboratories and development centers, no consideration was given to the problem of whether there was a competent staff available to run such a large-scale operation. The only consideration was to ensure that every congressional district could have a nearby laboratory that could be pointed out as an achievement for the particular congressman involved. In this way, congressional support for the enterprise was assured. It may well have been the case that available competent personnel might have been sufficient for staffing only two or three of these enterprises, but such arguments bore no weight.

Once the organizations had been established, some effort was made to eliminate those that showed virtually no competence. The regional laboratories were established as nonprofit-making corporations so, in theory, they could continue to survive without federal funds by taking in work on a contract basis, but those laboratories that lost their federal funding, died quietly without a struggle. The initial demise of five of the laboratories took place in 1968 and others have been eliminated since that time. Only half of the original laboratories still remain. Other organizations, however, have been added such as the Center for the Study of Evaluation at the University of California, Los Angeles. The surviving laboratories, centers, and newer miscellaneous organizations have formed a coordinating organization called the Council for Educational Development and Research, referred to as CEDaR. This council publishes summaries of the accomplishments of the organizations listed in terms of the products that are available. The listing is a catalog (see CEDaR, 1974) of what the organizations have produced.

The materials produced by the laboratories and research and development centers are quite diverse. They are, indeed, so diverse, and are produced from such a multitude of different educational viewpoints that the picture they present is almost one of chaos. There are packages of materials for teaching basic language skills, procedures offered for keeping attendance records, faculty and staff development programs, readers for children in Guam and in Eskimo villages, television mathematics programs for elementary school children, and so forth. The CEDaR catalog includes a section of summaries of what the catalog refers to as "Basic Research." The products in this section are mainly annotated bibliographies and summaries.

The CEDaR catalog also provides a section "Product Evaluation" after each product. Many of these are just blank. Those that have entries against them typically say that the product was tried out on children and the children seemed to enjoy the materials. One wonders how they found out whether the children did or did not enjoy the materials.

The CEDaR summaries of the products of the laboratories really do not do justice to the organizations. These summaries struggle to give the impression that there have been really worthwhile accomplishments in the few years that the organizations have been in existence. Only optimistic bureaucratic and ill-informed congressmen could hope for such products in such a short time. Also, much of the knowledge created by the laboratories is knowledge of what not to do. That is valuable knowledge, though it is not the kind that appeals to politicians. Consider the case of the Research and Development Center at the University of Pittsburgh that developed the program described as Individually Prescribed Instruction, in which all content was carefully sequenced and in which each pupil worked through the sequence at his or her own rate. The program took several years to develop, and one can hardly suppose that a finished program could come out the first time around. Only the federal government expected success of the first effort, and there was much disappointment in Washington when the program did not seem to produce superior learning. Nevertheless, much was learned by developing the program. The problem of how to sequence subject matter is an overwhelming problem in itself. In addition, the development of the program involved the use of various forms of record keeping, which need to be studied. The fact is that the record-keeping systems used in schools are primitive and studies in that area are valuable. The program also brought into focus problems related to the isolating effect of a program in which each child is working on a different aspect of the curriculum. Under such circumstances, children cannot easily work together, which they have to learn to do. The valuable knowledge achieved in such respects tended to be lost, because of the preoccupation of the federal government in obtaining a product that could be waved before congressmen. A set of work sheets is a visible product that can be presented to a congressional committee. A set of ideas, which may be far more valuable, is not so easily presented.

An overall evaluation of the federal government's venture in providing funds for regional educational laboratories and research and development centers is difficult to make. Even the government admits a high failure rate, having abolished half of these laboratories and centers. Those that remain do not seem to have made the same kind of impact on education that has been made by the research of Thorndike or Piaget but, of course, such individuals are rare jewels. The idea of a regional laboratory may be a good one, but there may not be a sufficient number of creative research workers available to staff even one, let alone ten or twenty. That may be the basic problem. The federal government, with its customary desire to have a big impact, may have produced a system that has had no impact at all.

Brief mention must be made at this point of the appearance on the Washington scene of the National Institute of Education, an organization designed to promote research and development in education. The National Institute of Education came into being in 1972 with a broad mandate to improve education in the United States. An institute of this nature had long been proposed by educational researchers who had viewed the National Institutes of Health as models that might be followed in the educational sphere. The National Institutes of Health have had a long history of promoting successful research and their policies have been set by panels of well-known professionals in the related scientific disciplines. The National Institute of Education was established as an independent agency in the Department of Health, Education, and Welfare, backed by the hope that it would have the same impact on education that the National Institutes of Health had had on research related to the health sciences.

The National Institute of Education, almost immediately after it was founded, embarked on an entirely different course from that which most research workers had hoped. It was virtually taken over by the same bureaucracy that had failed to produce a useful program of research in the U.S. Office of Education. Policies tended to be set by federal officials rather than by established research workers and scholars. Useless programs previously sponsored by the U.S. Office of Education were taken over wholesale by the new agency. As often happens, a new organization that offered great promise for producing change found itself doing only what its predecessors had done previously. The result was a general loss of support, not only from professionals outside of the government but from

Congress itself. At the present time the agency seems likely to survive, mainly because government agencies are hard to abolish.

The National Institute of Education and the branches of the U.S. Office of Education that preceded it have had enough money over the years to have built an outstanding program of educational research, but have failed to do so. Research has made an enormous difference to education, as this book tries to emphasize. But the useful and productive research has come from sources that were not funded by the federal government. A real need exists for a National Institute of Education with fundamentally different policies than those that have controlled the organization in the past.

Educational Research as a Source of Specific Practices

What the teacher hopes to derive from research is quite different from anything that has been discussed up to this point. Teachers typically want simple procedures for handling particular problems. What does one do if a child will not concentrate on his work? How does one deal with a child who is hostile to the school and everything in it? What do you do with a child who does not understand long division even though you have had several sessions trying to explain it to him? How do you handle a child who disrupts the work of other children? What is the best way to help a third-grader who cannot read at all? Teachers expect research to provide them with specific answers to such questions. When specific answers are not forthcoming to their questions, teachers are all too likely to conclude that educational research is a worthless enterprise. The capability of research to provide answers to these questions is now examined.

Let us first consider the problem of the child who may have difficulty concentrating on a task. The most common reason among schoolchildren for this difficulty may be that they find the materials uninteresting. A more unusual reason may be the child's inability to focus on materials close to his eyes for more than a few minutes. Numerous other reasons may also exist. The child may be genuinely hyperactive. The child may have strong social needs and prefer to relate to other children rather than to an intellectual task. The child may be intellectually unable to understand the task, and what he had to do.

Research provides suggestions of where to look for an answer to the child's problem, but even if an answer is found, there is still the matter of how to handle the child. Should the teacher determine that the child finds the materials for study to be dull, then research may suggest solutions to the problem, though the solutions may not be good solutions. For example, operant psychologists have proposed that children be kept working at dull tasks by offering them later opportunities to work at more enjoyable tasks as reinforcements. This solution has been criticized on the basis that there is no reason why any task that a child has to do in school should be dull. Critics say that the notion that some tasks are inevitably dull reflects a puritanical philosophy that divides life's activities into work and play, with the work activities being dull and virtuous and the play activities being fun and sinful. Critics of the operant solution suggest that the real answer to the problem is in finding tasks that the child enjoys.

What is generally called scientific research seeks to provide very general understandings and explanations of events in the universe. Such research seeks to establish general laws, though all scientific laws have limitations. Such general laws are used as very broad guidelines in solving problems. Thus, in the design of a manufacturing plant to produce some chemical, the design engineer will use his knowledge of chemistry, but he will also know that what happens in a test tube is not necessarily the same as what happens in a large manufacturing plant. In the latter case, chemical processes may occur that do not occur in the laboratory for many reasons. One is that the chemicals used will not have the purity of those found on the laboratory bench. The manufacturer cannot afford to buy chemicals of such purity. Another reason is that the temperature in the plant may not be as even as in a test tube. Still another is that the large vessels of the plant in which the reaction takes place may have walls that promote side reactions. The design engineer uses his knowledge of chemistry in a very general way to plan the plant, but he also uses a great amount of know-how derived from his years of contact with practical technology. The design engineer may be sufficiently unsure of how the plant will work, because of all the factors that limit the application of laboratory chemistry, to cause him to have a small-scale pilot plant constructed to determine whether his laboratory findings will hold up at a larger scale. But, as all engineers know, what happens in a pilot plant may not happen during large-scale manufacture. The further the engineer departs from the laboratory test tube, the less sure he can be that his laboratory knowledge will apply. The difference may be so great that, although in the laboratory he may be able to obtain 95 per cent of the output expected from the input of chemicals, in the plant he may obtain only 30 per cent of the theoretical yield. Chemistry does not provide a cookbook for designing manufacturing plants.

Psychological research similarly does not provide a cookbook for conducting classrooms, but it may provide some general guidelines, though these guidelines are much less specific than those provided by the much more advanced science of chemistry.

In the case of psychology, there is also the problem that one is much less sure than the chemist of where applications are appropriate and where they are inappropriate. A decade or more ago, psychologists applied, with little hesitation, knowledge derived from studies of animal behavior. Indeed, much of the knowledge of operant psychology is derived from studies of the behavior of pigeons and rats. Attempts to apply this knowledge to the solution of practical human problems has not been particularly successful (see the review by Travers, 1977). Many, if not most, contemporary psychologists would predict that such applications would be unlikely to achieve success, because psychologists have learned to exercise caution in generalizing their knowledge across species. Questions have even been raised concerning whether one can reasonably generalize from studies undertaken on children to adults, and vice versa. Most psychologists are learning to be cautious in making generalizations to situations that differ substantially from the situations from which the original knowledge was derived.

Although science has provided a general guide for many of man's most practical activities—the building of bridges, the manufacture of medicines, the design of communication systems, the production of energy, and so forth—much advancement has come from research that contributes little to basic scientific knowledge, namely, research related to the development of technology. New technology has long involved invention and a hit-and-miss, empirical approach, a kind of primitive research. In this way, for example, metal production slowly evolved from the primitive state in which a piece of ore was tossed into a fire roaring in a natural rock chimney, to the quite large furnace of the early nineteenth century. Each generation introduced some innovation, as adventuresome technologists tried one thing and then another, in the hope of improving the quantity and quality of the metal produced. Even some of the Roman plants had considerable capacity for production, yielding several thousand tons of metal a year. The slow accumulation of knowledge about the smelting of metals is comparable to the slow accumulation of knowledge about teaching that has also taken place over the centuries. Progress through informal experimentation, with no systematic way of leaving a record, produces very slow progress. In the case of the smelting of metal, the process of technological improvement was greatly accelerated when metal producers began to conduct systematic research on problems of technology. Such research came into being during the last century, and was made possible through the development of scientific techniques that made control possible. The manufacturer could not study the effect of various conditions on the metal produced until he was able to make an accurate analysis of the metal coming out of the furnace. This type of analysis was not possible until accurate methods of chemical analysis had been developed. These methods had to be very precise, because very small traces of impurities could make very large differences in the properties of the metal produced. Advanced sciences helped to refine crude technologies. Whether the behavioral sciences are advanced enough to refine our crude methods of teaching remains an open question.

In the last few decades attempts have been made to encourage technological research in education. In a sense, Thorndike's work on adjusting reading difficulty level and vocabulary level was of this kind, though it flowed directly from his scientific enterprises. Attempts to use the computer as an instructional device are considered, by some, to fall into this category. Many would doubt whether the attempt to adapt computers to the task of teaching has been anything more than an attempt to find a market for computers within school systems. Much of the public advertising that went along with this attempt was not far short of being dishonest. There is a great difference between conducting technological research to solve a particular practical problem and doing research to make equipment plausibly salable to a new market.

Much of the research undertaken by the regional laboratories, founded and largely funded by the federal government, has been an attempt to bring technological developments to education. Few would see their products as having had any notable consequences on education. The laboratories have had the potential for this kind of enterprise but, as was mentioned previously, many factors conspired against the success of these organizations. There is also the possibility that the sciences of behavior have not developed to the point where they can provide a base for the development of an educational technology. Technologies generally remain quite primitive, until they can be given the support of an advanced science. The science of learning is still quite primitive, despite the great strides that have been made in recent years. Perhaps the sciences of behavior are just developed enough to support the kind of program for building class-room materials that Thorndike undertook, or the kinds of curricula developments that the followers of Piaget have undertaken. Whether educational technology can expand much beyond that point, until the basic sciences expand, remains a question. Certainly the federal government should consider supporting the work of those basic scientists whose work seems to have implications for education.

Where Are We?

Looking back over the last seventy-five years of research related to education, one is tempted to draw the conclusion that research has had the least impact on education when it has been undertaken for the direct purpose of solving educational problems. On the other hand, the work of Thorndike, Skinner, and Piaget, which was undertaken mainly as scientific enterprises and with no immediate practical purpose in mind, has had a substantial impact. However, this may be a simplistic conclusion. If the Thorndikes, Skinners, and Piagets had been employed by regional laboratories, the picture might have been a very different one, but one cannot find out what would happen if outstanding scientists directed their efforts toward producing educational changes, for they are unlikely to change their way of life. Most outstanding scientists still prefer to work within the ivory towers of academic institutions rather than in practical problem-oriented establishments. The fact that academic establishments have some permanence will inevitably make them more attractive as work places than the research and development laboratory, which has had a hard time surviving over the last decade. The federal government has not been willing to ensure the laboratories a secure future, since they have been considered as experimental and probationary organizations. By making them experimental, the federal government has made it difficult for the laboratories to attract the talent needed and has stacked the cards against them.

One conclusion that can be drawn about the value of research to education is that great minds who conduct research on learning and related areas do have a real impact on education, and that this impact is particularly notable on the design of educational materials.

Issues of Value and the Persistence of Many Educational Problems

The spirit of the early part of the century inspired educators to believe that the major problems of education would be solved before many years had passed. Time passed without this hope being realized, but this lack of fulfillment of expectations cannot be totally attributed to the failure of research workers. What the early sponsors of educational research did not realize was that many of the most pressing problems of education involve issues of values rather than issues that can be intellectually solved through some kind of research. It is now apparent that most of the important problems of education are not problems to be solved through research, but are rather problems related to the goals and values of our society.

Our failure to identify our values in planning education, conflicts among us concerning our values, inconsistencies in what the values of our society are, and the values that apparently underlie so many of our school procedures, are all matters that impede progress in education. In the typical schoolroom, children are subservient to the will of the teacher and little is done to help the children become independent, responsible individuals. Yet our form of democratic society is built on the premise that each of us can become such an independent, responsible individual, but one does not become such an individual overnight, or on graduation from the controlling environment of the high school, where the control of the teacher determines what the student does and says. Many who are disturbed at the irresponsible behavior of youth blame the schools for not being strict enough, though the critics should be demanding that the schools demand responsibility from the student and reward him for responsible and independent behavior. The demands of society are unrelated to the disciplinary tradition of schools, which goes back to authoritarian forms of society.

Schools throughout the world have shown striking change during the last twenty-five years, not because of a mounting body of knowledge derived from educational research, but because leaders of education have come to realize that the schools must help children develop the values inherent in their society. Thus, Russian schools (see Bronfenbrenner, 1970) have become systems in which the children learn to live in a collective and acquire the responsibility needed for such a life. The entire Russian school system has been designed around the work of Anton Symonovitch Makarenko (1951), who designed an educational program in the early 1920s as a part of his task of running a camp for delinquent boys. Makarenko had great literary talent and wrote of his problems of developing a school program with warmth and vividness. The responsibility for running the camp, and its educational program, was ultimately taken over by the boys themselves who showed remarkable development within the system. Classrooms in Russia are designed as collectives with the children assuming the roles that are expected of them within the collective. Such responsibilities include contributing to group projects, helping members of the collective who are falling behind in their work, and administering justice under the guidance of adults. Life in the classroom collective incorporates the essential values of the adult collective.

Education in China has also undergone changes in the direction of bringing it more into line with the values of the adult community. This change has been particularly apparent since the Cultural Revolution, which closed down the schools for two years to provide a clean break between the old and the new systems. Chinese schools show some degree of the same socialization of children found in Russian schools, but there is also an attempt to tie schoolwork to the work of becoming a productive citizen. The children engage in productive labor part of the day from the earliest elementary grades. Kindergarten children undertake assembly tasks for local factories, and the schools are paid for the work undertaken by the children. Summer vacations for the older children are periods of work.

The values implicit in American education have never been well defined or analyzed. During the last century, and in the early part of this century, the schools were viewed as the basic social instruments for the Americanization of the immigrant, though how the schools were to do this was never entirely clear. The premise seems to have been that the acquisition of basic skills together with a knowledge of the history of American democracy was sufficient to Americanize the immigrant. Little attention was paid to the development of habits that might be crucial to democratic living, such as a tolerance for divergency of views, the exercise of self-control, and fairness and honesty in all aspects of the political process. It was hardly surprising that the immigrant child, living in New York City, grew up to support a corrupt city administration and to obtain a job with the city through a payoff to the official in charge. The schools in America at the turn of the century provided only token training for responsible living in a democracy.

A more impressive effort on the part of a Western country to develop an educational system related to the values of that country is found in France. The basic purpose of French education is to further what the French call the Perpetual French Revolution. The notion of a Perpetual French Revolution is that the ideals of the French Revolution were never fully achieved, and that each generation has the responsibility of bringing France nearer to these goals. The elementary school curriculum of France is focused on this goal of achieving national ideals, although the focusing is in a very intellectual way. Little or no consideration is given to the problem of inculcating either the self-control or the emotional responses that might be needed to achieve this ideal.

A central feature of American education, if not the central feature, is the competition of the individual against all other individuals. This aspect of education reflects a free capitalist society in which the individual must compete with other individuals for his purchase price in the market place. Although one cannot question the effectiveness of such a system in producing efficiently both goods and services, one can question whether the same principles should be applied to the design of an educational system for a democratic society. Democratic societies require more than individual competitiveness. They require individuals to cooperate, to work together, to give up individual goals for the sake of the community, and to understand that the common good often requires sacrifice on the part of the individual. The values of a democratic society are often in conflict with the values of a free enterprise system. The highly competitive system of the schools may not be a good system for training individuals to live a democratic way of life. This conflict between the values of a free enterprise system and many of the values of a democracy have resulted in a democratic government regulating some aspects of the economy.

Critics of the North American educational system, such as Illich (1972), point out that our schools serve the society to some degree by failing many and producing a class of individuals who feel worthless. These are the individuals who fit most willingly into an industrial complex, where they perform the simplest forms of routine work. Insofar as this criticism is sound, then education is serving the opposite purpose to that which it was hoped it would serve in the last century; that is, producing equality among Americans. On the contrary, the American educational system, according to these critics, is a mechanism for producing gross inequality. If this is true, then education is no longer serving the values and goals of a democratic society. That is a serious criticism.

The purpose of this discussion has been to point out to the reader, who is well versed in the psychology of measurement, that the central and most overwhelming problems of education have to do with issues that are related to the values that we hold. These are not problems that can be solved by research, though research workers may have some say in finding out which of the many possible solutions are best. Research workers may well explore the values of students who complete their education and compare these values with the values that are implicit in a democratic society. Research workers may also study whether new ways of planning school programs enhance or damage these values. What the research programs cannot do is to define the values that should underlie a school program. The research worker can also be sensitive to the values that are implicit in his attempts to apply research to school problems. Few research workers are sensitive in that respect.

Summary

1. The term *research* in education has been used quite loosely to cover a wide range of activities. Until recently, bureaus of educational research did little that might be described as the pursuit of knowledge. Nevertheless, the impact of research came from other sources.

2. In the early part of the century, the main impact of research on education came through the work of E. L. Thorndike. Thorndike is famous for his law of effect, but he also had an extraordinary influence on the design of educational materials. His work on transfer of training suggested that teaching should not be conducted by indirect means and that materials should be related directly to the objectives to be achieved. His work on word counts provided a basis for the selection of vocabulary for children's textbooks. Thorndike also built courses in arithmetic and algebra designed around his theory of learning. Thorndike later became involved in the development of intelligence tests, which, unfortunately, were used to bolster many of the prejudices of his time. A contemporary of Thorndike, Lewis Terman conducted studies of gifted children and disposed of the myth that such children were maladjusted or freakish in some way.

3. Before Thorndike had completed his own contributions to education, a new generation of psychologists was beginning to have a new impact on education. The most notable among these new names on the scene were those of B. Frederick Skinner and Jean Piaget. The name of Sidney Pressey will also go down in history as the inventor of teaching machines. Skinner's operant psychology was a close relative of Thorndike's connectionism, and Skinner too was interested in matters related to the design of materials. Skinner revived the interest of the schoolmen of the Middle Ages in the problem of the sequencing of subject matter. The resulting programmed

materials had a transitory impact on educational practice. Skinner's views of how behavior is controlled are so similar to that commonly expressed in a capitalist society that his views became easily accepted on this continent, even though they were rejected elsewhere.

4. The work of Ralph Tyler in the early 1930s represents another research-related trend that eventually fused with the operant position. Tyler understood, as Skinner understood, that objectives of education should be specified in precise terms. The fusion of these two sources of influence resulted in a great emphasis being placed on the definition of objectives, an emphasis that continues to permeate school systems of the United States.

5. Opposed to the reductionism of Skinner and Tyler was the position of Jean Piaget whose influence has been more recently felt. Piaget sees complex behavior as having its own laws and talks about the error of reducing the complex to the simple. Piaget sees the human brain as the instrument of a logical-mathematical intellect that permits the organism to adapt to a logical-mathematical universe. For Piaget, all development involves learning, for learning is the instrument through which development of the intellect takes place. Piaget has a great deal to say about the conditions that favor the development of the intellect and, hence, much of what he writes has implications for education.

6. Many other lesser psychologists have played a role in changing education. Of course, educational research is not the main avenue through which education is changed.

7. The emphasis of much educational research in recent times has been on the solution of important educational problems by attacking them directly through research techniques. Research rarely has this kind of direct impact on practical affairs. Direct attacks on educational problems often lead to superficial attempts at solution that may have bad long-term side effects. Attempts to attack educational problems directly brought a flood of studies of such problems as what makes teachers effective. This extraordinarily difficult problem does not yield to such a direct, simplistic approach. After hundreds of studies had been undertaken in this area, scientists have been able to tease out a few answers, which together yield a modicum of knowledge.

8. The federal government began to provide support for educational research in 1954. The early efforts of the federal government seem to have provided some encouragement for scholarly activity in this area. Later attempts were made to develop research and development centers and regional laboratories. These enterprises rapidly ran into difficulties and more than half of them were soon disbanded. The surviving enterprises have had much uncertainty as to their futures. Much was learned from some of these programs, but the centers and laboratories did not produce

the revolution in education that the politicians had hoped for. There was no way in which they could have achieved such a lofty goal.

9. The National Institute of Education was founded in the hope that it would provide a new and better focus for educational research. The institute has had a shaky beginning, but has survived early attempts to abolish it.

10. Educational research can never provide a cookbook for the teacher or educational planner. Like all other scientific enterprises, research can provide only a general guide for effective action.

11. The recent emphasis on the development of an educational technology represents an extension of the efforts of Thorndike. Much of modern educational technology represents an attempt to bring an industrial model of production to the classroom. Classrooms are not manufacturing enterprises and present very special problems in the development of a technology.

12. The applications of research in schools must always be subservient to the values of our society. An efficient method of teaching that may be appropriate to Russia may not be appropriate at all for North American schools. The American educational research worker needs to be sensitive to the values that the schools of our country seek to develop.

CHAPTER 2
The Impact of Research on the Philosophy of Education

In addition to the influence that psychologists have exerted on the way in which materials for schools are made and used, there is another subtle, pervasive, and often overwhelming way in which the great psychologists have influenced education. These psychologists are leaders of thought in their age and exert their influence, not only on their fellow scientists and other intellectuals but also on the thinking of the ordinary citizen. This is a relatively new role for the scientist, which began with the Age of Enlightenment and became of great importance during the last century with the work of Darwin. Before the age of the scientist, the religious leader and the philosopher had enormous influence on the way in which man thought about himself, and this influence still exists and must compete with the influence of scientific thought.

Although Darwin viewed with wonder the history of the evolution of every species and the extraordinary way in which adaptive mechanisms developed, his work was widely interpreted as a denegration of the human species. The human species, according to Darwin, could no longer be viewed as a creation set apart from the rest of nature, but as a part of it. For many, this was a humiliation of the human spirit and a way of saying that man was no better than a mere glob of matter. For others it showed that man was a mere mechanism and a part of the more comprehensive mechanism of life on this planet. Many saw a day, not far in the future, when the behavior of man would be reduced to a set of mechanical physical laws, and human behavior would be understood in the same way in which the behavior of machines was understood. All complex behavior and all the physiological workings of the body could be reduced to the same set of physical laws. This theory of reductionism, which was popular in the last century, was based on the faith that all complex phenomena can be reduced to the simple. We now know that this is a fallacious viewpoint and that the laws of complex organisms cannot be reduced to the laws of atomic physics.

Many influential psychologists in this century were quick to accept reductionism. For the father of behaviorism, John B. Watson, complex behavior represented only a chain of conditioned responses. Although Watson borrowed his ideas from Ivan Pavlov, he failed to note, as Pavlov had done, that complex behavior is far more than a sequence of simple muscular responses for it involved a set of events involving verbal and symbolic behavior. Pavlov had never seriously believed, as apparently Watson had, that human thought and problem solving could be reduced to the kind of conditioning that was shown by laboratory dogs. In many ways, Watson was more of an evangelist than a scientist. His works were speculative rather than based on research. Indeed, at the time when Watson wrote his classic work, entitled *Behaviorism* (1924), there had been very little research undertaken on the conditioning of the human subject. Watson was not disturbed by the absence of data, perhaps because he believed, in the Darwinian tradition, that whatever had been discovered through the use of animals could be directly applied to an understanding of human behavior.

Watson believed that his speculations could be applied directly to the problem of training the child to become an acceptable adult citizen, and strove to persuade the rest of America that this was so. The human was viewed as a stupid organism that could be trained to do whatever the trainer desired. All the trainer had to do was to arrange the environment so that behavior was appropriately conditioned. Neither Watson nor his followers ever demonstrated that the application of Pavlovian techniques ever produced knowledge acquisition or understanding of the environment, but this did little to deter him and his followers, during the 1920s, from promoting their cause. They were right that some learning had to take place by associating together stimuli, much as the bell and the food are associated together in dog conditioning experiments, but these represented some of the more trivial aspects of education and Watson had little to say about how learning by association could be improved. Nevertheless, Watsonian views did have some impact on the public's conception of the nature of the human, lowering him, as a learner, to the level of a laboratory animal, and placing the instructor on the level of an animal trainer. The time was not particularly ripe for the impact of such ideas, in that education in the 1920s was in the throes of a revolution known as progressive education. Nevertheless Watson founded a movement, the behavioristic movement, among American psychologists that was ultimately to have great impact on education during the 1950–1970 period under the influence of Skinner. Watson sowed the seeds that Skinner would later cause to germinate.

The influence of the Watson-Skinner tradition comes, not from the scientific discoveries of these two individuals, but from their philosophical position. Both made the assumption that the behavior of the child is under environmental control, though they would have disagreed on the nature of that control. Both took the positions that the teacher has to provide and plan an environment that will control the learning of the child in an effective way. Both took the position that the decisions concerning what a child should and would learn came from sources outside of the child. These are *assumptions,* and not scientific findings. Many scientists would not accept these assumptions. These assumptions are, however, quite useful for doing research, since they lead the scientist to look for causes of behavior that lie outside of the body of the organism being studied. Since the scientist has difficulty looking inside the animal that is the object of study, the psychologist is well advised to at least start by identifying all causes of behavior that are observable and outside the animal. This doesn't mean that there may not be important causes of behavior that lie within the organism, even in quite naïve organisms. Even infants may invent ideas that become enormously important for their subsequent behavior, but since these are difficult to observe, except very indirectly, it is often simpler to just assume that they do not occur.

The typical assumptions of behaviorism are good points of departure for research in the behavioral sciences, but they are probably a very bad point of departure for running a classroom or a school. Quite obviously, neither children nor adults like to be told that they are not in control of what happens to them. Only a foolish teacher would ever take such a position.

The central limitation of the Skinner model, or its predecessor, the Thorndike model, was that it failed to account for intelligent behavior. The model was excellent for accounting for the extraordinary stupidity that the human can show, but not with the brilliant genius that makes it possible to represent the complexities of the universe in mechanical, mathematical, and abstract terms. The generalization that because man behaves stupidly in some respects indicates that all behavior has the same simplistic base is not one particularly flattering of human nature. Indeed, the model has added to the belittlement of the human that had already been taking place for a century. How man thinks of himself is important and may be a major determinant of his behavior. The human who thinks of himself as stupid can be expected to behave in stupid ways. John Eccles (1973), the great neurophysiologist, has some interesting reflections on this point. Eccles asks why it was that the human had the same brain that he has today for at least half a million years before he began to use it in massive amounts of inventive activity, as he has in modern times. Eccles suggests that early man had just not discovered what he could do with his brain. By that he means that during all these early millennia, the human had not thought of himself as an inventive being. During that long period, man made small inventions, as he had to improvise solutions to problems, but he did not take time out from hunting just to see what he could invent. Man had to come to realize how clever a creature he was before he could fully use the brain that evolution had given him.

The human can almost certainly harm himself by considering himself stupid. The teacher who embraces the Thorndike or Skinner models is doing just that. Such a teacher is also transmitting to the children the idea that they should expect only stupid behavior of themselves. Such an attitude may even be extended to the point where the delinquent claims that he is not responsible for his own behavior, for do not psychologists claim that behavior is controlled by the environment and that individuals are not responsible for their own behavior?

This is the trap into which the practitioner falls when he embraces a model of human behavior that is suitable for research but unsuitable as a basis for the conduct of practical affairs. A model that emphasizes the stupidity of the human creature, although a suitable one for much research, may not be suitable for other purposes. The difficulty is that other models have been scarce. Furthermore, alternative models, because they help us to understand very complex forms of behavior, tend to be complicated. The extreme simplicity of the Skinner-type model makes it very easy to understand, and very easy to promote for anybody who wants to promote a cause, but the promoters do not generally make it clear that they are talking about very simple forms of behavior.

Only a few models have had some success in explaining complex intelligent behavior. The first model that attracted any real attention was that of E. C. Tolman (1932), which he referred to as purposive behaviorism. It never reached the point of having an impact on education, partly because it was difficult to understand, and partly because it never stimulated a program of research on human subjects. Although Tolman had a creative intellect, he was not, by disposition, an experimentalist. Many of his key ideas, such as those of expectancy, have been incorporated in many later models of learning, but his system is now only of historical interest.

During the last decade two new ways of representing the intellect and intelligent behavior have become dominant on the American scene. One of these new models, the one that has come to have a substantial impact on education, is that of Piaget, to which considerable reference was made in the previous chapter. Piaget, like Skinner, makes certain assumptions about the nature of human behavior, and these assumptions have tended to become incorporated into ways of teaching. A central assumption of Piaget is that the intellect is, first and foremost, an inventive system. There is, of course, no way to verify this assumption through an experiment. It is no more verifiable than Skinner's assumption that all behavior is controlled by the environment. It is just a way of looking at behavior. Piaget's assumption considered here is more easily accepted for teaching purposes than the assumption that Skinner makes about all behavior being controlled by the environment. Piaget's assumption is more consistent with common observation and popular ideas about behavior. That does not make it a true assumption, though assumptions made about behavior should show some agreement with common observation. Piaget's conception of intelligence as being inventive is quite acceptable to teachers who see children as clever, inventive creatures. Teachers have difficulty in viewing children as being under environmental control because so much child behavior seems to be spontaneous, and certainly not closely related to environmental events.

Piaget's assumptions about behavior are closely similar to those of John Dewey. Both view inquiry as the central process of learning. Both assume that the experiences provided by inquiry are organized and structured in a creative, inventive way. Both are highly acceptable to American educators because both base their work on a model of behavior that is consistent with one's own personal experience concerning behavior.

Although consistency with personal experience may make a model acceptable, such a criterion should be applied with caution. The theory that the earth is flat is quite consistent with the experience of those who live on the Great Plains, though it is not consistent with the experience of mariners who knew, more than 2,000 years ago, that the surface of the earth was curved. Nevertheless, where there are gross inconsistencies between a set of assumptions about behavior and what one observes in one's own behavior as well as that of others, then one must either find an explanation for these inconsistencies or discard the model. The early astronomers understood quite well why the earth often seemed flat to land dwellers. They also understood that the notion of a flat earth was a useful assumption to make when dividing up land for agriculture. Not until about 100 years ago did surveying become sufficiently accurate that the curvature of the earth had to be taken into account in locating particular landmarks.

This section has developed the idea that a major impact that the research worker has on education is that of providing a set of assumptions about the nature of learning and the nature of behavior. These are not verified facts, but convenient ways of viewing the child and the relation of the teacher to the child. Emphasis must be placed on the fact that such assumptions may be useful ways of looking at behavior for the purposes of research, but are not necessarily good ways of looking at pupils. The ways in which the scientist looks at behavior may also be in conflict with the socially acceptable ways of looking at behavior at this time in history. For example, most of us take the view that the individual is responsible for his own behavior, even though operant psychologists tell us that there is no such thing as personal responsibility, for behavior is controlled by the environment.

After Research What? Development!

A widely held view in education is that the results of the research should be taken and then used by individuals who convert the findings of the research worker into practical applications. Thorndike performed this extension of his scientific work himself, and even undertook the task of writing the definitions in his famous *Junior Dictionary*. Thorndike did not leave himself open to the criticism, that was later hurled against Skinner, that the scientific findings probably do not apply because they were derived mainly from studies of animal behavior, since most of the work that Thorndike applied was undertaken with human subjects. Skinner himself has suggested broad outlines for the application of his studies to education, but has left the work of making these applications to a devoted and enthusiastic following who are not bothered much by any line of criticism. Piaget has been completely unconcerned about the application of his work, preferring to devote his energies to the expansion of his scientific concepts, but, he too, has had admirers as well as many who have seen a profitable enterprise in his work.

This activity of applying the results of research has become known as *development,* but much development also involves an activity that is much like technological research, that is to say, trying one thing and then another until a satisfactory product or procedure is achieved. The assumption has commonly been made that development is a rapid process that produces results quickly. History does not support this contention. A classic case of development is James Watt's work on the development of the form of steam engine that became the driving force of the industrial revolution. Watt did not invent the steam engine. James Watt was an instrument maker for the University of Glasgow and there he had the experience of working on the Newcomen engine, a primitive and wasteful type of steam engine. Watt was impressed with the inefficiency of the engine and began work redesigning it. That was in 1763, but it was not until 1769 that Watt had worked out the basic principles that had to be followed in the design of an efficient steam engine. The resulting engine was a redesigned Newcomen engine. It was not until 1782 that Watt reached the point of patenting a double action steam engine, in which a crank connecting rod converted the movement of the piston into a rotary motion. Watt's engine became the basic form of the steam engine for the next 150 years.

Several points should be noted about Watt's research and development enterprise. First, it took place over a period of nineteen years. Although the invention of the crank seems to be such a simple matter today, it was perhaps Watt's greatest invention, and a climax to his years of work. Second, Watt was a genius and a man of great learning who was widely read. In addition to having mastered the principles of engineering and instrument making of his time, he was also well read in music and chemistry. He also designed various forms of gears, including the planetary system of gears, as well as various forms of heat gauges. The point here is that high-caliber development work is not something to be engaged in by individuals who do not have the capability of doing scientific work. It is an area that calls for its own form of genius and a time schedule that is generous. When the National Institute of Education finances proposals that call for the development of new educational products, within two or three years, only a very mediocre product can be expected. Perhaps if very large sums of money were available for such projects, dramatic technological developments might take place, as took place in World War II on the atomic bomb project, but this is doubtful. The atomic bomb project was able to be successfully completed because there already existed a solid body of scientific information that indicated the various approaches that could be taken. Actually, it is said that the only piece of new knowledge involved in the development of the atomic bomb was the size of the critical mass that would produce an explosion. The rest was a matter of experimenting with various processes for the manufacture of plutonium.

One can point to many important technological developments in our generation that have taken a decade or more to complete. For example, the use of lasers for a variety of purposes, from blasting fine holes in diamonds to providing a communication system, involved considerable work after the laser was first developed by Charles H. Townes in 1951. There are still many difficulties inherent in the use of lasers. Although the theory of the production of atomic energy by fusion is well worked out, it will be many decades before energy, on earth, will be produced by that means. A view that is commonly held is that there is a delay of about twenty years between the development of a scientific idea and its application to some practical field. This delay is sometimes called cultural lag, but its explanation may lie in the possibility that ideas may have to incubate in the human mind for a generation or more before their full implications are understood. Only bureaucrats hold out the hope that, if substantial amounts of money are spent, great technological developments can be made before the next election and in time for the incumbents in office to use these results to their advantage in an election campaign.

Summary

1. Research workers have influenced education through their development of understanding of how children learn and how materials have to be designed to produce effective learning. They have also influenced education in another way. Research workers, and particularly psychologists, have produced concepts concerning the nature of the human that represent philosophical positions. These philosophies have often been embraced as though they represented scientific positions.

2. Earlier in the century, behaviorism began to propagate a philosophical position that has had a marked influence on education. Indeed, the philosophical position of behaviorism has had a far greater impact than has any actual research. The philosophical position of behaviorism is not derived from research, but represents a set of assumptions that behaviorists

accept as a basis for their research. The assumption is made, for example, that behavior is completely under environmental control, a position that denies the individual any responsibility for his own actions. The assumption tells the research worker to find, in the environment, conditions that influence the behavior and learning of the child, and that is a productive avenue of investigation for research workers to follow. However, this may not be a good assumption for teachers to make. Teachers must assume that pupils can take some responsibility for their work. Indeed, it is hard to imagine any community functioning in which nobody assumed any responsibility.

3. It is important for all humans to make assumptions about themselves that emphasize their potential for competence and responsibility. Research workers may find it convenient to assume that the human is basically stupid, but this is a dangerous assumption to make outside of the laboratory.

4. Another source of influence on the philosophical position of educators is that taken by Jean Piaget. The assumptions of Piaget, which he makes for the purposes of research, are far more acceptable to educators than are those of the behaviorists. Piaget's assumptions are close to what common sense tells is a sound viewpoint, but that does not necessarily make the assumptions true.

5. The assumptions of research workers are not verifiable at this time. That is why they are called assumptions. Nevertheless, assumptions about human nature may have an immense impact on practice and should be examined carefully before they are made the basis for practice.

6. The conversion of research findings into practice is called development. This conversion is a very difficult task and often requires considerable genius. From research to development may take many years.

The Scientific Method—Myth or Reality

Toward the end of the nineteenth century, scholars began to take the view that scientists discovered truth about the universe through the pursuit of an identifiable strategy called the scientific method. Earlier in that century John Stuart Mill had laid a foundation for conceptualizing a scientific method by proposing that logic was derived from experience and was not innate, and that the application of logic to experience permitted the discovery of important truths. Mill attempted to describe simple procedures for arriving at truths and for testing hypotheses. Mill had had a classical education, obtained mainly from his father, and had little direct knowledge of how scientists went about their enterprise. Mill was right in his assertion that empirical knowledge, that is to say knowledge of the physical world and its events, was essential for the construction of a science. He was also right in asserting that scientific discoveries are made through the application of logic to findings. Mill's preoccupation with the nature of knowledge, and how it is acquired, represented a long-standing philosophical tradition. The limited value of Mill's pronouncements on the subject results from the fact that they were not derived from a study of how scientists arrive at what they call truth, and his views are also embedded in an early nineteenth-century conception of the nature of truth.

The late nineteenth and early twentieth century produced many attempts to describe what it is that scientists do. Elementary science books for children of that period were notably full of formulas for teaching the child how to behave like a scientist. Most of these formulas are misleading in that scientists do not follow a simple and rigid pattern in their work of producing scientific knowledge. Consider some classic examples of how scientific discoveries have been made.

No scientist would question the contribution that Darwin made to scientific understanding; the way in which he achieved scientific understanding has been well documented through the records he left behind. The crucial event in Darwin's life was his appointment as naturalist to *H. M. S. Beagle,* which had been given the mission of circumnavigating the Earth and exploring many uncharted areas on the way. Of all the events that took place on the trip, nothing impressed Darwin more than the observations he made about wildlife on the Galapagos Islands. These remote islands in the Pacific had been isolated from the mainland for millions of years. The islands had also been isolated one from the other. Darwin was puzzled by the fact that the same species could be found on the different islands, but the strains on the islands differed. Each strain seemed to differ in ways that made it particularly well adapted to the particular island and locality on which it was found. During his five weeks exploring the islands, Darwin began to make notes on what he referred to as the "Transmutation of the Species." The only explanation he could find for the variation in a species from island to island was in the idea that a species could slowly change in ways that would better suit it to the circumstances under which it was living. This led to the idea of natural selection. Darwin spent much of the rest of the voyage in collecting additional evidence that would support that point of view. In many ways, Darwin's life work was complete by the time the voyage of the *Beagle* had ended, but he did not publish his results for another twenty-two years, and not until he learned that another scientist was about to publish similar findings. During those twenty-two years Darwin made great efforts to collect additional information, spending five years studying the barnacles around the English coast, an approach that turned out to be unproductive. Darwin's entire approach was highly data oriented, with a lifetime search for more data that would support, extend, and improve his original concept of the transmutation of the species.

In contrast to the approach of Darwin to discovery is the approach of Albert Einstein. Darwin's thirst for data, and a life involved in its collection, is not at all evident in Einstein. Einstein never performed an experiment except as a student. He was not concerned with making extensive observations on natural phenomena. Even after he had developed a theory of relativity, he was not interested in finding experimental verification for this theory. Once when asked how he would react if an experiment produced results contrary to those expected of relativity theory, Einstein replied that in such an event he would conclude that there was something wrong with the experiment. Even before Einstein had left high school, his thoughts were already obsessed with the fact that the speed of light was always the same, whatever the conditions under which it was measured. In order to understand why this was so puzzling to Einstein, consider the matter of the measurement, not of the velocity of light, but of the wind. If one had a little device for measuring wind velocity, then the velocity would appear greater if one were walking into the wind than if one were walking away from it with the wind at one's back. In the case of light, one would expect, by analogy, that the speed of light should seem higher when one is moving toward the source of light than when one is moving away from it.

This is not what happens. When one moves toward a source of light, the velocity of the light is the same as when one moves away from it. Presumably, if one were traveling toward a source of light at half the velocity of light itself, and were measuring the velocity of the light coming from the source, the measured velocity would still be the same. Classical physics would have predicted that the apparent velocity would be multiplied by 2 under those circumstances, much as when one travels at 60 MPH along a highway and a car, traveling in the opposite direction at the same speed, passes one at 120 miles per hour. However, that is not what happens with light. The velocity of light is always the same regardless of how it is measured. Einstein was puzzled by this fact. Thus, classical physics describes what happens in the case of moving cars, but cannot explain the constant value of the velocity of light. Einstein's theory of relativity explains this paradox.

The work of Darwin and Einstein represents extreme differences between the highly data-oriented scientist and the scientist who is interested primarily in making logical deductions from the findings of others. Most scientists fall somewhere in between. Although one may think of Isaac Newton as a man who spent his life making mathematical deductions from the established facts of astronomy and physics, he also undertook many important experiments, including those that measured the velocity of sound and others that demonstrated the multicolored composition of white light. Ernest Rutherford's great contribution to our theoretical understanding of the nature of the atom was preceded by ten years of the most rigorous experimental work on subatomic particles. Typically, scientific careers involve a combination of periods of time when the individual engages in the collection of data or the exploration of interesting phenomena, and periods when theoretical ideas provide simplified explanations of complex sets of observations.

Another point to note is that the work of a Darwin, as the work of an Einstein, involves a set of disciplines. Most visitors to the Galapagos Islands would have seen the small animals that Darwin saw, and these same species can still be seen today, but they would not have observed what Darwin was able to observe. Darwin observed the animals within the framework provided by his training as a biologist. He was armed with such concepts as that animals must adapt to their environment in order to survive. Darwin was able to extend this idea to think of how a species might slowly change to provide a better adaptation to what would otherwise be hostile surroundings. Such interpretations of data were essential for Darwin to produce his discoveries. Raw data is not the essence of science, but the meaningful interpretation of that data is the essence of science.

Einstein brought to his life work skills that were very different from those of Darwin. Einstein sought to solve the problems with which he confronted himself with logic and that extension of logic known as mathematics. He did not have the disposition to be an observer or a laboratory experimentalist, but preferred to engage in reflective thought. Einstein's disposition for reflective thought seems to have been coupled with a rich fantasy life, and his scientific speculations were often accompanied by wild imaginings, such as that of traveling on a beam of light.

Scientists do not follow any simple routine that can be written down and communicated to others. Scientific inquiry represents a complexity of techniques and approaches to knowledge. Each scientist draws upon whatever personal resources he has available and uses those skills and techniques that are available to him. Even within a narrow discipline, the mode of attack of one scientist may be quite different from that of another. Within the field of chemistry, one scientist may bring to the research task a genius for accurate measurement and instrument design. Another may bring a capacity to conceptualize theoretical problems, and his actual experiments may be more crudely instrumented than that of his colleague. One educational researcher may be able to design and carry out experiments that give such clear results that there is no value in applying statistical analysis to the data, for the data are clear and unambiguous in themselves. Another educational researcher may be content to collect data that cannot be easily understood, for these data are contaminated with numerous variables over which the experimenter has no control. The latter research worker may resort to statistical procedures to determine what effects are statistically significant. Each of these educational researchers uses the skills at which he excels, and each may produce findings of interest and sometimes of practical significance. Other scientists, who have had an impact on education, have taken a still different approach. For example, the linguist Noam Chomsky has made contributions of enormous significance because he has had the ability of making an analysis of the problems involved in the use and learning of a language. Chomsky's contribution to education has been much like the contribution of the theoretical chemist to research on chemistry. The theoretical chemist has often provided the analysis that has to be undertaken before the laboratory chemist can undertake thoroughly significant experiments.

Whoever undertakes research in education should first equip himself with a repertoire of skills that he can bring to the scientific task. The skills should be consistent with his way of thinking and approaching problems. All too often the student of education is given a course or two on statistics, with the notion that those courses are all that is required to conduct worthwhile research. The end result is often the picture of the student who applies statistical methods, which he does not fully understand, to data that is so sloppy it should have been consigned to the wastepaper basket. The student of education should be exposed to the minds of those skilled in the analysis of problems and to those who have competence in designing ways to collect data. Schools of education show little recognition of the great range of skills that may enter into research.

The Empiricist and the Rationalist as Researchers

The distinction that has been made here is between the empiricist, who places emphasis on data collection, and the rationalist, who thinks through in very great detail just what the problem is before he collects data, or who develops theories to account for discrepancies among sets of data or discrepancies between what scientists had expected and what they actually found. Although one may think of the empiricist as a person who does not engage in any extensive theory building before he collects his data, he always starts out with some concepts that give order to his observing activities. In modern times, B. F. Skinner has been viewed as the prime example of the empiricist's approach to research. In an article written after he had ceased to be a productive research worker, Skinner (1959) describes some of the rules that the individual should follow in the pursuit of research that is closely tied to data. One rule is that the scientist, once he finds a phenomenon that interests him, should drop everything else and observe and experiment with the phenomenon. Many research workers may include very informal experiments among their early observations. Skinner describes how his wartime research found him doing experiments in an attic, where he began to observe some of the pigeons that nested outside under the eaves. He soon found the behavior of the birds to be enormously interesting. He captured a few pigeons and began to work informally at controlling their behavior. This activity soon became a subject of intense interest to him and the beginning of a program of research that provided a large amount of data. Surely, when Skinner saw those pigeons, he did not merely see a set of performing animals. He brought to his observations the ideas he had already derived from his studies of rats. Skinner saw the animals as creatures whose behavior was controlled by reinforcement. Thus, although Skinner the empiricist centered his efforts on the collection of data, he was nevertheless guided by primitive theories.

It should be clear that the work of the scientist is closely related to the use and making of theories. Darwin was guided by the general theory that living organisms adapt to their environment, slowly extending this idea to the idea of species adaptation. Einstein spent his early adult life searching for a theory. Skinner formulated a conception of behavior and the conditions that control it early in his career, focusing on the concept of reinforcement. Though his early work was centered on the behavior of the laboratory rat, Skinner's later observations were completely colored by the concept of reinforcement derived from the study of this single species. One could say that his life work was dominated by a primitive form of theory, though Skinner does not like to use the term *theory* in this connection.

All scientists construct or use theories of some kind. Those whose work is primarily focused on the development of theories are commonly called rationalists. Those who focus on the collection of data are referred to as empiricists. Most scientists are both rationalists and empiricists.

Let us turn now to a consideration of the nature of theory.

The Nature of Theory

The most useful work on theory for the purposes of educational research is the excellent article by Snow (1973), which was written specifically for educational research workers. Snow points out that the term *theory* has a multiplicity of meanings, and that it is often confused with the word *model*. Perhaps a good place to begin the consideration of the nature of theory is to consider what is meant by a theoretical statement. For example, Isaac Newton concluded that the planets were held in their orbits by the force of universal gravitation that exactly balanced the centrifugal force resulting from the motion of the planets around the sun. Such a conclusion is a theoretical statement in that it involves the term *universal gravitational force,* which cannot be directly observed but which is inferred from a great amount of other data. Theoretical statements always involve terms referring to events that cannot be directly observed. Useful ways of conceptualizing the nature of the universe have always involved the use of such terms.

What are first introduced as theoretical terms may later be found to refer to real objects or events. For example, when J. J. Thompson experimented with cathode rays, his data led him to the conclusion that the rays consisted not of waves of energy, as is the case with light beams, but of particles that were smaller in size than atoms. He called these particles electrons. Thompson could not see these subatomic particles, even under the microscope, but he inferred their existence from the fact that they behaved like particles of matter. They could, for example, be deflected by a magnetic field. Later, as the science of physics advanced, more and more direct evidence accumulated to show that electrons were real particles. Ultimately, the path of an electron could be observed with a naked eye through the invention of the cloud chamber, in which the passage of an electron draws a line through water vapor. In addition, a vast body of evidence slowly accumulated showing that the electron was one of the basic components of matter, and there was virtually no evidence to the contrary. The electron emerged from being a theoretical idea to being a reality. The most important theoretical ideas of the physical science of one generation have typically become the realities of the next generation.

The theoretical terms of a theory or theoretical statement are sometimes said to refer to what are called constructs. Thus, many theories of learning refer to a motivational factor in behavior. Now motivation is not directly observable. It is a theoretical term. Some psychologists prefer to say that the term *motivation* refers to a construct. The term implies that it is a *construction* of the scientist's imagination. Many of these constructs, or constructions of the imagination, have been of vital importance to the development of science. When Ernest Rutherford proposed that atoms were like miniature solar systems, with a positive charge in the center and small negative charges orbiting around the positive charge, he provided a construct which was consistent with all known facts and was of immense scientific value, and yet was not an observable entity. Sometimes the term *hypothetical construct* is used to stress that the constructs are hypothetical rather than real.

The behavioral sciences have been much less successful than the physical sciences in developing theoretical ideas that can later be shown to be realities. For example, most of the theoretical terms that Sigmund Freud tried to introduce are as theoretical and abstract today as they were when he first proposed their use. Freud's notion of a libidinal source of sexual energy remains an abstract concept for which there has not been a slow accumulation of supporting evidence; this concept remains as nebulous and obscure today as it was in Freud's day. Much the same is true of the theorizing of the Gestalt psychologists and such theory-oriented psychologists as Kurt Lewin. Indeed, a few psychologists have been so pessimistic about the possibility of productive theorizing in the behavioral sciences that they have taken the position that psychologists should stay so close to their data to make theorizing unnecessary. Skinner is one who has taken this position. He is right in asserting that most theorizing in psychology has led nowhere and has been little better than idle speculation, but he has been wrong in asserting that a science of behavior can be built without theorizing. No science of any consequence has yet been built without resorting to theoretical terms. Skinner's assertions in this respect are odd in that he himself seems to have given up data collection in the mid-1940s, and has since spent much of his time writing about the implications of his work in terms that imply that he has discovered a universal theory of behavior.

Thus, a product of all research in the behavioral sciences is a set of conclusions that involve or imply theoretical terms. These conclusions may be at a sophisticated level of theorizing, or at a level of theorizing that is quite minimal. Most psychologists would agree that it is wise to keep theorizing down to the level that involves a minimum use of abstract terms. Snow (1973) has suggested six levels of theorizing, and we follow his classification in this discussion.

Level 1. This is the level of hypothesis formation. Any hypothesis one may have that is to be used as a basis for research goes beyond the facts on which it is based. Suppose one has the hypothesis that school boards select superintendents for qualities that enable the superintendents to exert control over the teachers and supervisors of the system. The hypothesis is probably a hunch, based on considerable observation of superintendents, but there is no hard data to back it up. The hypothesis involves a theoretical notion that the members of school boards are influenced by particular characteristics when they select superintendents. This bias may not be obvious in the immediate behavior of school board members. The members of a school board may select a particular candidate for the superintendency but claim that they have selected him for reasons of superior professional knowledge, good administrative record, and pleasant disposition. However, the teachers in the system may see the selection as one that involves the appointment of a conservative bully. There appear to be forces at work that are not evident from an observation of the surface behavior of the board and what one can glean from a reading of the minutes of the meetings. The hypothesis assumes the existence of factors that cannot be directly observed, and, hence, introduces a theoretical concept. The problem could be studied in many ways. One would be to find out whether superintendents show qualities that might give them a position of dominance, such as tallness, impressive body appearance, dominance as a personality characteristic, and so forth. Incidentally, considerable research in this area supports this hypothesis.

Much of what is called educational research involves the determination of the nature of a particular state of affairs. Another name for this kind of research is *fact gathering,* but facts are not collected at random. Fact collectors are guided by a primitive theory of what to expect at level 1. Such studies involve what we call state variables, that is to say, measures of some particular condition as it exists at a particular time. The purpose is to establish the existing state of affairs. Nearly all surveys are conducted for the latter purpose. Thus, students of education may conduct a survey of what the pupils think of particular aspects of the curriculum, how much time is spent by pupils watching television, what are the facilities for providing audiovisual materials in one or more school districts, and so forth. Straightforward studies of states are probably the simplest types of studies to undertake, though this does not mean that they are easy to plan and execute.

An ambitious use of such state variables is found in the annual Gallup surveys of education published in the Phi Delta Kappan Journal. These surveys provide a great amount of information concerning the way in which the public views education at a particular time. Gallup's surveys also provide landmarks that can be used to follow, over the years, changes in the status in education in the eyes of the public.

School surveys, and the kinds of surveys undertaken by accrediting associations, involve the assessment of states. The recommendations of accrediting associations may include suggestions, often amounting to directives, that the state of a school should change or the school will lose its accreditation. Later assessments of the state of the school system are designed to discover whether the recommended changes have taken place. Thus, although each assessment of the state of the school system involves assessment of the existing state of affairs, successive assessments may show change.

Level 2. Snow describes such theories as being at the level of element-isms. Examples of theories at this level are primitive forms of classification, such as the classification of abilities derived from factor analysis, or the classification of teaching acts that may be the result of extensive classroom observation. The theorizing that produces such classification schemes may be quite primitive and, indeed, almost at the intuitive level. The classification of teaching acts is a long step from the development of a sophisticated theory of teaching. It may be a step in the direction of building a sophisticated theory, but, again, it may not be. Such categorizations represent some understanding, but it is a limited understanding. There is some difficulty in distinguishing classification activity at this level from classification at the next higher level.

An example of educational research that engages in theorizing at this level is a study by Halpin and Croft (1962) that was designed to discover ways in which schools differ in social climate. Halpin and Croft first assembled about 1,000 statements that describe teachers and principals in a school setting. Duplicates and ambiguous items were eliminated and then a statistical analysis reduced the pool of items to eighty. The statistical analysis also indicated that the items could be grouped into eight scales. Through further procedures, Halpin and Croft believed that they demonstrated that the climates of school could be classified into six categories. These were described as *open, autonomous, controlled, familiar, paternal,* and *closed*. This study involves a classificatory activity and a complicated statistical procedure that leads to a classification of school climates. Incidentally, the items in the scales all refer either to the behavior of teachers or the behavior of principals. Apparently, the behavior of children was assumed to be unimportant in determining the social climate of a school. The classificatory system, despite the fact that it is based on a sophisticated statistical technique, does not involve any sophisticated theory of behavior. It is about as sophisticated as making a classification of seashells in terms of their shape, color, and other obvious properties, but neglecting the nature of the organisms that lived in the shells and the way the organisms adapted to their environment. Perhaps much educational research has to begin with simplistic theories at this time. We have no good theory of how the people in a school create a social climate, so we may have to start by classifying climates in terms of their superficial properties.

Level 3. Snow describes this level as that of descriptive theories and taxonomies. An example of theorizing at this level is the taxonomy of human learning provided by Gagné (1970). Gagné classifies learning in eight different categories, which vary from the most simple to the most complex. However, this is much more than a classification of learnings in terms of complexity. The basic type of learning is signal learning, demonstrated by the infant who begins to smack his lips as soon as he sees his mother holding the bottle. At a slightly higher level is stimulus-response learning, as when an infant learns to empty his bladder when placed on the toilet. At the third level there is learning of chains of behaviors, each of which has already been learned in simple stimulus-response learning. At the next higher level is the learning of verbal associations. The next level involves the learning of multiple discriminations, as are involved in discriminating between and among objects that differ in many ways. Thus, a child will learn to recognize dogs as a class of objects and discriminate them from cats. Then come the final three stages of concept learning, principle learning, and problem solving. These eight categories of learning are related in that learning at each level always assumes that learning has taken place at lower levels. Thus, the learning of a principle assumes that the individual has already mastered the concepts that are involved in the statement of the principle. In order to understand the principle of the conservation of energy, the individual must already be familiar with the concepts of conservation and energy. This in turn has required an understanding based on the discrimination of objects radiating much energy and those radiating little energy. This understanding, in turn, requires that the individual understand the association between objects and words, such as the association between the word *hot* and objects that are hot. Thus, all understandings at complex levels call for learnings at lower levels. Gagné has more than a mere classification based on intuitively derived categories; he has a primitive theory of learning. That is what distinguishes theories at this level from theories at the next lower level. In the case of Gagné's categories, the theory that ties them together is derived by logical analysis. It is intuitively evident that the understanding of a principle calls for an understanding of the words and concepts that enter into the principle. Such understandings are a logically necessary prerequisite for understanding the principle.

Snow places the Bloom taxonomy of cognitive behaviors (1956) at this level of theorizing, but its location here is doubtful. The taxonomy is based on an intuitive understanding that some forms of cognitive behavior, that is to say, behavior related to knowing or understanding, can be arranged along a dimension of complexity. For example, knowing the name of the capital city of New York State is at a simpler level of knowing than is understanding the reason why the capital city is located on a river. The dimension of complexity is a questionable one. Evaluative behavior in the Bloom taxonomy is placed high on the dimension of complexity, but some evaluations can be at a quite primitive level, as when I say I prefer lamb to beef. Of course, the Bloom taxonomy tries to define evaluations in such a way that they involve complex forms of behavior. A dimension of complexity is about as simple a dimension as one can introduce into a theoretical system.

Snow implies that Skinner's operant psychology is at this level of theorizing. Skinner himself, of course, rejects the notion that his system of psychology involves theory, but when Skinner talks about theory he means any system that involves a large number of abstract concepts. Skinner's psychology is very parsimonious in the use of abstract terms, and the few abstract terms that he uses are closely tied to observable events. Reinforcers are defined as events that change responses in particular ways, but the term *reinforcer* is to some degree an abstract term in that it represents a class of events. A class of events refers to events that might be observed in the future as well as events that have been observed in the past. Hence, the term is tied only loosely to observables.

Most research on problem solving involves theorizing at this level. In most of this research there is the implicit assumption that particular processes are operating. Many studies of logic in children assume that children at particular levels of development can undertake some logical operations, but not others. Much of the American literature on the development of logical operations in children of elementary school age has been directed toward the goal of finding more efficient ways of developing better logical processes in children. The theory borrowed for this purpose is that of Piaget, but it is only a miniscule part of Piaget's theory of the intellect. The latter is nearer to a level 5 theory.

The logical solution to problems involve internal operations, that is to say, operations that cannot be directly observed. Theorizing at this level involves operations that cannot be directly observed. Level 1 research involves mainly the study of states, whereas level 3 involves the study of operations.

Despite the confusions between levels 2 and 3, the consideration of classifications as elemental and theoretical systems raises the issue of what forms of classifying and categorizing have a place in the scientific enterprise and which do not. There can be no doubt that a bad classification system can be a hindrance to the scientific enterprise. The classical case of the development of knowledge being prevented by the presence of an established but useless classification system is that of chemistry in the eighteenth century. At that time liquids were classified into oils and spirits. Thus, sulfuric acid was classified as an oil, and so too was olive oil. The system placed these two substances, which are entirely different one from the other, in the same category. In a parallel way, sulfur and cornstarch were also placed in the single category of *flowers*. The classification system was based on the superficial characteristics of the substances and had nothing to do with their more basic chemical qualities. As a system, it was worse than worthless because it concentrated the attention of the students of science on characteristics of substances that should have been overlooked. Classificatory systems have to have a deep, rather than a superficial, basis, and that deep basis often involves a very general theory of the nature of the phenomena involved. Thus, the present and extraordinarily useful classification of the elements is based on a theory of atomic structure.

In education, and in the behavioral sciences in general, there are no examples of the slow development of theory beginning with a simple theory that permits us to classify phenomena. Most classification systems related to behavior seem to have little power to stimulate further research. Many classification systems are barely at level 2 in terms of Snow's classes of theory. As a matter of fact, most of those who develop classification systems of one kind or another are not even aware of the need for having a set of theoretical ideas to underlie the classification. Yet it is this kind of theoretical underpinning that has proved to be essential for the development of a useful classificatory system. The classification of animals acquired significance only after it was realized that species could be fitted into a system in which the evolutionary relationships between animals became the basis for classification.

Level 4. Although the concept of evolution became a basis for the systematic classification of living creatures, the theory of evolution itself represents theory construction at a higher level. In this type of theorizing, abstract ideas are introduced to explain relationships between observed phenomena. Consider the idea that now finds considerable support that a person's self-concept is related to his motivation in performing particular tasks. There is now some evidence to support this position. The person's self-concept functions as a hidden element in his behavior. Although the self-concept cannot be directly observed, there are indirect ways through which it can be assessed. Much of theory of attitude is also at level 4 theorizing. Changes in attitude under particular conditions can be accounted for in terms of underlying conditions that can be only indirectly assessed. The classical conditioning theory of Pavlov, and the various Americanized versions of this theory, also fall into this class of theorizing. The dog learns to salivate at the sound of the bell because the sound of the bell and the presence of food are conditions that become linked in some unseen way in the brain of the animal.

Theories at this level are still quite primitive and crude, but perhaps they represent most good modern psychological theorizing. The state of behavioral and social science may be such that higher levels of theorizing cannot be undertaken at this time with much hope of success.

Levels 5 and 6. These are the levels of theorizing found in the physical sciences. At the highest level, a theory consists of a set of basic statements that are the axioms of the theory. For example, in classical Newtonian theory of physics, force is said to have both a point of application and a direction, and velocity (of a particle) has direction and is measured by the ratio of displacement in space (distance) traversed to time. These axioms tell one what the theory is about and they are also points of departure from which the rest of the theory follows. Such axiomatic statements, or *postulates* as they are sometimes called, include primitive terms. These are terms that are intuitively understood and cannot be otherwise completely defined. The use of the words *space* and *time* are primitive terms. Although one can measure both distance and time, these primitive terms are only fully understood through one's own experience of living in a universe that has the essential properties of space and time. Classical physics has a few primitive terms such as *mass, space,* and *time,* which are well agreed upon to be fundamental properties of the universe. In research on learning and education we have no agreement at all on what the fundamental terms of the system should be, and thus we cannot write theories that begin with a few basic postulates and then build theories on that kind of foundation. In the psychology of learning there have been a few attempts to build theories in this way, the most notable example of which is that of Clark Hull (1943). Some attempts to build mathematical learning theory are moves in this direction, but these tend to be minitheories, that is to say, theories that apply to a very small range of phenomena, in contrast to theories in physics that aim at being universally applicable theories. Snow places measurement theory as a candidate for theorizing in this category, but theory of measurement is not a theory about natural phenomena, but is rather a theory about how to measure natural phenomena. It is not a scientific theory any more than logic is a scientific theory. Closer to a behavioral theory in this category is that of Piaget, but he has made no attempt to state his theory of intelligence in formal terms. Piaget's basic axioms would be statements of the fact that the fundamental understanding of the universe calls for an understanding of the fundamental properties of the universe, namely space, time, and cause and effect. Another basic property of the universe is that objects have some degree of permanence. Objects do not suddenly disappear and then reappear, though they may undergo transition from one state to another. The infant does not understand any of these basic properties of the universe, and much of the first year of life is occupied in acquiring some limited understanding. The laws of Piaget's system have to do with the formation of various intellectual structures that permit a slowly expanded comprehension of the basic properties of the universe and properties derived from them. Interestingly enough, there is much in common, in point of departure, of Newton's theory of the physical universe and Piaget's theory of behavior. Piaget might expect this in that he assumes that the human brain has evolved as a system that has the capability of mastering the fundamental properties and laws of the universe, for such intellectual mastery has been man's means of survival. Piaget postulates a certain parallelism between the ability of the human to comprehend his physical environment and the nature of the environment itself. Intelligence is a mathematical-logical system that makes it possible to cope with a mathematical-logical universe.

Perhaps the main lesson to be drawn from the history of high-level theorizing is that it is undertaken by men and women of great genius. It is not an activity in which the typical doctoral student can hope to engage in successfully. Most competent research workers can expect to engage in successful theorizing at the first three levels, and perhaps occasionally at level 4. B. F. Skinner has long stressed, correctly, that one of the worst errors of psychologists has been that of attempting to engage in high-level theorizing while the science of behavior is still operating at a very primitive level. Skinner's view has been often taken to imply that no theorizing should be engaged in at all. Such a view is nonsense, for, as has been noted, even Skinner's own system of psychology involves theorizing at some of the lower levels discussed here.

An additional point needs to be made about the distinction between level 5 and level 6 theorizing. Snow reserves level 5 for incomplete theories or theories that are on the way toward obsolescence. Level 6 theories represent the ultimate in scientific creations. They represent the closest approximations to what one might call accurate descriptions of the laws of the universe. They will probably always be only limited reflections of reality and truth, in that the human mind is capable of only limited understanding of the nature of the universe. The human brain is probably one of the most complicated objects in the universe, but nevertheless it is probably not complicated enough to understand all of the complexities of the universe. A system can understand only that which is no more complicated than itself.

The graduate student who seeks a doctoral degree in education will have to produce a doctoral dissertation that involves some theorizing, either his own or that borrowed from others. Generally, he will borrow the theory from others, perhaps because the building of a theory is a very difficult enterprise. Many dissertations involve the use of a particular instrument that was built in terms of some kind of theory. For example, perhaps hundreds of dissertations have used the instrument known as the *Edwards Personal Preference Schedule*. This device attempts to measure needs in terms of a theory developed by H. A. Murray (1938). The user of such an instrument should know that the inventory does not do justice to the original theory. Murray took the position that needs had to be aroused before they could function. Thus, achievement need would influence behavior in those situations in which the need to achieve or excel was aroused. Achievement need could then be usefully measured only when the individual was in a situation in which this need was challenged. The inventory, although it purports to measure need, does not require the person taking it to be challenged in some way so that achievement need can be measured. Neither are any of the other needs challenged. The Murray theory of need assessment takes the position that needs can be usefully appraised only when they are aroused. The Edwards inventory, which attempts to measure Murray's system of needs, violates this basic condition. Most doctoral students who have used this inventory have not realized that the theory on which it is based virtually takes the position that the inventory cannot be a valid measure of need.

The doctoral dissertation is probably best undertaken through the use of data collecting devices that have already been developed on a fairly good theoretical foundation. Few doctoral students will have had enough sophisticated experience in developing knowledge to know how to go about developing theory. There is much to be said for the maxim that the doctoral student should stay as close as he can to his data, without failing to recognize that there may be theoretical ideas hidden in the data that he should recognize.

The student planning a study should be careful to identify the theory on which the study is based. If, for example, the student is undertaking a study on the attitudes of high school students toward their school, he should become familiar with current thinking about the nature of attitudes. He should understand that attitudes are considered to have several different components, a knowledge component, a feeling component, and an action component. The person making the study should also become familiar with the sophisticated theories of attitude change that have emerged in recent years. He should also be familiar with the major studies that have been undertaken within the various theories of attitude. He should not just develop an attitude scale according to a cookbook telling him how to develop an instrument to measure attitudes. Complicated procedures for developing attitude scales can be appropriately used after the student has mastered what is known about theory of attitudes that have been developed by social psychologists and sociologists.

The student of education should try to link his thinking with a theory that has proved useful over the years for developing research and which, perhaps, has even had some impact on practice. For example, those who are interested in conducting research on language development would do well to link themselves to the theory of language developed by Noam Chomsky, not because the theory is necessarily true, but because the theory has been enormously successful in stimulating productive research. The theory has led to the development of whole trains of important ideas. It has even had an impact on educational practice by stressing the production of language as a creative endeavor, rather than as the repetition of well-learned habits. The Chomsky theory of language development is to be contrasted with that produced by B. F. Skinner, which, although extremely ingenious, has led to little truly new research and has had almost no impact on practice.

However long a theory of behavior has been in existence, if it has not led to the development of knowledge, it should not be used as a basis for research. It would be hard to imagine a study undertaken on the basis of Freud's theory of psychoanalysis. The theory is far too vague to produce useful research, which is why it has not stimulated the development of knowledge. It is also far more complex than a productive theory should be at this stage of development of the behavioral sciences. Freudian theory has great appeal to the romantic in education, but its failure, after nearly a century, to stimulate productive research suggests that it is not a basis for useful work.

Models and Theories

The distinction between models and theories becomes apparent when one looks at examples of each. The reader is familiar with gravitation theory and with the theory that chemical compounds can be analyzed into their constituent elements. Such theories, and others, provide an understanding of the nature of the physical world and can be used to make scientific predictions. Theories provide us with useful ways of conceptualizing the world around us, but there are other ways of conceptualizing our environment. One can help a child to conceptualize the earth by showing him a globe with oceans and continents marked on it in different colors. The globe is more or less a small model of the earth made with a certain amount of license. The colors of the countries marked on the globe have nothing to do with the actual colors of the terrain represented, although the oceans are appropriately painted blue. The part of the globe near the equator is not hot and the poles are not cold. On some globes the mountain ranges are shown as raised ridges, but they are raised far out of proportion to their actual size. If the mountains were shown in a size proportional to the rest of the globe they would scarcely be discernible. The globe is a convenient *model* of the earth, that is to say, it represents important features of the earth in a way that is readily understood.

Chapanis (1961) pointed out that models are convenient analogies. Models may sometimes provide a close representation of whatever they represent, as a globe does; these are called replica models. Miniature plastic engines that are popular with children and show all the working parts are replica models. Models may be symbolic. The globe has some symbolic features, such as the little black circles that represent cities, but some models are completely symbolic, such as a table of organization showing the various positions, who occupies them, and the interrelationship of the positions. Another example of a symbolic model is an architect's floor plan for a building. This represents the building quite accurately so that the contractor can produce the building from the plans. Some historians have said that history is a symbolic model of the past built out of words.

All kinds of materials may be used to develop models of behavior. At one time efforts were made to develop mechanical devices that would show the same kind of learning that simpler organisms manifest. Thus, mechanical mice were developed that would learn and go and get a charge of electricity when their batteries ran down. The newest device for providing models of human behavior is the computer, which can be programmed to solve problems in quite human ways. Computer scientists can program computers in different ways and see which way produces problem solving that is most like human problem solving. In this way the computer can be used to model problem-solving behavior.

Models are very useful ways of thinking about complex phenomena. A good model can provide a very simple representation or quite complex happenings and make them more readily understood. A reader interested in learning about the great variety of models that have been used in different aspects of the behavioral sciences is referred to Stogdill's compilation (1970).

Two Aspects of Research Design

Theory is closely related to research design, but courses on the design of educational research given in colleges of education, however, rarely tell the student anything about the nature of theory. They are confined to the discussion of statistical methods and statistical aspects of research design. The result is that many doctoral dissertations and master's theses, which emerge from the colleges, use complicated statistical designs but are very naïve in terms of underlying theory. A dissertation that uses complex statistical designs provides the illusion of being a sophisticated study. This is just an illusion, but it may have a sufficient impact on a journal editor to have the study published. The author was recently on a committee to select an article for an award from a large number of articles on educational research. The difficulty in making a selection was to find one that had anything more than a sophisticated statistical design. The underlying theory was generally naïve and did not reflect any well-developed body of psychological theory. This is because the writers of the articles had all been trained in typical college of education statistical courses, with a heavy emphasis on statistics, but with virtually no contact with theory in the behavioral sciences. An exception to this is the area of counseling, which has long placed a heavy emphasis on theory of behavior. Any student of counseling at even the master's degree level has knowledge of operant theory, Rogerian theory, and so forth. Theses and dissertations in this area have a sophistication in the use of theory.

It is probably more important for the student to become familiar with the body of theory in the area in which he plans to work, than it is for him to become familiar with problems of statistical design. Most important discoveries in science have been made by people who never had a course in statistics and long before R. A. Fisher invented complex designs. Much of the best contemporary research in the behavioral sciences uses only the simplest designs. Such studies provide clear results because they are based on a well-developed body of knowledge and theory, which, though primitive by the standards of the physical science, are sophisticated in terms of modern behavioral science.

Assumptions Underlying a Study

Many graduate schools require the student to state the assumptions underlying his study. This is a difficult task because most studies involve numerous hidden assumptions. If one undertakes a study of the teaching of history to tenth-grade children, one is making the assumption that learning of history is, in some way, important; otherwise one would not be conducting such a study. The numerous studies of achievement motivation, the motive to achieve a personal standard of excellence, all make the assumption that such a motive is a worthwhile motive to have. In our culture, it probably is, but in many foreign cultures it would be looked upon as a character defect. The Russians and the Chinese would be much more interested in developing motivation that was group oriented. Every research involving behavior involves important assumptions concerning what is good or virtuous in our society, but such assumptions are not generally stated in the introduction to a research study.

Other kinds of assumptions are commonly stated. These assumptions generally have to do with the measures involved and their validity. Most survey studies assume that the sample from whom returns are received is representative of the total population to whom the questionnaires were sent. Sometimes one can make a few checks to see whether this assumption is a reasonable one. One may look to see whether those who returned the questionnaires were representative with respect to sex, geographical distribution, and other characteristics that one can readily identify. In the use of most measuring instruments one is likely to make assumptions about the validity of the measuring instrument. Suppose one were to conduct a study of the emotionality of counselors, and measured emotionality at the end of a counseling interview by determining blood pressure and sweating of the hands. In the interpretation of the results, the investigator would probably make the assumption that emotionality is a diffuse and general state of affairs and that the two measures used do actually measure the degree of general emotionality. When Lewis Terman conducted his famous studies of genius and selected a number of high-intelligence-quotient youngsters for subsequent follow-up and study, he made the assumption that intelligence tests can be used to identify those who have unusual intellectual powers that are of value in achieving success in life. He certainly did not undertake the study on the basis of the assumption that intelligence tests measure trivial characteristics. When rating scales are used, the assumption is made that there is some relationship between the ratings and how the individual rated performs in daily life.

One cannot assume anything one wants to assume. Every assumption that underlies a study must be a reasonable assumption. One may have to undertake an inquiry to determine whether an assumption is a reasonable one. Consider the case of the student who was interested in the writing ability of college administrators. This researcher decided to sample the writing of the administrators by collecting the memoranda they sent to the faculty. The assumption was that administrators wrote the memoranda as they appeared in the local mail. This assumption might be questioned. Surely, an administrator might well turn to his secretary and say, "Jenifer, draw up a memorandum asking the faculty to be more economical in using photocopying machines. By the way, also ask them to avoid using the machines for personal use." Then, Jenifer writes the memorandum, using all the finesse and tact she can muster. The assumption made about the source of documents needs to be checked in the case of such a study. A few secretaries could be asked about how their bosses prepared memoranda to the faculty.

Definitions of Terms

Most basic courses in research emphasize the point that all technical terms, or words used in a specialized sense, should be defined. This is good advice, but there is wide disagreement about how terms should be defined.

First, there is the difficulty that not all terms can be defined. Words, such as *after* and *before,* are intuitively understood. They can also be defined in terms of synonyms, which are also intuitively understood. Such terms are referred to as *primitive* terms, and all scientific discourse includes some primitive terms. There is also an intuitive aspect of understanding time and space, though both space and time can be understood at higher levels where measurement is involved, and at these higher levels precise definitions of their attributes, such as the attribute of distance, can be made. As a general rule, scientific discourse and the language of research use primitive terms to the minimum possible extent.

Second, there is some agreement that, as far as possible, the terms of discourse related to research should be defined through the use of what are called *operational definitions.* The term became widely known through the work of Percy Bridgman, the famous authority on high-pressure physics.

Bridgman pointed out that much of discourse outside of the physical sciences was vague because the language was vague. Bridgman took the position that terms should be defined by pointing to actual events in the physical world that represented the phenomena involved. Thus, the velocity of an object is defined in terms of a measured distance and the measurement of time taken to move through that distance. In an analogous way, one may define an individual's intelligence through his performance on an intelligence test. One can point to the performance of the individual on these items as the operations involved in defining intelligence. Although one can define intelligence in such terms, and the definition is an acceptable operational definition, it comes with no guarantee that the concept thus defined will be a useful one for research, or for any other purpose.

During the 1930s many experts on educational research embraced the idea that all terms should be defined in terms of operations. The hope was that in this way the vagueness of educational language would be eliminated and educational research could acquire the same respectability as research in the physical sciences. These hopes were not fulfilled. For example, although the concept of intelligence could be operationally defined through intelligence tests, the tests turned out to be far less useful than their makers had hoped they would be. It soon became evident that intelligence tests did not provide some pure measure of innate intellectual ability. Operational definitions may provide some clarity of discourse, but the discourse itself may not be worthwhile. It is all too easy to develop operationally defined terms that have very little significance. I may define a superintendent's "thrust" as his height, plus his weight, plus the loudness of his voice measured in decibels at a distance of two feet. This measure of thrust is greatest for the large, heavy superintendent who speaks with a loud voice. The measure defines the term operationally, but, as thus defined, it is a naïve and probably trivial concept. Problems in developing a science of education are not a result of any difficulties encountered in developing operational definitions. The difficulties derive from our inability to discover truly significant measures of what happens in education.

Although the doctoral student may be required to define terms in his dissertation, he should realize that this practice has rarely been adopted by the advanced scientist. In the physical sciences, a new subatomic particle may be postulated to account for the results of experiments that could not otherwise be accounted for. In the classic work of James Chadwick, the discoverer of the neutron, or the work of J. J. Thompson, which led to the discovery of the electron, the concepts of neutron and electron emerge from the work. There is no simple definition offered in either case. Research from a number of different directions pointed to the existence of such particles, and the work, as a totality, defines what these particles are. The definitions of these particles that one finds in dictionaries came long after the existence of the particles was well established, and long after the words *electron* and *neutron* had become common usage. Most of the terms used by Piaget, in most of his work, are not first defined and then used. The meaning emerges from the content within which they are used. One finds in Piaget no concise formal definitions of such terms as *assimilation, accommodation, equilibration,* and so forth. The reader brings to the writings of Piaget enough knowledge concerning the meaning of these terms in other scientific areas to enable him to understand the way in which they are used in Piaget's model of the intellect. Piaget does give examples of assimilation, but these examples are generally complex and lengthy. The meaning of a term such as *secondary schemata* is presented in his *Origins of Intelligence* (translated 1969) through lengthy descriptions of infant behavior from which the meaning of the term was derived. This is much like the way in which physicists have presented lengthy data and analyses to show that particular kinds of subatomic particles must be operating. The definition follows the research, rather than precedes it. In the case of Piaget, later workers have attempted to provide concise dictionary definitions of his terms, but these definitions are weak and nebulous compared with the definitions that are implicit in the context of his work.

This discussion of defining terms is concluded by considering the case of the student of education who wants to abandon all contemporary definitions of terms and decides that he is going to define words in his own way. Let us suppose that he is conducting a study of leadership among superintendents and decides to define leadership in terms of the absence of opposition to the superintendent's plans from school personnel. The student claims that he is entitled to define leadership in any way he pleases, and that is the way he has chosen. He is also careful to define, operationally, what he means by opposition from school personnel. Let us suppose that the student completes his study and finds that certain characteristics of superintendents are positively related to leadership as he defined this term. The student's study is, unfortunately, not buried in the archives, but is summarized in a nationally distributed paper. In that summary, the journalist writing the article explains that if school boards want to appoint superintendents with leadership abilities then these superintendents should have this and that quality. Soon school boards, with clippings of the newspaper article in front of them, are selecting superintendents in terms of these criteria. What the school boards did not understand was that the particular definition of leadership had nothing to do with leadership as it is ordinarily construed. What the doctoral student had been measuring, in common language, was the ability of a superintendent to bully his personnel subtly so that they stayed in line.

The story illustrates what happens when words that have common usages are used in special senses. The studies that abandon common meanings of terms are likely to be extremely misleading. Research workers do not have the right of defining terms in any way they please. In the physical sciences, terms with universally accepted meanings have become the rule. It is inconceivable that a physicist would give to a term some unique meaning. Defined terms in educational research should have meanings that are close to those they already have.

Summary

1. Although philosophers have long attempted to identify a procedure for achieving knowledge called the *scientific method,* no single useful procedure has so far been identified. Scientists differ greatly in the way in which they approach problems. Some search for new data and are continuously collecting facts, but others concentrate on unifying existing facts by building theories. The work of Darwin and Einstein represents fundamentally different approaches to the achievement of knowledge, and both made giant steps forward in the development of knowledge. Most research workers pursue knowledge with a variety of techniques, but their techniques depend upon their dispositions. Einstein did not seem to like to engage in actual experimentation, but depended upon facts discovered by great experimenters.

2. The overall field of educational research shows individuals who use a great range of techniques. Some of these contributors to research are primarily thinkers; others are collectors of facts and figures; and still others may design unusual ways of developing knowledge. The graduate student should equip himself with as many tools as he can for undertaking research. Above all, he should not look for some simple formula through which research can be undertaken.

3. Important research studies may begin with some unusual observations. Many research workers like to begin with a set of facts that happen to fascinate them, and then go on to collect more data in the same area. Such research workers are highly data oriented, and are sometimes called empiricists. Other research workers prefer to spend long periods thinking through the problem to be attacked before collecting any data. Those who emphasize theoretical analysis are called rationalists. There are successful contributors to educational research who are empiricists and others who are rationalists. Some scientists may even switch roles.

4. Scientific conceptions of the nature of things involve theories. The research worker should have some understanding of the nature of theory and should avoid trying to build theories that are too sophisticated. Theories always involve terms that refer to matters that cannot be directly observed. Gravity cannot be observed directly, though the effects of gravity can be. Gravity and gravitation are both theoretical terms. As science progresses, many theoretical terms come to refer to events that can be observed

directly. Motivation is an example of a theoretical term in the field of education. One cannot observe motivation directly, but one can observe the consequences of motivation.

5. Excessive theorizing should be avoided. An example of excessive theorizing is found in psychoanalysis, in which theorizing became so elaborate and so vague that it ceased to be useful as a guide to research. Theories should be built at the simplest level possible. All scientific knowledge has to incorporate some theorizing; it is a part of the nature of science. A few scholars in the 1930s argued that theorizing was unnecessary, but such a viewpoint has been largely discarded.

6. Theorizing may take place at different levels. At the first, and lowest, level, theorizing is no more than hypothesis formation. Research involving this level of theory building is very factually oriented and seeks to establish the nature of the existing state of affairs in some field.

7. Level 2 theorizing involves the development of classification systems in terms of some significant set of ideas or idea. Classifications of teacher behavior involve this form of theory. Classificatory systems that are useful are never arbitrary but are based on some form of conceptual system.

8. The third level of theorizing involves descriptive theories and taxonomies that are at a more complex level than mere classifications. Gagné's classification of learning functions into a hierarchy fits this level of theorizing. Although Bloom's taxonomy of cognitive behaviors is placed in this category of theorizing, because the categories used form a part of a system, some might view it as belonging to level 2. Skinner's operant psychology and reinforcement theory belong at this level.

9. Level 4 theorizing involves a greater use of theoretical terms than does level 3. Pavlovian psychology falls into this class as do the Americanized versions of this form of psychology. Theory of evolution represents theorizing at this level.

10. Levels 5 and 6 characterize mature sciences. Newtonian physics represents the highest level. There are a few attempts to build theories in psychology at level 5, but none have met with any notable success either for stimulating research or for providing useful applications. A small part of Piaget's work might be considered to involve level 5 theorizing, but most is level 4.

11. Doctoral dissertations should involve theorizing at the lower levels. Often a doctoral dissertation involves the use of a testing instrument that has been produced in terms of some relatively simple theory, and that theory gives unity to the dissertation. The doctoral student should read the manual for the measuring instrument he proposes to use and identify the theoretical position implied in the instrument.

12. Models differ from theories in that models are analogies that are useful in helping one to think about phenomena. Models may be either

replica models or symbolic models. The globe representing the earth is mainly a replica model, even though it has some symbolic features. Models help us to think about complex things in simple ways.

13. Research design involves two kinds of problems. One is the matter of the statistical design, the simpler of the two aspects. The other aspect of design is that of planning an investigation around important ideas. Many studies that use very sophisticated statistical designs involve quite trivial ideas.

14. The plan for a doctoral dissertation generally includes a statement of the major assumptions on which the study is based. Assumptions related to the validity of the data to be collected are particularly important to state.

15. The extent to which the terms used in a study need to be defined is a source of controversy. Some terms are intuitively understood. Some terms call for operational definitions. The fact that a term is operationally defined does not mean that the term has any particular virtue. Trivia may be defined operationally. Terms should be used as far as possible with meanings similar to those they have in common usage. A research worker does not have a special right to define his terms in any way he wants. Highly individualized definitions of words make comprehension difficult for the reader.

CHAPTER 4
Methods of Finding a
Problem to Research

In this chapter we consider the matter of how the research worker chooses a problem for study. This is mainly a concern for the beginning research worker, for the mature research worker never lacks a problem to study. Those who spend much of their time in research often find that they are confronted with a far greater number of problems than they can possibly solve. Each piece of research that is completed generates more problems than the researcher can immediately handle. There are also chance observations that are made in every laboratory that initiate new lines of research. For example, Roentgen did not set out to discover X-rays, but a chance observation showed him that an apparatus was producing radiation with highly penetrating characteristics. Minor discoveries, as well as major discoveries, are made in this way. The mature research worker finds his world filled with problems, and the only decision he has to make is to select the problems that are most likely to lead to productive research. This turns out to be a most difficult matter, and even great scientists have spent years working on unproductive lines of research. Darwin, for example, spent five years working on the adaptation of the barnacle to different environmental conditions, without producing findings that he considered to be of any importance.

The beginning research worker is in an entirely different position, which makes it difficult for him to identify a problem that is suitable for his research. He sees the world filled with unsolved problems and, all too often, views his task as that of selecting the problem that is of most interest to him. In doing this he ignores the fact that most problems are not researchable. True, one can go through a ritual with such problems that looks like research, but the results are likely to be trivial. Although every research worker should work on a problem that is of interest to him, the mere fact that he is interested in a problem does not necessarily make the problem researchable.

Large numbers of mediocre, or even worthless, theses have emerged from the process of the student undertaking research on a problem that was of the greatest personal significance to him. The author recalls a student who was deeply interested in group process and the effect of training in the area on teaching. The student argued that he was going to work on the problem, even though experienced research workers did not think that it would lead to productive findings. Research workers pointed out to this student that only the most crude methods existed for assessing the kinds of outcomes that one might expect from training in group process, and that these methods had generally failed to show that training had produced the expected outcomes. The student failed to recognize that there was such a matter as expertise in the selection of a problem and in the conduct of research. Indeed, the student felt that his own judgment was as good as that of any other person. All too often the student of education fails to recognize that there is expertise in the choice of a problem for research, though there obviously is.

A common source of a problem for a research study is the practical educational administrator, who typically loves to tell research workers what they should be doing. The administrator can identify the pressing educational problems that need to be solved. Educational administrators have even provided a list of problems to be solved (see American Association of School Administrators, 1966). However, the administrator, like the naïve research worker, cannot discriminate between the problems that can be solved today through research and those that cannot be solved. There is very little difficulty in preparing a list of important educational problems that need to be solved, but this does not identify a list of problems that can be solved at the present time. This, incidentally, is the way in which the federal bureaucracy develops programs of research. Problems that are voted to be important by administrators are placed on the list, and funds are then assigned to support research contracts to solve these problems. The result is a very large quantity of research that usually leads nowhere. An unfortunate consequence of this misguided procedure for developing educational research is that it leads to the false conclusion that research can make little contribution to the development of education.

The beginning research worker should rarely be encouraged to find a problem among the ideas that have personal appeal to him, but that does not mean that he has to work on a problem that has no personal appeal to him. The best single way for the student to find a good research problem is to attach himself to a program of research within the institution where he expects to finish his degree. The chances are that in doing so he will find a group of individuals working enthusiastically on some enterprise, and some of their enthusiasm will rub off on him. There are many advantages in pursuing research in such a setting. The researcher will find that he is among a group of individuals who are anxious to discuss related problems. He will find others who have had experience in tackling a particular type of problem, and who can help in telling the novice what can and cannot be successfully accomplished.

The main reason why the personally attractive problem is usually unresearchable is that there is no well-organized body of knowledge through which the problem can be solved. The alchemist could make no progress in solving the problem of converting base metals into gold, because all he could do was to try anything that came into his mind, without having the benefit of good reasons for what he was doing. The alchemist's experiments were based on vague hopes that perhaps some combination of treatments would produce the change, but often the treatments were based on little more than the hope that they contained some kind of magic that would work. Alchemists had a peculiar passion for magic, perhaps because their rational methods of dealing with reality were very limited in scope. In contrast with the alchemist, the modern atomic physicist knows exactly what transformations of one element into another are actually possible. The atomic physicist also knows something about the limitations of such transmutations and would be sure that the problem of changing lead into gold presents an impossibly difficult problem. The state of knowledge tells the physicist what is possible and also what kind of knowledge can be obtained. However, even if the physicist knows that a process is possible, this does not mean that the process is feasible. For example, physicists know that atomic fusion actually takes place in the sun, but the difficulties of producing atomic fusion on Earth are immense, and may perhaps never be overcome.

Since a research problem must be firmly rooted in knowledge, the student should first identify a general area in which he wishes to do research and then immediately set about reviewing the knowledge available in that area.

Looking Through the Research Literature

Professors advise the student to study the research literature as a step in identifying and pinning down a good problem. Most students of education have some idea about the sort of problem they want to investigate, and a review of what has already been done helps them to clarify their thinking. Some students of education will know only that they want to undertake research in a particular area, but have little idea of what type of research they want to do. A review of what has already been accomplished may help these students select a researchable problem of their own.

The research literature related to education may help the beginning research worker. Most students of education are unnecessarily overwhelmed by anything labeled research. Some are even overwhelmed by anything in print, as though the printing of a statement gave it some special significance or endorsement as the truth. Certainly, ever since the invention of the printing press, the printed word has carried enormous weight, and the weight carried has often been far in excess of its actual worth. The reader of research literature should be on guard lest his views become prejudiced by the status that printed material often has in our civilization.

The traditional view of research literature, represented by journals, was that the articles were selected by individuals of scientific competence who were able to appraise, objectively, the scientific worth of material submitted for publication. Social scientists are slowly beginning to realize that such objectivity in the selection of material for publication is not possible. Scientists have often submitted work and had it rejected, only for the work to be later recognized as being a basic and outstanding contribution to the science. The most famous case is that of Gregor Mendel, who submitted his famous findings for publication to the Royal Society of London, where the contribution was rejected and placed in a file. The Mendel manuscript lay dormant in the Royal Society files for thirty years until it was discovered by the distinguished biologist William Bateson, who immediately saw the significance of the work and had the results published. But for the curiosity of Bateson, Mendel's findings might have lain dormant until another scientist made the same discovery and found a more accepting publisher. The saddest part of the story is that the rejection of the material by the Royal Society killed all the interest that Mendel had for scientific work. The rejection killed one of the greatest scientific spirits of his century. The case is not an isolated one. R. A. Fisher had many of his early scientific contributions rejected for publication by the great Karl Pearson, a man who was considered a scientific giant in his time. Fisher remained angered by the way in which he had been treated by Karl Pearson for the rest of his life, making reference to it in personal conversation, and carrying on the feud that it generated with Karl Pearson's son. Fortunately, Fisher lived in an age in which more channels of publication were open than were available to Mendel. Fisher's work quickly blossomed and became the foundation of modern experimental design.

As a graduate student in Fisher's laboratory, I was surprised to learn that the maestro, for whom all had the deepest respect, had had manuscripts rejected. Later, I learned that many great men had had the same experience. When I worked for Edward L. Thorndike, a few years later, I was also surprised when Thorndike talked about the rejection of some of his manuscripts by notable journals.

The rejection by well-established journals of the work of such extraordinary men as these and many others, raises questions about where one should look to find the most innovative work of the era. The suspicion is that the well-established journals may not be the place to look. Kuhn (1970) has pointed out that the scientific innovator has had difficulties throughout history in being accepted by his contemporaries. At any time in history, there are established ideas, or paradigms as Kuhn calls them, that dominate the intellectual scene. Work related to these ideas are those that have easy entry into the published literature. The innovator often has to resort to publication in what are considered to be inferior publications, or may even have to resort to his own publication of his work. Kuhn also points out that the innovative ideas of one age become the established ideas of the next age. When these new ideas become accepted, they then tend to prevent a new set of innovative ideas from entering the field.

For these reasons, the student searching the literature for an idea, or for studies related to an idea he already has, should scan a wide section of the literature. He shouldn't just read what are accepted to be the "best" journals. For example, if the student is a psychologist, he would do well to scan the various sections of the *Journal of Experimental Psychology,* a high-prestige journal, but he should also consult journals of lower prestige. In the *Journal of Experimental Psychology* the student will find papers that are based on current theoretical ideas concerning behavior, which are accepted by most experimental psychologists. Few articles will be based upon ways of thinking that are unusual or innovative. The articles will show that the authors have mastered the ways of doing research in their age. The articles will be relatively free of flaws, extending knowledge cautiously and conservatively, and will be highly presentable in terms of the instrumentation used. The articles will present excellent tables and charts and the statistical methods will all be appropriate analyses, but they will rarely be particularly innovative, for to be innovative means that the author of the article will also be burdened with the task of convincing the journal editor that his heretical ideas are sound. Editors of journals are likely to be skeptical.

For these reasons the student should look beyond the high-prestige journals. A professor will tell the student which are the high-prestige journals in his particular field. These are the journals run by the scientific establishment of the time. They reflect the ideas of which the establishment approves.

The relatively low-prestige journals are not all delightful pieces of heretical thinking that were not accepted by the establishment. A few articles in these journals will be interesting and innovative. Some will be sound pieces of research that somehow did not manage to be accepted by the editor of a more prestigious journal. A few articles in these less prestigious journals will leave the reader wondering why they were ever published at all. Nevertheless, the search for the interesting and innovative idea will generally pay off.

The student of education must also be aware of another consideration that may influence his judgment concerning the worth of particular lines of work. Occasionally one comes across a review covering a large group of research studies that is highly destructive of the research involved. Every research article included in such a review is taken apart and shown to include one or more basic defects. The final conclusion is that the entire body of research is worthless. This type of destructive analysis can be done with almost any area of behavioral research, even with articles drawn from some of the most prestigious publications. Research in the behavioral sciences is rarely above criticism. The real issue in reviewing an area is whether the research, as a whole, generally points in one direction, despite a variety of defects in the research design. Of course, if all the research has the same defect, then one may conclude that the results may have been a result of that defect, and one may not know what the results would have been had the defect been remedied. If, however, the defects are varied, then the total picture may give some indication of what the real state of affairs is. There are some classic examples of the same error being included in each of a long sequence of researches. Thus one has to be very careful in evaluating such reviews. Sometimes damning reviews are justified, but sometimes they are not.

Those who write highly critical reviews of research are never unbiased. Sometimes such reviews reflect a game of one-upmanship on the part of a young research worker, who is overeager to establish himself by being critical of a more established member of the profession. Sometimes such reviews are motivated by a person who is trying to promote an alternative viewpoint to that presented in the articles reviewed. Sometimes a reviewer may display personal hostility. Reviewers are people, and they display all the prejudices and some of the irrationalities that are commonly displayed by all of us. Those scientists who have tried to build artificial intelligences, that is to say machines that will solve problems intelligently, have long ago concluded that it is much easier to build a machine that is coldly logical than a machine that is only partly logical, as humans are. Humans are only partly logical systems. Their irrationalities creep into the way in which they view the research of others.

Although research journals may publish reviews of research that are unflattering to those who undertook the research, they are not likely to print reviews that are overly accepting of research results. The latter type of review is more likely to be found in educational literature. All too often in such literature, one finds authors who have particular viewpoints that they want to bolster with whatever information can be gleaned from research. The result is a piecing together of odd bits of information, carefully selected because they support a particular position, and which are selected while ignoring the fact that most of the research in the same area supports a contradictory point of view. The user of research does not have the right to pick and choose as he pleases. If he selects a study from a particular area to support his position, then he is duty bound to examine the rest of the research in the same area and to discover the total picture that it presents. If a person is interested in exploring the possibility that children might develop just as well if they did not enter school until eight years of age, he might be able to find some studies that supported this point of view. However, he would be wrong in using these few studies to support the view that delay in entering school beyond the age of six is advantageous. What he should do is to weigh all the evidence, and all the evidence provides an overwhelming argument for children entering some organized form of education, at least by the age of six, if not earlier.

No educator, and no researcher, has the right to pick and choose the research and knowledge that supports a particular point of view. The first chapter of a thesis or dissertation should always be a fair presentation of all the available knowledge in the field, with studies being rejected only because they did not meet some criterion of competence.

Computer Searches of the Literature

A very old problem in the intellectual world is that of how to make knowledge available to scholars who need it. This problem became acute during the 1950s, when the growing volume of government-sponsored research seemed to be spawning scientific results at a much greater rate than could be quickly cataloged. Indeed, there seemed to be no useful way that was then available to catalog the findings. Scholars could not even find out what had been done in their own fields, and massive research projects often remained hidden in government files. Various initiatives were taken to solve this problem, one of the most promising of which was that of using the computer to store summaries of the literature and then to deliver selected summaries. Many computer retrieval systems have been designed to retrieve particular categories of information. The early retrieval systems delivered lists of references to the user, but later ones have provided printouts of abstracts of the studies that have been identified.

The method of locating studies from an inventory of studies stored on a computer tape or other device involves the use of key words that supposedly identify the significant content of the study. Thus, each study in the system has to be coded in terms of its content. In the case of studies in the behavioral sciences, there is generally a coding not only for general content but also for the nature of the population studied and for the method of approach to the problem. The classification of studies is inevitably crude. No discrimination is made between a well-done and thorough study and a shoddy piece of work. The classification of the studies is undertaken by individuals who have only a limited knowledge of the area. At best, the classification is crude and, inevitably, subjective. Most users find that the studies identified in any particular category include a rather large number of studies that are included only because they happen to use particular words in the title. Once the studies have been identified, the computer system then uses high-speed printers to print out the abstracts of the studies.

Abstracts of studies are typically written by the authors of the studies. The tone is likely to be optimistic. Few authors will write an abstract that says "Nothing of any consequence was found in this study." Abstracts are positive far beyond what the original study justifies, and even reputable journals lack guidelines for the writing of abstracts, which all too often are short commercials for the study that is allegedly described. Summaries and abstracts should not be relied upon to give useful information. The title of the article often provides more accurate information than the abstract.

The uses of computer searches of the literature remain controversial. Experts do not usually use them in areas in which they have some expertise. An expert reads the journal literature in his field. Most of the research that is publishable appears in such sources. The expert will also have friends who are active research workers, and who will send him drafts of their work that is awaiting publication. Some research workers have a distribution list of professional friends to whom they send drafts of their work. Young research workers in a field also often send copies of drafts of articles to more senior members of their research community. Such individuals form what are called invisible colleges. The term *invisible college* was first used during the seventeenth century, to describe the Royal Society of London in which information was circulated among members of the Society on an informal basis. If the research worker can tap the resources of an invisible college in his area of interest, he may find out far more information than he can derive from a computer search of the literature. He will probably find out about studies that will not enter into any computer system for perhaps another three to five years. Computer-based knowledge is rarely up to date.

My own experience has been that computer searches of the literature are most useful in areas in which one has little or no knowledge, and in which one does not know where to find competently undertaken recent reviews. In such cases, the computer search will indicate not only the general nature of the studies undertaken but also the sources in which newer articles may be found.

Although computer searches of the literature were designed to help the research worker to be thoroughly cognizant of the research that has been undertaken in a particular field, it is doubtful whether they have accomplished such a goal. Occasionally the author comes across an article describing research in a field with which he happens to be thoroughly familiar. All too often he finds that the references cited do not include important references from the past. All too often research repeats a study that was undertaken twenty years previously. Sometimes he may find listed among the references a work that he had failed to find in his own search of the literature. The difficulty of locating information is so great that two investigators may study the same problem and each may fail to cite the references that the other cited.

One final problem related to the use of information retrieval systems is that they do not contain the most up-to-date research and studies. Retrieval systems rarely include items that have gone to press, but are not yet in print. There is also usually some delay between the publication of the article and the entry of the article and its descriptors into the retrieval computer bank. For the author's own work, this almost rules out the use of retrieval systems for locating other research or related material. He wants to obtain articles either before, or within a month of, their publication. Most authors are willing to send to interested parties copies of articles that are in press, or that are even not yet accepted for publication. This is important to a user of such materials since a publication delay of a year or more is common, and books may take even longer than articles to get into print.

Statistics and the Evaluation of Research Results

The value of statistics in research in the behavioral sciences remains controversial, despite the fact that educational research, within schools of education, has long been dominated by academicians whose interests are largely in statistics. The greatest expertise in the area of applied statistics on a campus is often found in the college of education, and major textbooks in the area are commonly written by professors of education. Strong arguments have been voiced in opposition to the policy of placing statistics at the very core of educational research. One of the earliest critics of the use of statistics in behavioral research was B. F. Skinner (1956, 1959) who contended that most of the important discoveries of science were made without the use of statistics or complex experimental designs. This argument is quite persuasive. Ivan Pavlov presented data that were self-explanatory; his results were clear and beyond question. The same was true of Skinner's experimental work published in his *Behavior of Organisms* (1938). One can also point to the work of Jean Piaget, which has been undertaken almost entirely without the use of statistical analysis. For the most part, the results of Piaget, like those of Skinner, are so clear that any statistical analysis of the data would seem to be futile. Much the same is the case in the work of Edward Thorndike, who either found clear results or redesigned the experiment. Thorndike did write a textbook on statistics (1904) that had implications for measurement, but this was an area in which the work of Thorndike had least implication for anything practical.

There can be no question that research workers have to begin by finding reproducible phenomena. A phenomenon that is a will-o-the-wisp, and is sometimes seen and sometimes not, is a hopeless phenomenon to investigate. Skinner recognized this as a young man and designed his work around thoroughly stable phenomena. One can reinforce a rat or a pigeon for performing in a particular way and the response probability of the animal can be made to change from a low base rate to a high rate. No statistical methods of any complexity are needed to demonstrate this, beyond perhaps, the calculation of means. The results are clear and so reproducible that they can be demonstrated on unrehearsed animals in front of classes of students. The same is true of the experiments of Jean Piaget. One can perform the same experiments on uncoached and unrehearsed children and be almost certain that the children will demonstrate exactly what Piaget claims. Such results are clear and unequivocal and reflect ideal phenomena for research.

Although Skinner and his followers have obtained clear and reproducible results with pigeons and rats, attempts to reproduce the same finding with humans have not always been so successful. Many research workers have been interested in finding out whether one can reinforce human verbal behavior and obtain increased frequencies of the verbal responses that are reinforced. Much research was undertaken during the 1960s on this problem with the finding, of dubious significance, that the reinforcement effect on verbal behavior could sometimes be found, and sometimes could not. The phenomenon was so elusive that, after a decade of hopeless efforts to obtain reproducible results, research in the area was abandoned. The lesson to be drawn from this is that reproducible results found with subhuman subjects may not be reproducible with humans. Most studies in the behavioral sciences cannot be replicated with the same findings.

The state of affairs may not be as simple as Skinner makes it out to be. The admonishment to the student to discover clear-cut phenomena and then experiment with them is perhaps to be followed by a Skinner or by the few who have his genius for undertaking experiments that require no complicated statistical analysis of the results. Under some conditions, important findings may be produced as a result of statistical analyses. If one is dealing with a phenomenon that is influenced by many different events, but influenced by each to only a small degree, then one may have to undertake studies that call for efficient statistical analyses so that small effects can be identified in the data. The analysis of the conditions that make for effective teaching, that is to say efficient learning on the part of the pupil, may involve numerous different conditions, each one of which may make a small positive or negative contribution to the total performance. Rosenshine and Furst (1973) provide substantial support for this point of view. The smallness of the effect of each factor is evident from the individual studies that indicate that a particular factor is effective. For example, a number of studies show that a teacher who is businesslike is more likely to produce learning in pupils than a teacher who is disorganized, but the differences are small and not always consistent. Nevertheless, the trend in the data is clear. In the case of individual studies, the relationship between this characteristic and pupil learning is so small that one might wonder whether the result would be reproducible in another study, and that is where appropriate statistical analysis comes in. Through such analysis, one can estimate the probability that the difference found, or a larger difference, would occur on a replication of the study.

The student of education who embarks on a doctoral study would do well to choose some condition to study that has been shown to be reproducible. The numerous dissertations and theses dealing with Piaget's work on intellectual development fall into this class. Although one may start a study with some clearly reproducible phenomenon, such as the inability of the preschool child to conserve quantity, one may then want to find out some of the conditions that produce intellectual development in this field. One is then likely to find rather small relationships between the facilitation of intellectual development and actions taken to promote such development, though these relationships are not necessarily small. There are, of course, numerous studies that show that children in transitional states may show dramatic effects from exposure to single learning experiences.

One always has to be on guard against selecting for study a highly reproducible phenomenon that is trivial in character. Studies of the reinforcement of pupil behavior for the purpose of keeping pupils in their seats fall into this category. Only very naïve psychologists or educators are concerned with the superficial problem of keeping pupils glued in position. Free motion in a classroom is quite compatible with many forms of learning, though there may be times when a child has to stay in one place for a protracted period of time in order to acquire some particular understanding. The researcher can easily find some equally trivial aspect of classroom behavior that he can control through reinforcement, and perhaps even squeeze a doctoral study out of it. Before he does this he should ask himself, and others, whether the phenomenon he wants to study is really worth looking at. It is all too easy to become obsessed with the controllability of particular aspects of pupil behavior, and the nice clear studies of these behaviors that can be designed around them, and in so doing, forget that these behaviors may represent behavior at a trivial level.

Desirable Characteristics of the Problem

The problem that is eventually isolated for research purposes can be stated in terms of a question for which the proposed research is designed to obtain an answer. Sometimes the question to be answered is referred to as a hypothesis; sometimes it is called a deduction from a postulate. Certain criteria may be suggested for judging the merits of hypotheses, and these need to be discussed further at this point. It is assumed in this discussion that the hypothesis is firmly rooted in a framework of theory; hence this particular criterion is not discussed here at further length.

Hypotheses should be clearly and precisely stated. When hypotheses are clearly stated they usually avoid the use of common expressions such as good teaching, personality, favorable climate for learning, and others in the common vocabulary of education. On the other hand, one may refer to "personality as measured by the Minnesota Multiphasic Personality Inventory," or to "the climate of teaching defined as the number of positive reinforcing or encouraging statements made by the teacher during a given time period." The clear statement of a problem generally involves the use of a technical language that provides terms that are better defined than those in common language.

Hypotheses should be testable. One of the most common sources of difficulty for the graduate student who embarks on a dissertation is the selection of a hypothesis that is not really testable. The same difficulty is also apparent in the researches of some of the more mature members of the educational profession. For example, one educator selected for his research the hypothesis that secondary school teachers did not know enough algebra to teach pupils competently. This is not a scientific problem; nonetheless it was one of some interest. He proceeded to test this un-testable hypothesis by administering an algebra examination he had devised to a group of secondary school teachers. Because the questions in his test gave the appearance of having been devised to confuse, it is hardly surprising that most of the teachers achieved a very low score. His conclusion was that the teachers did not know enough algebra to teach with competency, which was just a reiteration of the opinion he had held in the first place. The data provided no genuine information to endorse or reject the conclusion. He wanted to "prove" a point. What was needed in order to make his hypothesis a testable one was a prior study establishing what mathematical knowledge was and what mathematical knowledge was not essential or desirable in an algebra teacher.

Hypotheses should state relationships between variables. A well-developed hypothesis that meets satisfactory standards should state an expected relationship between variables. Unless hypotheses can be stated in this form, they have not reached the point where they are appropriate as a basis for research. A hypothesis such as "Children who attend Sunday school show greater moral growth than children who do not" is not testable, because the term *greater moral growth* does not refer to a variable that is measurable at the present time, or likely to be measured in the near future. On the other hand, a hypothesis such as "Teachers who manifest aggression in the classroom have pupils who also manifest aggression" refers to a variable, aggression, that can be measured through such procedures as counting the number of specific types of aggressive incidents that occur. However, the reader should recognize the fact that it is often necessary to use indirect means of measurement. This is true of all sciences. The physicist measures the amount of various elements in the sun by studying the spectrum of its light. The psychologist may attempt to measure emotional disturbance through the response of the individual to an inkblot. Although hypotheses should state relationships between variables, it does not mean that these variables have to be measured by any direct method, although any indirect measurement should be based on a clear-cut rationale.

Hypotheses should be limited in scope. A common error of the graduate student of education in planning research is to develop hypotheses of global significance. It is perhaps natural for the beginning research worker to be overly ambitious in his initial efforts, partly because of his earnestness and partly because it takes maturity of viewpoint to realize how little can be accomplished in a lifetime. The more mature research worker is likely to choose hypotheses that are narrower in scope and, therefore, more testable. The student should seek hypotheses that are relatively simple to test, and yet are highly significant. He should try to bring order into a very limited corner of the universe—but it should be an important corner.

Hypotheses should be consistent with most known facts. Any hypothesis formulated as a basis for research must be consistent with a substantial body of established fact. It is too much to expect that it be consistent with *all* established facts because in so many areas the facts themselves appear to be inconsistent with one another.

Hypotheses should be stated as far as possible in simple terms. This is desirable in part to permit the meaning to become clear to others, but it is also desirable because, in order for a hypothesis to be testable, it must be stated in relatively simple terms. The simplicity of the statement has nothing to do with its significance. Some of the most important hypotheses ever tested could have been explained to an average child in junior high school. It is the simple truths tentatively formulated as hypotheses that form the fundamental cornerstones of science. For example, Pasteur's hypothesis that life would not be spontaneously generated from organic matter if all living matter were first destroyed is an easily understood concept, yet it is one that deals with an idea of fundamental importance. Newton's hypothesis, which he believed to be an axiom and obviously true, that a body continues in uniform motion until acted on by a force is a simple one, yet it became a cornerstone of physics.

Hypotheses should be simple from another point of view. They should avoid the use of vague constructs, however popular these may happen to be in current educational thought. It is quite useless to formulate a hypothesis such as, "The adjustment of the pupil to the classroom situation will depend on the total classroom situation." Such a hypothesis includes several vague concepts, one of which is *the total classroom situation*. To say that an event depends on everything else that is happening fails to do what the scientist has to do—namely, isolate a few aspects of his environment that have special relevance as factors in the production of the phenomenon in which he is interested. The specification of these characteristics must be undertaken in the formulation of a clear and simple and important hypothesis.

The hypothesis selected should be amenable to testing within a reasonable time. The student of education is too often excessively ambitious when he first seeks to undertake research. This is usually a result of the fact that he is in close contact with the pressing problems of education. He is frustrated by being perpetually confronted with problems that must be solved before major advances can be made, and to overcome his feeling of personal frustration he sets himself the goal of solving one of the major problems. Yet nearly all such problems cannot be solved for a long time to come. They are mainly problems of immense difficulty that cannot be profitably studied because the essential techniques for attacking them are not available.

The student should be warned against doing what is commonly done when the would-be researcher finds that techniques are not available for the study of a particular problem—that is, using what are often hopelessly inadequate techniques. For example, many who have wished to study personality characteristics of teachers related to their effectiveness have ultimately settled for studies involving the correlation of ratings of teacher effectiveness with ratings of personality characteristics. Such activity can be described only as pseudoresearch. It bears a relation to well-conducted research in that it involves the statement of a hypothesis and the collection of data, but the data have only a superficial relationship to the testing of the hypothesis. The serious research worker would find it hard to accept the belief that actual teacher effectiveness in achieving a particular objective is related, except to a slight extent, to ratings of effectiveness produced by an observer, for the judgments of an observer are likely to be very erroneous. Similar doubts may be expressed about the validity of ratings of the teacher's personality characteristics. Educational literature is full of examples of studies in which a student's enthusiasm for a problem has blinded him to the weaknesses of the techniques through which he has tried to study it.

Some Additional Considerations in Selecting a Problem

Some Practical Matters Related to Research

Before the final selection of a problem is undertaken, the student should ask himself a number of practical questions that only he can answer. The first of these is whether he is well equipped in terms of his background to carry out the research. A student in school administration may be fascinated with the idea of exploring faculty-principal relationships, or some phase of these phenomena. However, if the student has never undertaken work in social psychology he will rapidly find himself out of his depth. The would-be research worker must ask himself whether he has sufficient mastery of the area to undertake an attempt to advance knowledge. The advancement of knowledge can be undertaken only by those who have already covered all of the territory up to the frontier of knowledge.

A second question, somewhat mundane but important nonetheless, is whether the study falls within the budget the student can afford. For this reason, a careful estimate must be made of the cost of apparatus, tests and other printed devices, and other equipment called for by the study. In addition, the cost of computational work must be considered. Sometimes a study cannot be undertaken because adequate space is not available.

A third, very practical consideration is whether the necessary cooperation can be obtained from those who must participate in research as subjects. Many studies require the cooperation of schools, and although they will generally cooperate with faculty on major research projects, school districts are becoming increasingly unwilling to work with graduate students on research projects.

Indirect Versus Direct Approaches

A common error in educational research results from attempting a direct attack on a problem. For example, research on the development of improved professional training programs for teachers may not be a feasible enterprise until certain other problems are solved. For example, we probably know far too little about how children learn to be able to train teachers effectively. Research on learning in children might lead more rapidly to better methods of teacher education than would direct experimentation with teacher-training programs. In addition, the improvement in these programs may require that knowledge be first obtained of the difficulties that teachers have in communicating with children and the conditions that interfere with effective communication. The direct approach to the improvement of teacher education is likely to be much less successful than an approach that will develop bodies of knowledge about learning to be taught to students of education. Undoubtedly some improvements can be made in teacher education, but the major improvements will have to wait until more basic research has given us better insight into the conditions that make for effective learning in schools.

Another related problem derives from the fact that we probably have only the crudest of theories concerning what makes for effective teaching. One view is that effective teaching involves a large number of techniques that the student of education can learn, piece by piece. If this view is accepted, then teacher training should involve the communication of these techniques to the student of education. However, this view of teaching may be entirely fallacious.

Another view is that the effective teacher is not so much one with a repertoire of specific skills but a person who has certain broad traits of personality. If this is correct, then teacher education must draw upon the knowledge available about personality development and the techniques that are available for changing personality. However, basic research on personality is still in the embryonic stage.

Indirect approaches to problems are typical of all branches of science. The realization that the laws of falling bodies could be studied best by studying not free-falling bodies but such artificial situations as objects moving down inclined planes, opened an entirely new era in physical experimentation. The study of human genetics has been made possible through studies of the microscopic structure of plant cells. The development of radioactive materials has made it possible to investigate human metabolic processes that have defied any direct approach. Much scientific knowledge has to be acquired by indirect methods. Even the practical problem of measuring the diameter of the Earth does not lend itself to the direct approach, which would involve the stretching of a measuring tape around its circumference. All knowledge about the atom and its structure is acquired by extremely indirect methods, where the measurements made are connected only remotely with atomic phenomena and where the conclusions involve a long chain of supposed events.

Sometimes the indirect approach to problems involves the conduct of a study in a laboratory situation rather than in a real-life setting. Many problems of reading have been attacked successfully in this way, and subsequent classroom studies have validated the results. There are advantages in a direct approach whenever it is likely to yield results, but the student who finds that only an indirect avenue is open to him should not feel discouraged. He should remember that some of the most important discoveries of science were made by an indirect approach.

Research in administration is an area in which a direct approach is often not feasible but in which indirect attacks on the problem may be highly productive. I can recall the suggestion of a student who was interested in the question of how information was passed around in a large school district building. The suggestion was the simple one of keeping a record of who called whom on the telephone within the building. There was no intention of keeping a record of what was said, for the purpose was only to draw up a diagram rather like a sociogram that would indicate the channels through which information passed during the course of daily business. Of course, much laboratory work has also been conducted on the effect of various administrative practices on the morale of groups, and these studies are being slowly extended into the field of real administration. The choice of level of reality of a study, its directness or indirectness, is determined by a multiplicity of factors, including the amount that is already known about the phenomena.

The Advantages of Breadth and Narrowness
in Defining Problems

There are disadvantages in the definition of a problem in narrow terms, particularly in the early stages of exploration. Narrowness hampers the possibilities of an imaginative approach. This can be appreciated by presenting a concrete problem from a field other than education. The example is one developed by the late John Arnold, who, in his classes on creative engineering, stressed the importance of defining problems at first in broad terms. He points out that in one of his classes some students embarked on the engineering problem of designing an improved automatic toaster. By stating the problem in this way, the possible ideas that could be incorporated in a plan of action were restricted. If the problem had been defined as that of *developing new methods of providing the consumer with toasted bread,* a wide range of new ideas would have become available for exploration. For example, one can conceive of the possibility of providing the consumer with ready-packaged toast. Industrial methods of large-scale toast making could then be considered. There was also the possibility that some commercial substitute for toast might be developed. As long as the problem was that of *developing a better toaster,* these latter possibilities could not receive consideration. There is no question that ultimately a problem has to be narrowed before it can be worked on, but this should not happen until opportunity has been provided to explore the problem on a wide base with the full play of the imagination.

Similar disadvantages are attached to the early narrow definition of problems in the field of education. Thus, in the search for a problem to work on in the field of mathematics education, the researcher might well start by asking himself the question, "In what ways is it possible to improve the teaching of number operations?" rather than the question, "In what ways is it possible to improve the teaching of long division?" When the student begins to think in terms of the broad problem, he is free to identify some crucial aspect of the teaching of arithmetic, the improvement of which would result in the improvement of the teaching of arithmetic in general. On the other hand, if the student thinks only in terms of teaching long division, the outcome of the resulting research is likely to be applicable only to the teaching of long division. The student should direct his thinking in such a way that the ultimate product of the research envisaged is a principle that has at least the possibility of being widely applicable.

It should be pointed out that we are referring in this section to the early stages of developing research. As thinking progresses, it is necessary to consider more specific aspects of the problem.

Preliminary Explorations of the Problem

The selection of a problem for study is not usually undertaken in a single step, for it is commonly necessary to run a preliminary study before the final decision is made. The need for such a preliminary study does not arise when the problem requires the conduct of a research closely similar to one that has already been done, for it is then known that the research can be undertaken. However, when the field of inquiry is relatively new and does not have available a set of well-developed techniques, a brief feasibility study must almost always be run. Such brief trial runs demonstrate whether it is practical to undertake the research, whether the available techniques are sufficiently sensitive to measure differences that it is desired to measure, and whether one can obtain the necessary cooperation of others involved in the study. Negative results in any one of these directions may be sufficient to cause the researcher to change his problem.

A preliminary trial or pilot study also provides some indications of the availability of subjects, if human subjects are used, or of other needed materials. Certain studies may require specific population characteristics, and it is necessary to determine whether populations having these characteristics actually exist. For example, one study required a comparison of the performance of children who did not like their teachers with that of children who did, and each one of these categories of children had to be divided into a bright group and a dull group. A preliminary study was needed to determine whether enough children existed who would admit not liking their teachers to make the study possible.

In another study, a comparison was to be made between counselors with high scores on an empathy test with those with low scores. A preliminary trial showed that too few counselors scored low on the empathy test so the study had to be abandoned.

Preliminary trial runs involve not only the selection of a problem but also the selection of some kind of design for the study. In practice, the design of the trial run may be much simpler and less sophisticated than the design that is finally adopted. The trial run may provide much information that is needed for the final design.

Research on Individuals and the Infringement of Their Rights

Research with people introduces problems that are not involved when the material for research consists only of things. People have rights, and many kinds of research cannot be undertaken because the collection of the data, and perhaps even the reporting of the data, might infringe on those rights. The ambitious novice in research has to be particularly careful to select a problem that does not involve such difficulties, because his enthusiasm may lead him to choose one of the many attractive problems that should not be studied because of such considerations.

Until about 1950, few ethical issues were raised in the matter of the collection of data, but in recent times considerable attention has been focused on such issues, partly because many questions related to them have been raised both in Congressional committees and in state legislatures. The major issues that have been raised pertain to certain distinct areas, but any answers given here can represent only the moral judgments of the author.

Issues related to the questions that can be asked legitimately of captive audiences. This matter was brought to a head some years ago when anger was expressed in state legislatures because children were being asked questions on personality tests that were believed to invade their privacy. Considerable public irritation was caused by the fact that some of the questions were concerned with the relationship of the child to his parents, and such matters were considered to be strictly the concern only of the child and his parents except where a court had reason to believe that a child was being mistreated. An important point to note in the whole controversy is that the children who were given such tests in schools generally had no say as to their willingness to answer the questions. The children were captive in the situation and were not free to walk out. The situation involving the wholesale administration of personality tests in schools is entirely different from that of administering tests in clinics where children might be sent for treatment. In the clinic there is some guarantee that the relationship between the child and the therapist is one involving privacy. In the school there is no such guarantee. Renewed interest in the rights of children has been partly responsible for bringing this matter to the forefront, and the trend in both public sentiment and in the decisions of the Supreme Court has been to establish the position that children have essentially the same rights in many areas as adults.

Any research worker who wishes to obtain personal information from others, whether they are children or adults, must ask himself whether his questions will or will not invade their privacy. He must also ask whether he is taking advantage of the fact that he is dealing with a captive group that cannot readily escape from the situation. Sometimes the privacy of the individual can be protected by a guarantee of anonymity, but such a guarantee, if given, must be given with complete honesty. There have been too many cases in which anonymity has been guaranteed, but the experimenter has then gone on to establish the names of the respondents through some devious device. This is very easy to do, but it should not be done under any circumstances.

The ethical problems posed by the administration of personality tests are also raised when data are collected through individual interviews. Under this condition, the research worker does not have the right to inquire into the personal lives of individuals to the same extent that the therapist does.

The panel on Privacy and Behavioral Research appointed in 1966 by the President's Office of Science and Technology defines the right to privacy as the right of the individual to decide the extent to which he will share with others his thoughts and feelings and the happenings in his personal life. The essence of the right to privacy is freedom enjoyed in making a choice of what parts of himself he will or will not share with others. The research worker must behave in such a way that he upholds this right of the individual.

The use of deception in orienting subjects in experiments. A related ethical issue is that concerning the deception of subjects in experimentation. In most psychological experiments, the subject has to be given some orientation concerning the nature of the experiment and how he is expected to behave. If a subject is given a difficult task and is told that it is readily mastered by most first-grade children, his behavior in relation to the task is likely to be different than if he is told that the task is considered difficult by most adults. In most experiments, the experimenter cannot tell those involved in the experiment exactly what it is about. Most experimenters take the position that such deceptions are justified provided the subject is told, before he leaves, whatever information is needed to relieve his anxieties or feelings of inadequacy that the experiment has generated. Here again limits are set if the subjects are captive that do not have to be set if the subjects can walk out.

When college students are the subjects for an experiment, the research worker may feel obligated to reward the students for their efforts by making the experiment into a teaching situation. After the data have been collected, the research worker may send each subject a report of the experiment giving the true purpose of the study and the results that were found. This procedure, or its equivalent, should be followed whenever students participate in an experiment as a course requirement. An honest course requirement has to involve learning.

Developing a Research Plan

A stage arrives in the development of every research at which it becomes desirable for the worker to arrange his ideas in order and write them down in the form of an experimental plan. A few experienced and sophisticated research workers may never actually write out such a plan, just as most experienced writers do not start by making an outline, but most research workers need a formal plan just as most writers need to make an outline. The student of education who is embarking on his first research enterprise will certainly need to develop a research plan that will serve a number of different purposes.

First, the research plan helps the student to organize his ideas in a form whereby it will be possible for him to look for flaws and inadequacies. Many research studies appear to offer excellent promise until the details are laid out in black and white. Only then do the difficulties of executing the study become apparent.

Second, the research plan provides an inventory of what must be done and which materials have to be collected as a preliminary step to undertaking the study.

Third, the research plan is a document that can be given to others for comment and criticism. Without such a plan it is difficult for the critic to provide a comprehensive review of the proposed study. Word-of-mouth methods of communicating the proposed study are more time-consuming and less efficient than that provided by a written plan.

A research plan should cover at least the items discussed in the paragraphs that follow. Only a brief discussion is presented here, because many of the points are treated at greater length in other chapters.

1. The problem. The plan should include a clear statement of the question or questions that the research is designed to answer. These are the hypotheses. The plan should also provide a concise account of the background of the problem and the theory on which it is based. The questions must be clearly and precisely stated. The statement of the problem must be complete, and it must be presented in a form that makes absolutely clear just what information must be obtained in order to solve the problem.

2. The method to be used in solving the problem. This section of the plan provides an overall description of the approach that offers an avenue to the solution of the problem. Sometimes it is necessary to adopt methods that make special assumptions, and these should be explicitly stated in this section of the plan. For example, if the method involves the measurement of attitudes by means of verbal attitude scales, then it may be necessary to assume that verbal expressions of attitude are related to other expressions of attitude. In the latter case it might not be desirable to continue with the research unless evidence can be marshaled showing that the assumption was justified. Usually it is necessary to introduce assumptions about methods simply because direct attacks on the problem are not possible and the indirect nature of the approach that must be taken introduces the need for assumptions.

3. Procedures and techniques. Whereas the previous section describes the overall approach to the problem, this part of the plan is concerned with the details of the techniques to be adopted. If interview methods are to be used, an account of the nature of the contemplated interview procedures should be given here, as well as whether the interview is to be structured and if so in what way, and the characteristics that the interviewer should possess for the purposes of the study. If tests are to be given, the conditions under which they are to be administered should be specified, as well as the nature of the instruments that are to be used. This section is an appropriate place for describing apparatus to be used or to be built. If public records are to be consulted as sources of data, the fact should be recorded here.

4. The population to be studied. The population to be studied will depend on the population to which the results of the study are to be generalized. If the results are to be generalized to all seventh-grade pupils in a certain school system, the research plan should state this fact. Because it probably will not be possible to include all seventh-grade pupils in the study, but only a sample, the research plan should state how the sample is to be identified. The method of identifying the sample should be such that generalization from the sample to the original population is feasible. If textbooks are the subject of the research, the population of textbooks to which the results are to be generalized must be specified as must the method of identifying the sample of textbooks to be studied.

5. Methods to be used in processing data. A research plan should indicate the statistical and other methods that are to be used for processing data. Such methods should not be left until the data have been collected. Many students have completed considerable work on a study, only to find that statistical techniques did not exist for answering the questions that were asked. This part of the plan should be reviewed by a person expert in the field of statistics, because such a specialist can often suggest changes that result in substantial savings of time and effort.

Summary

1. Finding a problem is a first step in developing a research project. This is a difficult task for even great scientists have sometimes chosen problems that turned out to be poor ones to study. The student should have a problem that interests him, but interest in a problem is not enough, for the problem selected must be soluble.

2. Good research problems are most likely to develop out of ongoing research programs. Any good research enterprise turns up more problems than can be solved. Ongoing research programs are designed to add to knowledge already in existence. The relevant knowledge has already been reviewed and studied.

3. Early in the development of a research project, the related research literature must be reviewed. Although the most prestigious journals in the area should be reviewed for relevant material, other published materials should not be overlooked, for they may well contain some excellent contributions. Indeed, the research worker with novel ideas may have to publish his work in second-rate journals until his work becomes recognized. Of course, some of the articles published in second-rate journals are indeed

second rate. The student should realize that the research in any area of the behavioral sciences can be severely criticized. Perhaps all articles have some flaws, but a group of articles may show the same general trend in the results. It is all too easy to be hypercritical of research related to behavior. Of course, one should not tolerate work that is basically incompetent. Highly critical reviews are often a means of enhancing the ego of the writer.

4. The student who reviews the literature of an area is obliged to read all the literature. He cannot pick and choose the articles that fit his own particular prejudices.

5. The proliferation of knowledge has resulted in the development of means for searching the published material. The computer search system has become the most widely used. The search is made in terms of key words that describe the studies. High-speed printers may produce abstracts of the studies. Abstracts are not necessarily good descriptions of the studies and should not be accepted at face value. Experts rarely use computer searches in that they are already familiar with the literature and are in touch with those doing research in the area. If one has almost no knowledge of an area, then a computer search may be valuable. There is usually a lag of several years between research being undertaken and the abstract of the research being entered in a computer system.

6. Great research workers have had success in investigating phenomena that produce clear-cut results. With such data there is no need to apply statistical methods beyond the computation of means. Lesser research workers are likely to come up with data that are far from clear, and statistical analyses are necessary to sort out the findings. Of course, the fact that one is investigating a highly reproducible phenomenon does not mean that it is an important one. Research should be concerned not only with reproducible phenomena but with phenomena that are significant and related to important knowledge.

7. Problems should have certain desirable characteristics if they are to lead to significant research. These include

   a. hypotheses that are clearly stated.
   b. hypotheses that are testable.
   c. hypotheses that state relationships between variables.
   d. hypotheses that are limited in scope.
   e. hypotheses that are consistent with known facts.
   f. hypotheses that are amenable to testing within a reasonable time.

8. Before any research is undertaken, the student should ask himself practical questions about whether he has the resources and time to undertake the investigation.

9. The history of the development of knowledge through research

indicates that most useful knowledge is achieved by indirect means and that head-on attacks on problems rarely meet success.

10. Pilot studies play an important part in the development of research. They often indicate what is or is not feasible.

11. Research involving the use of other individuals involves ethical questions. In such matters investigators must show integrity and respect for the rights of others.

12. The preliminary development of a research project requires that a plan be developed. The plan must include a clear statement of the problem, an account of the general method to be used, a description of the techniques and procedures to be used, the population to be studied, and the methods to be used in processing the data.

PART II
THE ACHIEVEMENTS AND LIMITATIONS OF EDUCATIONAL RESEARCH

Before discussing techniques and strategies of research the student should become familiar with the kinds of research that have been undertaken and the relative success of these research enterprises. A comprehensive review of the large number of educational research studies that have been undertaken is beyond the scope of this book. A picture of some of the major thrusts of research related to education can be presented, together with a few comments on how productive each line of research seems to be. The discussion of research studies that follows represents the author's views, an appraisal by one person concerning the merit, or lack of merit, of particular lines of investigation. Many will disagree with the appraisals made here, particularly those areas of investigation that are viewed negatively.

This panoramic view of educational research has had to be undertaken in a historical context, because history has shown some lines of research to be productive and other lines to be unproductive. After nearly a century of educational research we know something about the characteristics of useful approaches. We now have examples of productive research workers who have had an impact on education, and a far greater number whose efforts have left no mark except for articles, which nobody reads, buried in the research literature. Research that has offered both promise and impact seems to have been characterized by one important overall feature, namely, the production of studies whose results can be readily reproduced. Most educational research studies, when they are reproduced, yield different results, much to the disappointment of the research worker.

Too many lines of research provide results that are will-o-the-wisps. Sometimes one sees them and sometimes one doesn't. Glass (1976) and others have attempted to devise methods for extracting information from assemblies of studies that show only very low consistency and have given their techniques the name of meta-analysis. Whether there is anything worth extracting from these studies is a matter of controversy. If a cornfield is overrun with weeds, the corn may be scarcely worth harvesting. The money invested in harvesting a meager crop might be better spent in planting a new crop.

Productive research also involves the use of well-developed techniques for the conduct of the study. For example, Jean Piaget has developed a form of clinical interview for exploring the intellectual development of children. These interview techniques have formed the core of a very large number of worthwhile studies that have provided results having considerable consistency. Good techniques enable one to explore important problems productively. Research without well-worked-out techniques is likely to provide just another meaningless study. In our brief, and perhaps hasty, review of major areas of educational research we look for lines of research that have produced consistent results and also point out some of the techniques that have evolved that have led to productive work.

The mere omission of particular programs of research from the review that follows in the next four chapters does not necessarily mean that the omitted research lacks merit. The author is not familiar with every program of research that has ever been conducted. There are many important lines of inquiry with which he is not familiar. In spite of such omissions the present review may still provide the reader with a sufficient overview of what has been accomplished in the past fifty years and of the shortcomings of the area.

CHAPTER 5
Research as It Relates to the Design and Use of Classroom Materials

Education, in contrast to technical training, has been linked from the earliest times to the technology of recording information. The recording of information called for the development of a system of signs for representing ideas and these signs had to be recordable in some permanent form. Once information had become recordable, word of mouth ceased to be essential for transmitting culture from generation to generation. The earliest written records are certainly lost, but we do know that the Babylonians used written systems for recording information nearly 5,000 years ago. With the invention of these systems of recording information, education became necessary for members of the elite so that they would have access to these written records. Education also became differentiated from training in those arts that were necessary for survival within the culture that continued to be transmitted on a personal basis from one generation to the next. Education became, to a great extent, the mastery of written signs and the world of ideas to which the sign system gave access. In modern terms, one might say that education, from the beginning, has been an institution closely tied to the technology of information recording, storage, and retrieval. One might also note that education has remained, until recent times, an elitist endeavor as it was in Babylon 4,500 years ago.

The early technologies of information storage were the preoccupation of a priestly caste, which also participated in the formulation and recording of laws. Collections of documents, which today we might call libraries or information systems, were maintained in temples. Often these collections were substantial in size. Woody (1964) states that most large cities of Babylon 4,500 years ago had such collections and that the one at Tello included 32,000 books, though the term book may not match our modern conception of what is a book. At the height of the Roman Empire, such collections probably contained hundreds of thousands of items, many of which may have been nothing more than records of various legal transactions.

From the beginning, education has been closely associated with the technology of information recording, storage, and retrieval. Indeed, from the earliest times, there has been a technology of education, which has been, in essence, the technology of handling information. What is referred to as educational technology today is still largely an attempt to improve the ways in which information can be stored and made available so that those who need the information can more readily master it. The form in which information is made available may determine the ease with which a person can use it or memorize it, and thus the form of storage should be compatible with the psychological characteristics of the user or learner. Most modern technology is concerned with problems of this kind. One such problem, emphasized by operant psychologists, is that of the ordering of subject matter, a preoccupation of the teachers of medieval times. Another, more notably modern, preoccupation of the modern educational technologist has been the use of audiovisual materials. The modern educational technologist is also concerned with the strategies that the learner uses in extracting information or in learning material.

There can be no question that the most important single invention related to educational technology has been the development of the printing press and the resulting availability of written materials. Perhaps one of the difficulties that the modern educational technologist has had, in making an impressive showing, is that he has to compete with one of the greatest inventions of all time, namely, the printing press. Of course, the printing press with movable type was not only a great invention, but it became instantly accepted by political powers because it enabled the authorities of the day, both secular and religious, to achieve a goal of great importance to both, namely, the distribution of the Bible. No item of educational technology today has such a powerful and widely supported goal.

Educational technology of the past, back to Babylonian times, sought to help the student gain access to the records that were available, but the modern trend in educational technology has been to study ways of presenting information that is already available in ways that will help the student learn most effectively.

Research on Producing Reading Materials

Teachers and educational administrators have long been concerned with the matter of how to improve educational materials. The classic example of this interest is shown in the preoccupation of the educators of the Middle Ages with the ordering of subject matter, and the arrangement of content into a question and answer form called the catechism. During that period there were no issues related to what should be taught. For most teachers the content was well defined. The only problem that remained was how to order the content. Catechisms represented the end product of deliberations concerning the ordering of the material to be learned. The resemblance of these materials to much that is modern is inescapable, but the resemblance also suggests that the problems related to the ordering of content are far from being solved, and that perhaps few useful steps have yet been taken in the direction of their solution. Many research workers today would not view the early attempts to arrange content in an optimum order as research, but the author takes the position that thoughtful activity is as legitimate a research enterprise as is the collection and analysis of data, which is often undertaken without thought.

Smith (1934, reprinted 1965) has reviewed much of the history of research related to reading, most of which, prior to the present century, involved attempts to design systematically materials for reading instruction. Perhaps the oldest approach to the improvement in the design of reading materials involved the development of strictly phonetic alphabets. The earliest systematic effort to do this was published in 1570 by John Hart who designed a new alphabet as a new manner of writing. Hart's phonetic alphabet was offered as a simplified system of orthography and was not developed to help the child learning to read. Many other efforts to produce phonetic alphabets followed, including one by Benjamin Franklin. These also were proposed for general use, rather than for instruction. Isaac Pitman and A. J. Ellis seem to have been the first to develop a phonetic alphabet for the purpose of helping children to read. Some schoolbooks were translated into this alphabet and were used from 1852 to 1860 in the schools of Waltham, Massachusetts. Other experiments followed, most of which led to claims that the modified alphabets saved one or more years of learning time. However, all cannot have been as good as the promoters of the enterprises claimed, for, despite the claims, the books using the modified alphabet were usually withdrawn from the schools after some years of use. If the alphabets had produced striking results, one would have expected that they would have remained as a part of the school curriculum. Instead, by 1925 all interest in the use of modified alphabets had subsided in America, and was not to return until the 1960s.

The idea of a modified, phonetic alphabet is an intriguing one, and one that has a continuing vitality. In 1961, James Pitman, together with C. N. Fellowes and D. H. J. Schenck, became interested in the problem and revived what had been a Pitman family enterprise for over a century. The original Isaac Pitman alphabet was taken and revised and emerged in a new form that was called the Initial Teaching Alphabet. With the financial backing of the Pitman organization, readers were prepared for elementary school, and were tried out in Great Britain. It is to the credit of James Pitman that the Pitman organization made no money out of the enterprise. Indeed, Pitman money was given liberally to the enterprise and to those who wanted to develop the use of the phonetic alphabet. At the present time more than 1,000 books printed in the Initial Teaching Alphabet, or ITA as it has come to be called, are available. These books are used in many different school systems throughout the world.

The revived enthusiasm for the use of a phonetic alphabet for the teaching of reading came at a time when educational research had begun to show some sophistication. Unlike the efforts of the last century to use such materials, the new efforts could be systematically evaluated, but the task soon turned out to be much more difficult than it had appeared to be on the surface. The results were generally favorable, though not to the extent expected. The transition from ITA to a traditional orthography, during the third year of schooling presented difficulties. The system has remained quite controversial. The use of the system has certain obvious disadvantages that need to be studied. Children raised on ITA do not have access to common materials in the daily newspapers, such as comic strips, and their opportunities to read are restricted to the school materials. The use of ITA also interferes with their reading in science and mathematics, where much of the available material is printed in traditional orthography.

This brief history of attempts to develop an easier-to-read orthography brings out two points related to educational research. First, the systematic analysis of a problem is a good starting point for educational research, and is research in itself. Second, much research serves the purpose of opening up the problems, understanding their complexity, and developing methods of approach, rather than solving them directly. Only politicians have dreams of solving major educational problems before the next election.

The attack on problems related to orthography represents one of the earliest attempts to improve educational materials. The work that has been done has taught us that this apparently simple problem is, in reality, a problem of great complexity. Other apparently simple problems related to the development of materials for teaching children to read have also turned out to be quite complex. One of these is the problem of the vocabulary to be included in books for children.

Authors of reading primers of the last century had an intuitive understanding that the choice of vocabulary was an important matter. Short words and common words constituted the bulk of the vocabulary in such readers. The difficulty of level of the vocabulary was arrived at by the judgment of the author of the primer, which proved to be a not very good criterion. The first systematic attack on this problem was undertaken by E. L. Thorndike, who provided an empirical basis for judging word difficulty. Thorndike's basic premise was that frequency of exposure to a word was a measure of its difficulty. Thorndike applied the obvious solution to the problem of measuring word difficulty. He decided to count the number of times that particular words appeared in printed materials to which adults were commonly exposed. Thorndike counted the frequency of occurrence of words in a wide range of reading materials, and from these data drew up lists of words classified in terms of the frequency with which they occurred. This activity occupied more than a decade, and eventually received the support from the Federal Works Progress Administration, which made available the services of several hundred workers, who spent their days counting the frequency of the occurrence of words. Millions of words were included in the tallies. The application of such word counts to the problem of developing reading material for children quickly followed. Perhaps the earliest of such applications was made by a student of Thorndike, Arthur I. Gates, who, together with Miriam B. Hunter produced the first set of such readers with a vocabulary controlled through the use of word counts. Other developers of reading materials were fast to follow the use of this practice, and within a few years virtually all reading materials for elementary school children were advertised as having been designed in terms of a controlled vocabulary.

Gates included another innovation that was also an extension of the idea that learning is a function of frequency of exposure. Gates believed that the quick recognition of a word by a reader was a function of the number of times the reader had encountered the word. Hence, the words in children's books should be repeated many times so that the child could slowly build up the ability to recognize these words rapidly. Frequency control of vocabulary was an important innovation and an important extension of knowledge gained from learning in the laboratory.

Another important extension of the use of word counts came in the development of methods for measuring the difficulty level of reading material. Almost all designers of such material assumed that vocabulary level was an important element in determining difficulty level, but it was obviously not the only element. Sentence structure was also important. This led to the development of measures of reading difficulty, which included a measure of the difficulty level of the vocabulary, but also other measures of sentence complexity. Most formulas for the assessment of reading difficulty also included measures of sentence complexity that were related to the number of embedded clauses.

Measures of readability have had many interesting applications. For example, Kilty (see Special Communication to *New York Times*, 1976) determined the readability level of printed materials found on the packages of merchandise in department stores and found them to call for reading skills and understanding far beyond that of the majority of consumers. The development of readability formulas have provided means of opening up communication within our society, though they have not been used as much as one might have hoped. Insurance policies are still largely unintelligible to the average citizen, as are the written proclamations of the Internal Revenue Service.

Thorndike, himself, participated in the application of his ideas to the development of reading materials in two ways. One was the development of dictionaries for children, which had extensive use in schools (see Thorndike, 1935). The other application was the revision of classic literature to make it more suitable for high school students. Thorndike sought to achieve that end by substituting the difficult words in that literature with words that were more commonly encountered. In the days of Thorndike, it was taken for granted that a scientist who made important discoveries should engage in applying those discoveries to the solution of practical problems. Research and development were considered to be intimately related.

Yet, despite all of the energy that was invested in this enterprise, and is still being invested, far more questions have been raised than have been answered. There are more reasons for believing that controlling vocabulary level and word frequency have improved the value of teaching materials than there are for believing that the use of phonetic alphabets has had an effect. Nevertheless, the Thorndike method of measuring the difficulty of a word leaves much to be desired. The method was a great advance in its day, and a poor measure is often better than no measure at all. The difficulty level of a particular word is derived from a count of how frequently the word appears in printed material commonly read by adults. Since the frequency reflects how often typical adults, or educated adults, read the word, the frequency may well indicate adult familiarity with the word. But is this a measure of the child's familiarity with the word? Probably not. The measure is not derived from the frequency with which the child is exposed to the word. Users of word counts commonly assume that the difficulty level of a word for an adult is related to the difficulty of the word for the child, but that may not be a good assumption. The most significant criticism, in this respect, has been raised by Dale and Eichholz (1960), who have proposed that the difficulty of a word for a child should be determined by finding out how many children at each age level actually understand the word. The collection of such data is an extremely laborious task, but some data has been collected. The difficulty indexes for particular words, based on this direct approach, show only a moderate relationship to the difficulty indexes based on word counts of adult literature. Word difficulty levels, based on data collected on children, seem to be much more defensible than difficulty levels based on word counts using adult literature.

Perhaps the ultimate application of the idea that children's reading should be based on the vocabulary that children know is found in plans for reading instruction in which the children tell their own stories. Sylvia Ashton Warner has done much to develop such methods. The stories produced by the children then become the texts that the children read. The teacher types out the stories with a special typewriter that has a large type face. A starting point for this kind of method is to ask children to give words they would like to learn to read. The children then see the words in written form, and the words can later be incorporated into narratives. Such a procedure escapes the questionable practice of using word counts that are based on adult reading material.

Research on alphabets, vocabulary, and frequency of use of words has been energetically pursued during the last ten or more years. New types of phonetic alphabets have been produced. One innovation in this area is the color coding of letters to indicate to the child the sound designated by the letter in the particular context. There has also been a proliferation of measures of reading difficulty, which, however, have many defects.

The research that has been thus far described, although it covers a period of more than a hundred years, has barely more than touched the surface of problems related to reading. Other, more indirect, approaches have also emerged. Perhaps the most promising of these involves the study of the perceptual processes involved in reading. Problems, such as whether letter recognition is crucial for word recognition in the early stages of reading, seems to be a crucial issue that the experimental psychologist is well equipped to study. The classic studies of Gibson and Levin (1975) and their students have been directed toward these issues. These studies have led to a better understanding of how beginning readers recognize and decipher words. These studies should help us to understand why certain words are confused, and possibly lead to a better choice of the initial reading vocabulary.

The content of reading material for children has been the subject of limited investigation. The content issue is avoided by having the children write their own stories or by providing a range of books from which the children can choose. Another way of avoiding the issue is to include only the most bland and innocuous content, such as is evident in many series of readers. The issue of content is an important one and is considered later in this chapter in the broader context of the content of the curriculum. The problem is a significant one and worthy of the consideration of educational research workers who have generally ignored it.

Research on the development of materials for reading is, at the present time, largely stagnant. Although the federal government has invested large sums in the development of such materials through the regional laboratories and research and development centers, there has been a notable lack of new ideas in recent times. The new materials look much like the old, though they often carry impressive descriptions that sound much like commercials. Nevertheless, the materials have not been demonstrated to be better than those already available or better than the informal methods that require no special materials at all. In addition, attempts have been made to develop readers for special groups. For example, the Northwest Regional Laboratory has developed a set of readers for the Eskimo in Alaska. These readers attempt to provide content derived from the environment of the Eskimo, but the content gives the appearance of being an office writer's assessment of what relevant content would be rather than the result of an investigation of the environment of the Eskimo. There is, at this time, no reason for believing that such materials are better for teaching children to read than are the materials available through regular publishers.

Although it is easy to become lost in one's enthusiasm for research related to the development of reading materials, this may not be the central problem that needs to be attacked in relation to the problem of reading. There is certainly ample research to show that experiences related to reading that the child encounters before ever entering school are of immense importance in determining the way in which the child enters into the role of learning to read. Probably more can be done to help children learn to read easily by giving them appropriate prereading experiences in the home than by any other means. Such experiences include the reading of stories to the child and showing the child that books can be interesting to him. The child who comes to school without ever having had a story read to him, who has never seen a book, who has no notion of what books are for, and who has never seen an adult consult a book is the child who is likely to see the task of reading as a meaningless routine. Of course it is for such a child.

Research Related to the Ordering of Subject Matter

One of the oldest problems that educators have attempted to explore is that of the ordering of subject matter. The early Christian teachers were deeply preoccupied with this problem. For them, there could be no dispute about the knowledge that the student should acquire as a necessity for his salvation. The only problem was that of ordering the subject matter in a manner so that it would become as intelligible as possible to the student. Catechisms were the product of such efforts to organize subject matter in the best order for instruction. In addition, Thomas Aquinas introduced the notion that there is a high degree of determinism in behavior and that the materials of instruction might control the thoughts of the students. Indeed, by the fourteenth century, education had become dominated by a theory of instruction resembling modern operant psychology.

Later educators, through the Renaissance and the period of the Enlightenment, seem to have lost interest in the problem of the ordering of subject matter, because the new central problem was that of selecting knowledge from the vast new range of information that had become available. Almost all later educators conceded that subject matter could not be presented to the student in any order, for some concepts were more difficult to understand than others. Also, in some areas, some concepts have to be learned before others. Thus, the understanding of the concept of *equality* would appear to have to precede the understanding of the concept of *democracy*. The magnificent attempt of John Comenius to organize knowledge in a manner suitable for everybody to acquire shows an intuitive understanding of some of the problems of ordering subject matter, such as that of moving from the familiar to the unfamiliar. Johann Pestalozzi developed a system of sequencing that began with the student acquiring knowledge directly through the senses and then moving to knowledge of a more abstract nature.

Mention has already been made of the efforts of Thorndike and his followers to provide carefully graded materials for teaching children to read. This was an important venture in ordering subject matter with respect to reading difficulty. The endeavor represented the major attempt of psychologists in the first half of the century to concern themselves with problems of ordering. In the second half of this century, concern for the ordering of subject matter has been largely a preoccupation of operant psychologists and a few other psychologists who were interested in a behavioristic approach to the study of learning.

Operant psychologists began their excursion into the field of curriculum after their experience with the training of animals. In their approach to animal training, they had found that the first step should be a careful analysis of the terminal behavior that was to be achieved. The next step was to develop an ordered set of prerequisite behaviors to be learned, one after the other, in an organized sequence. The psychologists planned out the sequence of learning to be undertaken by the animal, after making an analysis of the overall behavior to be acquired. Operant psychologists, in doing this, made the assumption that complex behaviors can be reduced to simple behaviors. The sequence of materials called for by the plan became known as a program of instruction.

Operant psychologists have generally made the assumptions that there is only one form of learning and that the general principles involved in the planning of learning, and in the analysis of learning, are the same for subhuman animals and humans. This involves a very primitive theory of knowledge, that is to say a primitive epistemology. All knowledge is assumed to have some kind of linear structure, and the discovery of that linear structure tells the curriculum expert the order in which items of knowledge are to be acquired. Operant psychologists have the notion that there is an optimum ordering of subject matter and that a program should include the optimum order. This is a set of assumptions about the nature of knowledge that has little real foundation in empirical research. A very limited amount of research has been undertaken on the search for optimum ways of ordering subject matter, but with no particular outcomes of great significance.

The development of programmed material for schools during the 1960s offered considerable opportunities for research into the problem of ordering subject matter, but most of the effort went into the commercialization of the material rather than into the development of methods of subject matter analysis.

A somewhat more sophisticated approach to the analysis of the problem of the ordering of subject matter has come from the work of Gagné (1970) who proposes that all knowledge can be arranged in a hierarchy, from the simplest forms of signal learning to complex problem-solving behaviors. Although the analysis proposed by Gagné may have some implications for planning learning over long periods of time, of perhaps many years, it has little to say about how to arrange subject matter for learning over the short haul of, say, a semester.

Most of these schemes for the ordering of subject matter are thoroughly subjective. Indeed, the typical operant way of making an analysis of subject matter is an "armchair" analysis, in which the analyst sits back and, out of his wisdom, there comes the analysis and ordering of subject matter that is sought. This is hardly the scientific approach that is so widely advocated by the proponents of operant psychology, but perhaps few of us practice what we preach.

Few who have considered the problem of the ordering of subject matter in a linear sequence have carefully considered how knowledge is structured. Knowledge, in almost any form, may be considered to have multiple structures. As an example, we can consider the subject of American history. Perhaps the most obvious structure to American history is the time structure. History takes place in time and the ordering of events represents a part of history, but time is only one of the ways in which history has structure. A part of the structure of American history derives from the way in which events happened in space. The great move toward the Mississippi and the settlement of the great plains has a space structure to it. Then there are the economic structures. The history of the South has to be understood in terms of an agricultural system that was dependent in its early days on a large source of cheap labor. One suspects that some of the various structures underlying a particular body of history could be determined by making a count of words in such categories, as words that had to do with time, space, economic conditions, and so forth. So far little has been done to use such word counts for the purpose of identifying structures in knowledge. Of course, the fact that particular structures do exist does not mean that they should necessarily be used as a basis for instruction. Children in first grade may be introduced to American history, but the understanding these children have of historical time is so limited that little effort should be made to present history as an historical sequence. In addition, children in this young age group may have little conception of geographical space and may have the greatest difficulty in comprehending the great migrations of history. The structure of much historical knowledge may be far beyond the grasp of most children in elementary school. Much of history requires a mature understanding of the world if it is to be appreciated. For this reason, the most avid consumers of historical materials, including the historical novel, are often people in the late part of their lives. Such individuals have lived long enough to appreciate what is meant by historical time for they have had direct experience of what constitutes a half century or more. They have lived a part of history and they understand history because they have had direct experience of a segment of it; this direct experience gives meaning to the rest of history.

Those who claim that subject matter has a simple linear structure have usually been concerned with the structure of mathematics. In a sense, mathematics can be considered to have a simple structure that is logical in character. Most mathematics is based on certain assumptions, from which particular deductions follow. Ultimately all mathematics can, presumably, be incorporated into such a deductive system. However, even mathematics does not conform to this simplistic view. Many kinds of elementary mathematics can be produced depending upon the assumptions with which one starts. Not all mathematicians start with the same set of assumptions. Also, the development of mathematics can be viewed within an entirely different structure. Some teachers may like to view mathematics within a historical context. The history of mathematics is a history of man's struggle to solve particular vital problems. The problems of simple measurement were first solved by the Egyptians who were faced with the problem of dividing up the land after the floodwaters of the Nile receded each year. Much of early mathematics in the Christian era had to do with the development of navigation problems and the related study of the heavenly bodies. Mathematics can be taught as part of history. Hogben's famous best-seller *Mathematics for the Million* (1936) did just that and the volume had immense appeal during the late 1930s. Hogben did not disregard the structure of mathematics as a logical system, but pointed out that much of it did not come into being as a coherent logical system, but as a set of bits and pieces of knowledge that evolved to solve particular pressing problems.

The most ambitious attempt ever made to use logic as a basis for the organizing of subject matter has come from the work of Jean Piaget and his associates. According to the Piaget view, the properties of the environment are slowly understood in a more and more comprehensive framework as the child invents logical structures for understanding the environment. Thus, a five-year-old may be shown a set of ten sticks, graduated in length, but, when he is asked to reproduce what he has seen, will merely draw a set of sticks that may be of the same length, but, if of differing lengths, they will not be arranged in order. Such a child does not understand the nature of a series or its general properties, and cannot comprehend a series when he is shown one. Thus, perception and logic are intimately related, not only at this five-year-old level, but at every other level of the child's development. In the same way a child of two years of age will not understand geometrical shape though he will understand some general properties of shape.

Piaget argues that the child's general state of logical development determines what he can understand about his environment. One can thus arrange a graduated set of tasks for a child to master, from the very simplest to those that require a mature understanding of logical structures.

Much of the application of Piaget's research to the curriculum has involved the development of a series of tasks suited to particular stages of logical development. For example, the Nuffield Mathematics Curriculum presents the child with a set of tasks to do that are within the child's capability of functioning as a logical being. Most mathematics curricula do not do this and the child ends up knowing how to carry out the mechanics of a mathematical operation, but not knowing the underlying logic. A curriculum based on the logical development of children would seem to be a significant contribution of research to educational practice.

Research Related to Management Concepts Used in Communicating Subject Matter

A considerable amount of research related to teaching has little to do with the choice of subject matter or the organization of subject matter, but has to do instead with the general management plan through which the program is conducted. Contract plans of the 1920s fall into this category, and so too do the operant plans of the 1960s. In more recent times, so-called competency based programs of education would be considered to fall into this same general class. Although there has been a great amount of research related to the production of such ideas, research has not been carried through to the point where it has been possible to show that these programs are better than those they have displaced or better than other programs administered simultaneously elsewhere. Here, as in other parts of this book, the position is taken that the creation of ideas is a legitimate research activity in itself, even though it is only the starting point for the development of substantive knowledge concerning the worth of the idea produced.

So-called competency-based programs of education have been the prime examples of this form of innovation during the 1970s. The fundamental idea underlying these programs is that education should be directed toward the development of a set of specific competencies, and that the student should, at the end of the program, be able to provide evidence that he can perform each of the specified competencies. Alternatively, the student may be asked to demonstrate his capability with respect to each competency soon after it has been acquired. In order to pursue this kind of educational program there must be careful scheduling of both learning and the tests for the competencies involved. Such a program is very similar to that advocated by Ralph Tyler in the 1930s, though some of the words have been changed to give an illusion of newness.

Administrative innovation at the classroom level is generally established today in such a way as to permit some opportunities for evaluation and research. Indeed, such enterprises are a part of a wider research program.

Let us consider, in this connection, the so-called competency-based teacher education programs, and specifically the one implemented at the Oregon College of Education in the elementary education area. This program was developed partly through the efforts of the college itself and partly through work undertaken by the Teaching Research Division of the Oregon State System of Higher Education. The original work for this enterprise grew out of a federally sponsored program referred to as the Model Teacher Education Programs. The work quickly became involved in the popular movement for competency-based models, and most of the development occurred within that framework.

The initial development of the program was focused on four efforts:

1. Any competency-based model must be able to identify the basic competencies that are to be trained. In this case, the effort was made to identify the competencies involved in teaching.
2. The development of means of determining whether the competencies were, or were not, achieved in the students in the program.
3. The development of a data collection and management system so that the progress of each student could be carefully tracked as he progressed through the system.
4. The design of a research system such that the data collected within the program could be used for the improvement of the program.

The problem seems to have been approached as though it were a simple one. Few questions seem to have been raised about whether the competencies of teachers can be that easily identified. Many have been trying to do this for a long time and have generally come to the conclusion that the problem is one of enormous complexity. There is also the issue of whether teaching competence consists of a set of small component competencies or whether it involves broad patterns of behavior. The model of the intellect of Piaget suggests that it involves broad ways of relating to children. The Oregon program of teacher education for elementary school teachers avoids this problem by accepting traditional assumptions concerning the nature of teaching. The program is similar in content to numerous others that have been provided for a long time, though it does differ in its administrative plan.

Consider, for example, the "functions" performed by the teacher in this program. These functions include defining the objectives of instruction in the five areas of reading, language arts, mathematics, science, and social studies. In many programs of instruction in school, there may not even be clear goals beyond those that are implicit in the immediate circumstances. In such a program, the teacher may see Jim, whose immediate problem is that of deciphering the directions on his model plane kit, as one who needs to be helped on that task, but who may need help on a different task next week. In such a program, the objectives are modified on a day-to-day basis as new needs arise. The teacher who planned the objectives in advance might well disrupt such a program. The Oregon program does not permit much flexibility and is strictly traditional.

Programs such as that at the Oregon College of Education have novelty in the management aspects, since each competency is measured in each student, as it is believed to be achieved. In many programs of this type there may be thousands of competencies and measures of their achievement, and the records have to be kept on computers, because of the massive amount of information involved.

The data obtained in these programs supposedly make it possible to identify the students in whom particular competencies have not been achieved and who would benefit from the subsequent use of additional training. In such a program there is also the hidden assumption that a competency mastered at one point in time, is mastered for all time. Much that is learned is soon lost for all practical purposes unless it is used. Learning achieved in college is, all too often, quite transitory.

The program does offer opportunities for long-term research. Students who have been through the program can later be studied in school settings. Data can then be collected to determine whether those who have the competencies specified are able to produce more learning in children than a control group that does not. The Oregon project personnel talk about undertaking such research, but research, as we already know, is extremely difficult to do.

The value of the administrative procedures developed in programs such as that at Oregon remains controversial. Despite the opportunities for research that the proponents of these programs proclaim, there is very little in the way of research results. Many are skeptical and doubt the value of developing new administrative procedures at this time. There is an old adage among administrators to the effect that if the administrator does not have an idea, he can still provide the illusion of moving things along, by inventing a new administrative procedure. Many competency-based programs survive on this illusion.

Competency-based teacher education would not have gone far without the substantial support given it by the federal government. The large size of this financial support blinded many to the shortcomings in the conceptual framework involved. It is all too easy to be blind to the rest of reality when a federal check for perhaps hundreds of thousands of dollars is being dangled in front of one's eyes. Yet solid critiques of competency-based programs have been devastating. That of Broudy (1972) is well worth reading, and a particularly interesting critique has been produced by Hamilton (1973) under quite strange circumstances. The Office of Planning, Budgeting, and Evaluation of the U.S. Office of Education wrote a contract to obtain a review of competency-based teacher education. The review by Hamilton was thorough and scholarly, but when it arrived in the U.S. Office of Education it produced consternation. The report would never have seen the light of day if copies had not been obtained and circulated by private individuals. The U.S. Office of Education had no intention that that should happen.

The Hamilton report states bluntly that competency-based teacher education has been oversold and that it has been presented with unrealistic expectations. The programs that illustrate this departure show little that is radical. Indeed, they are closely similar to programs that were in progress fifty years earlier. There is a basic lack of knowledge of the relationship between specific forms of teacher behavior and pupil achievement, and yet the programs have been promoted as though all the basic knowledge needed were readily available and that all that had to be done was to convert that knowledge into a training program and certification procedure. It is even doubtful that the research skills are yet available for producing the necessary base of knowledge needed to support such a program. Few programs have ever received such a devastating review.

Studies of the Curriculum

A central focus of research related to education should surely be in the area of the curriculum, conceived broadly as the sum total of the experiences to which the child or adult is exposed. In the narrow sense, the term curriculum is restricted to the experiences provided by the school. Psychologists who think in terms of conditioning view the curriculum as the stimulus end of the stimulus-response chain. They rightly point out that much too little attention has been given to the study of the stimulus end, perhaps because responses are so much more easily measured. There is little difficulty in giving a student a test to determine what he has learned about American history, but there is immense difficulty in measuring the kinds of experience in the area to which he has been exposed. For this reason, curriculum research has been vestigial compared with research on the response end. In this chapter we consider research related to curricula designed for school-age children. A later chapter discusses the preschool curriculum.

Curriculum research brings the research worker into one of the most difficult problems of philosophy, namely, the nature and structure of knowledge. Almost every teacher and curriculum worker assumes that knowledge has structure and that the mastery of a subject matter area involves the acquisition of far more than a mere collection of separate pieces of information. What the structure of knowledge is, nevertheless, remains debatable. This brings us up against the fundamental issue of whether knowledge has structure, as such, or whether knowledge is given structure by the human mind, because the human mind requires that whatever is learned be fitted into some structure in the memory system.

The most simplistic approach to the study of the curriculum is to assume that knowledge has some structure, in and of itself, and that the structure can be identified by examining books and printed materials in which the knowledge is recorded. These assumptions are commonly held by psychologists. The followers of B. F. Skinner, as well as those of R. M. Gagné, have based much of their work on this kind of presupposition. These psychologists, in designing a curriculum, have looked at the material to be learned and have first identified the final operations they believe the learner should be able to perform after he has mastered all of the materials. These are the ultimate result of the acquisition of knowledge. The assumption is then made that one can examine the body of material to be learned and then identify prerequisite knowledges that have to be acquired if the individual is to achieve these final accomplishments. Then the analyzer of knowledge seeks to discover prerequisites for the prerequisites, and then prerequisites to the prerequisites to the prerequisites, and so forth. Thus, in the analysis of the knowledge required for being able to undertake the operation of long division, the analysis might show that a prerequisite operation was multiplication, and prerequisite to multiplication was addition and subtraction. The analysis might be pursued further, and the prerequisite for addition and subtraction might be considered to be the ability to count. These kinds of analyses have been made extensively in the area of mathematics, which seems to lend itself to this pursuit, though it is not clear how such a process could be applied to an area such as geography.

This type of curriculum analysis seems like an obvious kind of activity to pursue in designing a curriculum and a teaching sequence, but the activity has certain flaws to it that need to be noted. A first point is that the procedure is dependent upon intuition and "armchair" analysis. The person engaged in the activity looks at the material to be learned and tries to discern structure in it. He looks for what appears to him to be a hierarchy of abilities. The analysis is intuitive and subjective, yet, oddly enough, it is commonly engaged in by those who most widely proclaim themselves to be the pioneers of an objective science of behavior, namely, the operant psychologists.

There can be no doubt that this form of intuitive analysis can be most misleading. Consider the example just given of the analysis of long division. True, long division presupposes the ability to multiply, divide, and add, but the prerequisites for addition and subtraction are much more than the ability to count. Addition requires an understanding of the nature of unity, and the understanding that, in addition, the operation does not change the number of units involved. Counting can be just a meaningless routine, as it is in most five-year-olds. In order for counting to be related to meaningful operations, then it must be based on a concept of number, which involves both the concept of a unit and the concept of a series. Most of those who have undertaken a typical armchair analysis of the operations involved in some aspect of arithmetic have missed such a point because their analysis has not been based on a study of the way in which children actually perform arithmetic operations.

The learning program, as designed for use in learning machines, or the programmed text, have been based, almost exclusively, on the intuitive analysis of the subject matter involved. The assumption is made that knowledge can be reduced to a set of statements that are most easily understood if they are presented in a particular order. Most programs that have been marketed, including an extensive series published back in the 1950s by Grolier, were prepared almost entirely on the basis of the intuitive judgment of the people making them. Almost no attempt was made to determine, through experimentation, the optimum order, if there should be one. The little evidence there is suggests that there may not be an optimum order in many subject matter fields. Even if one particular order seems to be effective, it may not be the order that is congenial to some learners who prefer to organize the knowledge in a different way.

Psychologists engaged in educational research have generally taken the position that there is a fixed body of content that all pupils should master. The only problem, then, is to find the most efficient means of presenting this fixed body of content. Such a view has had limited support by a few who are not psychologists. The great books curriculum was an attempt to identify, at the college level, the sources of influential ideas throughout history, and to base a curriculum on the study of those ideas. One can find much stronger arguments at the college level for a curriculum consisting of a fixed body of knowledge than one can at the elementary school level. The fixed body of knowledge, as an outcome of education, was also promoted during the early 1930s through a study known as the Pennsylvania Study developed by Learned and Wood (1938). This study was an attempt to survey what Learned and Wood and an advisory committee considered to be the essential knowledge that all students should acquire as a part of a general education. The survey of the knowledge of students was given to college seniors, sophomores, and to high school graduating classes, for the purpose of determining the deficiencies in these students. The findings were hardly surprising. Many graduating from high school knew more than many who graduated from college. Few had anything like the broad spectrum of knowledge that Learned and Wood thought they should have. Some teachers had less knowledge than their students. Despite these many interesting findings, the reader of the reports of this study has difficulty in knowing what to make of them. Were the students really worse off for the fact that they knew little of the history of their civilization? Suppose they didn't know much about Greek literature. What difference did it make?

Those who believe that there is a fundamental body of knowledge that all should master have never seen any problems in the design of curriculum. On the other hand, there are those who see the ever expanding body of available knowledge as raising ever new questions concerning what should be learned in school. Given the large and available body of knowledge, the problem of how to select a very limited amount of it for inclusion in the school curriculum can be solved in a number of different ways. One way is to emphasize skill acquisition rather than knowledge acquisition. The argument is that if a child can learn to read critically and effectively, to solve common mathematical problems, and to go about solving other forms of problems in a systematic way, then the school has performed an effective function. Although this argument is commonly encountered, it does not really solve any problems. Skills are not acquired in a vacuum, but in the context of problems. This context has to be chosen. Mathematics can be learned within the context of consumer problems or it can be learned within the context of elementary physics. Reading, beyond the most elementary stages, can be mastered at ever higher levels by using material that is literary in character, or the material can deal with sports events, history, popular science, science fiction, and so forth. The issue of selecting content cannot be avoided, for content is an inevitable part of the curriculum.

Studies related to the selection of content can take many forms. The traditional studies concerned themselves with what children like to learn and read about. Numerous studies have been undertaken on the problem of the types of literature that children enjoy reading. Such studies have generally shown that what children choose to read differs very widely from what adults think children like to read. Children's tastes in literature seem to be much more mature than adults expect them to be. Much work still needs to be done in this area. Studies of the humor of children appear to be particularly relevant for the choice of their reading materials. Certainly, the humor of children seems to be quite different from that of the adult. Little is known about the children's understanding of metaphor and analogy. Some research has been done on the moral understanding of children, which is also different from that of the adult. Since literature often has a moral implication, studies of moral development could have a considerable impact on the design and selection of books for children. At least we know something about the moral quandaries that are of interest to children of different ages. We also know that the thinking through of these quandaries is important for producing moral growth.

Traditional approaches to the selection of subject matter have involved either the study of the responses of the children to various kinds of material, but often an armchair approach has been used. Much of the material produced by the Regional Laboratories in recent years has been selected on an armchair basis, guided by a minimum amount of theoretical thinking. Sometimes some effort has been made later to determine whether the material actually did produce the learning it was supposed to produce, but such studies, after the content had been selected, hardly make up for a lack of careful planning in the selection of the content. There is still another very interesting alternative research method of selecting content to which we now turn.

Back in the 1930s, Seay and his associates (1944) were engaged in selecting content for schools in the back country of Kentucky. The contribution they made to this problem is classic and should have had a great impact on the whole problem of selecting content for the curriculum. Seay made the basic assumption that the content that was appropriate for these Kentucky backwoods children was that which would permit them to improve the quality of their lives and that of their families. Now, in order to find out what that content should be, a survey of the community had to be made. This survey sought to determine what the problems of the people living there were and what resources could be found in the community to solve the problems. For example, a medical study of the inhabitants in the experimental communities found that the children suffered from scurvy, among other diseases. The agricultural experts then had to determine what the people there could grow that would provide them with the necessary daily intake of vitamin C, which would prevent scurvy. Surveys were made in relation to problems of health, housing, clothing, and diet to determine whether the community, through the exploitation of the already existing natural resources, could improve the quality of life. The theory was that if the children learned in school to use the natural resources of the community, then they would, in turn, teach their parents how to do this.

Many books were written for the children designed to teach them how to use their local resources. A basic problem was that the ancestors of these children had come from England and had attempted to live in the mountains of Kentucky as though they were living in rural England. The entire argricultural program they brought with them from England was completely unsuited to the mountainous region in which they found themselves. The new books for the school attempted to teach the children a way of life that was better suited to the terrain in which they lived. For example, they had long raised pigs, but pigs do not live easily on mountainsides. What they should have been raising were goats, animals adapted to a mountain terrain and which would provide not only meat but also milk and cheese. Considerable expertise was brought into the experimental communities to determine exactly how the inhabitants could use local resources to advantage, and this expertise was used in the writing of books for the children.

This kind of curriculum research seems to offer promise, even though it has not been used to any extent. One can imagine similar projects undertaken in the inner-city ghettos with the ultimate goal of helping such children escape the ghetto. Survival, in the ghetto, prior to escape, requires that the children and parents know about all the social services that are available to them. The children must also learn how to function in relation to their local government and understand how to petition local government. Much also needs to be done to develop leadership among the occupants of the ghetto. A thorough study of such problems needs to be undertaken as a prelude to the design of instructional materials for ghetto children. The materials used at present in such schools has little relevance to any of the problems discussed here. Indeed, the standard readers used in inner-city schools have virtually no relevance to any of the problems that the children will have to face. Such readers may do little more than leave the children with the feeling that they are failures and that there is no way out of a world of failure.

In the case of the Seay study, elaborate plans were drawn up to evaluate the effect of the program on the communities. Some initial data were collected and showed promising results. The health of the community appeared to be improving. However, the full plan for the evaluation of the approach to curriculum development was never carried through to any extent. World War II, which followed the introduction of the materials, resulted in great changes in the communities. The program needs to be repeated today with a careful follow-up study of the results.

Problems related to the self-selection of curricula also need to be explored. In open classrooms there is some degree of selection by the pupil of the content that he is to study. An interesting theory related to how children select material for study has been proposed by Ruth Harring (personal communication). Harring spent many years running an open classroom at the fourth-grade level. She observed that children in such a situation seem to embrace a theme for a time that dominates their learning. For example, a child may become interested in the weather and how to predict it. He will read on the subject and begin to develop instruments for measuring temperature, wind velocity, and barometric pressure. He learns to do calculations related to the weather, such as how long it takes for a cloud to move from the one horizon to the other, given a wind of a certain velocity. He may keep records of rainfall and plot graphs showing cumulative rainfall totals over the month. For a period his whole mental life seems to be preoccupied with problems related to the weather. He may read books about the weather in other parts of the world and begin to understand how this is related to the form of vegetation found. He may even study the relationship between the weather and the cost of food in the supermarket. Harring proposes that children explore and develop such themes, but eventually drop them and then move on to other themes. Much more needs to be known about the function of themes in the intellectual life of children, how they find themes, and the conditions under which children move on to other themes. Some children may well become caught up so deeply in a theme that it may dominate their minds for the rest of their lives. Albert Einstein was an example of a child who became involved in a theme that dominated his entire life. In high school he became obsessed with the problem of what it would be like to ride on the front of a beam of light, how would such a person measure the velocity of another beam of light, and so forth. Such fantasizing ultimately led Einstein to the development of his theory of relativity, after he had pursued the theme for a dozen years or more. The theme involves the development of an organized system of knowledge about particular phenomena. The child develops his theme in a way that organizes knowledge in relation to it. The child is the active organizer of the knowledge and the developer of a system of knowledge related to it.

Studies need to be undertaken concerning the themes that attract children of different ages, the course of development of such themes, and the conditions under which these themes fade and become displaced by other themes. The child who does not have such themes in his life is also a problem of special interest, for such children are reported to present special and difficult problems for the teacher. The source of themes needs to be investigated, and so too does the relationship of themes to the development of understanding of traditional subject matter and skills.

Considerations, other than utility, should be introduced in designing curricula. One of these is the level of logical thought called for by the child who is using the materials. Thus, in a social studies curriculum, the student may be exposed to data concerning unemployment rates broken down by sex, ethnic background, economic level, and so forth, and attempt to solve problems that call for making inferences from the data. The naïve interpretation of the data may be simple as, for example, when the student is able to find the unemployment rates in the various categories. More subtle inferences to be made from the data may be beyond the abilities of some students, but within the capabilities of others. Some students may be able to infer that the high rate in certain categories reflects discrimination or educational disadvantage. Such an inference requires the student to perform certain logical operations on the data. These logical operations can be performed only if the student has already mastered the necessary prerequisites in logical thinking. The logical operations can be performed on any kind of data. The data themselves, in this instance, can be understood at one level at one stage of logical development, and at a much higher level, at a more advanced stage. Even at the simplest level of interpretation, the data require certain background information in order to be understood. Thus, the pupil who does not understand the concept of unemployment cannot have any understanding of the table at all. In addition, the concept of a *rate* of unemployment requires that the individual understand the concept of a proportion or ratio, which is a relatively advanced concept for an elementary school pupil, but equally within the grasp of the high school junior.

Most of the work on the analysis of content in terms of the logical processes required to undertake it has been undertaken by the followers of Piaget, who have emphasized the logical aspects of the curriculum, often to the neglect of other aspects. Many tasks designed for first-graders, for example, provide opportunities to classify quite trivial materials. Some time ago the author watched some first-grade children sorting into categories pieces of card of different shapes and colors. The teacher was most pleased with the task she had developed and so laboriously prepared with scissors and cardboard. She didn't have to go to all that trouble. A much better task was right outside the classroom window where leaves of various shapes and colors littered the ground. If the children had learned to sort the leaves into categories, they would also have learned that different trees have differently shaped, and differently colored leaves. They would also have learned that the size of the leaf has little to do with the size of the tree from which it comes, within certain limits. Also, they would have learned that only some leaves change to a brilliant color as they die. There is a basic error in designing curricula materials so that only the logical aspects of the tasks are stressed, for other aspects are equally important. Much more needs to be known about how children learn from, and respond to, tasks that call for important logic, but which involve trivial materials. There is also evidence that logical processes tend to be tied to particular situations. The physicist, whose logic is superbly correct in solving problems in his own field, may show only the competence of the fourth-grade child in applying logic to problems of politics. The mature human applies logic only as a last resort, but in a field of specialization such as physics, logic is not just the last resort, it is the only resort.

The determination of the order in which logical processes are to be learned is a matter that has to be settled experimentally. One can, of course, come up with good ideas, based on intuition, about how the various logical processes are ordered and sequenced. One may also go to philosophers to find useful hypotheses. However, regardless of where one derives one's hypotheses, the hypotheses have to be tested through experimental studies. For example, one may hypothesize that a child has to understand the idea of a unit and the idea of a series before he can give any meaning to counting. This seems to be a reasonable hypothesis, but until data are actually collected on children, it is but a conjecture.

The content of the curriculum, in contrast with the logical operations the curriculum calls upon the child to perform, presents much greater problems related to the selection of material. There are numerous different bases for the selection of content, but little agreement among the experts. The content of the school curriculum is also deeply influenced by tradition and by immediate social pressures. A fanatical legislature may include all kinds of requirements in the state curriculum, because they seem to be demanded by the times. Other content is excluded for similar reasons. Thus, sex education has been excluded by many communities and some communities have banned the teaching of evolution. Other communities have imposed a requirement that equal times be spent studying evolution and the biblical version of the origin of the world. Some states have introduced requirements related to the teaching of state history. Tradition has also established much of the content. Thus, American history is given priority and world history is very secondary. Anthropology has not yet found a place in schools. More rational approaches are those that build curricula on the basis of the requirements of the world of work, or what knowledge is needed to build a better world, or the skills one needs to have a satisfying life after the day of work is over. The choice of the approach used to construct a curriculum depends more on the political pressures of the time than on rational considerations. Thus, the present orientation of curriculum construction sponsored by the federal government is on what is called career education. This emphasis is a reflection of the government's policy to emphasize work skills and the related gross national product as the most important thing. The emphasis on what is called career education fails to recognize that perhaps as much as 90 per cent of the child population will end up in jobs that call for little education and which can be learned in just a few days. That is why some critics of the career education program protest that the central focus of education should not be on the world of work, but on how to live a satisfying life after one leaves the world of work. The critics point out that the world of work may occupy less than a third of the individual's waking hours and that preparation for work is not preparation for life, but only preparation for a small part of life. Studies are needed to determine the extent to which career education is related to the realities of the world, rather than to contemporary politics.

An additional approach to the selection of content is to let the children select their own content. This was the gist of the approach of the Progressive Education Movement of the 1930s that aroused so much criticism. Children were, to some degree, free to explore problems of their own choosing and an attempt was made to provide a wide range of sources of information that the child could consult. The present emphasis in some schools on learning centers represents a similar trend, but with much less freedom of choice, in that the centers themselves provide a restriction on the range of choices presented to the pupil. Studies need to be undertaken on the choices made by pupils in such situations and the extent to which behavior is structured by the presence of the materials selected for the learning centers. The children who select a focus of interest from outside the materials provided would be a particularly interesting group of children to study.

How to organize subject matter remains as controversial as how to select it. One position is that the subject matter expert should be the authority to undertake the organizing, but what is known about child development should be considered in doing this. Thus, the developer of a social science curriculum must take into account the fact that children in the first grade have very little concept of historical time, and no conception of a span of time such as ten years, let alone a century. The alternative approach is to let the pupils undertake inquiries and to permit them to do the organizing. In such a program, each child assimilates new knowledge to whatever knowledge he has already acquired. Thus, a first-grade child, learning something about the metric system, may understand the nature of a centimeter by relating it to the width of his thumb, but a fourth-grade child will assimilate the same information by relating it to the size of an inch with which he already is familiar. In addition, different first-grade children may assimilate the meaning of a centimeter in different terms. Although one child may relate it to the width of his thumb, another may assimilate it to the size of an M & M, or the thickness of a piece of bread. Should one tell such children how to assimilate the information, or should each child assimilate it in his own way? This is a problem that needs to be investigated. At all age levels there appears to be a great amount of individuality in how people assimilate the same information, suggesting that structured teaching, in which the teacher prescribes how information is to be learned, may not be effective.

Finally, there is a body of research related to the analysis of curriculum content that is of some interest. Most content analyses of textbooks are concerned with the frequency with which certain categories of ideas occur. The readers widely used in the mid-1950s have been analyzed to determine cultural bias in the content. For example, in such readers there were few references to minority groups and the illustrations were confined to white children. Later readers have far more references to minority groups and illustrations commonly show minority members, and sometimes show children whose identity cannot be determined. In more recent times, content analysis of readers has focused on the role that women portray. Curriculum designers are caught in the middle, between the problem of presenting women in traditional roles, or presenting them in roles that are strictly comparable to those of men. The former presents a realistic view of women as they are in the world, and the latter presents them as they would like to be. Should readers present a realistic or an idealistic view of the world? This is, in itself, a significant problem for study. How do children respond to a presentation of women in roles different from those which the children see around them? Do children presented with idealized roles of women treat them as fantasies, or do they accept them as presenting an ideal to be achieved during their lifetimes? Content analysis provides a means of tracing the changes in books designed for schoolchildren from one decade to the next, and there is an infinite range of characteristics for which content can be analyzed. At this time there is a need to look at schoolbooks to determine the kinds of values that are inherent in the stories and how these values correspond with those of the readers.

Research on the Form of Communications

Extensive research has been undertaken on the problem of the form in which communications are made to learners and the effect of the form of that communication on the efficiency of learning. At one time much research was undertaken on the form of typography used in children's readers, but this did not seem to lead anywhere. Later, research became concerned with the use of illustrations in readers, the utility of such illustrations, and the best form for illustrations. Work in these areas has been summarized by Travers and Alvarado (1970). Younger children do not generally like the kinds of stylized illustrations found in books designed for grades 1 and 2. The reason why such stylized drawings are used is that the books are selected by adults who have entirely different tastes in illustrations than first- and second-graders. Young children do like bright colors that are quite unrealistic, but there is a similar tendency among adults. The producers of color film have typically made their film with far brighter colors than occur in nature because the viewers prefer such unrealistic tones. Many of the illustrations used with young children involve the use of conventions to present motion. Thus, a ball in motion is presented with a wake behind it, though balls do not have a visible wake as does a ship.

Studies have been made of how children of different ages extract information from pictures. Travers (1969) found that children of preschool age tend to focus their attention on a single feature of a picture and seem unable to scan the picture and take in a breadth of information. A ten-year-old child, who looks at a picture, knows that the scene is a part of an ongoing set of events. Some state of affairs existed before the picture was taken, and another state of affairs will exist after the picture was taken. The ten-year-old child understands a picture as a part of a sequence, but the preschool child does not understand it in that way at all. The younger child is completely objective; he sees the picture as a static state of affairs. The ball in the picture is suspended in midair. It is not the ball that a child in the right-hand corner has just thrown. The young child's objectivity interferes with interpreting the picture as a part of an ongoing scene.

Much more work needs to be done to understand the way in which children interpret illustrations. Much of their difficulty would seem to derive from the fact that they are unable to comprehend many events simultaneously. Children also have difficulties in understanding the time dimension, which has to be understood in most picture interpretation. Studies also need to be undertaken on the effect of training young children to understand pictorial material.

Kennedy's (1974) excellent book on picture perception has brought together a great range of research findings related to picture perception that have implications for education. Kennedy does much to resolve the argument between those who believe that children need training in visual literacy and those who believe that no such training is necessary. The evidence indicates that infants under six months of age do not respond to a picture as a representation of the real world, but see it as a completely flat surface. These infants are responding to cues that indicate the flatness of the surface, but these are cues that the older child has learned to disregard. When an adult looks at an oil painting, he responds to information from the picture that tells him about a real world represented by it. The viewer disregards the reflections from the surface of the oils that emphasize the flatness of the surface he is contemplating. The young infant has to learn to disregard such cues, and when he has learned to do this, he can then see a picture as a picture. For the young infant, surface cues are important in learning to relate to the world around him. When the infant picks up an object from the surface of a table, he has to understand that the surface is there and he understands this by picking up cues from the light reflected from the surface of the table. Surface cues tell the infant where the boundaries of the world are.

Kennedy also brings together evidence that, once the infant has learned to disregard surface cues, he is able to view the picture as a picture. Further learning does not seem to be necessary to do this. Infants who have been raised in a world devoid of pictorial representation are able, at the age of two, to understand pictures immediately when they are shown them in the sense that they can identify objects in the pictures. This is a primitive understanding, for they still have to acquire the understanding that a picture represents a single moment from an ongoing sequence of events. This understanding cannot develop until the child acquires a better understanding of time and can expand his grasp of visual perception.

Substantial and interesting research has also been undertaken on the problem of how children and adults undertake a visual inspection of a picture. Eye cameras have been developed for this purpose. The classic work on the subject by Yarbus (1967) includes a great wealth of material concerning techniques for studying the process of visual inspection. Much needs to be done at the infant level where the first skills are acquired at undertaking visual inspections, but there are difficulties in using eye cameras at that level. Some interesting applications of eye cameras are found in studies of how children read.

As a general rule, children spend most time inspecting those parts of a visual display that communicate the most information. Thus, in the study of a map of, say, an island, most of the viewer's time is spent examining the boundaries of the island. Boundaries are generally filled with information and have to be studied first. Areas within boundaries are much less filled with meaning and are given only cursory examination.

The use of color is of particular interest in that colored pictures add greatly to the cost of school materials. A study by Travers (1969) compared colored with black-and-white reproductions of the same scene, with careful control being exercised over the degree of contrast found in the two sets of pictures. Preschool children found the colored pictures easier material for extracting information, even when color was not particularly significant. This finding has not been reproduced with film. Numerous investigations have shown that black-and-white motion pictures are just as informative as colored films. The exception to this is when color is of particular importance for the communication of meaning. A film on famous paintings could hardly be as effective in black and white as in color, for the particular color techniques used are crucial to an understanding of a particular artist and what that artist is attempting to do.

The use of color may also have a stimulating or arousing effect on the viewer. This is a matter that still needs to be explored.

An interesting set of problems related to the use of pictorial material is that of the coding of material into other forms. A person looks at a picture of a house and says to himself "That is a house similar to those that are built in Japan." These words code some of the information provided by the picture into words. The code is probably an auditory code, since we know that most verbal material is converted into an auditory verbal form. Verbal coding of pictorial material appears to be important for the retention of information. We know little about the age at which children begin to code visual material in a verbal form, and nothing about the trainability of that skill. Teachers presenting pictorial material often talk about it to the pupils and try to put into words what the picture presents. This is a form of coding that may be important in helping children to code pictorial materials for themselves. We don't really know whether such teacher coding is effective or whether it is best for the child to attempt to code the material for himself.

There are all sorts of other forms of coding that pupils undertake that need to be studied. Learning to use musical notation requires that the individual be able to code a printed note as a played note, or a played note as a printed note. Making a map is another form of the coding of visual information. The written description of a field trip or of a set of observations is another form in which the coding process occurs. Coding processes are universal in education and represent a neglected area of research. A few promising studies have been undertaken involving the coding of information from one sensory modality into another on the part of young children. In such studies children have had to match visually presented geometric shapes with tactilely presented visual shapes (see Jones and Alexander, 1974).

This discussion of recoding information into a different modality leads us to the consideration of the important question of the advantages of using more than one sensory system in the transmission of information. This is a very old problem in education. The classic works on audiovisual techniques, such as the early edition of the famous book by Dale (1946), took the position that more was learned when the same information was transmitted through two sensory channels rather than one. There was little evidence to support this contention, but it seemed a reasonable position to take. Research in this area has developed only slowly.

Two lines of research are related to this problem. One has been developed largely by psychologists interested in the problems of perception, and the other was developed by individuals who were mainly concerned with problems of learning in schools. Let us consider each of these separately.

The simplest form of the problem is the study of the extent to which the sensitivity of one sensory system is influenced by the stimulation of another sensory system. Does a person become more sensitive to slight changes in illumination if he is also listening to a tone at the same time? This is about the simplest form of the problem of the effect of one source of sensory stimulation on another source that has an impact on a different sensory system. This problem has been a favorite one for Russian psychologists, whose work has been summarized by London (1954). Later American research has been summarized by Loveless, Brebner, and Hamilton (1970). Visual threshold to light seems to be increased by auxiliary stimulation through another sensory system. Color vision is also changed by such auxiliary stimulation. Blue-green sensitivity is increased and red-orange sensitivity is decreased. Any source of stimulation appears to increase the level of arousal of the cells of the cerebral cortex and it is this arousal phenomenon that may well be the basis of the changed sensitivity. This explanation is not entirely without difficulties, one of which is that the auxiliary stimulation seems to lose its effect as it is repeated. An arousal theory does not allow for this kind of habituation.

Although this whole problem area may seem to be, on the surface, academic and unrelated to anything that happens in the classroom, in actual fact it deals with problems of extreme practical significance. Consider, for example, the long controversy in education about whether classrooms should be very quiet places in which children concentrate on their work, or whether they should be bustling with activity. Those who want the quiet classrooms believe that auxiliary stimulation is disruptive of important class work. On the other hand, those who run open classrooms believe that the noise of the ongoing activity seems to stimulate some children out of a state of lethargy. There are, no doubt, individual differences in response to auxiliary stimulation, and here is another important problem that needs to be studied.

Problems related to inputs through multisensory systems can be treated at a higher level of complexity. Freides (1974) has summarized much of the work involving more complex inputs than those considered in the Loveless, Brebner, and Hamilton (1970) review. One of the basic problems in this area is that comparable information that contributes to an infant's learning experience can come from both the visual and the touch-movement sensory system. The evidence suggests that the infant has to learn that the world, as explored by the touch and movement system, is the same world as that which can be explored with the eyes. The same is true of the visual and auditory world. Even at the nursery school level, children exploring objects through touch alone seem to learn little about the way in which these objects would present themselves visually. Some information did seem to be translated the other way. Visual information helped the children understand the touch world. Surprisingly enough, language seems to play little role with children in translating information from one modality into another.

The translation of information from one sensory mode into another is a common occurrence. When printed material is read, the visual speech information seems to be translated into an internal auditory speech. Young children engaged in reading provide very direct evidence of doing this when they read aloud, even when they are alone. Even simple lists of words, shown to college students, seem to be translated into an auditory-speech mode, because, in recalling the lists, there is a tendency to reproduce similar sounding words rather than words that are similar in appearance. Freides also brings out the point that there is always a tendency to translate information into that sensory modality in which the information is most easily handled. For example, suppose that I am in a strange town and have to ask my way. The person I stop for this purpose gives me a long verbal description of how I can get to the place where I want to go. As the description is given to me through my ears, I translate that information into a kind of visual map, which I later use in walking to my destination. I have translated the auditory information into visually recorded information, because the visual modality is the one that permits me to handle spatial information most easily. Other forms of translation are common. If somebody describes to me the texture of a particular fabric, I will translate the information into the tactile-haptic modality, and will arrive at understanding how that fabric feels when it is held and rubbed between the fingers. Translation is always into that modality in which the information is most readily handled.

Several additional points are of interest in this area. Information, at simpler levels, seems to be easily handled by any sensory system. At more complex levels, information often seems more easily handled by one sensory modality than another. This has implications for research on the teaching of children who have sensory disabilities. One needs to know more about the kind of information that is not readily communicated through any sensory channel. Furthermore, brain damage all too often seems to influence the processing of information in particular channels. Thus, many children with reading disabilities seem to have difficulty in processing visual information. This difficulty may be quite slight and involve only problems of directionality, as when the child cannot distinguish left to right from right to left. On the other hand, the difficulty may be very extensive as when the child seems unable to recognize the geometric features of visual materials and cannot discriminate common letters one from the other. In such cases there are obvious difficulties in trying to substitute other channels of information for the one that is malfunctioning.

Despite all the difficulties that are involved in substituting one sensory channel for another, highly motivated efforts on the part of a learner can result in extraordinary compensations for sensory deficiencies. Helen Keller is perhaps the most remarkable of the individuals who have had to find substitutes for lost channels of communication. One suspects that the remarkable performance of Helen Keller is as much attributable to her teacher Anna Sullivan as it was to Helen Keller's intellect and powerful motivation. This still remains a splendid and rewarding area for the educational researcher, for, despite the existence of great teachers such as Anna Sullivan, knowledge about how to go about teaching those with sensory deficiencies is still very limited.

The problem in the area of multisensory stimulation in which educators have focused their attention has been that of whether introducing the same information through two sensory channels produces more learning, or retention, than introducing the information through one sensory channel. The problem is a practical one. Indeed, the argument used to introduce the sound motion picture into the classroom was that the use of two sensory channels would produce more learning than would be produced by the silent motion picture that used only one. The argument has a certain surface plausibility to it. If the pupil is viewed as a kind of tank that has to be filled with a liquid, called knowledge, one can surely fill the tank more rapidly through two pipes than through one. Such analogies are always very tempting, but they can also lead one far astray.

A simple case for the study of this problem is that in which the child reads a paragraph either alone, or while another person reads the paragraph to him. When he reads the paragraph, and also listens to somebody reading it, then two sensory channels are being used at the same time. Traditional theory suggests that such a child should learn more than a child who either just reads the paragraph to himself, or who has it read to him. This looks like a simple problem to study, but it is not. In the case of young children, the performance of the children gives the impression that two channels are better than one, but this is because of an artifact in the situation. Some children may be virtual nonreaders, so reading the passage to them, while they are supposedly reading it, gives them a chance to acquire some of the information in the passage. Such children give the appearance of benefiting from two channels, but, in fact, they are using only one. Because of this effect, overlooked by the early students of the problem, the early investigators concluded that two channels were better than one. As the problem became better understood, the evidence became more and more clear that when the same information was introduced through two channels, no more was generally learned than when only one channel was used.

After more than two decades of research related to this problem, the full nature and scope of it only slowly became understood. The use of more than one sensory channel for the communication and reception of information involves a whole series of problems, of which the following are but a few:

1. A first problem is whether a single sensory channel can process several messages simultaneously or whether information is sequentially processed. For example, when one is presented with a three-word or a four-word sentence, does one process the information from left to right, a bit at a time, until the entire sentence has been read? The evidence is to the contrary, at least in the case of competent readers. Information from all the words is likely to be taken in at once and each of these sources of information is simultaneously processed. When this happens, information is said to be processed simultaneously, rather than successively. Such simultaneous processing is also typical of the way in which one may look at a familiar oil painting or a familiar scene. However, visual information may not always be processed in this simultanous manner. A child learning to read may start with the first letter of the three-word sequence, and then move to the second letter, and so on until the entire sentence has been deciphered. Such processing is sequential.

Auditory information is taken into the information system piece by piece. It has to be taken in sequentially. One can hear only one sound at a time, so verbal material has to enter the information system a sound at a time. There is no way of presenting a single sentence instantaneously to the ear, as one can present it instantaneously to the eye. Auditory information, despite the fact that it has to go in piece by piece, goes into a holding mechanism, where large amounts can be held for simultaneous analysis. In the holding mechanism the information is analyzed and meaning is extracted. The latter is a simultaneous process. To understand a sentence one has to understand the sentence as a whole. Thus, even within a single sensory channel, information is processed both in a sequential form and in a simultaneous form.

2. The evidence is substantial that the central information processing system in the brain is a system that can handle only a limited amount of data in a given time. Push more information into the system than can be handled and confusion results. This condition is referred to as overload, and the result of overload is confusion and a failure to learn. Overloading the system does not just slow down learning, but it stops all learning. The central information analysis system in the brain can handle only so much

information, regardless of the sensory system through which the information comes. For this reason, pumping in information through more than one system does not increase the amount of information that can be handled or learned if one sensory system is already receiving information at the maximum rate at which the information can be processed.

3. A sensory channel may receive stimuli with low informational value that may have use in arousing the learner to learn through another sensory channel. Thus, loud music at the start of a motion picture may arouse the learners so that they are better able to learn the material that is subsequently presented. Not much is known about this phenomenon, and there is also the related phenomenon of the disruptive effects of noise.

4. Multiple channels sometimes are used in such a way that the information presented through one channel can be coded in the other channel. Thus, many motion pictures present visual information that is then described in words. The word descriptions represent a coded form of the visual information. This kind coding seems to be very important for good retention.

5. The use of more than one sensory channel may be important to prevent monotony. Information that is presented visually today may be discussed verbally tomorrow. Teachers have long recognized the importance of presenting information in a variety of ways, and the use of more than one sensory channel is a way of producing variety. Here, again, is another set of problems about which very little is known.

6. Much more needs to be known about the effects of a person becoming specialized in the sensory channel through which he receives information. There is no doubt that, by the end of the elementary school years, some children can receive verbal information better through the visual printed form and some better through the vocal auditory form. How such specialization occurs is not known. One also does not know the effect this has on subsequent learning. Do those who prefer the auditory form read less and less, and do those who prefer the visual form become progressively more print oriented? A whole host of important educational problems lie in this area.

Computers as Information Systems and as Components of Educational Technology

Earlier in the chapter the point was made that education, from the earliest times, has sought to give the student access to information in the various forms in which it was recorded. It is hardly surprising that some modern educators have extended this idea to computer systems. Certainly, computers are major devices for storing information, though they do not as yet compete with books as sources of information in the sciences and the humanities. Nevertheless, the time may come when information in the latter categories may well be stored in computer memories and be presented on a screen to whoever needs the information. The home library may soon be a thing of the past. The home may well become equipped with a service that will enable the individual to obtain instantly a page from any book that has ever been written. All the home subscriber would have to do would be to dial the code for that page. The code would be available perhaps from a home catalog of sources or from a computerized catalog to which the individual would have direct access. Such information systems for the ordinary citizen are far into the future. For the present, the role of the computer as a source of information or instruction is very limited. Some educational research workers have been intrigued with that role and have attempted to explore its future possibilities with the aid of computer manufacturing concerns that see large profits in such an enterprise in the future.

Most of those who have been concerned with this problem have viewed the computer as a natural Pressey-type or Skinner-type teaching machine, but with rather greater flexibility than either Sidney Pressey or B. F. Skinner ever introduced into their simple models. Early research on the computer as an information system, to be used for instruction, tied itself to the Skinner type of programmed learning, with the usual preoccupation with the ordering of the subject matter. The computer permitted the use of devices that had hitherto seemed impractical in a programmed type of learning, and especially what is known as branching programs. The learner who cannot answer questions on a particular topic correctly is shunted to a special teaching sequence that helps him understand whatever he has failed to grasp. This special sequence is called a branching program. Then, when he has mastered the branching program, the learner is shunted back again into the mainstream program. On the surface, this sounds like a promising idea to pursue.

Very large sums of money have been invested in the study of this form of teaching. Millions of dollars of federal money have been spent, some of it by education agencies and some by the military. Indeed, the military have been intrigued by the enterprise since it offered promise of providing a completely mechanized form of training that could produce a technically trained army in a very short time during an international crisis. Much of the prompting for this enterprise has come from the producers of computers who saw this new educational thrust as a new market. The Radio Corporation of America went so far as to advertise it's computerized system of education on public television as though it were the most efficient system of educating children. IBM was more modest and reasonable in its approach and provided extensive facilities including computer time for experiments on computerized education. Some academicians, who are not insensitive to the possibility of funds, were quick to jump on the bandwagon. Research in the area was lavishly supported, and an academician can achieve enormous prestige by acquiring the reputation of having research funds at his disposal. A few academicians were genuinely intellectually absorbed in the idea that the computer might prove to be the ultimate in an effective teacher.

Now that the initial wave of enthusiasm of some academicians has died down and manufacturers of computers no longer see a large market in the immediate future, we can begin to take a more sober look at the future of the computer as a teacher. A first point to note is that the computer has a formidable rival in the form of the book, although much needs to be done to improve the book. The book is cheap, is always available to the purchaser, and information can be easily extracted from it. Books can also incorporate much illustrated material at moderate costs, and even include transparencies and overlays. Illustrations can be stored in computers but the mechanism for doing this is clumsy and expensive. The book still remains the prime invention of educational technology. Perhaps the most that can be said about the computer as a teacher and source of information is that the computer terminal may introduce some variety into the activities of the classroom. The research of Suppes (1968) and others provides little optimism concerning the immediate future of the enterprise, though the report of the Suppes study is written up in a mood of optimism far beyond that which the data justify.

There are negative features related to the use of computers as teachers and as sources of academic information. The most notable of these is that the computer isolates the child from other human beings. The child in isolation in the computer booth represents one of the ultimate products of an advanced technology, namely, a person who works in complete isolation from other individuals. Such isolation is a poor condition for the human as a member of an intensely social species. Humans need more contacts with others, rather than less. Technology isolates the individual and violates his basic social nature. The book has already done this to some degree; the computer does it to the final degree.

The use of computers in education for informing, instructing, and so forth helps to lead education down an unproductive path, in that most children need more contact with the real world to help them understand what they are trying to learn. The computer terminal, consisting of a sterile, isolated booth, separates the child from the real world that he is trying to master. Rather than spending money on a computer terminal, funds should be invested in equipping the classroom with a wealth of materials that the child can study, manipulate, and use as a basis for experiments.

A social species such as the human needs to have much contact with other members of his species if his learning is to be enjoyed. That is why incompetent teachers, who do not understand the social needs of children, may spend almost the entire day punishing children for interactions with other children. Such teachers should learn to find social situations in which the subject matter can be readily learned. Such an area is an excellent one for research, although it is not an easy one. We need to know about the social situations in classrooms in which learning can take place productively and those that tend to degenerate into gossip, horseplay, and other non-productive activities. We need to know how children can learn to exercise leadership in such situations. We need to design more tasks that groups can undertake. We need to develop general principles for the design of such tasks.

Computers have also been studied in school contexts as systems for keeping records. This has been an attractive theme for educational research workers, but other researchers should be finding out whether elaborate school records are ever used. Also, a record-centered school may be one run for the sake of the system rather than for the sake of the children. Computers are not just the instruments of bureaucracy. They are the weapons of bureaucracy that entangle the rest of the world in a jungle of records. The emphasis of research workers on how to keep records in schools needs to be replaced by a new emphasis on devising ways to elimi-nate the need for records. What would happen if the school were a record-free institution? Would it be worse or better? My guess is that it would be better. Also, the bureaucracy involved in record keeping would be better used elsewhere. One may perhaps be reminded that the enormous efforts of the FBI to keep records on innocent individuals used up labor that could have been used to combat crime.

Although the idea of developing a technology of education may be alluring, the basic problem of education is still that of helping the child relate, directly, to a complex environment. All too often technology pro-vides a barrier between the child and the environment with which he is learning to cope. Thus, a child in school may not be given the opportunity of seeing directly the countless organisms that live in the local pond, but he is shown a film of some of those organisms, which has a duration set by the filmmaker and not the child. In such a case, the technology is almost a barrier to knowledge for the child is denied the opportunity of collecting his sample from the local pond, examining it for organisms, growing the organisms, seeing them reproduce, and so forth. An educational technology that expands the things a child can do is needed, not one that restricts.

Summary

1. In ancient times, priestly castes learned to store information in a written code and slowly libraries developed. Later, education became the means of teaching people to decode the written signs. Education, at first,

was education for literacy. The manuscript, and later the book, became the keys to knowledge. The printing press is probably the greatest of all inventions in the area of educational technology.

2. Educators have long shown an interest in the problem of how to present written materials so that they can be easily understood. The early teachers of the Catholic Church became interested in the problem of the ordering of subject matter, and they developed the catechism. Some modern scientists have been interested in the same problem. Substantial research has been undertaken on the use of various modified alphabets for the purposes both of learning to read and for adult reading. The Initial Teaching Alphabet (ITA) is a modern attempt to do this.

3. The use of modified alphabets for teaching reading remains controversial. There is certainly no clear evidence that these alphabets are of value over the long run.

4. The choice of vocabulary for reading materials for schools is also an important problem that has been extensively studied. Thorndike initiated work in this area and developed a series of literary classics that had modified vocabularies. Later, students of Thorndike produced the first set of readers with a controlled vocabulary. The readers thus developed also controlled the frequency with which new words appeared.

5. The study of the control of sentence structure also occupied psychologists earlier in the century. Numerous measures of sentence complexity and readability were developed that were later used for the design of school materials. Then refinements took place both in the measurement of readability and in ways for measuring the difficulty of vocabulary. Newer methods of measuring the difficulty level of words were derived from studies of what words children could actually understand. An idea related to this is that children should develop their own reading materials by telling stories that are then typed out for them.

6. The content of readers and reading material for children deserves to be studied more intensively than it has been. Typical content is bland, innocuous, and hardly worth reading.

7. Research workers have been interested in the problem of how subject matter should be organized. Most modern theories of both learning and memory imply that knowledge consists of a hierarchy of skills that have to be learned in a certain order. Operant psychologists have been particularly active in the area of arranging subject matter in order. They refer to an ordered set of subject matter as a program and each item in the sequence as a frame. Such materials had a brief period of popularity during the 1960s. The slow disappearance of such materials is a result of many factors including their cost.

8. A problem that has not been faced by those interested in the ordering of subject matter is that most subject matter can be structured in many different ways. History has a time structure, a geographical structure, as

well as many other structures. Mathematics probably has a simpler structure than any other field, namely a logical structure, yet mathematics can be structured logically in many different ways.

9. Piaget has used logic as a basis for ordering subject matter, having demonstrated that different forms of logic are manifested at different ages.

10. Psychologists and educators have also been interested in designing and investigating management concepts related to the learning of subject matter. Competency-based programs of teacher education reflect one attempt to use a particular management system in an educational context. Attempted applications of operant psychology have also been in the sphere of the management of the classroom.

11. Curriculum research has had a long and quite unsatisfactory history. Approaches to the design of curriculum are intimately related to the designer's philosophy of education. The selection of the content may be related to children's interests, the needs of the community, or to other matters. The Kentucky study is particularly notable in that it attempted to build an elementary school curriculum that would improve the quality of life in a community. Attempts to build curricula in terms of the interests of children run into difficulties in that research has little to say about children's interests. Studies need to be undertaken concerning the themes that seem to preoccupy some children over long periods. The content of the curriculum may also be analyzed in terms of the logical processes that the material involves. There is also the important issue of whether logical processes should be learned by children with natural objects or with artificially simplified objects such as cardboard squares and triangles. The order of development of logical processes has been a productive area of research. The matter of the extent to which children should be free to choose content also needs to be explored. Another area that needs to be studied is the extent to which the materials themselves should be in sequence and the extent to which the pupil should himself attempt to organize knowledge. A child may learn more about trees by writing a short book on trees, digging out the information from various sources, than by being provided with a well-organized account of the subject.

12. An area of the analysis of curriculum in which numerous studies are, and have been, made is that of the sex roles portrayed by school materials. Other studies have been undertaken of the portrayal of race roles and stereotypes.

13. The form in which materials are provided for children has been the focus of numerous researchers. Studies have been undertaken of illustrations and how children respond to them. There seems to be a marked discrepancy in this area between what children like and what the adults who select the materials like. Children have difficulties in interpreting illustrations that adults do not have. Young children tend to focus on small elements of a picture and fail to understand the totality displayed. However,

there seems to be no argument in favor of training children in visual literacy. The difficulties they have in looking at pictures are just the difficulties they have in looking at the world. Very young infants have difficulty in seeing pictures because they are distracted by cues related to the flatness of the picture's surface. Studies of eye movements have shown how individuals inspect pictures. Most time is spent on the part of the picture that is least familiar and the part that contains the most information. Color seems to facilitate the extraction of information from a picture, but black-and-white motion pictures seem to be just as useful for educational pictures as those that are colored.

14. Classic studies took the position that more information could be transmitted to a learner through two sensory channels than through one. Recent studies have shown that this is not so when the two channels contain either the same or different information. However, sensory stimulation through one sensory channel may stimulate the individual and produce a heightened state of activity that may facilitate learning through another sensory channel.

15. An important issue is whether information is received by the senses, piece by piece in a chain, or whether several sources of information can be processed simultaneously. Both simultaneous and successive processing occurs, even though the central nervous system is a system of limited capacity for handling information.

16. The effective use of two sensory channels at the same time is when the information in the one channel is coded in the other channel.

17. Books may someday be rivaled by the computer as information storage systems. The computer has also been adapted for use as a teaching machine. Although much money has been invested in such a venture, there are few signs that computers will become widely used in classrooms.

CHAPTER 6
Research as It Relates to Development and Learning and Its Impact on Education

This chapter considers the development of attempts to measure intelligence along with attempts to develop theories of learning. The intelligence test movement developed as an attempt to discriminate those who could learn academic skills from those who could not, and intelligence tests are still used, and misused, for that purpose today. Most of the early developers of intelligence tests also had a theory of how children and adults learned and the tests were designed to identify what their developers believed to be crucial characteristics of the learner. In more recent years, measurement and learning theory have gone their separate ways, though a few psychologists have attempted to bring the two sciences together.

The Testing Movement

Learning and development have traditionally been studied separately as distinct areas of research. The separation was a result of the fact that until recently nobody knew how to relate the two areas. Traditional learning theory took the position that there was only one form of learning and, hence, babies were assumed to learn by the same kind of processes as adults. Thus, those who embraced the classical conditioning paradigm, as John B. Watson did earlier in the century, viewed all learning, from infancy through adulthood, as a matter of establishing particular classically conditioned responses; the general procedure for doing this was believed to be the same regardless of the learner's age. Operant conditioning psychologists have taken a similar position regarding the single nature of learning except for classical conditioning, which they consider to be a trivial case. They interpret all instrumental learning as the learning of operants. In all these theories, learning varies only in complexity, and not in the nature of the learning processes involved. Nevertheless, psychologists have had considerable difficulty in producing conditioned responses in the newborn despite the fact that such infants are obviously learning at a very rapid rate. Psychologists have had difficulty in relating learning to development, perhaps because most have made the assumption that learning represents a single uniform process at all levels of development. The fact that the assumption may not fit the facts has only recently become evident.

Another reason why psychologists have avoided considering the hypothesis that learning may involve different processes at different developmental levels is the delight that psychologists, like all scientists, take in providing grossly simplified pictures of the world around us. Psychologists provide a simplified picture of behavior much as the chemist provides a grossly simplified picture of, say, the chemical processes taking place in the soil. The idea that learning involves a single identifiable process, regardless of level of development, is an attractive one from the scientific viewpoint.

Those concerned with the processes of development have been equally obsessed with the separation of learning from those aspects of the life processes that stem from the natural processes of growth. The classic work of Arnold Gesell at Yale focused on the pattern of development as it was determined by the gene structure and modified by accidents such as brain damage at birth and other abnormalities. Gesell undertook to describe and inventory the sensory and motor process that emerged during infancy, paying special attention to the order in which they emerged and their functions. Gesell was not primarily concerned with learning for he assumed that normal learning took place provided the body mechanisms were there to permit normal learning to take place. Gesell described his observations in much the same manner that an embryologist would describe the development of the fetus. His descriptions provide few references to the environmental conditions that might influence learning except insofar as these conditions resulted in some form of traumatic damage to the nervous system. Gesell belonged to an era in which great emphasis was placed on the importance of maturational processes. In that age educators took the position that early childhood was a time during which little should be done except to let the child grow. Once this growth had developed the necessary structures to permit school learning, then would be the time to start formal education. This view was not universally held. Maria Montessori had attempted to inventory the important learnings that should take place during the preschool period, and Sigmund Freud had emphasized the importance of the learning of emotional responses during the early years of life. Despite these emphases, those who studied what they believed to be maturational processes remained apart from those who studied learning.

On the side of the maturationists were those who were concerned with the development of intelligence tests. From the time of Alfred Binet, psychologists interested in the development of tests of intelligence made the assumption that such tests measured the inherent intellectual powers of the individual, rather than the effects of formal training on the individual. Binet had many distinguished followers who took the same position including Cyril Burt and L. L. Thurstone. The latter even went so far as to suggest that the various components of intelligence, which he had isolated through factor analysis, might one day be shown to be related to particular genes. In recent times, as a result of controversy concerning the nature of the variable or variables measured by intelligence tests, efforts have been made to produce instruments that would be, as far as possible, uninfluenced by the particular learning experiences to which the individual had been exposed.

The criticism that intelligence tests were culturally biased also became the subject for extensive research, which demonstrated the obvious, namely, that competence depends upon the experiences one has had. Anyone who has any knowledge at all of the history of the human species would be acutely aware of this fact. The human brain reached its present state of development at least a half million years ago and yet, during most of the half million years, man has lived under the most primitive conditions. There was nobody to teach him to live otherwise, and half a million years of slow self-instruction were needed to produce the competence of the modern human. Probably the gene structure of the human of a half million years ago was essentially the same as that of the present-day human, but our far-off ancestor probably would have performed miserably on our modern intelligence tests. One should also perhaps reflect that modern psychologists would have performed woefully badly on the kinds of problems that our remote ancestors had to solve. Indeed, a modern psychologist dumped in isolation in the wilderness, and forced to live under the conditions that our early ancestors encountered, might not be able to survive at all.

Theory of testing, related to education, has probably reflected the values and cultural bias of those who have developed testing devices. All too often the developers of intelligence tests have failed to recognize their prejudices and have promoted them as though they were some form of scientific truth. At the end of World War I, American psychologists were invited to appear before committees of Congress to advise on matters related to the setting of immigration quotas. These psychologists generally took the position that the results of the Army Alpha Intelligence Test showed differences in intelligence among different national groups and that such differences should be taken into account in the setting of immigration quotas. The advice given to the Congress was that Eastern and southern Europeans produced substantially lower mean intelligence test scores than did the immigrants from Western and northern Europe, and hence immigration policies should favor those with the higher intelligence test scores. The notion that different European groups varied in their average level of intelligence was a view that had long been held by Western Europeans, and indeed, by many Western European scientists. Karl Pearson, the great mathematical statistician, had long argued that the Eastern and southern Europeans were of inferior genetic stock. The work done on the Army Alpha Examination was used to buttress this myth. The facts, as far as we can see them today, lead to the conclusion that there are no clearly established genetic differences between the various national and racial stocks.

Another lesson that may be learned from the history of intelligence testing is that research in its early stages can be misleading and has often been used to mislead legislators in setting public policy. Just as national legislation has often been badly misguided by research, so too has educational policy been led astray. The intelligence test movement did much to support ineffective practices in schools over a period of more than half a century. The view that intelligence tests measured innate intellectual capacity led educational administrators to take the position that children should be grouped in terms of what was believed to be their innate level of intelligence. Tracking systems became popular following World War II and reached their peak of use in the 1950s. Such tracking systems were well supported by the influential middle classes, because the intelligence tests placed the children of the lower classes in the lowest track. Middle-class prejudice had long held that the lower classes were intellectually inferior to the middle and upper classes. Intelligence tests seemed to provide support for this belief. Racial minorities also scored lower and this again conformed with the prejudices of the middle-class majority group. The scientists involved with these testing devices were flattered with the widespread support found for their materials. Large commercial ventures developed that brought considerable wealth to both the publishers and the individual developers of intelligence tests.

Some questioning minds believed that the intelligence tests that had been developed measured largely the cultural advantages that the individual had had. A few even attempted to devise experiments to demonstrate that intelligence test scores were influenced substantially by the quality of the environment in which the individual had been raised. Beth Wellman, at the University of Iowa, attempted to show in a series of studies, that exposure of young children to a rich nursery school program increased their performances on intelligence tests. Wellman's data were convincing, but her research was widely ridiculed and accepted by only a few. Her findings had little impact.

The area of intelligence tests is still controversial, but the former minority view has now become the majority view. Most psychologists take the position that intelligence test scores are profoundly influenced by the experiences a person has had. A few still take the position that at least some intelligence tests reflect basic differences in genetic constitution.

On the educational scene, the change in the views of psychologists has reflected a change in the practice in schools, though the schools themselves had come to realize that the intelligence tests could not be used to reflect the genetic constitution of the individual. In addition, intelligence test scores were not found to have the stability that they were supposed to have. A child who may test average in nursery school may end up with a doctoral degree from a reputable university. The tracking system, as it was practiced earlier in the century, seemed to penalize such children, sometimes just by telling them that they were viewed as inferior. The tracking system as it was used in large systems, such as the London County Council Schools (England), was shown to produce more problems than it solved and was discarded as a failure.

A useful model of the intellect and of development that educators could use with success, required a far more substantial backing of knowledge than that which the intelligence test movement had relied upon. The attempt to apply educational research, long before a substantial body of information had been acquired, undoubtedly did much harm to the lives of many pupils. However, the lesson that should have been learned was not learned, for later generations of psychologists were also ready to plunge ahead with practical applications of their work, long before their research was sufficient to justify such a plunge.

Although this discussion of the contribution of the immense amount of work undertaken on intelligence testing may seem negative, the enterprise had some positive contributions. It led to a rethinking of the whole problem of the assessment of intelligence. Indeed, the contribution of Piaget emerged from his consideration of the work of Alfred Binet and the questions that he (Piaget) had about it. The young Piaget went to Paris to work with Binet's collaborator Théodore Simon. Through the stimulation of these great test builders, Piaget was able to develop his theory of the development of the intellect.

Other positive contributions of the intelligence test enterprise include the development of a scientific study of the properties that useful testing devices should have. The intensive discussions earlier in the century concerning the nature of validity and reliability were derived largely from problems related to the building of intelligence tests, though the concepts that emerged were soon applied to thinking that was related to other forms of measurement, including personality measurement. The idea that behavior could be measured, much as the properties of material objects could be measured, has largely been a product of the present century. Although the concept of measurement had been used, with great practical success, in many other fields, its use in the area of behavior presented problems that had not even been considered elsewhere. The physicist does not have to be preoccupied with problems of validity and reliability, because he generally knows precisely what he is measuring and he also knows the precision with which measurement is made. Enormous effort was devoted in the last century to the improvement in the precision of physical measurement. By the turn of the century, physical scientists were able to measure weight to within one ten thousandth of a gram and length to within a thousandth of a millimeter. In the present century, even greater precision of measurement has been achieved. By comparison, the measurement of the educational researcher is quite crude. His error of measurement may be a third or more of the total range of measurements with which he is dealing. Work on the development of measures of intelligence brought all of these problems to the forefront.

Although the study of intelligence tests and their uses often did much to support and enhance prejudices related to racial, national, class, and sex, differences, the work also ultimately contributed to the destruction of these prejudices. From what is known today, there are far fewer and weaker arguments to support such prejudices than there were at the turn of the century. Much of the research indicates that desirable human genes are widely distributed throughout the world population and that no particular group or class has the monopoly of the genes that contribute to intelligence or virtue. The research has, over the long haul, contributed to a more reasonable and balanced view of the nature of others who may have superficial characteristics that make them different from oneself. Not all are yet convinced of this view, but if a poll were taken of psychologists today, an overwhelming majority would agree that there is little evidence to support the view that certain races, nationalities, or classes are genetically superior to others. Such a poll would probably have shown the reverse view if it had been taken early in the century.

The Testing Movement's Preoccupation with Reliability and Validity

The testing movement grew during World War I in a spirit of evangelistic enthusiasm. This soon permeated the marketplace where psychologists who had had contact with the army Alpha and Beta testing programs competed to sell intelligence tests to gullible businessmen. Most of the new tests showed considerable resemblance to the army prototypes that they mimicked. One of the most successful (of these) salesmen of the new psychological hardware was the late Arthur S. Otis, whose test was sold and promoted on a worldwide basis by Otis himself. Otis was a brilliant opportunist who had left behind him a collection of probably apocryphal stories. Some claim that he was the inventor of the group intelligence test. Indeed, the story told is that in the years before the United States entered World War I, young Otis was a student of Lewis Terman at Stanford University, where he took a course with Terman on the administration of the Stanford Binet Intelligence Scale. Students in the course were required to administer the test to twenty children individually, and Otis found more interesting activities to pursue than to administer individual Binets. The end of the semester drew near and Otis was faced with the mountainous task of giving the series of tests. Otis decided to short-circuit the process. He extracted from the Binet test the items that could be administered to a group and gave these to an assembly of twenty children. Then he wrote up the test results as though the tests had been administered individually and submitted his material to Terman. Later he told Terman what he had done and Terman was impressed with his student's invention.

When the United States entered World War I, a draft was instituted and the U.S. Army became interested in developing a group test of intelligence for classification purposes. The army found that there was only one expert on this in the entire country, an obscure student of Terman.

After the war was over, Otis spent much of the time promoting various forms of the group intelligence test that carried his name. His enterprise was most successful for his devices became the most widely used of their kind, though there were many successful competitors.

Whatever the enthusiasm may have been in the marketplace for the group intelligence test, scholars soon began to raise questions about whether such tests had all the scientific properties that a measuring device should have. Scholarly discussion of the matter centered on the words *reliability* and *validity*. Did these new tests have these important properties? This question turned out to be a difficult one to answer, for it took another generation of psychologists to find acceptable meanings for these terms. The problems involved were difficult, sometimes philosophical, and with implications for the scientific development of measuring devices as well as for their practical applications. A succession of committees of the American Psychological Association have wrestled with the meanings of these terms (American Psychological Association, 1954, 1965, 1966, 1974). The first of these committees must be given the credit for laying the groundwork on which subsequent committees have built.

Reliability. A measuring instrument used for either research purposes or for some immediately practical purpose, such as the measurement of the length of a piece of fabric, must have useful properties if it is to perform satisfactorily the task at hand. One of these properties is *reliability.* Although this is an abstract and theoretical concept, let us develop it, first, within a practical context. Suppose that we were engaged in measuring the height of some small saplings and that the measuring instrument available was a tape measure such as housewives use when they sew. We might start by checking our measuring tape against a highly accurate measuring rod that was known to be almost exactly sixty inches. Let us suppose that this standard was guaranteed to be within 0.01 inch. In comparing the tape with the rod we would probably note that if we stretched the tape by just the right amount, the tape and the rod would be precisely the same length. We might then go out and measure each of the young trees, each time trying to stretch the tape by just the right amount so that it would provide us with an accurate measure. However, try as we might, sometimes the tape would be pulled too taut and sometimes it would not be pulled tight enough. The result would be that the height of some of the trees would be overestimated whereas the height of others would be underestimated. The instrument is obviously not perfectly reliable. We might find that if we remeasured the trees on a later occasion that the two measures might differ by perhaps as much as two inches. If the trees varied from twenty-four to sixty inches in height, we might regard an error of measurement of this size to be unimportant. However, if we had been conducting an experiment on the growth of trees and the trees varied only from fifty-five to sixty inches, then this error of measurement might be too large for our purposes. We would then have to find a more precise measuring instrument—that is to say, a more reliable instrument. From this example it is also evident that the significance of errors of measurement depends on how much variability they produce in comparison with the total amount of variability among the objects measured. A useful measuring instrument is one in which the variability produced by errors of measurement is small compared with the variability of the objects measured. Another point to note, in this case, is that some idea of the size of the errors involved can be obtained by repeating the measurement procedure.

The tape measure is obviously a poor measuring instrument and, in any experiment involving the measurement of length, we should use a more accurate and reliable device such as, perhaps, a steel tape. The example of the fabric tape is of value here because it has similarities with measuring instruments used in the behavioral sciences. A psychological test, for example, provides us with a score for each individual to whom it is administered. However, we know that even when the same test is given again to the same individuals, they do not obtain exactly the same score on each administration. Scores vary from one administration to the next just as the measured height of the saplings varied. There would be even more variability if another measuring instrument, made as similar as possible to the first, were used for the second measurement. The point to note is that repeating the measurement permits us to estimate the general order of magnitude of the error of measurement.

A measuring instrument provides a score that can be regarded as consisting of two components: one is the true score and the other is an error component. When the measuring instrument has been applied and a distribution of scores has been produced, we would want most of the variability of the scores to be attributable to variations in the true score. The measuring instrument would be most unsatisfactory if most of the variability were only a reflection of errors of measurement. The degree to which the variation reflects variation in true scores represents the degree to which the measuring instrument is reliable. On the other hand, in a highly unreliable test most of the variation in observed scores is attributable to errors of measurement.

One cannot dissect each measurement into a true component and error component, for all one has is a single score for each individual that cannot be readily taken apart. For this reason, the reliability of a measuring instrument has to be estimated by indirect means. The key to the most common methods of estimating reliability has already been indicated and involves the making of repeated measures. The repeated-measures approach involves the use of either (1) parallel forms of the measuring instrument; or (2) reapplication of the same form; or (3) various split-half methods, such as where performance on the even-numbered items is compared with performance on the odd-numbered items. Let us consider each of these in turn.

Parallel forms of a test are two forms designed to provide instruments that match one another as closely as possible without using the same items in each. In terms of measurement theory, parallel forms can be defined as those on which the true scores for an individual are the same and on which the errors of measurement are, on the average, equal. This does not mean that when the same individuals are measured on both instruments that they obtain equal scores. They do not, because the error component of the score for the particular individual may vary from the one test to the other. This makes his observed score vary, but, if the instruments are reliable, then only a small amount of variation is to be expected. If, on the other hand, the individual's score varies a very large amount from the one parallel form of the test to the other, then the error of measurement is high and the instrument can be considered relatively unreliable. The measure of reliability commonly derived through this procedure is the correlation between performance on the one form of the test and performance on the other form. Thus, in a test manual one will find a statement such as, "The parallel-form reliability for the test was found to be 0.92 when the two forms of the test were administered one week apart to 350 fifth-grade children in a metropolitan area." In the interpretation of such a statement, the assumption is commonly made that the test measures a stable characteristic that does not change appreciably over a week. If the characteristic is not stable, then a low correlation may reflect merely that differences in the scores on the two forms of the test largely represent a change in the characteristic measured, rather than errors of measurement. There are methods available for discriminating between a variation in score, from form to form of a test, that is the result of a change in the characteristic measured, and a change that can be attributed to error of measurement. The reader who wishes to explore such methods is referred to Horst (1966).

Very often two or more parallel forms of a measuring device are not available and the procedure of administering the same instrument twice has to be adopted. This is not a very effective procedure for the estimation of reliability, partly because the individual tested often remembers how he marked the items on the first administration of the device and marks them in the same way on the second administration. The result is a spuriously high correlation between the performances on the first and second administrations. Thus, a test-retest measure of reliability tends to provide an excessively high estimate.

When only one form of a test exists, another method of estimating the reliability of the instrument is still open to us. One can regard the items of the test as consisting of two separate tests, each of half length. One can, for example, consider all the even-numbered items as one form of the test and all the odd-numbered items as another. If the test is highly reliable, then the scores derived from the one half of the items should be highly correlated with the scores derived from the other half. The correlation will be lower than if two full-length tests were used because, within limits, the generalization is true that the longer the test the higher the reliability. However, a formula can be applied to the correlation between the two half-length tests that will estimate what the correlation would have been if two full-length tests had been used.

Many methods exist for dividing up a test into two shorter forms for the purpose of estimating reliability. The purpose of the division of the items is to provide two tests that have, as far as possible, the properties of parallel forms. The odd-even approach does this by taking two samples in a systematic way that, one hopes, distributes the items in different categories appropriately over the two forms. An important point to note is that any split-half method of estimating reliability should not be applied if the test is speeded and not all persons complete the test.

Although we can regard the methods of estimating reliability considered to this point as ways of estimating the extent to which scores are contaminated with errors of measurement, we can also view the parallel-form method in another light. The latter method can be viewed as an attempt to discover the extent to which a score derived from one sample of items can be used to predict a score derived from another sample of items, when each sample is derived from the same "universe" of items. There is also another way of reviewing the problem of estimating reliability that brings us back to the problem of homogeneity.

The estimation of reliability by means of the Kuder-Richardson type of formula refers again to a different type of phenomenon. Cronbach (1951), who has made a careful study of this approach, refers to the coefficient derived from this procedure as *alpha*. He has also shown that alpha refers to an internal property of a test, which is a product of the statistical relationship among the items. This property is known as homogeneity, and refers to the extent to which all the items on a test can be considered to contribute to the measurement of a single common variable. The coefficient alpha is for this reason now most commonly referred to as a measure of homogeneity rather than as a measure of reliability.

There are also other approaches to the problem of estimating reliability and some of these approaches make it possible to investigate far more complex situations than have been discussed. Consider, for example, a problem investigated by Stanley (1962) of determining the reliability of an essay test. Let us suppose that two essay tests, A and B, were administered to 200 students. Let us suppose that, on the first day, half of the students took Test A and the other half took Test B, and that on the second day those who had previously taken Test A took Test B and those who had previously taken Test B now took Test A. Let us suppose also that the papers were retyped before the scoring was begun, and that the papers were assigned at random to the examiners except for the added restriction that no examiner ever scored both essays of the same student. In addition, let us have four examiners who read the tests; each examiner reads twenty-five of the A papers and twenty-five of the B papers from the first day and a similar number of each from the second day. After all the papers were scored, a study of the marks would probably show quite clearly that many factors entered into a student's mark. One might be the examiner, some examiners are tougher than others. Another factor might be whether it was the first day of the examination or the second. An additional factor, and the one in which the examiners were interested, was the ability of the students to perform on such a test. The examiners would hope that the scores on the essays would indicate primarily the differences in ability of the students to perform, and not differences between examiners or other irrelevant features of the testing and scoring situation.

A technique known as *analysis of variance* (commonly called Anova) can be applied to these kinds of data for the purpose of sorting out the various factors influencing the final scores. Through the application of this technique, one could determine from the data the extent to which examiner peculiarities influenced scores, the extent to which the day of the examination had an effect, and the extent to which students showed consistency of performance from the first test to the second. If the procedure were further complicated by requiring that each paper be scored independently by two different examiners, then the analysis of variance could also be used to determine the extent to which two examiners agreed with one another, a further aspect of reliability that has not been considered up to this point. The advantage of the analysis of variance procedure is that it permits the sorting out of the various factors and an estimation of the relative effect of each on the scores given to papers.

Validity. The term validity seems to have been derived from philosophers concerned with what they refer to as the validity of knowledge. At the most naïve level, the validity of knowledge refers to whether facts are true, but no modern philosopher would accept such a naïve meaning. Indeed, many would say that knowledge does not consist of facts. Piaget (translated

1972) takes the position that knowledge is action on an object. When one says that one knows the French language, it means that one can speak or read French and use the language to reach some appropriate goal. A knowledge of French is not a stored set of facts about the French language, but an action system that permits one to perform meaningful activities. The validity of one's knowledge of French is whether one can use the language to achieve some goal such as that of reading a book to extract meaning from it, or to speak the language to ask for food. Knowledge is an action system. The validity of knowledge is shown in whether the action system achieves anticipated goals. The validity of my knowledge of French lies in whether I can use the language effectively. Perhaps this will be made clearer by pointing out that I can read Russian, in the sense that I know the Russian alphabet and can read the words from a page. However, I cannot extract any meaning from the page because I have no other knowledge of the Russian language. Other than reading the words, I have no knowledge of the Russian language and no action system that I can use for any useful purpose. Thus, I have no valid knowledge of the Russian language except that involved in deciphering the letters. In a sense, the validity of knowledge is determined by what one can do with it.

Knowledge may have limited, but useful validity. The belief that the world is flat was a useful basis for making simple maps in the days of the Roman Empire. Up to a point this belief had validity in that it led to useful action, but it became quite useless once exploration of map makers went beyond a small part of the earth's surface. The discovery of the New World required a new conception of the shape of the earth for map makers to use. The flat model of the earth had no validity for mapping large areas. Thus, knowledge may have validity for certain limited purposes but lack validity for other purposes. The concept of the validity of knowledge developed in philosophy is very much the same as the concept of the validity of a test. A test score has validity because one can use it as a basis for relevant action.

Most measuring instruments are used on the assumption that a score derived from the instrument can be used to predict some aspect of behavior in situations different from that in which the measurement has been made. College admission tests are given on the assumption that they will predict success in college and that, on the basis of a student's score, one can make true statements about the probability that the student will complete a college degree. If one cannot make true statements of this kind it would be said that the test has no predictive validity. Such statements involving predictions from a test score do not imply a cause-effect relationship. Although one may be able to say that the score on an aptitude test predicts scholastic success in a particular educational institution, this statement must not be interpreted to mean that high aptitude *causes* high scholastic success. This concept of validity is called either predictive validity or criterion-related validity.

Statements that pertain to predictive validity have to be based on sufficient quantities of carefully collected data, but these statements hold true only for those situations that are closely similar to the situations in which the data were collected. If, for example, a measure of motivation were shown to be related to scholastic achievement in the case of children in middle-class elementary schools, one could not assume that the same relationship would hold for children in underprivileged areas, or even for children in different geographical regions. Until one has a sound theory about why predictions can be made, great caution has to be exercised in making any generalizations from data showing that a particular prediction can be made in a particular situation.

A distinction must also be made between predictions of immediately occurring events and the prediction of events occurring at a later date from the time when a particular instrument was applied. The fact that a measuring device can be used to predict other immediately occurring events does not mean that it can be used for making predictions over greater time spans. For example, a simple test measuring interest in each school subject given in elementary school can predict the grades of pupils in related subjects, because the interest test scores reflect the immediate success that the pupils are enjoying. However, the same test scores may be useless for making predictions during subsequent school years. As a general rule, it can be said that the longer the period over which predictions are made, the less likely an instrument is to be an effective predictor.

Psychologists sometimes use the term *concurrent validity* when referring to statements about the prediction of events that occur at roughly the same time as when the instrument is applied. These statements are to be contrasted with statements involving the prediction of more remote events to which the term *predictive validity* is applied.

Although statements that a test or measuring instrument can be used to predict this or that have a certain practical utility if they are true, they still present only fragmented pieces of knowledge that do not constitute an organized body of scientific knowledge. A measuring instrument useful for research has to be one that has produced at least some findings that fit into a body of knowledge. Consider an example from another field of knowledge: The statement that the prolonged elevation of sugar in the blood after a test meal indicates diabetes represents much more than the discovery of the simple empirical relationship between the appearance of the symptoms of diabetes and the elevation of the blood-sugar level. The statement is one of a set of interrelated statements representing knowledge about the metabolism of sugar, the function of the pancreas in producing insulin, the storage of sugar in the liver, the glycogen cycle in the muscles, and so forth. It is not an isolated statement representing some odd but interesting experimental finding, but a part of an organized body of knowledge. This situation is to be contrasted with most of the statements that can be made about measures used in the behavioral sciences and in education. For example, although it can be said that a measure derived from a test of intelligence enables one to predict performance in school, only rather vague statements can be made about the conditions, genetic or environmental, that produce intelligence. In addition, one cannot make any statements about how intelligence test scores are related to the structure and functioning of the nervous system. The statements that can be made about intelligence-test scores are very limited in scope and fit into a poorly organized body of scientific knowledge at this time—in contrast with the statements about level of blood sugar, which are not only clear and precise but also fit into an organized body of knowledge about physiology.

When statements can be made about a measuring instrument that fits into an organized body of knowledge, the instrument is said to have *construct validity*. When this term is applied to an instrument, it implies that the measure represents a variable that has a role in a scientific theory. Very few of the measures used in educational research can be said to have construct validity in this sense, although construct validity is always a matter of degree. In the case of some measures of anxiety, such as the Taylor Manifest Anxiety Scale, a considerable body of information has emerged suggesting that the variable measured has many properties similar to a drive and that predictions can be made of limited validity based on the assumption that one is dealing with a variable that is, essentially, a measure of the extent to which behavior is energized. This is the beginning of construct validity. The measure is on the threshold of fitting into a theoretical framework, but it is still far from fitting into a tight system of ideas, as measures in the better-established sciences do.

Studies of Learning and the Development of Theories of Learning

Research on learning may be considered to have taken two distinct forms. In one form of research, studies are undertaken on learning in school settings. The Eight Year Study was an example of a research of this type. A second form of research involves studies of learning in laboratory settings, which, in general, have been far more influential than those undertaken in school settings.

Studies of school learning, in school settings, that have had impact on educational practice and educational policy are relatively few. The famous Coleman Report (Equality of Educational Opportunity, 1966) is a rare example of such high impact research. However, the impact of this study is probably not a result of the contribution of the study to knowledge, but rather because the document arrived at a time when the Washington bureaucracy was looking for sources to support the proposed plans for the integration of educational opportunities through busing and integrated housing. Many questions have been raised about the validity of the findings, but there can be no question about the impact of the study. The study itself came into being, not as a part of a program designed to increase knowledge related to education, but as a result of congressional action. The Civil Rights Act of 1964 (Section 402) had required the commissioner of education to produce such a report within two years of the enactment of the legislation. The report showed inferior facilities in schools that catered mainly to blacks and what was believed to be a resulting deficit in achievement. For example, schools that catered largely to blacks were shown to have slightly larger classes than those that catered to whites. This was taken to mean by many readers of the report that the achievement deficit was a result of the poorer educational facilities, at least that was a popular interpretation. No account was taken of the fact that these same black children often lived in overcrowded and unhygienic conditions, that their diet was inferior to that of whites, and that they commonly lacked even the simplest medical care. Such facts were of much less significance to the U.S. Office of Education in the late 1960s than were the facts related to the differences in educational opportunity for blacks and whites. In this case, as in many others, legislators and bureaucrats seized barely relevant facts to support legislation and social action. Neither fully understood the impact of what they were doing or the limitations of the data that was being used to support their actions.

The Coleman Report was a significant contribution to education in that it provided a mark of how things stood during the 1960s. A similar report ten years from now will provide new data that will be compared with that collected by Coleman and his associates. The application of what he had learned in such programs as busing and integrated housing had consequences that Coleman never could have predicted. It was not a document that provided, through research, clear solutions to problems, but rather it was a benchmark in the history of education that came to be used as a hot political document. Other studies could be cited that have had an extensive impact because of the timely political nature of the material involved, though few have had such extensive impact as the Coleman Report. The impact of research related to learning on educational practice has generally come through another channel, namely that involving the diffusion of learning theories developed in laboratories.

The Coleman Report led to a great number of political innovations, including the use of forced busing. Since that time many have questioned whether the data provided by the report should have been used for such extensive changes. The discovery of unequal opportunity for blacks and for whites was hardly new in the educational field, but the causes go far beyond differences in the amount spent on educating white pupils in contrast with the amount spent on blacks. The differences in academic learning between the two groups is a result of complex social conditions.

Learning theory was developed as a science in the laboratory rather than as a tool for educational reform. There is always a long step from the laboratory to application. Even well-established facts that can be repeatedly demonstrated in the laboratory may not have any direct bearing on the practical world. Classically conditioned reflexes were well established late in the last century, but there is a long step from establishing conditioned reflexes to that of providing evidence that classical conditioning is the mechanism of all learning, as John L. Watson and Edwin Guthrie proposed. The operant experiments, begun by B. F. Skinner in the late 1930s, and subsequent experiments on pigeons, primates, humans, and other species, provide some evidence of particular conditions that influence learning, but the step from these experiments to the assumption made by operant psychologists that all behavior is controlled by the environment is a far longer step than can be justified in terms of the evidence.

Teachers have often embraced the theories of learning developed by psychologists, despite the fact that these theories have been designed for the purpose of conducting research and not for the purpose of running classrooms. Teachers have embraced such theories because teaching requires that the individual instructor bring to the task a broad conception of the nature of learners. Such conceptions have always been implicit in the teaching role. They have, in the past, been derived from religion rather than from the work of research workers. In the last century, a common conception of the nature of the pupil was that he was capable of learning whatever was taught to him, provided he could undertake a moral commitment to the task. A teacher who embraced such a conception of the learner interpreted failure to achieve as a result of the pupil not trying hard enough. This view implied that academic failure was moral failure. Children were punished for failure just as they might be punished for other moral transgressions. Although such a view is primitive, it is still held by some sections of the American community. I have even encountered university students who told me that their failure was because of the fact that they had not tried hard enough, although all the evidence indicated that they lacked the intellectual quality that was necessary for success. There are also parents who view the academic failures of their children as moral failures. Such views are on the wane, for modern political philosophy takes the position that failure on the part of the pupil is failure of the teacher to instruct by appropriate means. Of course, any simple formula that attempts to account for pupil failure is almost certainly faulty, for academic failure is a complex matter.

Earlier in the century, a global conception of the nature of the pupil came to be extracted from the work of philosophers. Certainly few men have had such an extraordinary influence on education as had the philosopher John Dewey. One of the reasons that Dewey had influence was that his philosophy was in so many ways compatible with the American view of the nature of existence. Truth was to be discovered by experimentation and inquiry, not by appeal to authority. Children had to learn to discover knowledge for themselves and to become masters of the process of inquiry. As an individualistic and antiauthoritarian system, such ideas had much in common with values widely held in the United States. Unfortunately, what Dewey had to say about education was widely misinterpreted. The fact was that popular versions of Dewey were gross misrepresentations of the message he had to give to the world. He came to be viewed as one who wished to see an educational system with little intellectual aspirations and a permissiveness that amounted to chaos. Dewey did not represent either one of these ideas. Dewey stood for a disciplined intellectualism in education. Most of his discussion of education focuses on intellectual achievement. Even his best-known volume, *Democracy in Education,* is almost entirely devoted to a discussion of the acquisition of what most people would call subject matter. There is hardly a reference to *adjustment,* which is the word through which Dewey has so often been attacked.

The attacks on the influence of Dewey on education were so devastating during the 1950s and 1960s that few teachers were willing to admit that their thoughts had been influenced by this eminent philosopher. A search for a conceptualization of the nature of the pupil in other terms became a political necessity for survival on a school faculty. Some teachers solved the problem by turning the clock back and embracing the moralistic views held during the last century. School boards commonly did this and sought to employ superintendents who held similar views. By the early 1970s many schools seemed to have taken a direction that moved them toward the past. The opposite reaction was evident in some alternative schools, overreacting to the conservative educational philosophies of the age. Such alternative schools tended to find their unifying ideas in the work of the existentialist philosophers, viewing personal experience as the all important factor in education. The nature of the experience of the individual was considered to be far more important than even social interactions, although such schools commonly proclaimed that they were concerned with the socialization of the individual, and with whatever gave the individual satisfying personal experiences. For this reason, these schools introduced such curricula items as the making of pottery, weaving, and leather crafts. The utility of such skills over a lifetime seems to have been scarcely considered. Intellectual activity of a logical nature, such as is involved in mathematics and science, tended to be discounted, though many would regard these skills as some of the most satisfying to acquire. Of course, Dewey had not denied the importance of personal experience and, indeed, has said that life in school was a part of life and should be satisfying as should be other parts of life, but he had seen satisfaction as residing in intellectual and moral development.

Conservative and traditional views of education found, in the late 1960s, and to some degree since that time, a powerful scientific ally in the form of operant psychology. The conceptualization of child behavior promoted by operant psychologists became integrated into the views of tradition-bound educators. Traditional views of education were thoroughly simplistic, but in operant psychology it seemed that they could be stated in a form that at least gave them the appearance of sophistication. Traditional teachers had believed that they were in control and what the pupils learned depended upon that control. Traditional teachers used rewards and punishments to control the behavior of the pupils and believed that such control was necessary for effective learning. In traditional education, as in education designed by operant psychologists, what the pupil wanted to do was irrelevant to the educational process, for the teacher was the one who decided what pupils were to learn and how they were to learn it. Operant psychologists and traditional teachers agreed on these basic premises and, thus, the traditional teacher, who had previously been embarrassed by the lack of novelty of his methods, suddenly found that he was working right at the frontier of knowledge. The curricula for schools that were run along operant lines were developed along the most traditional and conservative rut. Operant psychologists embraced all the traditional goals of education of the last century. The claim to novelty lay in claims that the new methods of the operant psychologists would be more efficient than those of the Victorian teacher. Whatever the operant psychologists lacked in knowledge of pedagogy and its history they made up for in enthusiasm and a driving evangelistic spirit. Some of the materials that derived from this spirit were placed on the open market and had substantial sales. An example of the latter is the DISTAR reading program, which is a good illustration of the application of operant techniques to education. A DISTAR reading class reminds one of descriptions of reading instruction from past generations.

What traditionalist educators embraced in operant psychology was a conception of behavior that had been evolved for the purpose of doing experiments. The conception they embraced was not a theory that had evolved as a result of research, in the way in which nuclear theory had evolved as a result of systematic experimentation, but it was a conception that had utility in devising experiments. It involved generalizations that were extremely broad and that went far beyond the facts, such as the generalization that all behavior was under the control of the environment. Of course, nobody knows whether this is, or is not, so. Situations can always be found that will lend support to this particular view of behavior, and operant experimenters were ingenious in finding such situations and in using them for experimental purposes. They also chose species and specimens on which to experiment that would fit their particular view of behavior. Pigeons and laboratory rats were the subjects for much of their experiments. Since the average human does not shape up well in operant experiments, much of the work with human subjects was restricted to very young children or the mentally retarded who seem to conform somewhat better to the operant point of view. There is no doubt that a body of important data was collected on such subjects, and one should not minimize the genuine experimental work of the operant psychologists, but this should not keep one from being extremely skeptical about the justifiability of much of their work in the applied field. In the latter area the efforts to have social impact were so remote from the data on which operant psychology was based that one has every reason to doubt that the enterprise had much scientific standing. Some success was inevitably achieved, for the old-time theory that behavior is controlled by rewards and punishments is a partially correct theory. Restating it in terms of the language of operant psychology does little to improve its applicability.

The major deficiency in operant psychology, insofar as education was concerned, was the fact that it had little to say about problem solving, an activity that many believed to be central to education. It had much to say about the learning of specific simple responses in specific simple situations. Thus, operant psychology had much more to say about learning the letters of the alphabet than about the comprehension of a sentence from which meaning had to be abstracted. It also had virtually nothing to say about how knowledge was organized except that specific pieces of information should be learned in the order in which learning was most efficient, but there was absolutely no theory concerning the nature of the structure of knowledge, for operant psychology barely recognized that knowledge had any structure.

Since conscious experience was deliberately excluded as a part of the operant system, operant psychologists in schools paid no attention to the kind of subjective life that children led in them. This was a contrast with Dewey's system, which placed great emphasis on the value of life as the child perceived it. What this attitude of operant psychologists did to life in schools has not been carefully studied, though the factory-whistle quality of life was quite evident in schools run along these lines.

The enthusiasm that operant psychologists displayed for their system eventually became the millstone around their necks. Ever larger and more ambitious applications had to be attempted. These reached their peak of adventuresomeness in the massive performance contracts in schools undertaken in the late 1960s and early 1970s. These programs were developed by operant psychologists who had the deepest faith that their position was a correct one and that the application of operant psychology to schools would inevitably produce great improvements in the efficiency with which children learned traditional subject matter. The ventures were pushed by contracting organizations that offered their services in return for guaranteed results in terms of pupil learning. The proposals advanced by these organizations seemed to be ones from which the schools could not possibly lose, and many systems negotiated contracts that included the provision of guaranteed results. This was to be the massive test of the usefulness of operant psychology as the guiding science for education. Superintendents, principals, and school boards held out great hope that these ventures would produce substantial gains in pupil achievement, and the enterprises were entered into with great enthusiasm, widespread publicity, and high acclaim through the media. Teachers were more skeptical, often saying privately that performance contracting was only ballyhoo. The federal government provided the means of determining the success of the project by setting up an evaluation program to determine the results of this massive social experiment. The federal government, which had invested millions of public funds in the enterprise was deeply concerned with the outcome. The results were deeply disconcerting to the Washington bureaucracy, who looked to the program as a means of bringing educational research into favor in congressional circles. The results reported in two mimeographed communications, which look more like office memoranda than like official reports, are the climax of a massive attempt of the federal government to have impact on education (Office of Economic Opportunity, 1972a, 1972b). The reports showed clearly and unequivocally that the effect of performance contracting on pupil achievement was lacking. There was absolutely no indication that the large amounts of money spent on performance contracting had any effect. The federal bureaucracy no doubt hoped that the mimeographed reports of the enterprise would rapidly disappear in wastepaper baskets, but academicians looked upon them as reporting results of the greatest significance to education. They came to be considered documents of importance and the data in them have been carefully preserved.

The findings were received with mixed reactions. The federal government was interested in forgetting about the whole affair. The contracting agencies claimed that they could now do a better job with what they had learned and sought another round of contracts. The schools went back to conducting programs similar to those they had long undertaken, and the teachers felt comfortable again with tradition and well-learned ways of teaching. Operant psychologists continued to pursue their ventures with the evangelistic zeal that had now characterized them for a generation.

The experience with performance contracting had another very important impact. The contracts had been entered into with complete naïveté on the side of the schools, and perhaps too on the side of the contractors. As the contracts were pursued, evidence slowly accumulated that some of the contractors were loading the dice in their favor by teaching the specific items included in the tests used to evaluate performance. The majority of the contractors were honest, both in their efforts and in their appraisals, and were interested in finding out what they could accomplish.

The few contractors who were not honest demonstrated how easy it was to convert a performance contract into a corrupt venture. This factor alone makes it unlikely that performance contracting, involving large sums of money, will be attempted again for a long time to come. Also, school administrators will look with skepticism on any psychologist who claims that the school only has to pay for what is accomplished. Schools were also left with a certain amount of skepticism about the value of complete package programs that included everything from detailed statements of objectives and detailed curricula to tests for measuring outcomes. The taste left by performance contracting was sour.

Some, but by no means all, teachers and educational institutions began to search for other guiding models. Many teachers had probably never heard of the reports of the Office of Economic Opportunity on the effects of performance contracting.

Nevertheless, some teachers and administrators have continued to cling to an operant model of the pupil, perhaps, because they could not find any handy alternative. They also saw in government and industry a movement known as management by objectives, which seemed to have much favor and was a system of behavior control that had been developed along operant lines. The promise of behavior control offered by operant psychologists has also retained tremendous appeal, for many of the problems of the classroom teacher provided the illusion of being a result of the failure of the teacher to exert appropriate control. Few of these teachers considered the possibility that their problems were created by excessive control rather than by lack of control.

Teachers and administrators with a taste for operant psychology had also found an ally in the work of Ralph W. Tyler, who had long been one of the most influential people in education. Tyler had prestige in education, not merely because of the contributions he had made but because he was a distinguished educator, who came from the education fold. Tyler was not an outsider psychologist who could be accused of not understanding the problems of the teacher. Tyler's ideas and those of operant psychologists became fused into a single approach to education, and it was this fusion that gave both sets of ideas a life that was longer than either would have had alone. Nevertheless, even the overall combined system of ideas had to give way to new ideas and new approaches.

Teachers and administrators did not have ready access to alternative models. In contrast, the operant model had been so thoroughly promoted that much of the technical language of the model had become incorporated into common speech. Existentialism had had some popular vogue during the 1960s, but the concepts underlying it were hard to digest. The writings of the most eminent existentialist, Jean Paul Sartre, were written for professional philosophers, and even his literary works had philosophical implications that were beyond the understanding of the ordinary educated reader. Also, an age dominated by technology and scientific ideas required educators to derive their models from the scientific area rather than from philosophical analysis. However, in the early 1970s, a large number of books began to appear on the horizon that attempted to bring to the attention of American teachers and administrators the work of the Swiss scholar Jean Piaget. The books claimed that the work of Piaget had important implications for education. Piaget's own works previously had been translated into English and many other languages, but they had not attracted attention except among scholars. Anyone who attempts to read the original work of Piaget can readily see why these works did not stir the imagination except of a few. The reason is that the works are some of the most difficult ever written in the behavioral sciences. They are filled with references that even most behavioral scientists have never heard of. Piaget is one of the most prolific readers of the academic world and has a penchant for reading works that only professional philosophers ordinarily read. He has produced an extraordinary blending of philosophical ideas and behavioral research that is unique in the history of the academic world. The result is a set of works that is unreadable to most academicians who are either acquainted with philosophy, but who have no knowledge of behavioral science, or who have the reverse combination. Interpreters of Piaget have to have some knowledge of philosophy, with a special emphasis on logic and epistemology, as well as a general knowledge of behavioral science, in order to understand his message.

Those who became the popularizers of Piaget ranged from educators who had had some brief exposure to Piaget in a university course, to scholars who had spent years studying his original works. Some of the popular works on Piaget were tainted with an evangelistic zeal for educational reform. Some saw Piaget as the scientific counterpart of John Dewey, and as one who could provide a scientific basis for Dewey's conception of human nature. Strangely enough, Piaget acknowledges only a superficial contact with the works of Dewey, and yet has admitted that this contact has given him a sympathy for Dewey's ideas. American and British popularizers of Piaget, who wrote for an audience of educators, tended to emphasize those ideas that both Piaget and Dewey shared in common. Both emphasized inquiry as the basis of intellectual development and the acquisition of knowledge. Both saw the child as an active explorer, formulating ideas about the nature of the environment. Both avoided viewing the child as a passive system that would learn as it was acted on by the environment. Both saw logic as a construction of the child. The appeal that the ideas of Piaget had for educators was very much the appeal that the ideas of Dewey had had earlier in the century. It now became possible for educators to embrace these ideas again without encountering the criticism that they were embracing what was alleged to be just Deweyan speculation. The ideas now have a scientific status that gave them acceptability in a scientifically oriented society.

Although Piaget's general conception of the nature of the human was closely similar to that of Dewey, Piaget was also able to provide a model of the development of the intellect that was far more detailed than any that had previously been developed. This model came to have particular impact on education, perhaps as much as anything because there were no competitive models. A description of how the intellect develops has enormous appeal to teachers, most of whom focus their efforts on the intellectual development of the child.

Piaget's model of the intellect, and his entire research program as well, has been based on certain assumptions that may not be entirely valid. His basic assumption is that the mature intellect can be described in terms of the ability to perform logical operations such as logicians have described. That is Piaget's starting point where he embraces a view of logic that is essentially what philosophers call neo-Aristotelian. He then works backward and forward through the development of the individual trying to identify the sequence of prerequisites of a functioning, logical, mature intellect. His work involves both an analysis of what the prerequisites must be and then an experimental determination of whether he was right in his conjectures. Critics of Piaget's model point out that there is a certain looseness to the system. A reader of Piaget's works is never quite sure when he is reading about the results of experiments and when the discourse pertains to Piaget's analysis of the prerequisites of mature, logical thought. The confusion between analysis and experimentation is not a unique attribute of Piaget's work for a similar criticism has also been justifiably leveled against Skinner's system and that of operant psychologists. Perhaps the important point to note in connection with the application of Piaget's system, as in the application of all other systems, is that application involves a great amount of judgment and that the applications have only rather remote relationships to the actual experimental data on which they are tied.

There is much misapplication of what Piaget has to say, just as there is much misinterpretation of what he actually says. Some application involves no more than teaching children to do the experimental tasks that Piaget used in his laboratory. They make interesting instructional exercises, but hardly represent an attempt to apply Piaget's model of the intellect.

Learning and the Curriculum of the Infant and Preschool Child

Learning on the part of infants has been a difficult matter to study. The literature of a quarter century ago described the difficulty of producing even conditioned responses in the first few weeks of life. From such data the conclusion was commonly drawn that the maturation of the newborn infant was not sufficient to permit learning. The apparent inability to learn was ascribed to the fact that the nerve fibers of the infant's brain had not yet become entirely enveloped in an insulating layer of myelin, which was supposedly necessary for learning. The conclusion was not warranted, for as psychologists became more astute in the study of infants, they found that infants were capable of learning vastly more than anyone had dreamed possible. The difficulty of studying learning in young infants is that the infant does not demonstrate easily what it has learned. Its outputs are extremely limited, and often hidden from view.

Techniques for the study of infants have centered on observing the simplest responses as indicators of learning. Some of these techniques are so obvious that one wonders why they were not used before. For example, Fantz (1958) in a classic study investigated what infants look at. He was able to show that infants in the first few weeks of life could recognize a pattern they had seen before. He was able to do this by showing infants two patterns simultaneously, one of which they had seen before and one of which was new to them. The eyes of the infant became fixated on the new pattern, demonstrating that they recognized the other pattern as one that was familiar. Another sensitive technique for the study of learning in infants involves the use of changes in heart rate. A new object will produce a very slight change in the heart rate, which is easily recorded with modern equipment.

The reader interested in some of the new techniques available for the study of cognitive learning in infancy is referred to the book by Bower (1974), which is full of ideas and novel suggestions. Anyone who reads this short book must come away from it impressed with the present capability for studying the infant in the first few weeks of life. A summary of much of the knowledge available about the young infant is found in the large and comprehensive volume edited by Stone Smith and Murphy (1973), which provides a large quantity of materials drawn from the research literature. The latter is also an impressive presentation of what is known. The approach of most of the studies is typically eclectic. Often the experimental techniques are drawn from operant psychology and the theory of the study is drawn from Piaget, a very strange combination of sources. Allegiance and loyalty to particular theoretical positions is largely lacking, perhaps demonstrating that the area of research is coming of age.

Research has also been conducted on the development of a number of curricula for infants, particularly infants who were raised in underprivileged environments. Such curricula have been developed on three very different foundations, namely, classical conditioning or associationism, operant conditioning, and Piagetian cognitive psychology.

Associationism or classical conditioning represent the basis used by Russian psychologists for the design of such curricula. They emphasize associating words with objects, and situations with particular habits. The pursuit of such a curriculum requires that the infant frequently be brought into contact with objects, which are then named by the attendant. Play is supposed to become associated with cooperative behavior, and thus the toys of even the youngest tots are so large that they require more than one child to move them or to use them as playthings. Russian psychologists have criticized Piaget's notion that the child is self-centered. They believe that any self-centeredness in Western children is caused by their living in a bourgeois society.

Associationism has had a long and quite successful history as a basis for the development of a curriculum for infants. It does have limitations, which stem from the fact that it represents a very simplistic theory of how children learn. It may explain how children come to associate particular names with particular objects, but it does not explain how the infant acquires the idea that objects have names, and that the names can be used to designate the object when the object is absent. It also does not explain how children acquire the rules of a grammar that permits them to generate new sentences they have never heard before.

Operant psychology has also been used as a basis for an infant curriculum. The latter position assumes that infants can learn virtually anything, given enough time and provided that one makes a sufficiently detailed analysis of what the learning requires. Of course, the analysis may involve a sequence of learning that would take a lifetime. Operant psychology takes the position that the manipulation of reinforcement is all that is required to produce learning, but there is very little useful theory concerning how the content of the curriculum should be selected. The notion is generally introduced that skills can be ordered from the final skill to be acquired to the simplest prerequisite skill. The ordering of the skills to be accomplished involves some kind of subjective analysis of the skills. Since reinforcers are difficult to find for infants, operant psychologists have commonly used food or hugging the child for this purpose. Both of these supposed reinforcers may lead to problems. The use of food as a reinforcer is believed by some psychologists to lead to a preoccupation with food and, ultimately, to the production of overweight adolescents. The hugging of the child, when the child responds correctly, is also not entirely free from potential problems. Such hugging, though appreciated by the infant, may well have the effect of disrupting the learning process. There is surprisingly little evidence concerning such matters which need to be explored experimentally.

Operant psychologists have virtually nothing to say about the content of the infant curriculum, and most of the ideas they propose in this respect are rooted in tradition and folklore. Though many infant schools have been set up by operant psychologists, there is virtually no acceptable evidence to indicate that these schools have produced any special results. One may note in this connection that Skinner has made many pronouncements concerning the way in which infants should be reared, and has designed a special crib that has been used by many of his followers for the rearing of their infants. The basic principle underlying the Skinner crib is that the infant should be in a temperature-controlled environment and that he should not be encumbered with clothes. The infant is able to see the rest of the world through a glass panel in the side of the crib. Those who are critical of the Skiner crib point out that a controlled temperature may not be the answer to any question of any consequence. The crib certainly does not provide the kind of contact with warm soft objects that seems to be important. Also the crib does not provide the swaying motion produced by picking up the child and found in the colonial rocking cribs, which is also believed by some to be important for infant development. Skinner's crib is certainly not designed in terms of what is known about conditions that are favorable for infant development, and Skinner seems to have been mainly concerned with eliminating crying behavior when he designed his crib. We do not know whether crying behavior is useful or harmful in the case of the infant. It does seem to be a basic form of communication between infant and mother.

The third basis of an infant curriculum is the cognitive psychology of Jean Piaget. Gordon (1972) has developed such a curriculum. A central assumption of this psychology is that all understanding of the environment on the part of the child begins with an understanding of space, time, cause and effect, and the permanence of the physical world. This position derives from the philosophy of Immanuel Kant and is one that has been of great influence on psychology in recent years. Much of the cognitive learning of the child during childhood involves the expansion of these understandings. Thus, the infant first must learn that the spatial world involved in touch is the same as the spatial world of vision and hearing. The various sources of knowledge about space have to become coordinated through learning. As they become coordinated, the infant becomes able to grasp an object he sees, although he cannot do this in the first two months of life. Later the child comes to understand the geometrical properties of space, and then more complex properties such as are involved in the measurement of distance, area, and volume. Then space becomes related to time when the child learns the concept of speed. At a more complex level, the child will learn the idea of relative speed, and that an object can be motionless with respect to one object, but moving with respect to another. Still more complex is the concept of acceleration. None of these more complex concepts and ideas can be acquired unless the infant first learns the fundamental properties of space as they come to be understood in infancy. The argument is highly persuasive and Piaget has substantial evidence to show that the various properties of space are learned in sequence. Indeed, they have to be, for these properties to be learned otherwise would be a logical absurdity. The argument is so obviously true that one wonders why other psychologists never hit upon the ideas before.

This theory leads to the design of a curriculum for infants. Tasks are developed that call for the exercise of abilities related to the development of understanding of space, time, cause and effect, and the permanency of objects. Thus, the three-month-old infant may be shown objects that attract his interest and which he attempts to grasp. As he succeeds in grasping them, the infant learns the relationship between visual space and tactile space. Although the theory underlying such training is clear, the effects of such training are not. Studies need to be undertaken to observe the effects of such training. It may well be that the typical infant's exploration of his own body, as when he learns to grasp one hand with the other, and the explorations of his crib, may provide him with all of the training related to space from which he can profit. Even if the latter is so, there is still the possibility that special training may be needed for children who have sensory or motor handicaps. The infant with cerebral palsy, who has little control over his hands, may well have difficulty in learning that there is only one spatial world, even though it is revealed through different sensory systems.

The understanding of the basic physical properties of the environment is but a foundation for the development of the child as a rational, logical being. He must go on to understand differences in size, color, texture, and in other important properties of things in his environment. This kind of perceptual development ultimately teaches the child to be able to perform simple logical operations such as are involved in the classification of objects and the ordering of objects. Such abilities go far beyond the sphere of infant development, but the foundation for such abilities, involving logic, are laid in the very earliest learnings about the environment.

A striking feature of research in this area is that the play activities that the mother enters into with the infant do seem to make a striking difference to later development of the infant. Indeed, Gordon (1973) followed up a group of underprivileged infants, whose mothers had been taught how to play with them, and found that the effect of such play on the development of intelligence was quite striking at least up to the beginning of elementary school.

Reinforcements have no place within this system except that they play a part in determining the objects to which the child turns his attention. They are assumed to play no role in learning itself. Learning is automatic in the sense in which the learning of a conditioned response is automatic. Piaget does not deny the kind of learning that Pavlov and Skinner have observed, but he views these, even at the infant level, as being quite trivial.

Although there are curricula for infants based on all three of the positions described here, very little work has been done to compare the effectiveness of the curricula. Very often the curricula involve quite different objectives. Operant psychologists, including Skinner, have emphasized the importance of providing conditions that will lead to a minimum of crying behavior. Piaget's followers have emphasized skills related to the under-standing of space. Classical conditioning workers have emphasized signal learning, that is to say teaching the infant that certain events, such as a word spoken by the mother, are signals for subsequent events, such as feeding. None of the three positions has anything of much importance to say about language acquisition, even though language is one of the greatest accomplishments of the infant in the first two years. Skinner's book on language acquisition (1958) is filled with delightful anecdotes and superlative examples of his humor, but it is wholly lacking in any data base that might give it the status of a scientific work.

Finally, the point must be made that the great influence on research related to language acquisition has been that of Noam Chomsky. The body of research that has been stimulated by his work will, as it grows, become an important basis for designing curricula in the area of infant language acquisition. However, the research has probably not yet reached the point of development where it can have an impact on practice.

New Models of Learning

Most American and Russian ways of viewing learning, that is to say, models of learning, have been related to conditioning concepts. In Russia this has been so because Pavlov was a leader of the Russian revolution and his research has been viewed as Marxist inspired. In the United States the popularity of Skinner's outlook is partly attributable to the fact that it closely reflects the views of traditional and conservative capitalism. Psychological theorizing, like philosophical theorizing through the cen-turies, has been closely related to the dominant ideas and values of the culture in which it emerges. There is probably no complete escape from this capture of psychology by the local culture. Nevertheless, our own civilization does have some diversity of ideas, and a far greater diversity than is found on the Russian scene. At the present time, in the American civilization, and to a lesser degree elsewhere, research activities have developed related to information processing. These activities have been made possible because of the development of the computer as a giant information-processing device. From the impact of the computer there has emerged a whole new set of concepts concerning how libraries and other information systems should be managed. So preoccupied has the culture been with the processing of information that the thought developed in relation to computers has permeated a great variety of scientific fields. For example, much of the recent research on the human brain, and on neural mechanisms in general, has viewed the nervous machinery of the body as a complex information-processing system. Indeed, the cerebellum, a small mass of tissue to the rear of the brain that controls motor skills, is now looked upon as a very complex and compact computer with programs for performing motor skills. Somewhat less success has been achieved in viewing the cerebral cortex as a computerlike system.

Computer models of behavior have been developed largely by psychologists interested in the perceptual systems, that is to say the systems through which information enters the brain, such as the visual system, the auditory system, and so forth. Psychologists interested in perception have been interested in how the perceptual systems receive information, analyze it, and use it in some way. Those who are not psychologists are likely to respond to the latter statement by saying that there hardly seems to be a problem there at all. Don't we look at the world and see whatever is there? The problem is not so simple. We look at the world, and see our environment, but we respond to but little in all that we see. Thus, we may see the full front page of the newspaper as we unfold it, but we only notice the words "Great Sea Disaster." We see much but recognize little. The eye does not just register a picture of the outside world and transmit that picture, in its entirety, to the higher centers of the brain. What reaches the higher centers is but a selected and miniscule portion of the total visual world. Each of us is highly selective in the part of the visual world that is actually recognized and seen in detail. Seeing is a selective matter, and what is selected depends partly on one's training and partly on the native mechanisms that determine our priorities. Thus, priority is given to anything that moves. A part of the information-processing problem is the reason for the selective processing of some information and the rejection of other information. Much of teaching involves this problem. How can one ensure that children will process information that is relevant to their development and not be preoccupied with information that is trivial or of only transitory interest? Information-processing models of learning attempt to contribute to the solution of this problem.

The classic work on this subject is that of Gibson (1969), but a very large literature has developed on the subject in recent years. Some of the contributions have been by computer experts who have attempted to draw an analogy between the way in which computers process information and the way in which the human nervous system processes information.

The selection of information is only one of the problems considered by information-processing models of learning. Another is the problem of how we recognize objects correctly and sometimes incorrectly A part of the task of learning to read is that of learning to recognize words without paying attention to every detail of every letter. In the case of reading, the good reader recognizes words while paying attention to very little detail. That is why he will not recognize errors in the printing of particular words. The fast reader can skip over the page quickly, because he has learned how to pick up the meaning on the basis of minimum cues. Indeed, he may skip over words or groups of words and be selective in the words he actually reads. The slow reader, on the other hand, may decipher words letter by letter. He requires a great amount of information from the page in order to extract the meaning, and the extraction of the information takes a great amount of time. Considerable research has been undertaken on reading as an information extraction and processing skill (see Della Piana, 1973, and Gibson and Levin, 1975). All education can be viewed as an information extraction and processing venture. The student who goes out into the forest to explore biological processes has to extract from the vast array of information available that which has relevance to the problems he wishes to solve.

One of the areas in which information-processing theory has had the greatest impact on research, and perhaps too on practice, is that of memory. The memory system is viewed as a system for the storage of information and from which information can be retrieved. The memory can be compared with other systems for storing and retrieving information and the properties of different systems can be compared. Thus, a library is an information storage and retrieval system. In order that information can be retrieved from a library, it is absolutely essential that the system have organization. A library in which the books were placed on the shelves, without respect to any order, would be one from which one could not derive the information needed to solve a particular problem. Libraries are organized and books are placed in categories, and the card file, which uses these categories, becomes a retrieval system that permits one to find the information one needs. The library, as a system, suggests how the human memory must be structured. The library shows us quite clearly that an information system can be searched efficiently for information only if the information in the system is organized. The human memory is such that information can be drawn from it with incredible speed. This fact means that the human memory must be a highly organized system, for it is theoretically impossible to draw information rapidly from a system that is disorganized. All information systems have a set of common properties that can be used to understand the human memory. What is the organization of the human memory? Do different individuals have different forms of memory organization? How can children be helped to develop a well-organized system of memory? These are all problems that information-processing models of the human intellect attempt to solve.

Information-processing models of the human intellect also open up a whole host of other problems. Much has been done to study the amount of information that the human intellect can handle and what happens when the individual is provided with more information than he can readily handle.

Information-processing models have brought to the attention of educators the fact that efficient information-processing models have to be extremely selective in what they store. Libraries have to avoid becoming cluttered with trivia and have periodical reviews of their contents, with consignment to storage or for sale those items that no longer have some relevance. The human long-term memory system does not seem well designed to get rid of information already contained in it. It is selective in what goes in there in the first place. The human is equipped with a short-term system from which important items are selected for long-term storage, the rest of the information there being discarded after a short interval of time. Much research has been undertaken on how information is transferred from the short-term memory to the long-term memory. Generally speaking, information that is recognized as having future use is retained as is information that is called for frequently.

Children obviously do not transfer to long-term storage much that the teacher hopes would be a permanent part of the child's inventory of information. Much needs to be done to discover ways in which the teacher can ensure that such transfer of information occurs. Research on memory has reached the point where it seems to have some practical implications for education that need to be checked out.

Information models of memory also have something to say about why particular pieces of information become used for solving some problems, to which they are relevant, and yet are not used for solving other problems to which they are equally relevant. Information-processing theory suggests that when information is placed in memory, then it is *tagged* to indicate the kinds of situations in which it can be used. The piece of information tends to be used only in those situations for which it is tagged. Teachers have to be sure that information is tagged in such a way as to make the information of maximum use.

It is all too easy to apply information-processing models on a sweeping scale without understanding their limitations, which must be mentioned briefly. Information-processing models also have little to say about the way in which information is used in very specialized ways by the artist. Eisner (1972) has taken the position that at the core of art education is the education of artistic vision. This involves teaching the child to see the world as the artist sees it, and involves a special kind of information processing that is not described at all by those who have developed information-processing models of the intellect. Artistic vision requires not that the individual perceive objectively that which exists in the world, but that he pay the closest attention to his inner responses to the objective visual world. When the objective world is viewed in this way, elements that would otherwise be considered trivial suddenly come to have enormous significance. Thus, the face of an old man may suddenly become far more than the face of an old man and may become the carrier of a picture of accumulated wisdom or sadness, or fortitude.

The Psychology of School Subjects

Educational research of half a century ago concentrated much effort on developing what was referred to as the psychology of school subjects. This was an enterprise, not so much directed to discover new ways of organizing and presenting subject matter, but to discover good ways of teaching what was believed to be the inevitable and eternal content of the curriculum. The belief was that if a teacher were faced with the problem of teaching, say, long division, then somewhere in the psychology of arithmetic could be found an excellent way of doing this. The psychology of arithmetic has never been prescriptive in this way, yet the hope was that it would be, and this hope still lingers on in the minds of those who promote competency-based teacher education. The latter viewpoint includes the seductive suggestion that the teacher's mind should be an inventory of tricks related to teaching this and that, and that these tricks of the trade have been discovered through research on the psychology of school subjects. There is such a science as the science of the logic and psychology of mathematics. A great amount of knowledge exists concerning the way in which mathematical concepts develop. It is known, for example, that a useful concept of number cannot be acquired until the child has grasped the idea of a class and the idea of a series. The concept of the number 6 involves the idea of a class having six objects in it, and only six objects. Also 6 is different from 4 because of the position of these numbers in a series. Children may learn to count before they have the concept of a class or the concept of a series, but counting means little to them at such a rote learning stage. Teachers need to understand the difference between counting and understanding the concept of number, and that there are innumerable ways of acquiring a concept of number. Each child may acquire the concept in a different way.

Though some good work has been done on the psychology of arithmetic, the psychology of school subjects is still one of the most sterile of enterprises though it consumes much federal research money. Nevertheless it may have some potential if it can become divorced from the problem of how to teach children items of traditional subject matter. There is a possibility that epistemologists may make some contribution in this area. Epistemologists are scholars concerned with the nature of knowledge and the structure of knowledge. Only slowly have we become aware of the fact that the structure of knowledge as adults conceive it may, in itself, present difficulties related to learning. For example, a common structure for organizing history is the time structure. History is taught as a sequence of events located in time by dates that the student is often required to remember. We now know that children in the lower elementary grades have only the most limited concept of time and, hence, have only the most limited comprehension of history as taught within a time structure. However, history does not have to be learned within a detailed time structure, in its early stages. History can be learned through acting plays, through art (as Colin Clark has shown us), through short attempts to live with the implements and tools available in past times, and so forth. The time structure of history can be largely neglected.

From what is known about the nature of logical development one can also infer something about effective ways of teaching science to particular grade levels. This too is an advance from the traditional studies that involved research on the best of ten ways to teach Newton's first law of motion, and the like. The focus is now on how to develop in the growing child a scientific conception of the world around him by exposing him to concepts at the level at which he can master them.

Summary

1. Most learning theories are grossly simplified representations of the learning process. Watsonian behaviorism reduced all learning to classical conditioning. Operant psychology reduces all learning to the learning of operants. Those who studied humans from the developmental point of view early in the century tended to emphasize the maturational factor. The early developers of tests represented an outgrowth of the maturationist point of view, stressing the belief that the intelligence quotient represented the individual's inherent capacity to become an intelligent adult, and de-emphasizing the role played by training and education. Some even went so far as to suggest that there existed a number of separate intellectual factors that might be related to particular genes.

2. The ideas of those who built intelligence tests had enormous influence, even to the extent of having an impact on immigration policies established by Congress in the 1920s. These policies assumed that certain individuals were inferior because they came from groups that tended to have low intelligence quotients. Tracking systems in schools were also established on the assumption that low intelligence quotient groups had inherent incapacities to learn. Evidence to the contrary was largely rejected and failed to have the impact it should have had. The early intelligence testing movement should have taught the lesson that psychology, in its early stages of development, should not be applied to the solution of practical problems, for by doing so great injustice can be produced. The research that ultimately ensued demonstrated that there is a much wider distribution of desirable genes than the early workers assumed, and that learning accounts for much of the differences between individuals.

3. From the testing movement there developed an interest in the matter

of the validity and reliability of measurement. The merchandising of poor measures eventually aroused many to recognize the need for setting standards by which such devices could be evaluated.

4. *Reliability* is an abstract concept related to how a test or measuring instrument performs. It pertains to the error of measurement inherent in the instrument itself. A satisfactory instrument has a small error of measurement in relation to the range of measures. Thus, any score consists of a composite of a true score and an error of measurement. There are various ways in which the reliability of a measuring instrument can be appraised.

5. The term *validity* implies that the test produces valid information or knowledge. The validity of knowledge is the validity of an action system. A test is valid if it can be used successfully to achieve a particular purpose. A common purpose of using a test is to predict how the individual will perform in particular situations. Validity in this sense is sometimes referred to as predictive validity. A distinction is sometimes made between the ability of a measuring instrument to predict immediate events and the ability to predict events in the future. The terms *concurrent validity* and *predictive validity* are applied to make this distinction. The term *construct validity* is used to describe the extent to which the theory underlying a test fits into a more general theoretical framework and provides data that fit that framework.

6. Studies of school learning have rarely thrown much light on how children learn and most of what is known has been discovered in laboratory settings. The Coleman Report is an example of a study that has had an impact on education. However, questions have been raised about the validity of the data of the report and the inferences made from the data. Many believe that the report should not have had the impact it had.

7. Laboratory studies of learning have generally been undertaken for the purpose of developing a theory of learning, rather than for the purpose of producing educational change. Well-established laboratory phenomena are a far step from educational reform. Unfortunately, psychologists have been too willing to generalize their findings to practical situations. Laboratory scientists make assumptions that are convenient for experimentation and then undertake experiments based on those assumptions.

8. Teachers have often embraced theories of learning, and the assumptions they involve, despite the fact that these theories have not necessarily been validated in classroom situations. All teaching requires the teacher to accept some form of theory of how children learn, so teachers are all too prone to grab any theory that happens to be available. Philosophy has also provided assumptions concerning the nature of the learner. The assumptions made by John Dewey have been particularly influential in the present century. Other sources of philosophical impact come from existentialism.

9. Conservative views concerning education tended to be linked in the 1960s with operant psychology. The emphasis of operant psychologists on the use of rewards and punishments, or on reinforcements as they like to say, was highly acceptable to conservative teachers who attempted to control learning through the use of rewards and punishments. Materials also became available for classroom use based on an operant approach. Operant psychology had little useful to say about problem solving, but this did not bother the conservative teacher who was not centrally concerned with problem-solving skills. Operant psychologists also showed no concern for what John Dewey emphasized, namely, the worthwhileness of life in the classroom.

10. The impact of operant psychology on schools reached its peak in the massive performance contracting experiments of the late 1960s. The experiments showed clearly that operant psychologists could not deliver what they had claimed. The contracts did demonstrate the fact that a system in which the monetary rewards are tied to measured pupil achievement is all too likely to be corrupted. Despite all of these problems, some teachers have continued to cling to an operant view of learning, perhaps because they knew of no other.

11. A new source of impact of psychology on education comes from the work of Jean Piaget. The impact of his research has been slow, partly because his contributions are so difficult to read. In many ways the assumptions made by Piaget are similar to those made by Dewey. Both viewed the child as an active explorer formulating ideas about how the environment operates. Both viewed intellectual development as a prime goal of education. There is much misapplication of the ideas of Piaget in the educational field.

12. Studies of learning in infancy have advanced greatly in the last decade and suggest applications for child rearing. The techniques of the operant psychologists have been applied to the study of the infant, though such work on infants has not been influenced much by operant theory. A number of curricula have been developed for infants. The Russians have developed curricula influenced by associationistic theory. Some North American curricula are based on operant psychology and some on a Piaget type of psychology. There is evidence that the Piaget type of curriculum for infants does produce superior development. The latter curriculum helps the infant master space, time, cause and effect, the permanence of objects, and their general properties.

13. Another way to view learning in humans is to consider it as an information analysis and storage activity. Research on memory has made great strides in the last twenty years and some of this research has had important implications for education. The memory is an organized system of knowledge. Education has to help the individual achieve such an organized system. The study of problems related to the building and operat-

ing of computers has led to a better understanding of how an efficient information-processing system must work.

14. A traditional approach to educational research was that of attempting to develop knowledge concerning how to teach particular school subjects. Edward L. Thorndike contributed to this field in the areas of arithmetic and algebra, and later research workers attempted to develop knowledge related to teaching in other school areas. However, the psychology of school subjects has not flourished. No set of tricks has emerged that teachers might use in teaching a particular school subject, nor has there been developed a set of principles specific to the teaching of particular areas. Some knowledge has been achieved related to the psychology of school subjects, but such knowledge is marginal.

CHAPTER 7
Research as It Relates to the Social Setting of Education

All education takes place in a social context. Indeed, education as an institution can take place only because the human species is a highly social species, with one member learning from another member and with one generation communicating its wisdom, and also its follies, to the next generation. Yet research related to education has typically ignored the social factors that make education efficient or inefficient, although these factors may have such an extraordinary impact on the nature of education itself. Educational researchers almost seem afraid to tangle with the essentially social nature of the process, even to the extent of designing educational setting to minimize social processes, as if they wanted to deny the powerful social nature of man. Thus, psychologists have designed schools in which students worked alone in isolated booths that minimize social contact. The fact that solitary confinement is considered a painful punishment in other settings has not deterred the educational research worker from viewing it as a condition favorable to education. The isolation booths of some schools, of the 1960 to 1970 vintages, were direct descendants of the rows of desks, all facing the teacher, that were used to isolate the children, one from another, earlier in the century. There are other ways too of isolating children. Some individualized programs of education achieve isolation by having each child working on a different level and on a different enterprise. In such a school there is no basis for one child interacting with another child. Much individualized instruction has this isolating effect, though some degree of individualization is possible without achieving such complete isolation.

The isolation booth of ten or more years ago also sometimes provided a strange partner for the child in the form of a computer terminal. Teachers were alleged to be too busy to communicate with children, so the computer was provided as a teacher surrogate, much as little monkeys have been given substitute cloth mothers to hold and clutch.

The reason for the emphasis of educational research workers on isolation techniques is probably the pressure from teachers and school administrators to have schools that impress the visitor as being orderly.

One way of maintaining order is to isolate the pupils from each other. Pupils incarcerated, each in his own study booth, isolation cell, or computer terminal, are not likely to engage in disorderly behavior with other pupils. This is, of course, one of the ways in which a semblance of order can be maintained, but it is surely not the best way in terms of the development of the pupil. Perhaps the oldest technique for producing control is for the leader to isolate each from all so that individuals who might threaten the authority of the leader cannot develop a following. College administrations commonly use this technique by not arranging for faculty meetings or for having meetings where only the administrator speaks, or by making it difficult for faculty to interact. A simple way of doing the latter is to ensure that there is no faculty room where faculty can obtain coffee and interact. School administrators have often used similar techniques for maintaining complete control, and sometimes even occupy the time devoted to faculty meetings by scheduling the discussion of such trivial topics as the location of wastepaper baskets in classrooms.

The federal government has been as guilty as administrators and teachers in sponsoring research that has resulted in the isolation of pupils from each other. Although large sums of money have been devoted to research on the use of booths with computer terminals as teaching devices, very little has been done to investigate the effects of cooperation and competition on learning.

The emphasis on individualism, and individual achievement, in our own society has also the effect of distracting our attention from the social processes at work in education and in the broader society. Many believe that individuals have to achieve success through their own initiative, and that the place where they learn to achieve as individuals should be the school. Thus, the parent, who visits the teacher, asks how the child is achieving, and not how well did he contribute to the group. In contrast, in Russian schools the child learns to be concerned, not with this own achievement, but with the contribution he makes to the team to which he is assigned. The Russian child who achieves a low score on an arithmetic test is not admonished for individual and personal failure, but with failure to contribute to his team. Such a child is likely to be coached by other members of his team to improve his performance. The Russians, in their educational research, pay little attention to the development of the individual outside of his contributions to the group, and a parallel neglect is shown by the American research worker in his failure to investigate social aspects of education.

Social factors influencing schools can range from individual interactions to the impact of society on the policies related to schools that are adopted by Congress and state legislatures and school boards. At one level of research there is the study of the impact of the social context within which school administrators work on their policies. At another level there is research that has to do with the social interaction of children in class-rooms, which also reflects the standards of conduct prescribed in other sections of the community. The latter set of problems brings one close to the issue of whether the classroom should be the place where children learn to relate to others within the code of standards prescribed by a demo-cratic society.

Research on Who Runs or Influences the Schools and on How to Improve School Management

Studies go back to the early 1930s on the matter of who exerts the greatest influence on schools. A favorite topic has been to study boards of trustees of colleges and school boards. The outcome of the research in the area has not changed much over the years. The information generally shows that although bodies controlling schools are supposed to represent the public, they do not in fact do so, regardless of whether they are elected, as school boards are, or appointed, as is the case with most boards of trustees. They do represent a small, powerful, and influential group within the community, which may be referred to by some as *the establishment.* A college board of trustees, for example, typically includes mainly wealthy businessmen or unusually successful professional people, who are also wealthy. Such boards are sometimes self-perpetuating, and thus appoint more of their own kind. They generally exclude large sections of the com-munity, including the black section. Even when a college is located in an industrial town, the board of trustees or regents is unlikely to include representatives of organized labor.

School boards also tend to be selected from a very limited section of the community. One could understand the rationale of electing to school boards those who have special knowledge related to schools such as psy-chologists, physicians, and perhaps publishers, but such individuals are rarely found on these bodies and indeed rarely seek public office. More needs to be learned about what the public expects from a school board and the kind of expertise the public believes is needed there.

Characteristics of superintendents of schools was also a source of re-search back in the 1930s and 1940s. This line of research did not produce any notable results except to indicate that school boards selected super-intendents on the basis of superficial qualities. The most notable charac-teristic for which superintendents of schools seem to be selected is their size. This is quite obvious to anybody who has ever attended an annual meeting of the American Association of School Administrators, though this impression is less marked today than it was thirty years ago. One can understand the security that school board members feel when they can sit behind a large and physically impressive superintendent who seems to overwhelm his staff by his imposing size.

In more recent times, the role of the school administrator in producing innovation and change has become a source of study. Studies of this problem have been undertaken by the laboratory at the University of Oregon. Studies generally confirm what is obvious from history that an innovative superintendent can be a great force for educational change. This problem has received extensive treatment in Boles and Davenport's book (1975) on educational leadership.

This leads to a brief mention of the area of leadership, which is both glamorous but extremely difficult to attack from a research standpoint. The chief promoters of research in this area have been the armed services, but the research done under their auspices is not necessarily applicable to educational situations. Even within one branch of the service, the leadership role involved in one situation is quite different from the leadership role played in another. The captain of a battleship, sitting in an office, working with a staff, and remote from enlisted personnel, plays an entirely different leadership role from the captain of a submarine who knows each enlisted man personally and provides a personal model of behavior for each and every person under his command. Much of the research on leadership has been summarized by Stogdill (1974). This research brings out the fact that the early studies tended to concentrate on a search for personal characteristics that produce leadership. Later research has been focused more on situational features, and particularly the conditions that result in the emergence of leadership. There is a clear interaction between these two classes of variables. A person may be an effective leader in one situation, but quite ineffective in another.

Much of the research related to leadership involving the social climate of schools emerged out of the work on the military. This has been largely the work of Halpin (see Halpin, 1966, and Halpin and Croft, 1962). This research has attempted to isolate characteristics of schools, teachers, and administrators. These characteristics could be related to leadership. Since the instruments are easy to administer, they have formed the basis for innumerable master's theses and doctoral dissertations. The results of this flurry of activity are difficult to discern. Perhaps the main knowledge derived has been that a useful instrument produces few results when used indiscriminately. Even a hammer is a useful tool unless it is used indiscriminately to hit whatever happens to be around. The Halpin instruments may well be useful devices, but it is difficult to separate out any useful results that may have been achieved with the devices from the vast quantity of trivia.

Research on the management of schools and the role that teachers, administrators, and others play in it is becoming progressively more difficult to undertake. Teachers and administrators feel threatened today by the prying eyes of research workers. There is considerable fear that the results of this research may be misapplied or even misused for political purposes. Often there is a lack of trust in educational research workers who, in the past, have often occupied the time of school personnel, without bothering to go back and report the results to them.

Mention must also be made of the extensive attempts that have been undertaken to train administrators through the application of various techniques involving role analysis, group therapy, transactional analysis, and related techniques. Much of this work came into being through the research of Kurt Lewin on the dynamics of groups. Lewin believed that the way that groups and their leaders operate could be reduced to certain basic psychological principles. Lewin was able not only to encourage and produce original research but he also developed a group of devoted followers who went on to develop and expand his ideas after he died. One activity undertaken by this group of Lewin students was to establish the National Training Laboratory, which existed for the purpose of providing practical training in the area of group functioning and group leadership. Summer sessions attracted school administrators and also teachers from across the country, where they participated in a group experience designed to enhance their understanding of themselves and how they functioned in relation to groups. A little research has been undertaken with respect to the outcome of this form of group process, but the results are not clear (see Smith, 1975). Also research is extremely difficult to conduct because the participants come from a great variety of jobs, and little is known about how they performed on the job before they came, and whether their job performance improved after training. For this reason such studies are generally limited to an exploration of how the individuals thought they were changed as a result of training. It is unlikely that a person would be willing to admit that he wasted his summer on a profitless training program. Two things are clear about the outcomes of such training programs. One is that many leave the program believing they have had an important, soul-changing experience, almost like a religious experience. Another point is that the training experience is likely to be extremely stressful, and a good trainer may remove some of the participants to engage in an observer role, if he thinks that the experience is more stressful than the participants can tolerate. Nevertheless, there are some whose behavior deteriorates as a result of the experience and may require individual therapy. There can be no doubt that such group experiences can have an enormous impact. The problem is to arrange them so that the impact is beneficial. This is a training problem that still needs to be solved.

Power in the Classroom: The Role of the Teacher

Substantial research has been undertaken related to the teacher's place in society and the way in which this influences behavior in the classroom. Bidwell (1972) has brought together much of the research related to the social psychology of teaching, pointing out that teaching is a variety of social relationships. Teaching involves various norms of behavior that are sanctioned by various sections of the community. The teacher also has the power to sanction various forms of pupil behavior. The teacher sanctions this and that form of behavior on the part of the student and disapproves other forms of behavior because the teacher has a commitment to certain values. Thus, a first-grade teacher will sanction all behavior related to learning to read, but disapproves of behavior of pupils related to pushing and shoving and the assertion of the self through physical force.

Studies of the social background of teachers in public schools have been useful in clarifying the influence that background may have on the aspects of student behavior that the teacher sanctions. Such studies have typically shown that teachers represent a group moving up the social ladder and are seeking status that their parents did not have. McClelland (1975) has some evidence that teaching is a power-oriented occupation and that the teacher's function in the classroom may satisfy certain needs for power, particularly in the case of male teachers. Certainly the teacher is one who wields power, and this power may be exercised in ways that are despotic or benign. Arbitrary despotism is not uncommon in classrooms where teachers tell pupils what to do and the pupils try and carry out the commands as precisely as possible. This does not mean that the teacher in an open classroom is not also exercising power, for such teachers do, but in a more subtle and agreeable way. The teacher in the open classroom may be of enormous influence on what pupils do and how they interact both with the teacher and with other pupils.

The McClelland studies also bring out important differences in the way in which men and women exercise power. Men exercise power through asserting themselves physically. Women exercise power by more subtle means, influencing others by the resources they bring to particular situations. Thus, a woman may exercise power by being charming, or persuasive, or insightful, but a man is more likely to attempt to dominate the situation. These differences need to be studied within the context of the classroom, and also within the administrative structure of schools. The differences between men and women in this respect are probably a result of a long history of the human species extending back to primitive times. Changes in the way in which men and women exercise power may well be on the verge of a change. Courses and programs for women are now available to make women more assertive. How such programs influence the classroom behavior of teachers exposed to such training needs to be studied. Assertiveness on the part of a teacher in a classroom would hardly seem to be a blessing. Indeed, the traditional power role of the woman, in which she exercises power because of the resources she can provide, would seem to be ideal for operating many types of classroom, and particularly those run along informal lines. The typical assertive male role would seem to be most appropriate for operating within a traditional classroom in which the teacher is an assertive leader.

The teacher derives some prestige in relation to students because of the attitudes that children bring to school. Young children in kindergarten and first grade hold their teacher in awe, partly because the teacher, as a substitute for the parent, is viewed by the child as having all the power and authority of the parent. This power, derived from the role of being a parent substitute, wanes rapidly as the child goes through the elementary grades, perhaps reflecting the waning prestige of the parent as the child matures. In some cultures, the teacher derives prestige from other sources. In France, for example, the teacher is viewed as being the most prestigious citizen of every small community. Children come to school prepared to view the teacher as a person of great influence. Studies need to be undertaken on the prestige factor, how it varies in the United States from one community to another, and how this variation is related to the way in which classrooms are conducted.

In some countries the teacher is held in universal high esteem. In few countries is the teacher held in low esteem, but in the United States the status of the teacher in the public eye is equivocal. In terms of some measures the status of the teacher is high. For example, George H. Gallup's organization has held an annual poll to determine what the public thinks of education, and the results of this poll generally show that the schools are held in high esteem and that the public believes that teachers are doing a good job. On the other hand, when the public is asked to indicate other occupations that have the same status as teachers, the occupations named are not other professions, such as law or medicine, but trades such as that of electrician and plumber and service jobs such as that of policeman and fireman. The public thinks that teachers do a good job, but the level of their work is not very high on the status scale. This situation is to be contrasted with other countries where the teacher often ranks above the doctor.

Since the teacher is a prestigious figure, some pupils compete for the opportunity to relate to the teacher, and thereby derive prestige for themselves. Not all pupils do this, but some do to the point where the teacher may become exasperated. Studies need to be made of this problem and of ways in which teachers can cope with it effectively. The problem is particularly acute in open classrooms where a single pupil may sometimes seek to occupy most of the time of a teacher.

The expectations of the pupil influence the way in which he will behave toward the teacher. Indeed, all social relationships are partially structured by such expectancies. There is also a reciprocal relationship with the teacher, bringing to the classroom a set of expectations concerning the way in which the pupil is expected to behave. Teacher expectations are complex in that they include expectations of how the pupil will actually behave and also expectations concerning an ideal form of behavior that the teacher believes pupils should manifest if the classroom is well run. The effect of the teacher's expectations on how pupils will actually behave has been the focus for a long series of studies, beginning with those of Rosenthal and Jacobson (1968) who believed that he had demonstrated that teacher expectations influence learning. The general thesis was that teachers who believe that their pupils are stupid or unmotivated, or in some way poor learners tend to produce pupils who behave stupidly or lethargically, or who are poor learners. The thesis was important because many educators believed that one of the problems of the ghetto child was that his teacher viewed him as incapable of learning. They also believed that if the teachers could change their attitudes, there would be a corresponding change in the child. Barber (1973) has reviewed the evidence and can find no support for this contention. Nevertheless, the issue is not entirely settled. The effect of the attitudes of one teacher may not be impressive, but when a child is raised in a whole subculture in which he learns to believe that he is an inferior learner and that, even if he can learn, he will not gain any particular rewards, then the effect over an entire childhood may be overwhelming. Clinical psychologists have long held the view that the attitudes expressed by adults about the child slowly help form the concept the child has of himself, and that the child's self-concept influences his learning. Some evidence supports this statement. Rosenthal and his associates may well have had correct intuitive feelings about the matter, but sought to find verification in situations in which evidence for it could not be found.

Expectancies may have devastating effects outside of particular situations. The treatment of the black during the last century, which virtually denied him an education, is an example of what such expectancies can do on a large scale, for legislation followed that indirectly denied that group an education. This denial to blacks of equal opportunity for education is much less likely to happen today than during the last century, and, when it happens, it is much more likely to be subtle and hidden. The expectancies of pupils and teachers cannot be considered without considering the expectancies of parents. The annual Gallup poll related to public attitudes toward the schools throws some light on this. Generally, parents have a positive attitude toward teachers and public schools and do not blame them for the shortcomings of the younger generation, as they have been blamed by businessmen and, to some extent, by legislators and by the press. Parents expect the schools to provide opportunities for their children to learn and generally find that these opportunities are, in fact, provided. Failure to learn is not generally considered to be the fault of the school. The public blames the students, the society at large, and the parents for a child's failure in school. The accountability movement takes a different point of view and tends to point an accusing finger at teachers.

Brookover and Erikson (1975) summarized a series of interesting studies on how teachers relate to principals. Teachers, like other groups that are moving upward in the social structure, stand in awe of authority. They view the principal as a person who is in authority above them and consider him as a person who should not only have authority but who should show considerable initiative and leadership. Teachers generally favor having the principal appointed by the superintendent or school board and do not think that they should participate in the decision. The unionization of teachers is likely to change this attitude.

Brookover and Erickson point out that although teachers have gone a long way in achieving political power, through unionization, they are still quite subservient to authority. They are very traditional in the way they view the role of power and authority in the management of a school.

Moral Development and the School Culture

An important part of the socialization of the individual is the acquisition of ethical standards and a code of behavior that includes some element of morality. Over the years, numerous studies have been conducted showing, in general, that the actual standards of conduct of children and adults do not meet the desired standards. The classic studies are those undertaken by H. Hartshorne and M. A. May during the 1920s, which showed that schoolchildren lacked consistent standards of conduct. In these studies, children were exposed to various situations in which they believed that they could cheat without being found out, take money that did not belong to them without being caught, and so forth. Of course, the experimenter knew who had cheated and who had pocketed the money that did not belong to him. The children showed an extraordinary lack of consistency in their behavior from one situation to another, demonstrating a lack of any overriding standard of conduct. The Hartshorne and May studies set the stage for studies that were undertaken in the next forty years, which mostly showed similar results. Training procedures that were tied to particular theories of learning also failed to show any notable changes in any broad standards of morality. E. L. Thorndike's psychology would have led teachers to expect that whatever morality was learned would be learned in specific situations and would be applied to those, and closely related, situations. Thorndike found little experimental evidence to support the view that broad rules could be learned that would be applied to a wide range of situations. He expected specific responses to be learned to specific situations and did not advocate training or education that was designed in the hope that the responses would be generalized to a broad range of situations. Skinner seems to expect more generalization to new situations, provided they contain enough of the elements in the old situation to trigger the response. Thorndike and Skinner, on such matters, are pure speculators, having only remotely relevant data to back up their positions.

Certainly, the work of Hartshorne and May gave support to the Thorndike position and perhaps also the Skinner position, though studies of the effects of training have been largely lacking. Despite the lack of an experimental base, training programs have been set up along a Thorndike-Skinner line, and some have even been advertised as though their validity could not be questioned. Most of these programs have not come to grips with the basic issue, which is that freedom and autonomy of choice are essenital and central to any conception or discussion of morality, but Skinner regards these as figments of the imagination. Morality involves making choices. A person trained to give away everything he has, because he has been consistently punished for retaining personal belongings, is hardly making a moral decision when he has personal possessions and someone to give them to. He gives them away, much as a machine designed to give away whatever is stored in a bin will automatically give away whatever is stored in it. Machinelike behavior is not involved in moral choice, and neither is Skinner's automated human being involved in moral decisions. Despite the fact that religious educators have based some programs of moral education on operant psychology, the Skinner position does not include a conception of morality involving an autonomous free-choosing decision maker.

Programs for moral training that involve the doing of good deeds and then being rewarded for them have not been properly evaluated. Aronfreed (1968) has summarized the evidence that can be gleaned, but it is meager and not enough to arrive at any conclusions. If reinforcements function in this respect, then they are not the obvious kinds of reinforcements. It is hard to understand how a Saint Francis, who was raised in a culture of luxury, should take vows of poverty and find joy and fulfillment in living the simple life and helping others. Operant psychologists try to handle this situation by imagining inner reinforcements, which are figments of the imagination of the operant psychologist.

While Hartshorne and May were undertaking their classic studies of morality at Yale University, a young man in Geneva was beginning his research in the area of morality, which was later to have a great impact on the field. The young Jean Piaget had been concerned with the development of the intellect, and had been much influenced by the German philosopher Immanuel Kant in this pursuit. Piaget had learned from Kant that the basis of the intellect lies in an inherent ability of the individual to understand space, time, cause and effect, and the underlying reality of the environment. In addition, Kant proposed that there was an inherent moral factor in intellectual life, which he referred to as the categorical imperative. Piaget became intrigued with the idea of an inherent moral factor but saw an alternative to Kant's nativistic idea that a moral sense was inborn. Piaget viewed morality as a construction of the human intellect, proposing that the human constructs a moral code because he has an inherent capacity to do so. For Piaget there is no inborn morality, but there is an inborn capacity to construct a system of morality. Piaget began to pursue this idea by conducting a number of studies of how children make rules for the games they play. He saw in the rule making of children and, in their games, the seeds of adult morality. Adults play games that are conducted according to very strict rules. These rules represent the moral code of the society. Piaget noted that children are quite uniform in the rules they invent and the conditions they insist are required for the application of the rules. A child of five may be quite rigid in his insistence that the other child, with whom he is playing, should follow the rules precisely, but he may invent all kinds of new rules to justify his own behavior.

A striking feature of Piaget's work on morality is that it implies that morality is not learned in the kinds of situations that have been typically used in an attempt to teach morality. Many churches have taken the position that morality is learned through instruction that is much like the instruction given in any other area. Religious instruction is often thought of as being synonymous with the teaching of morality. Such instruction given in Sunday schools or as a part of instruction in many parochial schools has long been believed to constitute the basic teaching of morality in Western culture. Piaget brings some new thoughts to this matter, stressing the importance of social activities such as games in providing the basic understandings of moral concepts. The child ultimately learns that games are possible only when the players agree on a code of ethical conduct, which includes such principles as that one does not cheat, one tries to be fair in interpreting the rules, and that the behavior of a player has to produce trust in the other players. Without such a code of conduct games become unhappy forms of interpersonal strife. Piaget's position is that the child constructs a conception of morality from his experiences with games, broadly conceived. This would explain why children's conceptions of morality are extraordinarily similar across the world despite differences in religious background or even culture. A six-year old in a tribe remote from modern technology is likely to have the same moral concepts as a six-year-old raised in a North American city and in a family that has a strong Christian or Jewish tradition.

Piaget published a single book on the morality of children (1932), but he then seems to have abandoned the topic, turning his attention to the study of the more traditional aspects of the intelligence, such as the development of logic. Fortunately, Piaget, unlike most notable psychologists, has had a group of followers who dedicated themselves to expanding the work he had begun.

A following did not form readily around Piaget and his work. Indeed, in the case of his research on morality, Piaget's work remained buried in libraries for more than thirty years. Of course, American academicians had heard of Piaget's book on morality, just as they had heard of his work on intellectual development, but few of them had read anything he had written. European psychologists were more familiar with Piaget's work, but there were very few psychologists on the European scene. Opportunities for psychologists had been so scarce in Europe in the first half of the century that many of the notable ones had migrated to the United States including E. B. Titchener and William McDougal. Thus, much of the work of Piaget remained dormant until American psychologists slowly came to realize that he had made highly significant developments. The American psychologist who was to rediscover Piaget's work on morality and to expand and systematize it was Lawrence Kohlberg, who produced a dissertation on the topic (1958).

Kohlberg's study identified three major stages of moral development, each of which is divided into two substages. The infant starts with an amoral level of conduct seeking to obtain what it can for itself by whatever means are open to it. Toward the end of this stage, the first glimmerings of a system of morality appear in the form of "If I do this for you then you, will do this for me." Morality at the level of simple bargaining is not just found in infancy, but is found at all age levels. The politician's kind of bargain, whereby he gains by making concessions to competitors, is clearly morality at this simple level. All of us engage in conduct that is at about this level of morality, but most of us are able to achieve the middle stage of the three major stages. In this middle stage, the morality adopted is that of the group. At the lower level, it is that of the immediate peer group, which is exemplified by the morality of the early teenager. Whatever is sanctioned by the peer group is right, even if it comes into conflict with the code of conduct of the adult. This is part of the basis of the conflict between the adolescent and his parent. At the second level of this middle stage the moral code accepted is that of the society at large, rather than that of the peer group. This level of moral development has been referred to as the law-and-order level. The individual in this stage upholds rigidly the law of the land, even when it results in obvious injustice. "My country, right or wrong!" reflects this view of what constitutes right behavior. The chauvinist, who is typically at this level, cannot imagine that his country could be wrong, or that a law should be disregarded in the interest of justice. This level of morality is completely rigid in terms of what is right and wrong because justice and the laws of right living are believed to be a part of the social system.

In the third stage of moral development, right and wrong are judged in terms of general principles. At the higher level of this stage, principles are individually evolved. At the lower level they are generalities that are widely accepted. Thus, the golden rule would be an example of a principle at the lower level. For example, at the lower level of the third stage, a person might help rehabilitate a criminal even though by doing so he might disobey laws related to the cover-up of a crime. The general principle thus takes precedence over the socially sanctioned law. At the higher level of this stage, the individual evolves his own generalities. Thus, the writers of the United States Constitution would be placed at the highest level in that they were evolving moral principles that were to form the basis of government.

The work of Kohlberg has had a great deal of impact on various forms of moral training and research on moral training because he has formulated a theory of the conditions that move an individual from one stage to another. In this respect, Kohlberg is strictly a follower of Piaget. The individual moves from one stage to another by formulating his own ideas about the nature of good and evil. He will stay at one stage so long as the system of morality appears to work and does not involve contradictions. Thus, the individual will remain at the law-and-order stage unless he begins to see that this may involve gross injustice. Perhaps he is most likely to recognize this possibility if the law, as it is, brings him some great injustice. Then he is likely to reconsider his position and to begin to question the standards he has upheld in the past. A state of doubt about one's beliefs is a powerful motive for the reformulation of those beliefs. Piaget refers to this state of doubt and attitude of questioning as a state of disequilibrium.

Kohlberg has produced extensive research over the years. His more recent productions have tended to be related to the training of children in moral behavior (see Kohlberg, 1975). His position has been extensively criticized (see, for example, Peters, 1975), but alternative positions have not thrived because they have been largely unsupported by research. Most of Kohlberg's research in teaching settings have involved the use of discussion techniques that were designed to lead children to the formulation of higher levels of moral concepts. The 1975 article describes a school in which children had discussions related to what were fair practices as a basis for formulating policies. These discussions seem to have been effective in promoting a form of participatory democracy in the school. Kohlberg points out that most systems that involve student participation in the running of the school have failed. This failure is often caused by the fact that the student participation is modeled after the U.S. Constitution in the form of a student government. Such student governments are generally viewed by students with apathy, and often with disdain, and do not generally serve the purpose they were designed to serve. This is even true at the college level. The time has certainly come when new forms of student participation in the running of schools should be attempted, but they have to involve situations that produce learning and raise students to higher levels of moral development. Typical forms of student government do not do this and are viewed by students as ritual, and often meaningless ritual.

Followers of Kohlberg have produced all kinds of materials for moral training. In so doing they have sometimes come up against those who take the position that the school is not the place for moral education. The latter position is, of course, absurd. One cannot study the Constitution of the United States without recognizing that it is an attempt to cope with great moral issues of equality and freedom. Those who would deny the right of schools to discuss moral issues would also have to deny them the right to consider the great moral issues that underlie the history of the United States.

Some critics of Kohlberg have taken the position that he ignores the affective aspect of morality, and that his theory is coldly intellectualistic. The criticism is sound, but there is some evidence that moral development is intimately connected with intellectual development. Turiel (1973) has accumulated evidence to show that moral development and intellectual development go hand in hand. They surely must. One can hardly imagine an individual formulating abstract principles of moral behavior, at the highest level of moral development, unless he had previously mastered the skills involved in abstract thought. Failure to develop intellectually should result in failure to develop morally. Nevertheless, the critics have a good point. Surely the ability to help others who are in less fortunate positions calls for an ability to place oneself in their position and to experience their feelings of desperation. This is far more than merely intellectualizing their plight. The morality of the confidence man is at least partly a result of the fact that he has absolutely no feeling for his victims and can take them for all they are worth without any pity or anguish on his part. There is obviously a strong feeling element in moral behavior. True moral behavior is not cold and calculating, as is much immoral behavior. Moral behavior has its own special gratifications that involve deep feeling elements.

Kohlberg disturbs many religious educators because he dissociates moral development from religious belief. He claims that all children in all cultures and in all religious groups move through the same stages of development. Investigators in other countries and other cultures have provided some evidence to support the claim, but there are alternative explanations of the data.

Research in the area seems to have special significance at this time. Thinkers of today express doubts about man's ability to develop further without the development of a new moral posture. Kay (1975) expresses this by saying that our present age is, perhaps, the last phase of the Neolithic age. Of course, we are not used to thinking of ourselves as late Neolithic men, but Kay's arguments are persuasive. Neolithic man is man of the late Stone Age who has used his intellectual capacity to invent all kinds of ways of dealing with nature. He developed all kinds of tools, invented agriculture, domesticated animals, and slowly evolved technologies that permitted him to make ceramic objects and, later, objects out of metal. The age has represented a mastery over nature through the ability to solve problems rationally. During this age there were also some important social inventions such as the development of various new forms of government and the invention of such institutions as universal education. Despite these great social inventions man's moral stature in a general way barely moved beyond that of the herd, in which there is some protection of each member by all and a set of conventions that make for survival. Kay, and other writers like him, argue that the next stage of humanity, if there is to be a next stage, must be one of great moral development, and education must play an important role in that development. Kay does not expect any dramatic change within a few years. He writes that we must not think in terms of ten years or even ten centuries, but we must think in terms of a cultural evolution that will take at least tens of thousands of years in the future. Moral education is not just a matter of combating crime, but a matter of changing the whole nature of human existence. Research is just at the beginning of such change.

Aggression, Assertion, and Competition

An important field for educational research has to do with the direction of the energies of the students into productive rather than nonproductive enterprises. American schools have had a long history of aggression disrupting learning. Horace Mann, in his annual reports, commented many times on the large number of disruptions of the schools that occurred in his State of Massachusetts. In some years he reported hundreds of closings of schools because of conditions that were not far off from being riots. Mann pointed out that most of these disruptions and closings were a result of actions initiated by students, but some were a result of disruptive behavior on the part of the teacher. Horace Mann offered no specific remedies except to imply that, as the curriculum became more meaningful to the students, disruptions would decline in number. Mann's thesis was that schools should provide a congenial environment for the student, rather than the forbidding one that schools so commonly presented. Mann not only carefully documented the number of school closings caused by disruptive behavior but he also tried to make an analysis of the causes of these events. Modern supervisors are much more likely to cover up such events and to gloss over them in their annual reports. The result is that such problems are not recognized and studied as they should be. Also, schools are not closed down when students get out of control, because state funds would be lost by a school closing.

There may be obvious aggressive behavior of students against the school as is evident from the widespread occurrence of vandalism, but more often the hostility of students is shown in a sullen kind of anger that appears in what might be described as sulking behavior. The student may attend classes, but often puts his head down on his arms and appears to doze throughout the class session. Sometimes the behavior is accompanied by remarks that ridicule the content of the class or the teacher. The entire behavior pattern is a protest against the school, and often is as disruptive as overt physical aggression. A student may show this behavior for weeks or months, or throughout his entire high school attendance. Very little is done to cope with this type of behavior, perhaps because it calls for more inventive capacity than the teacher can muster. Although the dropout has received some attention from research workers, little has been done to study the student who stays in high school, bored and frustrated, though the recent report of Flanagan (1976) has produced some relevant data on this problem.

Some aspects of this type of school behavior must be understood in terms of some of the basic human characteristics. Primates, unlike most lower species, show prolonged emotionality when faced with frustration. A dog may show instant anger, but gets over its anger in an instant. Sometimes a dog will even sulk for an evening. On the other hand, the human may show prolonged anger accompanied by extraordinary meanness of disposition. The human can spend a lifetime angry at some incident that happened in childhood. To some extent this prolonged anger is a result of the fact that he has a memory that permits him to recall, again and again, events of the past. The human can live with this past in a way that is not possible in the case of animals further down the evolutionary scale. This ability to recall the past at will makes it possible for the human to profit from the past. It also makes it possible for him to have his whole life dominated by a single earlier episode. Superior memory carries with it disadvantages that we are only slowly recognizing.

The author has summarized elsewhere the evidence indicating that modeling is a powerful influence in releasing aggression (Travers, 1977). There is little doubt that aggressive teachers release aggression in their students. The aggressive behavior released may not be toward another human being but toward an object, as it is in the case of school vandalism. Unfortunately, schools provide ample opportunity for venting aggression toward objects.

The origins of aggression in primate groups has been closely studied, but the findings are easily misinterpreted in relation to problems in schools. In natural settings most aggression is seen in males competing for the females. The natural habitat of most primates virtually does not provide opportunities for competing in relation to food. Food is abundant. There is even some sharing. Economic competition did not arise in the case of the human band until some individuals became capable of amassing food or other desirable objects. In early human groups there may well have been aggression related to the selection of mates, as there is in all social species, but food was probably communal property. The killing of large game required the group to cooperate in order to make a kill possible. Once the game was killed, there was no possibility of one member claiming ownership since the meat would not keep. The meat had to be shared communally in order for the group to survive. Thus, competitiveness, and aggression related to competitiveness, was almost certainly a matter that was confined to sexual mating and to the formation of sexual partnerships. It may well be that the most competitive were those that had the greatest number of progeny. In this way, over a few million years, the human species may well have acquired a high degree of competitiveness that ultimately became directed into channels other than those related to sex. This line of reasoning suggests that much competitiveness is simply a residual of primitive sexual behavior that served the human species well far back in history, but that now it may not be as valuable an asset, if it is an asset at all.

Studies of the causes of pupil aggression in schools would be likely to show that much of this aggression is instigated by incompetent bureaucratic controls. Consider a single case history. A fifteen-year-old boy was sitting in class. The teacher said that she was going to dictate an assignment to the class. The boy asked for some paper on which to write out the assignment, and the policy of the school was to provide paper. The teacher told the boy that there was no paper available that day and went on to dictate the assignment. The boy didn't know what to do and pulled a pen from his pocket and scribbled down the assignment on the first flat surface he could find, which happened to be the top of the desk. The teacher saw him writing on the polished surface, became angry, and sent the boy to the principal's office with a note saying that he had been destroying school property. The boy was thereupon suspended for a week. Of course, the boy was angry, and became a likely candidate for destroying more school property. This incident, together with other incidents, eventually led to the boy's withdrawing from school, and in the years that followed, he was able to find only the most menial jobs. Now, as a young adult, he is angry with society and for good reason. He is a capable young man. In school he showed himself to be an excellent machinist, yet he never received enough training to qualify in that field. He also showed talent as a draftsman. But his whole experience with schooling led him to hate all formal education and everything associated with it. Sad to say, his teachers had no conception of what they were doing to the boy.

Far more research needs to be undertaken on the use and misuse of competitive situations in education. The school systems of most countries of the world are intensely competitive. In some countries the competitiveness produces extraordinary tension in students. In many European countries, annual competitive examinations are followed by waves of suicides, for to have failed an examination is to be an outcast. In the United States, a common reaction to failure is in complete apathy toward the school system, the community, and the system of laws. So intent has the educational world been on developing competitive tasks that little has been accomplished in the way of developing curricula around cooperative tasks, in which several children can make contributions to a project. Cook and Stingle's excellent review of research on cooperation (1974) brings out the vast ignorance existing about this area. They point out that we do not even know at this time the conditions under which cooperation will occur. The application of simplistic theories to the production of cooperative behavior have generally had negative results. Thus, attempts to reinforce cooperative behavior have also resulted in an increase in noncooperative behavior. There is also the question of whether children can be readily taught cooperative behavior in a society that is basically competitive. The cultural atmosphere permeates even the play of children. For example, Cook and Stingle bring out that the play of Mexican children does not involve the rivalry shown by American children. Mexican children shrink from such rivalry situations, but American children approach such situations with enthusiasm. The American child, in the American school, is expected to work in isolation from other children. Intellectual sharing is discouraged, except when it is under the direct supervision of the teacher, as in recitation sessions. For a child to ask another child to help him solve a problem may even be characterized as cheating.

Competition and cooperation have been viewed by most research workers as representing opposing processes. Johnson and Johnson (1976) take this view in their excellent review of research on the subject, and in their attempt to draw together some materials for training in the area of cooperation. Johnson and Johnson consider three categories of attitude as falling within this general area. When several individuals are together in a work situation, the attitude of a particular individual may be cooperative or competitive, but it may also be individualistic, that is to say the individual may become absorbed in the task and take no notice of the fact that there are others present. The individualistic worker may be competing with himself, trying to raise his level of performance, or he may be relaxed and content to do whatever he can in the situation.

Johnson and Johnson make some important observations about the cognitive aspects of cooperation and competition. For there to be cooperation or competition there must be a sense of mutual causations and a sense that the individual's own behavior influences the behavior of the other. A completely self-centered individual is neither able to cooperate nor to compete for he does not understand the effect of his actions on others.

Children come to school with certain ideas concerning how one behaves in relation to other children. Johnson and Johnson point out that research indicates that children in America enter school expecting to have to compete with other children, and that they are probably more competitive than those in other countries. Of course, it is difficult to make cross-cultural comparisons because other cultures, such as that in Russia, combine competitive and cooperative situations. The Russian child works with a small group of other children cooperatively but the group competes with other groups. The longer children are in American schools the more competitive they become. This may be because as they grow older, they become more discerning about their relation to the work of others and more able to pick up cues concerning their own accomplishments and the accomplishments of those around them. A six-year-old, who has produced a painting, may be so preoccupied with this own work that he never compares it with that of another child.

Within the United States, some children are more competitive than others. The most competitive children are the Anglo-Americans, and those of Mexican and African origin are generally less competitive. Presumably such differences are not the result of any inborn differences, but a product of the subcultures and the historical events that gave one group greater capacity to compete successfully than another group.

Another finding of great interest is that urban children are more competitive than children raised in the country. This is hardly surprising in view of the fact that life on a farm calls for a great deal of cooperation between all concerned, and children and adults must cooperate together in order to keep the farm operating. No such cooperative situation exists for the city family in which each person functions as an independent individual.

A sad reflection on the state of American schools comes from research that Johnson and Johnson say indicates that American schools provide almost no opportunity for children to cooperate. Indeed, the situation is so bad that a child may devote most of his time devising ways to lower the rewards of other children. Helping behavior toward other children is often viewed as wrong. Sometimes this kind of wrongdoing is institutionalized, as when at West Point, any help on take-home examinations is considered cheating and against the honor code. One wonders how an honor code would work if there were a requirement for one student to help another.

Competitiveness in schools seems to have the effect of raising the anxiety level of the individual. This seems true, not only for children in schools but also for adults working in industry. Competitiveness is also damaging to interpersonal relations.

Competitiveness is highly destructive of human relationships. A competitive society is one in which individuals are relatively isolated and alienated from one another. Johnson and Johnson give as a reason for this that individuals like other individuals who help them achieve their goals and dislike those who frustrate them. In a competitive society individuals frustrate one another. The individual who succeeds frustrates all those who do not. Cooperative societies, by their very nature, involve collections of individuals who are helping each other achieve goals of importance to them. Even those who do not succeed very well, and who pull down the level of competence displayed by the group, do not seem to be treated with antagonism. A cooperative learning atmosphere increases trust, task orientation, and an involvement in the learning activities.

Johnson and Johnson report much more in their excellent review of the literature. Perhaps enough of their findings has been presented here to motivate the reader to study their excellent book. This field is a rich source of important ideas, and yet the most important problems have not yet been studied. We know almost nothing about whether the competitiveness described in the research studies is an irreversible condition. Can one take sixth-graders and build in them persistent cooperative work habits? If children are taught cooperative work habits in kindergarten, will these habits persist, or do they require continuous strengthening in higher grades? What do teachers do to foster competitiveness? Can parents be enlisted in a program to develop a cooperative climate in the schools? How early can competitive tendencies be detected, and what is the origin of these tendencies? Is the competitiveness of the parents a crucial factor in the level of competitiveness shown by children? Many other interesting questions can be asked which may form a basis for a research study.

Attitudes and Values

Social psychology has long focused on the study of attitudes and values. These are necessarily derived from the individual's social environment. One can hardly imagine a person raised in isolation from all other individuals as having attitudes or values. Significant attitudes necessarily pertain to relations between members of a society. Attitudes are complex structures underlying behavior that result in behavior related to the approach or avoidance of particular classes of objects or situations. Thus, a person may have a positive attitude toward religious institutions and act in ways that are supportive of those institutions, or at least make comments indicating such support. Attitudes are generally considered to have three main components. First, there is the cognitive component, that is to say the component that has to do with the person's knowledge about the class of objects toward which he has an attitude. Thus, a person may have a large body of favorable information about the contribution that religious organizations have made, or are making, toward communal welfare, and this knowledge may be the basis of his attitude. Second, attitudes have a feeling component, referred to as the affective component. A person may feel strongly for or against a particular institution. It is not just that his views are pro or anti, but he has strong feelings on the matter. Most people who have attitudes toward busing as a means of achieving school integration have strong feelings with respect to the matter, often so strong that rational argument is precluded. Sometimes the feeling elements are much less strong. One may have a strong intellectual commitment to some cause and yet not have very strong feelings in the matter. The feeling elements seem to be quite independent of the cognitive component. Indeed, an attitude may have only a small cognitive component but strong feeling elements, or vice versa.

The third component of attitudes is the action component. One can have prejudice-loaded information related to a particular issue and even strong feelings and yet one may never undertake any action. Perhaps a majority of Americans believe that religious institutions do some good, and feel strongly supportive of such institutions, and yet they may go to churches or synagogues or other religious establishments only on very special occasions, if they go at all. In such cases the attitude lacks any action component. Attitudes may lack action components, just as they may lack feeling components.

The great problem for schools in this area of attitude education is to develop an action component. In social studies classes children may learn to feel positively about their right to vote and may acquire a great amount of information related to the significance of exercising the franchise. But when they reach the age of majority less than 50 per cent of them actually vote. The attitude was learned without an action component in about half the students. Such data are easily misinterpreted, for one must remember also that about half the graduates of high school did learn an action component and did actually vote. The failure to produce an action component was only in certain students. In others, the action component was successfully developed.

There seems to be a weak relationship between beliefs, feelings, and related actions. The relationship is sufficiently weak that one cannot assume that action will follow a program that attempts to build up beliefs and feelings related to an attitude, and yet beliefs and feelings are important for the establishment of actions. The mere practice and reinforcement of related actions, as is undertaken by student government elections, seem to have little effect on the development of the action component that has to function later in adult life.

Attitudes are essentially approach and avoidance responses. A child said to have a bad attitude toward academic work means that he shows avoidance responses to such work, preferring to engage in other activities. In terms of definition, there is no basic difference between interests and attitudes. The term *interest* is commonly reserved for approach and avoidance responses to objects and particular activities, such as stamp collecting or doing science experiments, whereas the term *attitude* is reserved for responses toward institutions such as church, or school, or particular political parties. The distinction is merely a convention. Since the life of the individual is controlled to a great extent by the institutions of the society in which he is born, attitudes toward those institutions are important for his adjustment to life's circumstances. One of the functions of the school is to develop good positive attitudes toward those institutions valued by the society, and negative attitudes toward those institutions that the society rejects. One can expect that schools should play a part in developing positive attitudes toward a just legal system, toward freedom of speech, toward exercising the franchise, and toward other fundamentally distinctive aspects of our democratic society. One hopes also that schools will develop negative attitudes toward such institutions as the use of a secret police by the government, intolerance for the deviate thinker, and restrictions on the freedom of the press. The success of the schools in achieving these goals seems to have been quite minimal, and the recognition of this fact has resulted in extensive research on the problem of educational conditions that make for educational change. The effort is a long-standing one that goes back to the early 1930s, when it enlisted the energies of such well-known research workers as H. H. Remmers and L. L. Thurstone.

The early studies concentrated on the development of measuring instruments, which typically measured the affective responses of the individual to some custom or institution. The early studies also demonstrated that exposure to films and other educational experiences did produce changes in scores on these instruments. The changes in scores tended to slip back over weeks or months, as one would expect them to do. These early studies provided much encouragement to those concerned with attitude education. Later studies also showed some relationship between the type of college education pursued and changes in measured attitudes. Students at some liberal arts colleges showed a liberalizing change as the students completed their bachelor degree courses. Students at highly conservative colleges tended to show the opposite change. Despite such changes, the research also showed that the student's home was vastly more influential on his attitudes than any educational influence to which he might be exposed. Though the school might have some small impact, the techniques of attitude change that are available to teachers seemed to be weak. Still another fact that dulled the optimism of the early workers was the consistent finding that the changes in attitudes as measured by the attitude scales was all too often unrelated to the other forms of behavior of the students. The school experiences changed his verbal behavior in a test situation, but did not necessarily change other action components of his behavior. The attitude scales primarily measured the affective component of attitude. They asked questions about how the individual felt about particular aspects of the institution or customs involved. Thus, in many of these early studies little relationship was found between the action component and the affective component. This led to considerable discouragement among educational research workers who began to abandon the field in the mid-1940s, leaving it for further study to social psychologists and sociologists.

The major difficulty that educational research workers had encountered was that they had no useful theory concerning the mechanism underlying attitude change except that of Thorndike (1935), which was not widely adopted. The theories they had had were quite primitive. L. L. Thurstone had assumed that the presentation of ideas sympathetic to a particular attitude position would result in the formation of attitudes favorable to that position. His work involved the presentation, through film, of views of minorities that were favorable to those minorities. He did find some change in the attitudes of high school students in the desired direction. Remmers took the position that any material that teachers judged to be an effective means of producing attitude change had a good chance of producing an effect. Mere exposure to suitable materials was considered to be the prime educational means of producing change, though Thorndike had long stressed that likes and dislikes were learned through the manipulation of rewards and punishments, an idea that has been reborn in operant psychology.

During the last twenty-five years, after educational researchers had abandoned the field, social psychologists and sociologists have been busy developing theories of attitude change. A very large literature has since accumulated that focused on a number of different theoretical positions. The major theoretical positions are those referred to as dissonance theories, self-perception theories, and information theories of attitude change. These theories have been presented in a number of books that summarize the field.

The classic volume summarizing what are known as dissonance theories of attitude change is that edited by Abelson et al. (1968). A review of many different theories of attitude change is found in the work by Insko (1967). Triandis (1971) also reviews theories of attitude change. Lemon's book (1974) provides a review of techniques for measuring attitudes. A volume that is highly critical of all previous research on attitude change is that by Nuttin (1975).

The educational research worker who wishes to conduct research in the attitude field should become cognizant of the different theoretical positions, each of which has some experimental support.

Educational researchers need to take a new look at the formation of attitudes in schools in the light of the work that social psychologists and sociologists have undertaken. Armed with new theoretical positions, the results achieved might be of far greater significance than those undertaken in the 1930s.

Public opinion polls are attempts to provide crude measures of public attitudes, usually for the purpose of demonstrating changes over the years. Gallup has conducted his public opinion polls of attitudes related to education. Remmers initiated an opinion poll of high school students as a means of determining attitudes of adolescents, not only toward education but also toward issues of the times. Such enterprises are always of current interest, but they have done little to advance our knowledge of education. The materials produced may well be of greater significance as historical records than they are as contemporary sources of information.

A problem related to that of attitude development and change is the problem of the acquisition of values, which, in turn, is also related to the problem of moral development. Values are discussed briefly here, rather than in the section on moral development, because they have been the object of study of psychologists who are interested primarily in attitude research rather than by psychologists interested in problems of moral development. One of the outstanding contributions in this area is a volume by Rokeach (1973).

Rokeach takes the traditional position that values represent organizations of attitudes. They are like attitudes but are much broader in scope. Thus, a person's life may be dominated by the value denoted by the word *freedom,* but he may have specific attitudes toward such matters as freedom of religion, freedom to hold highly deviant political beliefs, and economic freedom for private enterprise. The value *freedom* is much more encompassing than any of the specific attitudes to which it is related. Rokeach also takes the position that a value is a standard by which an attitude is judged.

Rokeach distinguishes between terminal and instrumental values. Terminal values represent ultimate goals. Thus, freedom is an ultimate state to be achieved, but is unlikely ever to be fully achieved. In contrast, honesty is an instrumental value and a way of life that one may actually hope to achieve in one's daily transactions. Rokeach has attempted to provide an inventory of the common terminal values and the common instrumental values. The terminal values include a world at peace, salvation, wisdom, equality, and freedom. His list of instrumental values includes ambition, courage, honesty, lovingness, and self-control. Neither list is claimed to be comprehensive, but it is presented as a list of the common values that play a role in the life of Americans.

The method used by Rokeach to measure values is so simple that one is amazed that such simplicity could have produced such interesting results as he has found. Rokeach simply gives his individuals a list of either the eighteen instrumental values or the eighteen terminal values and asks the individuals to order them from those that are the most important to them, as individuals, to those that are of least significance to them. The task takes less than ten minutes. This procedure for the assessment of values has none of the complicated statistical methodology that characterized the early work of Thurstone on attitudes, and neither does it involve any complex scaling procedure; it simply produces a rank ordering. Yet the rank ordering does bring out very important differences between groups. For example, political conservatives are found to rate freedom very high, and equality relatively low. The political radical left places equality high, and freedom low, whereas Rokeach suggests that the genuine liberal might be defined as one who placed both equality and freedom high in relation to other values. There are, of course, immense difficulties in constructing a society in which there is both equality of individuals as well as great freedom. Some aspects of freedom, such as freedom in the business world, result in great inequalities, with some people accumulating wealth and others losing their money. Much depends on how equality is defined. The conservative tends to think of equality as meaning equality in terms of the right to vote. The radical left considers equality in terms of equal wealth or equal access to services such as those involved in the maintenance of health. Other important differences are found between men and women and between various occupational groups.

Even more important than these general findings is the finding that values may be changed and that the changes may have a very durable impact. Rokeach has conducted a number of experiments in which a brief experience has been provided to change the values of students, and then a follow-up has been used to determine whether the experience changes behavior related to the value structure involved. One such study involved students for whom the value denoted by the word *freedom* was high and the value of *equality* was relatively low. A brief lecture was given explaining that in a democratic society, equality was a very important state to achieve. Many months later the students and also a control group were sent a letter inviting them to join the National Association for the Advancement of Colored People. Those students who had been exposed to the ten-minute lecture showed a greater tendency to support this organization than those who had not. In addition, the students tended to enroll in college programs that were more highly related to social goals.

Rokeach argues that values have powerful and direct influence on behavior, and that they are highly related both to motives and to actions. As the value system of the individual changes, so too does the behavior in which the individual engages. Attitudes do not seem to have the same direct tie to action.

The Rokeach study suggests a great range of problems that need to be attacked in a school setting. Little is known about the values of children and how those values develop. There is virtually no research on the conditions within the school that result in the development of values. One suspects that much that goes on in a typical school results in the development of values that are not beneficial either to the student or to the society in which he lives.

Summary

1. Education takes place in a social context, but social factors in learning have been all too often ignored by research workers concerned with the schools. Educational technology has generally had an isolating effect on the pupils, just as most technology is isolating. Little has been done to facilitate pupil interaction related to school learning. Even the faculty have tended to be isolated the one from the other. The social context of education in the United States encourages individualism and individual achievement, and a child may learn that he can gain by not helping others to learn. A highly competitive society produces a highly competitive atmosphere in the classroom.

2. Educational research workers have long studied such problems as which section of the community exerts the greatest influence on the schools. Studies over fifty years demonstrate that those who are supposed to represent the public in matters of educational policy actually represent a very limited section of the community. These individuals tend to come from an affluent and influential group that exerts considerable political power. In recent years, there has been considerable interest shown in the area of leadership, though much of this research has been undertaken in a military context. Instruments have been developed for measuring aspects of the administration in schools. Though these instruments have been widely used, they do not seem to have accumulated any substantial body of knowledge. Attempts have been made to develop social skills of educators through various forms of sensitivity training, but the value of this training has not been clearly established. There are very real difficulties involved in the conduct of research related to sensitivity training.

3. Sociologists and psychologists have become interested in the social role of the teacher in the classroom. The teacher can exert power and control pupils in the classroom partly because society sanctions certain of the teacher's activities. The teacher, in turn, sanctions certain behaviors on the part of the pupil. Studies have also been undertaken of the power motive in teachers and how it operates. Men and women exercise power in different ways and this may influence the ways in which men and women function in the classroom. The ways in which women exercise power are far more subtle than the ways typically used by men. Assertiveness training is an interesting new development that may change the way in

which women exercise power. There is the possibility that men may need to change their power tactics more than women.

4. The effect of teacher expectations on pupil performance remain controversial. The flurry of interest in this problem in the late 1960s has been followed by a certain skepticism that the research fails to show a consistent relationship. There may well be no short-term effect even though there is, perhaps, a long-term effect.

5. The relationship of teachers to principals is a worthwhile area of research. The relationship seems to be one of deference on the part of the teacher for a figure of power.

6. Only in recent times has the public school come to be recognized as a source of moral development. The extent to which there should be a balance between competitiveness and cooperation in the classroom is a moral issue. History cannot be studied without understanding the moral issues involved. The area of moral development has become one that has attracted research workers in recent years, although Hartshorne and May created interest in the area in the 1920s. Most recent research finds its foundation in some of the early work of Piaget who, following the thinking of Kant, proposed that there is an inherent moral factor related to intellectual development. The work of Kohlberg has been the most influential on the modern scene, and his stages of development have been widely used as the basis for much research. The theory has advantages over that of its predecessors in that it incorporates a theory of how moral change is brought about. Many studies have been undertaken on conditions related to moral change.

7. Aggression in schools has long been a problem as it is in other areas of human activity. Anger has special problems in the case of the human, because of his ability to remember and continually recall the original situation that produced his anger. Much anger on the part of students has to do with the way in which they are controlled by teachers and school administrators. Much needs to be done to understand better the causes of anger in school situations.

8. The area of competition and cooperation in schools has produced interesting research in recent years, but much more work is needed in this area. Schools have almost no aspects of their programs designed to produce cooperative behavior in pupils. There are even fewer learning tasks that call for any cooperative behavior. The longer children are in American schools the more competitive they become, except for those who cannot compete successfully and who may give up and become lethargic. Competition is highly destructive of human relationships.

9. The area of attitudes and values has long interested educational research workers. Values are complex in that they include an affective component, a cognitive component, and an action component. Each one of

these components may vary from being strong to weak. One cannot assume that an attitude with a strong affective and cognitive component will have any action component, except a verbal one. The term *interest* is closely akin to that of *attitude*. The distinction between the two terms is relatively minor. Early studies of attitudes sought to discover a relationship between exposure to various forms of educational materials and attitudes, as measured by verbal attitude scales. These scales measured mainly the affective component. This aspect of attitude was changed by educational experiences, but the change tended to be dissipated as time passed. The early research, undertaken in prolific quantities, was deficient in that it was not guided by any useful theory of the nature of attitude change. This deficiency in attitude research has been remedied in recent years through the development of a number of theories of attitude development and change, which should form the background of anyone wishing to undertake research in the area today.

10. Research related to values has had a long history and has recently acquired new vigor through the work of Rokeach who discriminates between terminal and instrumental values. Rokeach adopts the long-held view that values represent the underlying organization of attitudes. His method of measuring values, through a rank ordering procedure, is extremely simple and requires only a few minutes in time. Rokeach has provided some evidence that values can be changed through brief experiences in an educational setting, and that the change will manifest itself in changes in action.

CHAPTER 8
Research as It Relates to the Observation and Evaluation of Learning and Teaching

A very large fraction of the work undertaken by educational research workers involves work on problems related to learning in the classroom. The pupil and the teacher and the classroom represent the focus of educational research, for the ultimate goal of all educational research is to help the learning and life of the pupil in some way. Many do not agree concerning the way in which the pupil needs help. For some, the goal of helping the pupil is to improve the efficiency with which he learns. For others the goal of efficiency in learning is trivial, for they see that the primary need for improvement in the school environment is in the improvement of the quality of life of the pupil. For the one group of researchers, the cost of education is of the greatest concern. For the second group, cost of education is unimportant provided the children lead full and worthwhile lives.

Research on the classroom tends to be compartmentalized. Some research workers, have concentrated on studies of behavior of the teacher, whereas others have focused on the behavior of the pupils. Still others have attempted to study the characteristics of the school environment and the educational materials. Of course, those who study teachers, and who have built elaborate instruments for doing this, have also been interested in the relationship between the behavior of teachers and the learning of pupils, but their measures of pupil learning have all too often been perfunctory or commonplace. Those who focus on the behavior and learning of pupils, such as the personnel of the National Assessment Project, have shown little interest in the behavior of teachers or the characteristics of the educational environment. The compartmentalization of research is evident, but all research related to pupils and teachers has one element in common, involving difficulties related to the problem of how to define variables. Research on teaching materials also has this problem.

The Early Period

The problem of defining pupil variables has been viewed as that of defining objectives related to learning and the extent to which they are achieved. The area is one of high controversy dominated, at present, by dogmatic statements concerning how one should go about defining such pupil variables. The issues are best understood by considering briefly a history of the problem. A good point to begin is the work of Ralph Tyler at Ohio State University in the 1930s. Tyler went to Ohio State to participate in the famous Eight Year Study. In this project, thirty innovative schools were selected for study. These schools had programs that in those days would have been identified as *progressive,* and were part of the progressive education movement, which became institutionalized through the establishment of the Progressive Education Association. Although progressive education of the 1930s assumed many forms, there was some agreement among the various schools that had such a program that the schools were attempting to develop a curriculum and set of procedures along the lines proposed by John Dewey. In these schools, children had considerable responsibility for their own learning. Work was commonly undertaken in units referred to as projects, and there was considerable individualization both in the choice of projects by the pupils and the way in which the projects were developed. The Eight Year Study was designed to investigate a group of schools with such a program and to study the merits and limitations of their curricula.

When Tyler arrived at Ohio State University, the Eight Year Study was in a condition of chaos. Almost no systematic efforts had been made to collect data on the thirty schools. There had been many visits to the schools by staff members and a massive volume of case history material had been accumulated, but the data provided little information concerning what the schools were achieving or whether they accomplished what they believed they were accomplishing.

In a series of articles, Tyler (1934) offered solutions to the problems that the staff of the Eight Year Study had encountered. The major problem was that the staff had not been able to specify the objectives of the schools in terms that might permit research workers to determine whether the objectives were or were not achieved. Tyler took the position, which today is a familiar one, that the objectives had to be operationally defined if they were to be identifiable and comprehensible. The form of the operational definition was to be a set of specific behaviors that would identify the pupil in whom the objectives had been achieved. The emphasis in the formula was on specificity, in that specificity implied identifiability. Although the formula has usually been stated in this way, and was thus stated by Tyler, his formula was much more complex when it came to be applied. One did not determine the extent to which a particular objective had been achieved by merely watching a child to determine whether the child did or did not behave in a way specified. What one usually did was to confront the child with a particular problem and then determine whether the solution reflected learning related to the objective in question. The problem might be presented in a formal way, through a test, or the pupil might be led into a problem situation, as when he is taken to the cafeteria and is confronted with the task of selecting a meal. In the latter case, one might determine from the pupil's responses whether he understood and was willing to apply what he had learned about nutrition, assuming that the cafeteria presented a range of choices consistent with both poor and good nutrition. The Tyler system of defining objectives requires that a problem be specified and that one or more acceptable solutions to that problem be identified.

Tyler developed his system for defining objectives operationally in terms of what have come to be known as specific behaviors through work in the area of critical thinking. All thirty schools agreed that critical thinking was what the curriculum should stress, but none of the faculty seemed able to provide a clear definition of what critical thinking was. Tyler attempted to remedy this deficit by defining components of critical thinking through making an analysis of what those components were (see Smith and Tyler, 1942). Critical thinking was analyzed into such components as the ability to interpret data, the ability to apply principles of science, the ability to apply principles of logic, and the understanding of the nature of proof. It is of interest to note that these categories are quite similar to the categories that Jean Piaget and his associates have stressed in their model of the intellect.

Tyler and his associate Louis Raths worked on an analysis of each of these areas of critical thinking. For example, the area of interpreting data was broken down into such components as the ability to perceive relationships in data and the ability to recognize the limitations of data. Each of these components was then broken down further. The *recognition of the limitations of data* was broken down into the ability to identify additional data needed for drawing a given conclusion, the ability to make justifiable inferences from data, and so forth. These latter elements are the specifics of the system. They are not specific behaviors at all, but are categories of behavior that may be observed when the individual is exposed to a particular class of problems. The term *specific behavior* is really misleading, for the problem that Tyler pursued was that of identifying classes of behaviors such that behavior can be placed in a particular class.

Tyler and Raths developed a whole series of tests for the measurement of particular classes of thinking skills. The tests were developed for appraising the extent to which the thirty schools were effective in producing these thinking skills in their pupils. The performance of the students on the tests in the thirty schools was then compared with the performance of pupils in other schools, with programs designed along traditional lines. The data generally favored the thirty schools, but differences were not dramatic and were small enough to cause statistically minded psychologists to engage in some wrangling concerning the meaning of the results. One unpublished piece of evidence indicated that the development of the tests had another important effect that was perhaps more important than any it had on the evaluation of the schools. This effect was that the teachers became more aware of the nature of this objective critical thinking, which they all endorsed and few understood. Within the thirty schools, the use of the tests was followed by year-by-year increments in the scores on the tests. One interpretation of this finding is that the nature of the tests became popular knowledge, but those connected with the study were inclined to believe that the teachers began to actually teach the skills involved. The work undertaken on the Eight Year Study was of tantalizing interest, even though it may not have produced the clean results that many hoped to see. Perhaps the most important finding of the study was that the progressive curriculum did not produce detriments in learning as so many of its critics thought it would. This study, together with others undertaken during the 1930s, gave strong support to a curriculum that abandoned drill and much of the tedious work of rote memorization that had characterized education since scholastic times.

The Eight Year Study, despite its lack of clear-cut results, brought hope that educational problems could be solved through careful analysis and research. The study did much to dissipate the disillusionment concerning the worth of research that had developed in the 1930s. During that decade, innovation, based on the ideas of John Dewey, had tended to overshadow the role of the research worker. Systemwide "experimental" programs were developed, including the introduction of a new program into seventy of the New York City schools, which in today's terms would be described as a system of open classrooms. In those innovative programs, in which some attempt was made to collect data, the new programs stood up well in comparison with the old. Those who looked at the data were generally disappointed, for the hope had been that the revolution in education would also increase efficiency of learning with respect to traditional objectives. The fact that it did not led many to believe that the data did not show the true state of affairs. Those who took the latter position were inclined to the view that the new programs were accomplishing much that the tests did not measure. The faith in the new programs was such that it overrode any concern that might have been felt concerning the lack of data pertaining to outcomes. Faith can be a substitute for data in maintaining enthusiasm.

Later Impact of the Work on the Eight Year Study

Through the 1940s and 1950s, the thinking that Ralph Tyler had brought to the Eight Year Study was applied to the development of different aspects of education. Tyler expanded his influence by writing a book on curriculum (1950), which stressed the importance of defining objectives in operational terms as a first step toward developing a curriculum. Test construction became dominated by the Tyler approach. This influence nevertheless presented an interesting paradox. Although the initial work on defining objectives in "specific" terms had been undertaken within the framework of progressive education, during the 1930s and 1940s the work was developed as a part of a reactionary movement in education that revived traditional objectives and de-emphasized the objectives of the Progressive Education Movement. Standardized tests in traditional subject matter fields were developed on the basis of detailed specifications of the objectives they were to measure. Despite the effort expended on this enterprise, one cannot see any great gains achieved in education by this process during the 1940s and 1950s. Indeed, this period was extraordinarily devoid of innovation in American education. The standardized test, built on the basis of detailed specifications, often became the teacher's curriculum guide, and instruction became directed toward the improvement of children's scores on tests. This pattern of education is still apparent. A memorandum that was recently distributed by a school superintendent's office to teachers in the system advised the teachers to have their children well prepared on the use of the encyclopedia since the next statewide test would contain questions on that topic.

The development of curricula, testing, and the statement of instructional objectives in terms of what people called specific behaviors had become institutionalized in American education by 1960. At about that time the movement found another powerful ally in the form of the operant psychology of B. F. Skinner.

Operant Psychologists and the Evaluation Movement

Although operant psychology began in the thoughtful, technical, and scientific publications of Skinner during the late 1930s, Skinner attracted a following of individuals who sought either to reform aspects of society on the basis of his work, or who saw that operant psychology was a marketable system that could be applied universally to the solution of problems of society. Operant psychology stressed the importance of analyzing the behavior to be produced in terms of a set of prerequisites. In a simple matter, such as arranging for a rat to press a lever to obtain food, the operant psychologist would list a whole sequence of behaviors that had to be learned such as:

1. Learning that a buzzer indicated that food had dropped into a trough and was available.
2. Orienting the body so that the head of the rat was near the lever.

3. With the rat in that position, the rat next has to raise itself upon its hind legs.
4. Once raised on its hind legs, the rat must place one or both of its front paws or legs on the lever.
5. The rat must then put its weight on the bar to depress the bar.

The operant psychologist of the 1960s would train a rat to press a bar by working through such a list of behaviors, reinforcing those behaviors that were appropriate, and slowly extinguishing both inappropriate behaviors and partially correct behaviors. Operant psychologists proposed to apply the same kind of analysis and reinforcement procedure to the instruction of children. A few psychologists pointed out that even the method of training a rat to press a bar was inefficient, for the easy way to bring the rat into relationship with the bar is to give the bar an odor that will attract the interest of the rat. Such a simple procedure can result in the almost immediate shaping of the behavior of the rat. Behavior in the child can also often be produced immediately without any elaborate shaping procedure.

The operant position was also joined by many other psychologists who had viewpoints that did not entirely agree with Skinner's position. The most influential of these was Gagné (1970), who took the position that the development of curriculum first required the identification of what he called the *terminal behavior,* that is to say, the complete behavior to be acquired by the learner. A second step was to identify prerequisites to the terminal behavior. Then, if necessary, prerequisites to the prerequisites would be specified. This process would be pushed back into increasingly simpler learning until the point was reached where the behaviors listed were such that the beginning pupil had already mastered the skills. At that point the pupil had to begin to learn to master the sequence leading to the terminal behavior. Thus, reading with comprehension involves an ability to make the analysis of a sentence to extract meaning. The ability to make this analysis requires that the individual be able to recognize the printed words. Word recognition is possible only if the pupil has already mastered the perceptual skills of form recognition, because if the pupil cannot discriminate form and shape, he cannot discriminate words. Form discrimination requires that the individual have already learned some of the basic properties of geometrical shapes, and this in turn calls for at least a primitive understanding of visual space, which calls for the ability to fixate points and to move the visual fixation of the eye along a line.

Gagné's argument is persuasive. Most of the work that has been carried out on the basis of this viewpoint has involved the analysis of objectives in the mathematics area, where the skills involved can be arranged in a hierarchy, from the simple to the complex. Such an ordering of skills is, however, a very subjective matter and is based on an armchair analysis of what seems to be involved.

The idea is so seductively attractive that it has been embraced not only by the federal government but also by state and local governments too. The term *seductively attractive* was chosen for use here with care. It is taken to imply that honest individuals have been led astray by the idea and have embarked on projects that have been far from desirable and healthy. The notion that this procedure can bring to education a clarity of thought that the area has so often lacked was and still is an attractive one, but simple formulas often attract because of their simplicity rather than their usefulness.

The idea that objectives can be precisely specified, together with their prerequisites, has become the very foundation of performance-based evaluation of schooling, performance-based evaluation of teachers, and performance-based teacher education.

Instruments related to this conception of behavior can be grouped into those that have to do with the performance of the teacher and those that are concerned with the performance of the pupil. Other instruments reflect attempts to analyze the behavior of effective supervisors, such as principals, into specific components, but these have not had much impact on the course of education. Let us consider the problems of defining teacher performance and then of defining pupil performance.

What Happened to the Specific Criteria of Teaching Effectiveness?

Research on teaching effectiveness during the 1940s and 1950s consisted of a search for teacher traits, broad categories of teacher behavior, and specific teacher behaviors that were related in some way to various criteria of teacher effectiveness. The literature of this period on the subject represents a conglomerate of ill-conceived studies undertaken without much research competence and without any inspiration. The several hundred studies of the era have been listed in an annotated bibliography by Domas and Tiedeman (1950). The faults of most of these studies are so obvious that it hardly seems necessary to list them. Yet it is necessary because more recent studies show the same faults. We now briefly summarize the most common of these faults.

1. The most common fault among the older vintage studies of teaching and teacher effectiveness was that they lacked an acceptable criterion of what was to be considered the mark of an effective teacher. Many of these studies used a supervisory rating for that purpose, but supervisory ratings have not generally been demonstrated to have much relationship to how much children learn.

2. All too often the studies involved rating the teacher for what prejudice dictates to be the constituent elements of effective teaching. These ratings were then compared with overall ratings of teacher effectiveness,

which were also based on a conception of effective teaching, which was also largely a product of prejudice. This procedure is like having people rated for overall size (big or small) and then having the same individuals rated for height, weight, girth, and other components of size. Of course, the two sets of ratings will be closely related.

3. Many of the studies showed what has come to be referred to as data contamination. The most common form of this is when the same person rates teachers for overall effectiveness in producing learning and then rates the same teachers on various characteristics that have been hypothesized as being related to teaching effectiveness. When this is done, the rater is likely to see some teachers as being generally effective and they are given good ratings both on the scale for overall effectiveness and on the various scales describing personality traits. Other teachers are rated uniformly low or uniformly mediocre. The uniformity of the rating of the teacher across all scales is a result of a perceptual distortion on the part of the rater. He fails to discriminate between the teacher's strong and weak points, and his failure to discriminate means that each rating given is a result of an overall impression. The effect of this phenomenon on the data is to produce high correlations between all of the characteristics rated. In this case the result is a set of high correlations between the rating of teacher effectiveness and the ratings for personality characteristics. The problem can be solved partly by using one or more persons to rate the teachers for effectiveness and other persons to undertake the ratings for effectiveness. The effect is not entirely overcome by this means because the appearance of some teachers may have such an overwhelming effect on all raters, for good or for bad, that this appearance tends to overwhelm the rating process.

During the 1940s and 1950s two solutions to these problems began to emerge. One of these was to emphasize the need for obtaining objective measures of teacher effectiveness, through the measurement of pupil learning by tests. The argument in favor of doing this is strong, but in recent years political considerations have often led researchers to use student ratings of teachers as criteria of teaching effectiveness. The latter is popular with student bodies and student activist groups, and is often popular with college administrations, but such ratings have much of the weakness of the earlier studies that used the ratings of experts. Competent research workers today prefer to use objective measures of student achievement as a means of assessing teacher effectiveness. The main argument against such measures is that they often do not sample well the behaviors represented by the objectives of teaching. Sometimes this is a persuasive argument.

A second attempted solution to some of the problems of the studies was less successful in overcoming their limitations. Around 1950 those who reviewed the earlier studies of components of teaching effectiveness came to the conclusion that the procedure of using ratings was a mistake. These ratings were believed to represent too broad and too vague assessments of behavior. What researchers believed to be necessary as one way of improving teacher effectiveness studies was to identify aspects of teacher behavior that observers could observe. This approach came from those who embraced the idea that all complex behaviors could be reduced to a set of specifics, which were the components to be worked with, much as the chemist worked with elements or pure compounds of elements.

The most ambitious attempt to reduce teacher effectiveness to identifiable components was the research of Morsh, undertaken with air force personnel. Morsh had a situation for studying effectiveness that was far superior to that which had been open to most other investigators. He had access to a group of instructors, all of whom taught the same course, and all of whom were confined to the same specified curriculum. The instructors had some latitude in how they handled subject matter and how they related to trainees taking the course. All students of the course took the same final examination.

Morsh compiled lists of specific behaviors that previous literature had suggested were related to learning on the part of students. Most of these behaviors were extremely specific and identifiable such as, "Writes key term on the blackboard." Armed with such a list, Morsh had observers spend time in classrooms and record the frequency with which each event occurred. Observers also made record of specific behaviors that were manifested by the students. The latter were also identifiable and included such items as "Student yawns." Morsh then went on to find the relationship between the frequency with which each behavior occurred and the performance of the class on the final examination.

The Morsh study showed very little relationship between the specific behaviors of the teachers and the learning of the students. At the time when the study was undertaken the findings produced surprise, but there would be little surprise today.

Morsh did find that the specific behaviors of the students were more significant for indicating the amount of learning than were the specific behaviors of the teachers, perhaps because symptoms of boredom are so clear and overwhelming. The student who yawns, or who goes to sleep, has provided overwhelming evidence of lack of participation in the learning process. The teacher who does not write a key term on the blackboard has not provided evidence of anything much.

What went wrong with the specific behavior theory? Did the Morsh study and other studies tap the wrong specifics? Why had the clarification of the vague qualities rated in the earlier studies, by reducing them to identifiable behaviors, failed to produce a clear and valid measure of teaching competence? The answers to such questions are not known with any finality, but one can now make some guesses. The doctrine that significant aspects of behavior are reducible to a set of specifics has many flaws in it, some of which are obvious. Take the case of the item, "Teacher writes key term on the blackboard." The teacher who does this does not do it as an end in itself, but merely uses the board as a device for impressing on the students the importance of the term. There are many ways of making such an impression on the students. One way would be to forget about the blackboard and ask the students to write down the key term themselves. One might even argue that it is more useful for students to write down the word than for the teacher to write it out. Another way might be for the teacher to ask the students to underline the word in their books. There are many ways of making an impression. In the assessment of teacher competence one could, perhaps, prepare a list of many alternatives in the case of this item and use the list as a means of assessing competence. If one were to try and do this for all the specifics and their alternatives, one would find oneself with a list as long as the New York City telephone directory. Even then the list would not be complete. The behavior of teachers shows an infinite variety in the achievement of specific ends. There is no short list of critical specifics that can be used to identify the competent teacher and discriminate him from the incompetent. Looking for such a list is a search for a nonexistent talisman.

Before leaving the Morsh study and before discussing further the matter of why specific teacher behaviors do not predict the learning on the part of the pupil, a few additional comments must be made concerning the Morsh study. One point to note is that instructors who produced the large gains with one section of students also tended to produce large gains with other sections, and a parallel conclusion can be drawn about those who produced the smallest gains. In other words, the final examination was a fair appraisal of teacher effectiveness. Some instructors were consistently good at producing learning in their students and some instructors were consistently poor. This means that teacher effectiveness with these instructors was a reality.

The situation is almost certainly more complicated than one in which teachers can be arranged along a simple dimension of effectiveness. Some instructors were probably more effective with some students than they were with others. Later work has suggested an interaction between teacher effectiveness and student characteristics. Most studies of teacher effectiveness do not take this interaction into account. Where there are large differences between students in aptitude and background, this may well become an important factor. When students are very uniform in their aptitudes and the knowledge with which they start the program of instruction, then this interaction factor may have a minimum effect.

The Second Research Era on Problems of Teacher Effectiveness

During the 1950s relatively little research was undertaken related to the problem of discovering components of teacher effectiveness, or competence, as it later came to be called. The new era came into being largely because the federal government finally began to sponsor research that was related to education. Washington bureaucrats, with a certain amount of scientific naiveté, but with some political shrewdness, saw the area of measuring teacher competence as one with potential for producing results of immediate value to education, and also as an area that would have appeal to Congress. Over the years that followed, the Washington bureaucracy was wrong on both scores. Nevertheless, a large number of studies were given the support of federal money and a host of new instruments were developed. These instruments, together with some earlier instruments, have been assembled and published by Research for Better Schools. The compilations have been prepared by Simon and Boyer, but only the third compilation (1974) is referenced here, since it makes the earlier versions obsolete and incomplete. Each edition of this compilation has been designated the title of *Mirrors for Behavior* to indicate the idea that each one of these instruments is to provide a mirror image of the behavior of a teacher or a pupil, or a teacher-pupil interaction, whose behavior is recorded thereon. The instruments form an extraordinary conglomerate with a great variety of different purposes. Some of the instruments are for the recording of the behavior of a teacher or a pupil alone, but some focus on the interaction. Some are strictly cognitive, relating to intellectual goals and achievements, but others are concerned entirely with affective dimensions. A few of these instruments list relatively specific behaviors, but most handle rather broad categories of behavior. Some require the use of observers, but others call for a videotape or sound recording that is later analyzed by technicians trained in the task. One only has to thumb through the volume to realize that much effort has been invested in the development of these devices.

Data is extraordinarily lacking on most of the systems listed in *Mirrors for Behavior III,* but the material is of interest in that it reflects a great variety of ways of looking at teaching. Some of the observation schedules show originality in their attempts to find new ways of conceptualizing teaching. There are many ways in which one may categorize these conceptualizations, but some are only scatterbrained assemblies of ideas about teaching that fall into no conceptual category at all, except the scatterbrained category. Let us look at a few categories, beginning with instruments that are based on a logical analysis of the nature of teaching.

The best developed of the systems that view teaching as a logical process is that of B. Othanel Smith, which was originally developed by a team under the guidance of Smith (Smith et al. 1967). Smith had long been interested in viewing teaching as a logical process and had published an earlier monograph on this problem (1962). Smith views teaching as the extension of knowledge through logically structured dialogue. He also shows the influence of the philosopher Ludwig Wittgenstein, in that Smith refers to the teacher and pupil as making certain "plays." This term implies that cognitive learning is a game, much as Wittgenstein viewed philosophical dialogue among philosophers as a game played according to certain rules. Smith has nothing to say about affective aspects of learning, except for the implication that learning is a game that is fun. The original system of Smith, described as *The Logic of Teaching,* codes behavior into episodes, each one of which is categorized as (1) defining, (2) describing, (3) designating, (4) stating, (5) reporting, (6) substituting, (7) evaluating, (8) opining, (9) classifying, (10) comparing and contrasting, (11) conditional inferring, (12) explaining, and (13) directing and managing. Coding is undertaken from a record so that it can be undertaken with care.

The system was later revised into a *Strategies of Teaching* instrument. This method of analyzing teaching uses a larger unit of teaching than the episode. This larger unit is called the *venture,* which may be a discourse between one or more persons, or a monologue. The venture is more inclusive than the episode. One venture ends and another begins when there is a complete change of topic. Ventures are classified into the categories of (1) causal, (2) conceptual, (3) evaluative, (4) informative, (5) interpretive, (6) procedural, (7) reason, (8) rule, and (9) system. An explanation of just one of these categories will help to explain the general nature of all the categories. Consider category 8, the rule category. Ventures fall into this category if they involve the identification and the use of a rule, or the discovery of a rule, or the making of a decision based on rules.

Other instruments have been based on a logical analysis of classroom monologue or discourse. Bellack (1966), among others, has produced such an instrument. These instruments present an interesting analysis of one form of teaching. What one needs to know is whether teaching in the style described by Smith results in a better logically structured system of knowledge in the pupil than would result from other forms of teaching that did not place emphasis on logical structure. Smith and others who have pursued work along this line have made the assumption that teaching that shows logical structure is more effective for achieving cognitive ends than is teaching that lacks that structure. In addition, the teacher who pursues this line of teaching is, presumably, able to communicate to the student important components of logical thought such as those of using terms with clear meanings, making inferences that follow from data, stating assumptions underlying particular arguments, and so forth. The evidence available with respect to the latter does not indicate that logical thinking is learned by being exposed to a model, but much more needs to be done to explore this matter.

The Smith type of observation schedule makes assumptions about the nature of cognitive processes that are quite similar to those proposed by Piaget, though it departs from Piaget in the implied specifications for what are good teaching procedures. Smith advocates discourse, presumably led by the teacher, but Piaget recommends experimentation on the part of the child, with the adult serving the role of providing the materials or providing the child with an opportunity to explore particular materials.

The instruments under consideration ask observers to classify teacher and pupil behaviors and interactions into very broad classes of behavior. There is nothing as specific as the use of a chalk and blackboard for writing out a key term. Considerable judgment must be exercised in deciding whether any episode or venture is to be placed in one class or another, or in several classes. The instruments developed in the 1960s and later abandoned the idea that validity and precision could be usefully achieved by dealing only with behaviors as specific as that involved in pressing a lever. Studies of rats ceased to be the model of developing observation instruments for the classroom, though they still remained the model for producing some types of classroom materials, mainly in the form of the programmed textbook.

Large amounts of federal funds were available during the early 1960s for the development of such instruments, but most of these devices have remained almost unused ten or more years later. Changes in federal policies concerning the kinds of research projects that were to be sponsored meant that many of these promising projects were cut off from sources of research funds. Yet, a few of these projects represented some of the best thinking of recent years concerning the nature of teaching.

Before considering other forms of observation schedule that are designed for classroom use and based on other theoretical viewpoints, mention should be made of a primitive class of instruments that show a minimum amount of theoretical underpinning. A group of such instruments was developed by Ned Flanders and modified in various forms by others who have been interested in the enterprise. The Flanders Interaction Analysis has also been extensively studied, largely because of the simplicity with which data can be collected using the system. The simplistic theory of teaching that underlies the device has also had appeal to the unsophisticated research worker.

The Flanders system uses trained observers to collect classroom data. Verbal behavior in the classroom is recorded every three seconds in one of the following categories:

(A) Teacher talk
    1. Clarify feeling constructively.
    2. Praise or encourage.
    3. Clarify, develop, or make use of ideas suggested by students.
    4. Ask questions.
    5. Lecture.
    6. Give directions.
    7. Criticize.
(B) Student talk
    8. Student talk in response to the teacher.
    9. Student talk initiated by the teacher.
(C) 10. Silence or confusion.

Flanders has developed an elaborate system for analyzing the data. Through the use of the Flanders system one can determine the percentage of the behaviors that are initiated by the pupil and the percentage that are initiated by the teacher. In most classrooms in public schools, the teacher is the main initiator of verbal behavior and only occasionally does the pupil initiate an interaction with the teacher. Typical data would show the teacher initiating behavior, and hence activity, in about 70 per cent of the time and the pupil in about 20 per cent of the time. Most research workers who have used the instrument have made the assumption that better learning occurs in classrooms in which pupil initiation is at a high level and teacher initiation is at a low level.

The device has been used extensively for the training of teachers, generally for the purpose of increasing the amount of pupil-initiated behavior, but sometimes for the purpose of encouraging the teacher to use more indirect approaches to instruction. Such indirect approaches are found in teaching in which the teacher engages in such activities as clarifying a pupil's ideas or encouraging a pupil to pursue ideas of his own. Despite the extensive use of the interaction analysis system for the training of teachers, there is little or no evidence that the use of the device has produced better teachers, either through becoming more effective in producing learning or in providing an improved quality of life in the classroom. Some positive results are almost certainly a result of artifacts of the research procedure. Classes that show high gains in achievement may well show a high degree of pupil-initiated behavior and substantial so-called indirect behavior on the part of the teacher, but the main reason for this relationship is that these classes of children consist of relatively high IQ students who initiate much activity on their own and who want a teacher who helps them with their thinking rather than one who tells them what to do. Coats (1966) brings out this relationship rather clearly.

On the other hand, there seems to be quite substantial evidence that the style of teaching reflected in the interaction analysis data does have marked effects on the extent to which the children enjoy school and feel positively toward learning. The influence on the pupils seems to be much more in the affective area than in the cognitive. Such a finding is of very limited utility in that it does not provide us with any sound theoretical basis for understanding what makes a classroom a pleasant place in which to learn. It is nothing more than an odd, and perhaps unexpected, relationship.

The discussion of the Flanders Interaction Analysis system sidetracked our consideration of the various theoretical foundations that can be used for building classroom observation instruments. The Smith system was presented as one that had been built on the basis of the logical processes involved in classroom discourse. Such instruments seem to carry with them the implication that teaching should be pursued by a Socratic method in which thoughts undergo a logical development. The main alternative approach to the study of teaching assumes that it is a psychological-social process and that one must begin understanding teaching by studying the behavioral processes that are related to it. Many instruments have been developed along these lines. Most of the instruments have as their foundation an intuitive analysis of what are believed to be the significant psychological processes underlying teaching. Opinions with respect to this matter vary enormously. Operant psychologists limit their discussion to such events as the reinforcements and the contingencies when reinforcement is provided. Concern for the characteristics of human cognitive learning is limited because the vocabulary of operant psychology does not permit much discussion of such a topic. Those with a broader background in psychology, and with some knowledge of the difficulties the teacher encounters in helping children learn, include a long list of psychological factors in teaching and learning. There is some agreement among the various schedules concerning the factors that should be included in a list of components of teaching, though different styles of teaching would involve different amounts of the different components. Such lists generally include negative factors, such as aspects of behavior that might be expected to disrupt learning. An example of such a negative factor is accusatory behavior, or behavior involving a verbal brush-off on the part of the teacher.

The following categories of behavior in the Hughes system are presented here as an example of an attempt to make a systematic behavioral analysis of teaching:

1. Structures.
2. Regulates.
3. Sets standards.
4. Judges.
5. Admonishes.
6. Reprimands.
7. Accuses.
8. Refuses request.
9. Checks.
10. Demonstrates.
11. Clarifies procedure.
12. Informs (not requested by pupil).
13. Acts as resource person on request of pupil.
14. Stimulates by offering alternatives to pupil.
15. Clarifies idea.
16. Interprets (a more detailed process than clarification).
17. Evaluates.
18. Supports (praises, reinforces positively).
19. Is solicitous (shows concern for welfare of pupil).
20. Encourages.

21. Does something for (highly personal rather than connected with class work).
22. Moralizes.
23. Gives verbal brush-off.

Each of these categories is carefully defined for those who classify the behaviors or interactions. Those who code the materials have to be carefully trained and recordings have to be used, since a coder may have to play back a piece of the record several times in order to arrive at a correct classification. Hughes codes the recordings of classroom events in units referred to as teaching acts, which she also takes great pains to define.

In this instrument, as in the others considered in this chapter, there is virtually no evidence that the measures derived from the use of the instrument are related to the achievement of the pupils over a short period of time such as a school year. Such data needs to be collected as does data on the long-term effect of being exposed to particular styles of teaching. Both of these types of studies are expensive to undertake and will not be undertaken without the financial support of federal or state authorities. Studies of long-term effects are unlikely to be sponsored by government agencies for the additional reason that government agencies want quick results in such a controversial field as educational research. A study that will take five or more years to complete is unlikely to be supported for political reasons. Yet such long-term studies of the latter type are probably the most important that can be undertaken. There is now evidence that the short-term effects of a particular educational program may be quite different from the long-term effects. Programs that drum into unwilling learners material that they master from the sheer pressure of the teacher may mold the learner into an unwilling and rebellious student in later years. The schools are full of students of this type. One can see them in droves dozing in high school classrooms, vandalizing the building, and disrupting the learning of other students.

Rosenshine and Furst's Analysis of Components of Teaching Competence: Specific Components Versus Broad Traits

Rosenshine (1970), and later Rosenshine and Furst (1973), have made one of the most significant contributions to our understanding of the relationship between component aspects of teacher behavior and teaching competence. Rosenshine began the series of studies in this area while still a graduate student at the University of Illinois. Rosenshine sought to discover the relationship between personality traits, specific behaviors, and other supposed components of teacher competence on the one hand, and objective measures of achievement on the other. He saw clearly that unless one had a defensible criterion of how much the pupils learned, one could not possibly achieve any understanding of how the teacher's behavior influenced gains in achievement. He also had the perspicacity to observe that teacher behavior could be assessed accurately and objectively in terms of specific behaviors, such as the teacher writing a key term on the board in chalk. The teacher's behavior could also be assessed for the presence of broad classes of behavior. What are referred to as ratings pertain to broad classes of behavior. Let us consider this further.

Consider a category of behavior *businesslike behavior on the part of the teacher*. This class of behavior can be manifested in a great variety of forms. One teacher is businesslike in the sense that he runs a highly structured classroom and each child knows what he is supposed to be doing and, for the most part, is doing it. Such a teacher keeps careful records, has the materials to be learned well identified and available, and keeps track of the work of each pupil. Another businesslike teacher adopts different procedures. He is orderly, but requires the children to keep most of the records. He does not tolerate excessive social play, but persuades children who engage in it to settle down to serious work. His conversations with children focus on the work of the particular child. Sometimes he spends time, while the children are working, in designing new tasks for them to do. When a child asks a question, the child is directed to a source where he can find the answer, and the child is expected to go to that source.

When the observer watches the teacher and rates him for the extent to which he is businesslike, the rater observes numerous incidents that vary from teacher to teacher, and which vary from day to day in the same teacher. From these incidents the rater must arrive at an overall impression of the extent to which the teacher is businesslike. In doing this, the rater functions much like a computer into which complex data is fed. The computer then decides what weight to assign to each item of information in order to arrive at some kind of estimate of the strength of a particular trait. The human rater must make an inference about the strength of a trait on the basis of the incidents observed. The human brain manages to weight each incident in the total, though not as systematically and consistently as does the computer. The human brain often performs this function quite well, but those who do it well are not generally able to communicate to others how they do it. The computer has the advantage in that the operations performed by computers are undertaken, not only on the basis of a set of identifiable specifications but also the computer functions with complete consistency. Ratings involve the combining of a large number of items of behavior, giving a weight to each item in the total.

This process makes it possible to rate ten teachers on the same trait, and yet the behaviors observed may be entirely different in each of the ten teachers.

In the development of rating scales one does not usually just list a sample of the positive behaviors that are evidence of the trait. Generally we are concerned with traits that range from positive to negative. Innumerable behaviors characterize the businesslike teacher, but such teachers range in their behavior from very businesslike to the disorganized and scatterbrained. A sample of the behaviors of the disorganized and scatterbrained teacher should be given, although these specific behaviors may never be seen in a teacher, though other behaviors that are judged to fall into the same sample may. Scatterbrained teachers may conduct a discourse that hops from one topic to another, without any real connection between topics. Such teachers may have classrooms that are as chaotic as their own behavior. Their records may be confused, or even utterly wrong. They may also show none of these characteristics, but will show instead characteristics in the same general class. The reader must not lose sight of the fact that we are dealing here with classes of behaviors rather than with certain limited and well-defined particular behaviors.

In the case of ratings, the rater has to make an inference about the relevance of a set of behaviors as indicators of a particular trait. Ratings of this kind involve inference, and Rosenshine and Furst (1973) refer to such measures as high inference measures. On the other hand, if one is observing specific behaviors on the part of the teacher, then there is little inference involved. A teacher either performs a particular act or he does not. One can count the number of times that such an act is performed by the teacher. Counting, again, does not involve the making of an inference.

Rosenshine and Furst have found that high inference measures derived from the observation of teacher show greater correlations with the objectively measured achievement of students than do measures derived from counts of specific behaviors referred to as low inference measures. The data they have assembled indicate that a broad spectrum of behavior may be a much more important predictor than a very narrow spectrum. The entire position that one should deal with highly specific behaviors that are thoroughly identifiable is brought into question.

The Rosenshine and Furst analysis suggests that the essence of teaching competence is a set of broad traits, which permeate every aspect of the teacher's behavior. If this is so, then the acquisition of basic competence, as a teacher, involves the acquisition of broad personality characteristics. This view is contrary to the present trend, which demands that teacher education begin with the identification of specific behaviors that produce learning in the pupil and then develop the capability of the prospective teacher to emit those specific behaviors on appropriate occasions. This is the theory underlying competency-based teacher education. In order to achieve this goal, some institutions have listed hundreds of specific teacher behaviors believed to be the basic competencies of teaching. Courses have been designed to produce those specific forms of behavior in the student of education and large amounts of federal funds have been spent on this seductive idea. The whole concept is politically attractive in that it is easy to present to a congressional committee the idea that a teacher, like a plumber, has to know certain specific things, and that these things can be incorporated into a course that teaches them one by one. The simplicity of the idea has great appeal, but like many simplistic ideas, it has tended to prevent good ideas from entering the field. The problem of developing specific behaviors is a simple one. Just teach the student of education how to handle the 2,500 common problems that occur in the classroom, and then we will have smoothly running classrooms in schools! What could be simpler!

A much more complicated problem is that of developing broad traits of personality. How does one help a student of education become a well-organized classroom teacher, whose language relates clearly and intelligibly to the needs of children, who shows enthusiasm both for the job and for activities of the children, who is flexible and is able to vary behavior from day to day, and who is supportive of the children, particularly when they become frustrated with their inability to solve a problem and the other forms of behavior that are related to learning on the part of the pupil?

Travers and Dillon (1975) have proposed a general approach to the training of the teacher with respect to these broad classes of behavior. The general theory underlying this approach is that the characteristics that the teacher should possess constitute a role, and that role development has already been well developed in the theater arts. Some of the techniques developed in the theater arts appear to have relevance for the training of students of education in a teaching role. The essential procedure for such training involves the study of the role, the search of the individual's own personality for characteristics that can form the basis of the role to be acquired, and the incorporation of those characteristics into the role.

Much research needs to be done in relation to this problem. Studies need to be undertaken on the success of various techniques for developing broad and permeating characteristics of behavior in teachers. Such research should not be too difficult to undertake for one suspects that presently available ways of changing the classroom behavior of teachers may have quite striking effects in relatively short training periods. Of course, this may not be found to be the case, but it probably is the case. The research has to be conducted on the impact of the role thus developed on the learning of the pupils. There is also the more complex problem, namely, that the role that is most effective at one grade level may not be the best role for another level.

There are other ways in which research in the entire area could be invigorated and drawn out of the rut into which it has fallen. Sociologists have some interesting concepts concerning the nature of teaching that should be explored. Anyone interested might do well to start by reading

Brookover and Erickson (1975), who have attempted to focus on the knowledge that sociologists have accumulated related to education. The teacher is not an isolated professional performing in a classroom sealed off from the world. On the contrary, the teacher is subject to all sorts of social pressures, just as the children are. The community of the classroom reflects to an extraordinary degree the community at large. If the community values learning, then the children will realize that schooling is a special privilege. A community that is concerned primarily with the accumulation of wealth will send to school children who may not be interested in learning as an end in itself. These children may see learning either as a means of joining the society of the affluent, or perhaps even as an activity that is barely worthwhile. The teachers in such a community may lack status, for their values are ones that the community does not consider to be of real worth. Teachers may well need status in order to perform their role successfully. One would expect that there has to be some degree of compatibility between the values of the pupils, the members of the adult community, and the teachers, for there to be an effective educational system.

Some Contemporary Problems in Assessing Pupil Achievement

The problems that have been considered as being related to the study and assessment of teacher behavior are paralleled in studies and assessments of pupil behavior. The original Tyler approach of defining broad categories of behavior in terms of specifics was first applied to the problem of assessing pupil achievement in the thirty schools of the Eight Year Study. Tyler later extended the same line of thinking to the development of curricula and began a movement that has had great popularity in state departments of education throughout the country. There have been some productive outcomes of this theoretical approach to curriculum design and pupil assessment, though much of the application has resulted in sterile curricula and meaningless evaluation studies. Let us consider some of the problems related to the application of this approach by considering an extreme case of its misapplication.

In one state where this approach to educational problems has become the bureaucratic way of life among educational administrators, from the state superintendent of education down to the level of classroom teachers, efforts have been made to define what is to be learned down to the last detail. Teachers in this state have held prolonged meetings during the summer recess when they have attempted to list all of the specifics to be mastered in each aspect of the curriculum at each grade. As a result of this process, elementary mathematics has been reduced to a set of nearly

10,000 specific problems that the pupil should learn to solve and be able to solve. Tests have been developed that sample these specifics. The teacher is supposed to guide the child through the sequences of activities that achieve the 10,000 objectives.

A list of 10,000 objectives is bewildering to any teacher, let alone to any pupil. Indeed, if I had been told in the third grade that I would learn 1,200 arithmetical operations, I would probably have given up trying to learn mathematics. An elementary school teacher faced with a list of 10,000 objectives in mathematics, along with similar lists in other subject areas might well decide that teaching called for a span of comprehension that was far beyond anything available to the ordinary teachers.

Fortunately, such bewilderment is unnecessary, as is the process of listing 10,000 objectives on elementary arithmetic. Those who engage in these rituals of breaking down subject matter into very large numbers of component understandings do not understand that they are making the complex out of the simple. Most arithmetic can be reduced to very simple logic, and the pupil has to understand only a relatively few logical processes in order to master all of the arithmetic taught in the elementary school. Unfortunately, the children are not taught the logic of arithmetic but rather are taught the application of formulas. Let us give an example of how the logic of underlying arithmetic may completely escape children who are taught the usual formula for dividing one fraction by another. Here is an example and the procedure derived from one arithmetic book for elementary school-age children:

The problem $\dfrac{1}{2} \div \dfrac{1}{8}$

Here is how the book solves it:

$$\frac{1}{2} \div \frac{1}{8} = \frac{\frac{1}{2}}{\frac{1}{8}} = \frac{\frac{1}{2}}{\frac{1}{8}} \times \frac{\frac{8}{1}}{\frac{8}{1}} = \frac{1}{2} \times \frac{8}{1} = 4$$

The student may learn the routine and may be able to solve the problem on a test, but the logic of the problem escapes him. He may not even understand what the dividing of one fraction by another means. He should not have learned first an algebraic manipulation that he cannot relate to anything he knows. He should have been brought to understand the problem as a first step. He should have begun by understanding that the problem is that of finding how many eights there are in a half; a half is four eights, so how many eights are there in four eights?

The difficulty with the complicated demonstration of how the formula is arrived at, is that it is dependent upon algebra and algebraic substitution. The latter involves a level of abstraction that is beyond that of which the typical fourth- or fifth-grade child is capable. The problem has to be understood by such a child in terms of logic at the concrete level. This is quite easily done. Circles can be drawn representing units, and segments of the circle can represent fractions. The problem can then be formulated in concrete terms. Many children never understand the meaning of the problem "Divide a half by an eighth," though they learn to solve the problem. However, the solution is readily forgotten because it is not assimilated into the child's understanding of the logic of arithmetic. That logic may be completely absent.

Having mastered the basic logic of the division of fractions, then more complicated examples can be considered. Keep in mind the basic logic of finding out how many times one fraction goes into another. Then there will come a time when the pupil will have to move to the more difficult form of problem represented by the following task:

$$\frac{1}{4} \div \frac{1}{2}$$

This problem also can be solved by the typical meaningless routine. Here it is best to introduce the basic logic by asking the pupil to consider the problem of $2 \div 4$ or how many times does 4 go into 2.

The actual number of logical operations that need to be understood by the child in order to understand all of grade school mathematics is probably quite small. The 10,000 objectives can be reduced to a rather small number and, if those objectives are really achieved, then the child has virtual mastery of much of elementary mathematics.

After World War I an effort was made to reduce elementary mathematics to just a few simple concepts. At that time, this was to be accomplished through the reduction of all mathematics to mathematical sets. This came about because Bertrand Russell had once suggested that all mathematics could be reduced to set theory and many mathematicians became intrigued with the idea of doing just that. Elementary school children were not to be left out of this experiment in mathematics. Soon large and often well-funded mathematical projects were set up in order to bring these new mathematical concepts to the elementary school child. Not far behind these evangelists of the new mathematical curriculum were the "quick-buck" entrepreneurs in both universities and publishing houses, dashing out their materials on the new mathematics for children, teachers, and even parents. No stone was left unturned to make every dollar that could be made out of the new enterprise.

The reduction of elementary mathematics to set theory was doomed to failure. Indeed, the first to become disillusioned concerning the value of set theory were the mathematicians themselves who soon demonstrated that all mathematics could not be reduced to set theory. There was also evidence that the level of abstraction of set theory was not appropriate for elementary school children. The glorious reduction of elementary school mathematics to a simple logical system turned out to be beyond the comprehension of most elementary school pupils, some teachers, and many parents.

The reduction of elementary mathematics to what Piaget calls the logic of concrete operations, or what John Dewey has referred to as the logic of action, avoids all of these difficulties.

These are all problems for research, as is the bewilderment of the teacher confronted with such documents as those that list 10,000 objectives of elementary mathematics. We also need to know a great deal more about the kinds of documents that help teachers guide learning. Guides to the teacher probably need to be quite simple, and there is thus a need to reduce elementary mathematics to simple logic that can form the basis of all elementary school mathematics instruction. Guides to behavior always have to be simple, if they are to have any chance at all of being effective. That is why, in the moral area, great teachers have always attempted to reduce morality to a few simple rules, such as the golden rule. Learners of mathematics also need to have this kind of simplification. When learning can be fitted into a framework of a few strong concepts, then there is a chance that learning will be effective and relatively permanent. If elementary school mathematics involves several thousand formulas, which to the child have little connection one with another, then learning will be chaotic and lack permanence. A major thrust of educational research should be the discovery of simple structures into which knowledge can be fitted. There is little place for a brand of educational research that proliferates huge lists of specifications for learning. The institutionalized sterility of much educational research stems from this approach.

Evaluation Studies—The New Emphasis in the Use of Observational Techniques

During the 1930s considerable excitement was expressed concerning the possibility that the value of educational programs and specific teaching procedures could be determined by systematic study. The formula for doing this emerged from the formula developed by the Eight Year Study for appraising the outcomes of the educational program of the selected thirty schools. The objectives of teaching were established and then defined in as specific terms as could be devised. Means were then determined for establishing whether the objectives were or were not achieved. This procedure was followed by the evaluation staff of the Eight Year Study, though exactly what was done is not clear from the record left of the project. Supposedly the teachers, or the administrators of the schools, should have been the ones to define the objectives, but this does not seem to have been the case. At least, a large share of the work of defining the objectives seems to have been undertaken by the evaluation staff, though the teachers had some opportunity to make some inputs and to concur, or not concur, with the objectives as they were stated.

This immediately raises a problem. Suppose teachers do not have clear objectives. If that is the case, then against whose standards is the program evaluated? If teachers have clear objectives, then one may be able to evaluate the outcomes of the program in terms of the objectives of the teachers. Were the teachers' objectives achieved? However, if one looks at a program and says to oneself, "These seem to be the objectives of the program," or the like, then all one can do is to determine whether these imaginary objectives are achieved. To some extent, this was what was done in the Eight Year Study.

Education may be a purposive process, with goals and objectives to be achieved, or it may be a ritual, established by tradition. A third alternative is that education may be a process of first seeking out goals and then taking steps to achieve them. Perhaps the first step in any study of a particular program is to determine the extent to which it is a ritual, that is to say, a process engaged in because that is what has been done for a long time. The famous satire entitled the *Sabre Tooth Curriculum* (1939) satirizes this form of education by describing an imaginary prehistoric culture that derived its educational program from an earlier age, when effort was made to teach children how to hunt the sabre tooth tiger. In the satire, the sabre tooth tiger had become extinct, but the curriculum designed around the hunting of the animal had become well established. I do not know of any studies of contemporary American education that have sought to discover the extent to which the curriculum is a ritual derived from a past age, but studies of that kind could well be undertaken. Of course, one can always read into an obsolete curriculum objectives that make some kind of contemporary sense, but these read-in objectives may have little to do with reality. The author was raised in such a system in which Latin was taught because it was said that a knowledge of Latin would be useful in understanding how biologists named plants and animals, how doctors wrote prescriptions, and other implausible reasons, which convinced neither the pupils nor the teachers. Another example of ritualized education used to be found in Texas where children had to learn the names of everybody who died in the Alamo and exactly where they died.

Accrediting associations have long been confronted with the problem of how to do away with ritualized education. Usually, these associations do not formulate the problem in this way, but rather see the problem as one of having educational procedures unrelated to the needs of the students.

Students of education in the 1930 and the 1940s were taught in every graduate school that evaluation was the key to educational improvement.

All that had to be done was to find out what each kind of educational program achieved, after which one could construct new programs that would be far more efficient than any program in existence for achieving educational goals with efficiency. The argument was persuasive and had wide appeal, particularly among professors of education, but the attractiveness of a goal has little to do with whether or not it can be achieved. The pressure to conduct evaluation studies during that period produced a flurry of activity that soon ended for several reasons.

The death of systematic evaluation as an enterprise of the academic establishment was first and foremost the result of the inadequacy of the measuring instruments. Measuring techniques that were available then, and are still available today, are crude and measure the less important rather than the more important achievements. Certainly, one can measure aspects of reading skill, but this does not mean that the child has learned to use reading as an important skill in life. A study of the effect of reading instruction should delve into the use to which the pupil puts the skill. One can gain some information about this matter by finding out the extent to which the pupil uses the library and the kinds of books he takes home, if he takes any books home at all. This still tells us little about whether the pupil obtains information from books to solve the problems he encounters. Tests also tell us little about the extent to which the pupil enjoys reading for pleasure. Through an evaluation study one can find out about the extent to which the child has mastered American history and civics, but one will know little about the extent to which he has become a responsible person who exercises the franchise and takes a part, when necessary, in local government. Ways of undertaking these more significant aspects of the evaluation task need to be explored and developed.

Related to this first problem is the fact that the introduction of tests in schools makes teachers test conscious and more and more prone to teach the items on the test. As a result of pressures from school administrations, all kinds of ruses are surreptitiously introduced in order to help the children to show up well on the tests. For example, in one school system tests are given early in the fall semester and in the spring. The differences in the scores on these two tests are supposed to indicate how much the children have learned. In this system, in the fall testing, every child is encouraged to come to school that day. In the spring testing, children are told to come if they feel well and are instructed to be particularly careful to be well rested and to have a good breakfast on that day. The teacher only has to make a few statements about how important the test is, to scare away some of the children who would not do well. This causes the spring testing to be conducted under conditions that are more favorable for producing good test scores than the conditions in the previous fall testing. Pupils as well as teachers have thus learned certain tricks related to the taking of tests. Administrators have also not been above using certain tricks to produce an apparent improvement in test scores. One result of these activities is that the test scores often give the impression that the children have made large gains during the school year, but the scores then appear to slip back to an extraordinary degree during the summer recess. The summer slippage is largely an artifact of the manipulation of the test scores by all concerned.

Another very serious problem related to the evaluation of pupil achievement is that immediate achievement seems to be little related to long-term achievement. An educational program that produces efficient learning over a semester may not produce efficient learning over a longer period of time. Beller (1973) brings this out in his review of studies of early education. Programs for the teaching of reading, which provide outstanding results at the end of the first grade, may turn out to be the poorest when their outcomes are studied in the third grade. What appears to happen is that the children can be taught reading by highly efficient methods that also teach them to hate reading. The result is that they learn to read, but then do not want to use the reading skills they have acquired, and slip further and further back as the years go by. One suspects that the same kind of effect appears in other areas. If learning is not exciting, and to some degree fun, the pupil may learn to regard the activity as something not worth doing. Also related to this is the possibility that, in some areas, children may learn by rote information that is retained efficiently until the final examination. Then it is dumped because it has not been learned as a part of an organized body of knowledge. The quick method of learning is not always the most worthwhile method. The search for quick-service education produces a program about as palatable as the foods that come from quick-service food enterprises. This is a matter that should be studied and provides a vast number of possible subjects for doctoral dissertations.

Another difficulty of conducting evaluation studies soon became evident. However well one might try and define the objectives of education, some ambiguity always remained. Suppose one had as an objective the ability to read and interpret correctly an editorial from the *New York Times*. First, there is the problem that these editorials are not uniform in content, difficulty, degree of technicality, style, presence or absence of humor, and innumerable other characteristics. Measuring the ability to understand such editorials would involve trying to draw up specifications for the particular editorial to be presented to the student for interpretation. Let us suppose that this hurdle has been overcome. Then one has to decide what aspects of interpretation to use in the evaluation study. Interpreting editorials represents a wide range of skills. Merely being able to understand the gist of an editorial might be viewed by some as representing the ability to interpret correctly the editorial. Other teachers may take the position that the student who really understands the editorial should be able to tease out all the subtle innuendo in it and the assumptions on which it is based. Teachers are not going to think in such detailed terms in helping students to interpret newspaper editorials correctly. Teachers will probably take the students along the road to the correct interpretation of such editorials as far as they can in terms of the time available and of the ability of the students to do such work. Also, the problems presented by one editorial may be quite different from those involved in interpreting another. Teachers cannot use detailed objectives in such work with students, but rather they need broad guides. Thus the use of highly specific objectives becomes a game played by the specialist in evaluation, and this game may not be too closely related to what teachers actually do. There is a gulf between the activities of the outside evaluator and the teacher that needs to be understood and which makes typical evaluation studies of dubious significance. Whether objectives appear to be achieved or not to be achieved depends upon how the evaluation expert interprets the teacher's goals.

Another difficulty with so-called evaluation studies is that they do not seem to exert any influence on education. A study can be undertaken and conferences held with teachers when deficiencies in the achievement of students are pointed out. The teachers will probably protest that they are already doing their best to achieve the objectives. They probably are. The result is an impasse between teachers and evaluators and little comes of the evaluators efforts.

Evaluation Studies—Death and Then Resurrection by Congressional Edict

The movement started by Ralph Tyler in the early 1930s was quite short lived. It failed to live up to the expectations that it would lead to an orderly improvement in educational practice through the use of research methods. Most of those who had felt enthusiasm for this movement in the late 1930s and 1940s had lost all enthusiasm by 1950 and they had moved on to other fields. It was not merely the lack of enthusiasm that produced the flight, but a deep disillusionment with the result of all the effort that had been devoted to the enterprise. Nevertheless, the Tyler arguments remained persuasive at higher levels of government, and these arguments began to assert their influence again in the 1960s when the federal government began to sponsor such large educational programs as Head Start.

The new federally funded programs raised strong voices in the halls of Congress demanding that evidence should be collected to determine whether the money spent on these new educational programs led to the anticipated gains. The result was that the congressional bills setting up the new educational programs, and those funding them, included statements that evaluation studies had to be conducted in order to determine whether the goals of the program were achieved. Representatives voting for the programs and the evaluation studies of them did not concern themselves with whether their demands fell within the realm of what was possible. The important thing was that money now became available for evaluation studies, regardless of whether such studies could, or could not, be undertaken, and money attracts experts challenged by the problem.

The new era of evaluation studies begun in the 1960s attracted a new generation of research workers, few of whom had been associated with the evaluation movement of the 1930s. The money that became available permitted the new generation of workers to do much that the earlier workers had been unable to do. Some extremely competent professionals became interested in the field and a new era seemed to be dawning. The extent of the work that was stimulated in this field is evident from Struenning and Guttentag's *Handbook of Evaluation Research* (1972). Other extensive works reflecting the new evaluation-of-education era were a handbook edited by Bloom (1971) and another extensive work by Popham (1974). These works collectively reflected a new vigor in the field. One of the obvious features of this literature is that it is an attempt to develop a vocabulary for talking about problems in the area. Many concepts that had been used under a melee of designations acquired accepted designations. For example, the term *criterion-referenced tests* came to be used to designate tests that indicated identifiable levels of performance and skill. A criterion-referenced test for typing indicated levels of performance called for by particular jobs. However, the concept is not new, having been used first by Thorndike (1904) in his work on psychological measurement.

Important terms that came to be used in the field were those of *developmental, formative,* and *summative* evaluation. One can appraise in some way the process that goes into the development of a curriculum. Then, as the curriculum is put into use, one can appraise the learning of students at various levels of proficiency and also determine the effects of changing various parts of the new curriculum. That is *formative* evaluation. Then there is the evaluation of the final and total effect of the curriculum, called summative evaluation. Summative evaluation is supposed to provide a final verdict on the worth of the package. These terms have had widespread use, but many do not use them. The terms have caught on, perhaps because they facilitated discussion of the area, though they do not represent any profound reflection on the nature of evaluation.

The new evaluation experts showed a level of sophistication in thought that their earlier counterparts had not shown, because earlier thought had been based on relatively primitive conceptions of the nature of research. The new writers, such as Nunnally (1972), pointed out all the difficulties inherent in the Tyler model. They also noted that the earlier evaluation studies could all too often be described as experimental studies that failed to include a control group. Thus, the earlier investigators would collect evidence to determine the extent to which the graduates of a program showed evidence of having achieved the objectives of the program, but there is a flaw in this design. The graduates may well manifest all of the behaviors that are to be accepted as evidence of goal achievement, but these may have little to do with the program. The participants may have learned these behaviors elsewhere, or they may even have learned them before they entered the program. If the measures of outcomes are to be related to the education provided, then there must be a control group. The earlier model failed to introduce this important component. Some cynical reviewers of the evaluation field have even said that an evaluation study is an experiment in education that fails to include a control group.

Although the modern evaluator has a wider range of measuring instruments to use than did his predecessor, instrumentation is still extremely crude. Few measuring devices are available that can be applied without the awareness of the person whose behavior is being evaluated. Webb's excellent book (1966) on what he calls unobtrusive measures has inspired many to develop measuring devices that can be applied without the person measured being aware of what is happening; few such measuring devices are available. Much needs to be done to develop unobtrusive measures related to the outcomes of education.

Evaluation, as an activity, also became broadened. Its earlier counterpart had concentrated on school programs, generally academic programs, though there had been some effort to evaluate such enterprises as health education and driver education. In the case of the latter, ample studies have shown the effectiveness of driver education in reducing the accident rate of those who have received such training. Modern evaluators have been interested in applying their models and techniques to a great range of programs including mental health programs, rehabilitation programs, law enforcement programs, and so forth. Most of the effort of the professional evaluator is directed toward programs other than those involved in public education. The application of evaluation procedures and methods to new areas offers many possibilities for the graduate student of education, and numerous theses and dissertations have come out of the area.

New models for the guidance of those who wish to conduct evaluation studies have proliferated. The models are the end products of the thought that has focused on the problem of conducting evaluation studies. Most of these models do not represent, at this time, procedures that have been shown to produce useful results, which is all the more reason why students of education should attempt to use them and discover the difficulties that are inherent in their use. The term *model* is probably not well used in this connection in that it does not refer to the kinds of models that have already been discussed. The term *model,* as used in connection with evaluation studies, refers to a set of procedures and not to some kind of analogy that is useful for structuring thought. The models do suggest a structure to thought, but the ideas are expressed directly rather than through analogies.

Most models of evaluation are built around the idea that all evaluation programs are undertaken for the purpose of making wise decisions related to programs. Thus, administrators have to make decisions related to the continuation of programs, the revision of programs, and matters of the group to whom the program is to be made available. Evaluation studies are designed to provide data to improve the validity of such decisions. The central problem in all evaluation studies is to produce data that is truly useful in the making of such decisions, and that task is a very difficult one. Many would argue that because of the nature of measurement techniques very little can be provided for decision makers. The decision-making process is also confused by the political considerations that must be taken into account in the making of decisions. Poor programs are sometimes retained for political reasons. Data are often not even examined by school boards because they might demolish one of the school board's sacred cows. The relationship of evaluation to decision making is complex and a matter that could be the subject of research studies.

What are referred to as evaluation models are broad procedures for conducting studies. These models list the conditions to examine and particularly the conditions that yield variables. Stuffelbeam's CIPP model (personal communication 1975) is an example of such a model. The letters C-I-P-P refer to the following four phases of evaluation:

1. Context evaluation.
2. Input evaluation.
3. Process evaluation.
4 Product evaluation.

Let us consider each phase, keeping in mind that each can constitute an evaluation study in itself.

Context Evaluation. In the educational setting, context evaluation consists of studying the conditions that lead to the selection of particular objectives. Context evaluation may include a study of the stated or implied intentions of those producing a particular educational program and the values of the subculture that influence the entire course of the program itself. Data are very difficult to obtain about matters related to context evaluation. Although the stated intent of the developers of a first-grade program may be that of providing efficient conditions for learning to read, close examination of the program may suggest that it has been unduly influenced by public pressure to have a highly traditional, regimented program. Thus, the intent of the makers of the program seems to fit the notion that they were trying to palliate public opinion. Human intent is a difficult condition to study because it is internal and one must generally infer intents from the total context, a dangerous kind of inference to make.

The values of the social context also tend to be elusive and difficult to measure. Few engaged in educational development are willing to admit the underlying political pressures.

Input Evaluation. This category refers to the evaluation of the materials and the plans for using them. In the case of an educational curriculum, the inputs would be the curricular materials, the equipment, the plans for activities, and so forth. Evaluation at this stage may involve an examination of the general strategy of the program. For example, some science programs are designed around the Piaget model of the intellect, whereas others stress the acquisition of interesting information or information that has direct applicability in the lives of the students. The Piaget model attempts to build a scientific conception of the environment with long-range applicability, but the main alternative model aims at immediate and local applicability. Books on curriculum have a great number of ideas on how evaluation studies of this kind can be undertaken. They are very difficult to undertake because they are biased by the personal values of the person who undertakes the study. Read, for example, Illich's (1970) biting analysis of the typical American curriculum, which he sees as having only one purpose, namely, that of maintaining a class society, and compare it with the kind of analysis that a school administration might make. One can hardly believe that the two sets of evaluations pertain to the same curriculum.

Process Evaluation. This stage has to do with the monitoring of the actual program itself. This phase of the evaluation may be undertaken by observing the process and collecting data related to the ongoing process. In the case of a classroom one may record what is happening, what teachers do and what pupils do, and make inferences concerning the effectiveness of the process to the objectives of the program. In some areas of activity, good criteria can be applied to establish the effectiveness of the ongoing process. In medicine, a medical student can be observed in the late stages of his training to determine whether he diagnoses the complaint of a patient in a systematic way. One can record the information the student seeks to collect, whether he follows up important clues, whether he orders appropriate tests for the patient, whether he is good or poor at eliciting information from the patient, whether he is able to relate to the patient in an understanding way, and so forth. Problem solving in medicine is understood to the point where it is possible to observe a student and determine whether his problem-solving skills are or are not effective. Gross errors can be noted. In the case of the classroom, there are no clearly defined effective ways of teaching and there is even controversy concerning whether the teacher is a problem solver, transmitter of information, model for learning, or something else. One can study the process of teaching in typical classrooms, but there would not be substantial agreement among experts concerning what positive features to observe and record, though there would be agreement on the negative features that interfere with learning. Most professors of education would agree that learning is disrupted by the teacher shouting, engaging in hostile behavior, being sarcastic, punishing harshly, failing to explain or providing a confused explanation, ridiculing, enforcing an unnecessary degree of order and silence, and so forth.

The study of process can also show up defects in the materials. Teachers may find the materials or equipment provided difficult or awkward to use. Printed materials may need more explanation than should be necessary. Scientific equipment may not be well designed so that the pupils can make their observations easily. Equipment may be difficult to maintain, easily broken, or present problems related to its distribution. All of these considerations, and others, have to be taken up in the process evaluation of a program.

This phase of the evaluation influences decisions related to the design of the program, and it is typically undertaken with an early version of a program. Most school programs that are marketed are tried out and evaluated by identifying the difficulties encountered during the tryout. The teaching materials are then "debugged." Sometimes schools will introduce programs on a trial basis for the purpose of assessing their suitability, and this assessment involves process evaluation.

Product Evaluation. This is the crucial test of any program. Were the objectives achieved? In the case of education, one is likely to use the misleading metaphor and to think of the pupil as the product, much as an automobile is the product of a factory. The pupil's behavior may be influenced by the educational program to which he is exposed, but he is much more than a product of the program, for he is also a product of his own initiative in using the program. In the case of a mental health program, the behavior and well-being of the client can be viewed as the product.

Numerous other decision models of evaluation can be found in the literature. For example, Edwards, Guttentag, and Snapper (1972) have what is essentially a decision model. Nevertheless, this emphasis on using data derived from evaluation research for the purpose of making decisions is not without its critics.

The main criticism is that the data derived from single evaluation studies is weak data; at least it is weak compared with all the other sources of knowledge that can be assembled to critique a program. If a program of education has been well described, and if the materials are all available for inspection, then one can evaluate a program in terms of what is known about human learning. Much knowledge is available concerning what makes for effective learning and what does not. On the basis of such knowledge, one can critique a program. Such knowledge is not the most substantial knowledge, but it is strong compared with the information that is likely to come out of a single research.

A second and related criticism is that most evaluation studies cannot be replicated. One only has to review the numerous studies conducted on such programs as the DISTAR reading program to find evidence for the extraordinary lack of replicability of typical evaluation research. The research varies from that which is highly favorable toward DISTAR to research that is extremely negative. Evaluation research is not peculiar in this respect. Research in the behavioral and social sciences often seems to be quite inconsistent from study to study. What this inconsistency means is that there are uncontrolled and unrecognized factors operating that influence one study in one direction and another study in another direction. Thus, the data derived from any single instance of evaluation research should not be used for making decisions of any consequence. Only after many studies have been undertaken, using many different programs, should the results be assembled, and only then, and only if there is some consistency of the results, should a decision be made on the basis of the data. Decision models of evaluation are a little unrealistic in terms of the data that can be collected.

The graduate student of education who wishes to conduct an evaluation study should not be discouraged by what has been said here. Such studies should be made, but the student should not plunge in and advocate the application of his results, unless his results are well supported by other data collected elsewhere. There is much to be said for making attempts to reproduce evaluation studies that have already been undertaken.

A final point to note in this connection is that production followed by evaluation is not the usual way in which any form of program is made in our society. Engineers do not proceed in this manner. Silk stockings for women were not slowly improved by making studies of the holes worn in them. Stockings were improved by the invention of an entirely new manmade fiber named nylon. Transportation was not improved by studies of the horse and buggy and its defects, but by the invention of mechanical means of providing power. No meaningful improvement in lighting resulted from the study of the candle or the oil lamp, though such studies did produce a longer burning candle and a brighter burning oil lamp. The real improvement came with the invention of the electric generator based on Faraday's experiments. Perhaps the same is true of education. Important steps forward in education seem to have come through the creative work of such individuals as Maria Montessori and John Dewey rather than through the careful data collections of the evaluators. This form of criticism cannot be taken lightly.

National Assessment of Educational Progress

The topic of evaluation cannot be left without considering one of the most expensive and ambitious evaluation programs ever developed, namely, the National Assessment of Educational Progress. The data collected in connection with this program might well be used for a large number of doctoral dissertations and other researches. Indeed, researches of the latter kind may be far more valuable than the National Assessment project itself. What is said here about the history of National Assessment is based on the account provided by Hazlett (1976) who was formerly administrative director of the project.

The beginnings of National Assessment are found in legislation passed by Congress in the 1960s. The Commissioner of Education, Francis Keppel, became concerned about the problem of obtaining information on the quality of education and the effect of federal programs on that quality. The piecemeal collection of data did not seem to provide an ongoing monitoring of the state of American education. The assumption seems to have been that education would make progress and that such progress should be well documented with facts. Hazlett states that Keppel had a conference with Ralph Tyler and asked him to prepare a memorandum on the matter of collecting systematic data in relation to the problem. The memorandum established the basic plans for the National Assessment of Educational Progress. The next six years were occupied in developing details of the program including the development of measuring devices and the working out of sampling procedures. During that period most of the funding was provided by the Carnegie Corporation and the Fund for the Advancement of Education, but in 1969 funding was taken over by the federal government, which has funded it ever since and has permitted it to become the most expensive educational project ever funded by the federal government, or by any other source of funds.

In the program as it has been developed, data are collected in ten areas of the curriculum on a three- to five-year cycle. Data are collected on children aged nine, thirteen, and seventeen, and also on young adults. Those included in the sample are selected by region, sex, parent's education, and type of community. Children are distributed across schools and the data cannot be used to evaluate particular schools. Those who have developed the program seem interested in the data from particular items as much as total area scores. The data to permit the comparison of regions for the ability to respond to particular test items is not yet available, although similar kinds of data are already available from other sources.

The National Assessment program introduced the concept of objective-referenced tests, which is a revival of Ralph Tyler's original notion of the 1930s that instruments could be developed that would indicate whether an objective has, or has not, been achieved. Some of the difficulties related to this concept have already been discussed. At the risk of being repetitive, let us ask again the question of what it means to be able to interpret a newspaper editorial correctly? Those who build objective-referenced tests seem to believe that it is possible to build a test that will tell whether a person can, or cannot, interpret a newspaper editorial correctly. Interpreting an editorial involves a range of activities from crude interpretation to the interpretation of subtle innuendo. Then there may well be messages written between the lines of the editorial that even the maker of the test has not noted. Most outcomes cannot be defined with any precision and, hence, objective referenced tests cannot be referenced to objectives except in the most crude way. National Assessment has a certain naiveté in the thinking that underlies it that is disturbing.

National Assessment is mentioned here because it is an area in which some may want to do research. Interesting studies can be undertaken in this area, though not necessarily using National Assessment data. There is some interest in readministering tests that were given twenty-five, fifty, seventy-five, or even one hundred years ago in order to see the changes that have taken place. The interpretation of the findings is always difficult. National Assessment was undertaken on the assumption that the findings would provide information about the quality of education, but there may well be far more powerful factors that influence the scores. For example, over the first six years of the use of National Assessment tests, there has been a decline in scores in the science area. This decline probably cannot be ascribed to a decline in the quality of science instruction, but is much more likely to be a result of the rejection of science and technology as a guide to life. There has even been a decline in interest in science at the college level and an increased interest in the humanities. Much more needs to be learned about the attitudes of children toward science and technology if the decline is to be understood. A comparison of the attitudes of children in areas of the country where science scores are high and where science scores are low would throw some light on this problem. National Assessment data might be used as a basis for such studies even though the National Assessment data is worth little in itself. There is an equally mysterious increase in the reading skills of children, which is also difficult to understand. This increase may be the result of improved methods of instruction, but equally plausible is the explanation that there is greater pressure from parents to develop reading skills in their children. Reading is an area in which conditions in the home seem to be far more crucial than what happens in school. The change in reading scores is all the more surprising in view of the fact that newspaper reading is on the decline. Much more needs to be known about the demands placed on children in the reading area. The uninterpretability of data from National Assessment presents a whole range of research challenges.

Evaluation in Open-Ended Education

The evaluation movement, beginning with the work at Ohio State University in the 1930s, looked upon education as a closed system. Objectives were established, educational programs were developed, data were collected to determine whether the programs achieved the objectives, and, where this did not happen, the program was changed in the hope that the modified program would achieve that which it was planned to achieve. Many have questioned this whole view of education, regarding it more as an open-ended exploration of the world and the self-development of means of coping with a complex environment. For those who take the latter view of education, the systematic type of evaluation study that has dominated research in the field is quite pointless. The Progressive Education Movement of the 1930s took this position, but nevertheless pointed out in its numerous works on curriculum that evaluation should be an integral part of the day-to-day routine of the classroom. In other words, value judgments should be made concerning the worth of the child's accomplishments and the child should be the one who should judge himself in this respect. This kind of evaluation is implicit in Jean Piaget's approach to education. The child is either satisfied with his solutions to problems or he becomes frustrated, perturbed, and in a state of disequilibrium, in which case he seeks out new solutions that restore his intellectual equilibrium. According to the latter point of view, intellectual development follows its own inexorable track regardless of what the program of the curriculum maker may be.

The search for outcomes, unguided by the use of objectives, presents some interesting problems. If two outsiders collected evidence related to the outcomes of a program, would they discover the same outcomes? Probably not! I remember watching a group of zealous operant psychologists running a nursery school program in which they handed out small marshmallows to those children who looked in the direction of the teacher. The psychologists insisted that they were teaching attentive behavior. My own suspicion was that they were teaching the children that this is an odd world in which one way to obtain a piece of candy is to look at the teacher. A pediatrician, who also viewed the program, decided that the children were learning to indulge themselves in unnecessary eating and that the main product of the program would be a group of overweight adolescents. Of course, all three opinions might have had a modicum of truth to them; data could have been collected to determine the extent to which each opinion was true.

A good place to begin open-ended evaluation studies may be to find out whether independent observers of the program can agree on what they expect the outcomes to be. The distinction should certainly be made between immediate outcomes and long-term outcomes since these may be substantially different.

Sometimes open-ended evaluations are performed by simply fishing for outcomes. I recall a teacher, who ran an excellent open classroom, who decided to give the Metropolitan Achievement Test to all the children in her class. This teacher did not subscribe to the educational philosophy represented by the test, being more concerned with both the child's ability to reason logically and the development of the child's values. Nevertheless, the teacher had the suspicion that the children were picking up a great deal of conventional subject matter and the giving of the test was an attempt to see how much subject matter they were picking up.

International Studies and Intercultural Studies

Numerous studies have been undertaken in recent years that compare the outcomes of education in different nations and different cultures. The international studies have been undertaken through the initiative of Torsten Husen. Some of the data developed by the International Project for the Evaluation of Educational Achievement located at the University of Stockholm is summarized in Husen's book (1974). Substantial support for the enterprise has come both from the United States government and from American psychologists, many of whom have played a central role in the studies. The data from the international studies are available for further analysis and can be readily obtained. The findings of the studies are intriguing curiosities, showing that school subjects, such as mathematics, which in some cultures are regarded as areas of knowledge that only a small elite can master, in other cultures are regarded as universal and necessary knowledge to be mastered by large proportions of the population. The latter view is, of course, in line with the position long taken by Jean Piaget that mathematics can be mastered by most children. The differences between countries in such outcomes is puzzling. Differences in teaching may well be a factor, but probably not the major factor. Cultures also differ in the extent to which they encourage learning in the young. Much more needs to be known about how these cultural factors work. What kinds of pressures do the Japanese exert on their children to produce so much learning of mathematics in their children? Such problems need to be investigated by those with backgrounds in anthropology and sociology.

Although the international studies have appeared as glamour projects, which governments were willing to finance generously, the end products have tended to present differences between countries that were so ill understood that the studies have remained little more than collections of odd and interesting facts. There have also been suspicions that the data themselves are far from being as valuable as they should be. The supervision of the collection of data across the world is an impossibly difficult undertaking. Even the collection of data in different parts of a single country presents difficulties that often makes it necessary to discard much of it because facts about the conditions of collection come to light that throw doubt upon its usefulness. Limits on tests are often not properly observed. All too often there is a subtle form of pupil selection that raises the mean score unduly. The children least likely to do well are excused from the testing for trivial reasons of health such as "You don't look well today, dear. Hadn't you better go home?" In order to make the data from different countries comparable, corrections have to be made and these are often little more than good guesses. As an illustration of this problem, take the case of comparing the high school mathematics performance in two countries, one of which has a school-leaving age of fourteen and the other a school-leaving age of eighteen. In the former, only a select few will pass through high school, but in the latter, most will go through high school. A comparison of the crude scores of seventeen-year-olds in these two countries would be a comparison of a highly select group with an unselected population in that age bracket. Statisticians can help us to adjust the data, but all adjustments involve making assumptions of various kinds that some might dispute. Indeed, there is no truly satisfactory way of making these adjustments in ways that do not involve assumptions that some will object to. International evaluation studies have even greater problems than evaluations conducted in the local community.

The international studies have been paralleled by cross-cultural studies in the United States comparing the intellectual abilities of white, black, and Chicano children. These studies are even more controversial than those in the international scene. Although the international studies focus on typical school achievements, those in the cross-cultural areas have been concerned mainly with measures referred to as aptitudes, which can be interpreted in many ways. Jensen (1974) interprets these aptitudes as basic components of innate intelligence, but others see them as forms of achievement that are not specifically linked to school learning. The nature of measured aptitudes remains obscure, and the results of such studies are highly controversial.

The issues raised by the Jensen studies are familiar, having been discussed for more than half a century. Today, as it was fifty years ago, there are a few who believe that these studies demonstrate inherent and genetic superiority of whites. Most psychologists would not draw such a conclusion and would most likely take the position that the source of the test score differences among racial groups cannot be determined at this time and that controversy with respect to the issue is of no value.

Studies in this area, like studies in the international field, are not to be encouraged, unless the research worker has a design that will permit him to determine the causes of particular differences in test scores.

Summary

1. Educational research ultimately focuses on problems related to learning in the classroom. Research on such problems has had a long history. Of particular historical importance are the studies undertaken by Ralph Tyler at Ohio State University in the 1930s. Tyler's task was that of developing techniques for evaluating pupil progress in a group of thirty schools.

2. Tyler initiated the procedure of defining objectives in terms of the behavior of those in whom the objective was achieved. This form of definition later became standard practice, though many now have reservations about its usefulness. Tyler and his associates developed a series of tests designed to measure various aspects of critical thinking. These tests were given in schools and the results were believed, by some, to support the practices of progressive education. The strategies developed in the Eight Year Study were later applied to many subsequent investigations. Tyler went on to extend his ideas to curriculum design and wrote his well-known monograph on the subject.

3. The developments initiated by Tyler later found an ally in the form of operant psychology, which also placed emphasis on defining objectives in terms of specific behaviors. Operant psychologists had had extensive experience in animal training activities in which they had attempted to analyze complex animal performance, to be learned, into simple components that could be taught by the well-known shaping procedures. Operant psychologists proposed to apply the same procedures for analyzing behavior to the analysis of human learning. Terminal behaviors were to be broken down into lists of prerequisite behaviors that were to be taught piece by piece. Gagné also proposed a similar analysis.

4. A related form of analysis was also applied in the case of studies of teacher behavior. Early studies of teacher behavior seemed to involve vague variables, so the new studies of the 1940s were to focus on specific aspects of teacher behavior. The early studies had not only been vague but they had manifested a number of basic defects including data contamination. The new generation of studies were to focus on specific teaching acts and were to relate these to student achievement. Despite the promise offered by the new generation of studies, they yielded little knowledge, and such studies ceased to appear for the next fifteen or 20 years.

5. In the years that followed, numerous new instruments were developed for conducting studies in the classroom. Many of these reflected excellent analyses of teaching in terms of particular theories. Many, of course, were thrown together without any great effort of thought. The chapter presented two instruments that reflected a worthwhile analysis of what teaching may involve. Very little has been done to exploit the use of such instruments for research, though many should be used as components of research

studies. The most widely used of all the instruments developed during this period was Flander's Interaction Analysis. This device was widely used because it is easy to apply and was the basis for probably hundreds of theses and dissertations. Nevertheless, the device represents only the most superficial analysis of teaching. There is little evidence that what it measures has much relationship to pupil learning, though it is related to the pupil's affective responses.

6. Later analyses of the relationship between the behavior of the teacher as recorded by observers, and pupil achievement led to the discovery of interesting relationships when all the data were put together. Broad and pervasive characteristics of the teacher seemed to be of much greater consequence than assessments of much more specific aspects of behavior. Ratings of such characteristics were related to pupil achievement in certain instances.

7. This discussion of teacher observation led to a consideration of the nature of the rating process. In the case of the rating of overall characteristics of behavior, that is to say, permeating characteristics, the rating process involves the weighting of many specifics within a composite. Raters do not know how they do this, and the process may vary somewhat from rater to rater.

8. The data extracted from studies of teacher behavior and its relationship to student achievement suggest that teacher education should attempt to develop in students of education these broad personality characteristics that seem to be important for helping pupils learn.

9. The final application of the Tyler approach, extended to the level of absurdity, is found in efforts of state departments of education to reduce objectives to thousands of specifics. Such a reduction of objectives may reflect a lack of understanding of the nature of the subject matter to be taught. Elementary arithmetic may involve the understanding of just a few important logical operations. A much more important matter is the discovery of means of representing the abstractions of mathematics in concrete terms. The reduction of mathematics to set theory, as has happened in the so-called new mathematics, also fails to identify the basic logic that the pupil has to master.

10. A new era of evaluation studies started in the 1960s, as a result of the money that was made available for this enterprise by the federal government. Interest in evaluation, manifested in the 1930s and 1940s, had died because evaluation studies could not produce the knowledge expected of them. Techniques had not advanced notably during the intervening years, and evaluation, as an enterprise, would not have come to life again so quickly had it not been for the availability of federal funds. The techniques available for appraising student progress provided the most solid information about the least important aspects of education. The new emphasis on standardized tests in schools in the 1970s brought with it all

of the problems that earlier testing programs had fostered. Such programs have always carried with them suspicions that there was some tampering with the measurement procedures, always for political purposes. The new programs showed the same evidence of tampering. The new programs of evaluation also failed to take account of the fact that the short-range measurement of achievement tells us little about what happens over the long haul. A reading program that produces a high level of learning in the early stages may have negative effects several years later. The new era of evaluation studies has produced prolific writing and some rethinking of what is involved. Much of the new thinking attempts to view evaluation studies as a part of a decision-making process. The new era of evaluation has developed its own vocabulary and also a large theoretical literature. The new effort to think through the problems involved is excellent, provided that nobody concludes that the problems have been solved. Instruments are still crude and little has been done to develop unobtrusive measures. Also, the vital matter of the long-term effect of educational programs still suffers from neglect. The federal government seems interested in funding studies that have to do with the immediate effects.

11. There are many new models for conducting evaluations. These models are guides to action rather than models in the scientific sense of the term. One model was presented, known as the C-I-P-P model, which seems to represent a good general procedure for planning evaluation studies. The letters in the name for this model represent the terms *context, input, process,* and *product.* The model is much like a mnemonic device, which tells one about some of the things to remember when one is conducting an evaluation study. In the past, most of those who have conducted evaluation studies have thought largely in terms of outcomes, that is to say, products, but other aspects of programs need to be studied and evaluated. One may find, for example, that the content of the textbooks in a particular program are unrelated to the outcomes as stated in the objectives. If that happens, product evaluation hardly seems necessary.

12. A major difficulty in using an evaluation study as the basis for making a decision is that most studies in the behavioral sciences, conducted for the first time, cannot be reproduced. Only a very unwise administrator would make an important decision on the basis of a single evaluation study. Perhaps he might consider the study as one small, and weak, piece of evidence. Also, the point must be made that most improvements in products in our society do not take place through product evaluation, but through inventions that make new products possible.

13. The National Assessment of Educational Progress is a controversial enterprise developed largely through federal sponsorship, though private foundations played a role in its initiation. The program has introduced the concept of objective-referenced tests, though whether there can be such tests is open to question. Just what the program can ever show, if any-

thing much, is open to conjecture. However, the data collected may be available for others to use. Scores on the tests used in the program reflect a complexity of conditions in our society. There will be real difficulties in determining the reasons why scores are increasing in one area, but declining in another.

14. Traditional approaches to education have assumed that education is a closed system, with instruction directed toward the achievement of certain objectives specified in advance. A part of education is like that, but some aspects of education represent an open system. One does not know what the outcomes will be or what opportunities the pupil will create for himself. Open-ended programs call for open-ended evaluations.

15. Studies of education across nations have also had incorporated in them evaluation components. The data from such studies are tantalizing in the differences they show between nations, but accounting for the differences is a much more difficult matter.

PART III
THE TECHNIQUES OF EDUCATIONAL RESEARCH

Up to this point, the discussion has focused on the nature of research and the kinds of problems that have occupied the efforts of educational researchers. Almost nothing has been said about the techniques and strategies of educational research, yet little can be accomplished by the would-be research worker unless these have been mastered. A parallel is found in the training of the musician. A person may know a great deal about music, but be unable to play an instrument because he has never mastered the techniques involved. The techniques of educational research are the intellectual tools that the research worker brings to his task. He must select the best technique for his purpose and know how to use it. Without research techniques he can no more undertake research than can an individual play a musical instrument without a mastery of the techniques of musicianship.

Techniques of educational research are the techniques of the behavioral and social sciences. The techniques may be such that they pertain to details of research or they may provide gross strategies. For example, there are techniques for developing measuring devices. These are techniques at the detailed level. There are also techniques related to the overall design of studies, once suitable instruments have been developed or have been obtained from those already available. We do not concern ourselves with instruments at the detail level, but rather devote our energies here to a study of the broad strategies. There are, for example, strategies or techniques related to the conduct and design of experiments. There are ways of designing experiments so that they have some chance of providing useful results. Most experiments involving behavior have some flaws in them. Those who understand experimental techniques will design them so that they contain no very obvious flaws. The reader may have been struck with the previous statement that all experiments contain flaws, but this is a matter that cannot be expanded upon at this time. Perhaps it is enough to say that when the first edition of this book was published, much less was known about the flaws in experimental design than we know today, and there are certainly flaws in educational experiments that have not yet been identified. Experiments that would have been acceptable twenty years ago may not be acceptable today.

Genuine experiments are often difficult to undertake in education so, fortunately, other techniques are available. The most widely used are survey techniques, which are also, however, the most widely misused. Here again many of the flaws in studies undertaken are easily identified, but others are not. Once again many flaws that were not fully recognized twenty years ago are well recognized today, and there are certainly other flaws that are not recognized at all. Progress has been made even though one can say, with some certainty, that survey methods are still crude in many respects. Unfortunately, the survey gives the appearance of being an easy approach to research, but it is not. Even the experts in conducting surveys, who sell their products to the newspapers, have been caught at times making serious errors in their designs, or their data have been contaminated by sources of error that even the experts do not understand. For example, in the famous Dewey versus Truman election, the polls showed Dewey winning. Even when a poll was repeated after the election asking how the individuals had voted, Dewey still won. Of course, Truman won the actual election.

A third area in which techniques for undertaking research have been extensively developed is the area of discovering means of making predictions. Oddly enough, prediction studies have often been looked down upon by scientists because they do not seem to have the same potential as experimental studies for advancing knowledge. Yet prediction studies are of vital interest, and in some areas have the potential of providing information of the greatest consequence. Studies of problems of prediction have been undertaken outside of education and are continuing in such vital areas as earthquake prediction, weather prediction, and disease epidemic prediction. Some of these studies have added greatly to our knowledge of natural phenomena. In the case of weather prediction, studies have developed an entire theory of factors that control weather changes and a general theory of climate. Earthquake prediction studies have led to a better understanding of the nature of the earth's crust. Prediction studies in education, designed to discover who is most likely to succeed in particular programs, have contributed much to the development of testing devices. Prediction studies are very practically oriented but they usually do have a spin-off in the production of knowledge of a theoretical nature, though such studies sometimes have a strong tie to theory. A particular theoretical position may lead one to believe that a particular prediction is possible. If the prediction can be made, then the theoretical position is validated. For example, the theory that the position of high-level jet streams of air determine climate over long periods has led scientists to expect that changes in climate will result from changes in these jet streams. Thus, when changes in the jet stream have occurred, scientists have predicted changes in the climate over considerable periods. Such long-term forecasts have been shown to be quite accurate and have validated the theory that the jet streams are important determinants of climate. Theories of prediction of achievement in education have a potential for contributing knowledge to the conditions that make for success or failure in these programs.

CHAPTER 9
The Conduct of Experiments

The scientific experiment has become the most prestigious method of advancing scientific knowledge, though much knowledge has been acquired by techniques other than that of the experiment. Different areas of knowledge, such as astronomy and geology, have developed as sciences through the accumulation of knowledge by nonexperimental techniques. Nevertheless, the experiment is still a technique of very special importance in the advancement of knowledge.

All humans are natural experimenters. Indeed, Jean Piaget has collected observations to show that even children as young as two years of age may do experiments, of a kind. Piaget noted that when a child aged two throws an object on the floor, he will watch the results with the closest attention. When the object is given back to the child, he is likely to throw it down again, but this time he will throw it harder or less hard, or perhaps in a different direction. The throw is again followed by the deepest concentration on the results. He will continue to throw down the object again and again, as often as the object is retrieved for him. The infant is concerned with varying the way in which the object is thrown and then seeing what happens. The infant is an experimenter, and the results of his experiments give him a knowledge of the world necessary for understanding how common events take place. The scientist conducting an experiment conducts his enterprise at a rather more sophisticated level than the infant, but the essence is the same. The scientist varies some condition and watches for the effect. There are also certain other basic differences between what the scientist does in conducting an experiment and what the infant does. The scientist is generally interested in adding to a public body of knowledge, whereas the infant is adding to his own personal knowledge. The scientist records what he finds, but the infant is satisfied with general impressions. The scientist also introduces a number of checks to help keep him from jumping to faulty conclusions. Nevertheless, despite these differences, one must recognize that the experimental method is one that has been used by the human race for hundreds of thousands of years. Scientists have merely refined this powerful way of extending knowledge.

Credit for the basic refinement of this basic way of achieving knowledge is generally attributed to Galileo, who was interested in refuting an idea originally advanced by Aristotle that large bodies fell more rapidly than small bodies. Galileo's famous experiment involving the dropping of bodies from the top of the Leaning Tower of Pisa was a first attempt to study this problem. The Pisa experiment left much to be desired as a scientific investigation. For one thing, the bodies fell so fast and time measurements were so crude that it was not at all clear what the demonstration showed. The experiment was, in fact, little more sophisticated than some of the experiments undertaken by the children that Piaget observed. Nevertheless, Galileo continued to ponder the problem, but it was not until nearly twenty years after the original Pisa experiment that he came up with a new experimental approach that was to provide a milestone in the history of science. Galileo had the idea of slowing up the rate at which bodies fell by using balls rolling down an inclined plane. Galileo could make the rate of descent as slow as he wanted by making the slope of the plane less steep.

In this simple form of experiment Galileo had done something very important. He had discovered that one way to acquire knowledge is to use a grossly simplified situation. This is what all scientists have done in their laboratories since the time of Galileo. Objects falling naturally in space, like the stones pushed off the Tower of Pisa, do not provide very good situations for gaining knowledge. Such situations are often too complicated and not subject to good controls. Galileo could control all kinds of conditions when he rolled balls down the plane, and he could make sure that his results were not influenced by such factors as the wind on the particular day. The balls could also descend slowly enough so that they could be easily timed against the ticking of a clock.

The tremendous advantages of Galileo's form of experimentation were not immediately appreciated. Indeed, it was not until at least 200 years later that there was any real understanding among the world of scholars of the extraordinary invention related to experimental method that Galileo had made. One perhaps may even say that today much of the world of education does not yet appreciate the advantages of experimenting under simplified and controlled conditions, for experiments in schools, under natural conditions, are still the order of the day. The tendency in schools of education has often been to ridicule laboratory experimentation on the grounds that it is "ivory tower" and remote from reality. That was one of the criticisms leveled against Galileo in his day.

There is no single, simple formula for conducting experiments under controlled conditions, and those who followed Galileo have produced many variations of the theme he started. Many so-called experiments of great historical importance would be thought of today as being more demonstrations than experiments after the pattern of Galileo. For example, the famous demonstration of Henry Cavendish undertaken in the eighteenth century showed that when oxygen and hydrogen were combined in proper proportions, all that was left was a small residue of water. Cavendish showed that it required twice as much hydrogen as oxygen, by volume, to make the combination with only water as a residue, and thus established that water is composed of oxygen and hydrogen. Cavendish's demonstration was an experiment in that it was known that other quantities of oxygen or hydrogen left a residue of one gas or the other. Cavendish demonstrated the precision with which the two elements had to be present in order to leave no residue.

Most textbooks on chemistry that refer to the work of Cavendish refer to his demonstrations as *experiments*. Some modern students of the behavioral sciences also refer to demonstrations of behavioral phenomena as experiments. For example, Jean Piaget has shown that when four-year-olds are shown a ball of clay and the ball is rolled out to form a thick sausage, the four-year-olds insist that there is now more clay. When the same demonstration is repeated with eight-year-olds, these older children show they understand that the quantity of clay does not change as its shape changes. The experiment is not like most experiments in that the one factor that is altered in the two demonstrations is the age of the children, and yet age is not the crucial underlying variable. What is crucial is the child's ability to conserve the volume of the clay and to understand that shape may have nothing to do with quantity. Piaget's writings contain very large numbers of such demonstrations of basic ways in which the child develops an understanding of the world around him. They are highly reproducible. Indeed, they are as reproducible as Cavendish's experiment involving the combination of oxygen and hydrogen to form water. Modern behavioral science in America, which conceives of an experiment as involving the study of the effect of varying one condition on another condition, is not likely to view the demonstration of Piaget as representing experiments, yet much of the scientific world does regard them as experiments and sees them as belonging to the scientific experimental tradition.

Some of the most important moments in the history of science have involved demonstrations. One can count among these moments John Priestly's demonstrations that oxygen is a gas involved in combustion, Newton's demonstration that white light is composed of components of different colors, and J. J. Thompson's demonstration of subatomic particles. The student may be overwhelmed by these examples, and yet there are examples of graduate students, and even undergraduate students, developing demonstrations of important phenomena. For example, Fantz (1958) demonstrated that infants shortly after birth are selective in what they look at, surely a remarkable phenomenon. Kohlberg (1958), while still a student, produced demonstrations of basic phenomena in the moral judgment of children. Other examples could also be given. Identifying what are the very important phenomena in a field of study is a very basic activity. All too often we engage in research without really knowing what the important phenomena are. Perhaps no student should be discouraged from trying to identify, and demonstrate the important phenomena

of, an area, even though the task is difficult. Students may be encouraged
by the idea that one such enterprising student at Oberlin College, Charles
Martin Hall, succeeded in demonstrating how aluminum could be produced and then went on to found the Aluminum Company of America.
Perhaps the reader too can undertake a study that will demonstrate a
phenomenon of fundamental importance in the behavioral sciences, but
it would probably be better for him to undertake a more conventional
study or experiment as a thesis or dissertation.

Conventional American Experiments

In the conventional experiment in American behavioral research, a particular condition is manipulated, that is to say, varied by the experimenter,
and the effects of this manipulation are first recorded in some way and
then studied. When Galileo rolled balls down an inclined plane, he varied
(or manipulated as we say today) the size of the balls and the weight of
the balls. His purpose was to be able to infer whether large and heavy
bodies fell more rapidly than smaller bodies of the same density. In a
modern behavioral science one might be interested in determining whether
the size of the reward made a difference to the rate of learning. In such an
experiment one might use such a task as learning the vocabulary of a
foreign language. A randomly selected group might be given five cents
for each word learned correctly, under the experimental conditions, and
another randomly selected group might be given ten cents. Otherwise the
two groups would be treated identically so that one could say that other
things were equal except for the size of the reward. In all experiments one
has to be able to say that, apart from the experimental conditions, other
things are equal. The other-things-are-equal concept is one of crucial importance in designing all experiments.

Let us discuss again the little experiment on the effect of the size of
rewards. This kind of study has been undertaken many times in laboratories
with undergraduates as the guinea pigs. When such studies are undertaken
in the laboratory, the materials used are very carefully selected, the words
to be learned are presented through some mechanical device in a systematic
way, the amount of time involved in the task is carefully controlled, and
so forth. That is why a laboratory setting is so useful. One can control many
conditions that might influence the outcome of the experiment.

Experiments do not have to be undertaken in laboratories. The same
kind of experiment might be undertaken in classroom settings. Indeed,
educators have a preference for undertaking experiments in classroom
settings arguing that if one wants to know how to influence learning in the
classroom, then one should undertake experiments in the classroom. Of
course, as soon as the experiment is undertaken in the classroom setting

one finds that numerous conditions are not equal for the groups that are paid differently for learning. One cannot usually assume that the two groups are selected at random from a pool of students. The morale of the children in one room may be much higher than that in another room. Indeed, the pupils in one classroom may be reluctant to learn anything at all, having been demoralized by the teacher. Often the experimenter who wishes to undertake an experiment in a school setting may give up in despair for other things are not equal. Indeed, conditions in the two groups available for the experiment may be clearly, and all too obviously, different.

When Galileo decided to study falling bodies by means of bodies moving down inclined planes, he had a logical and rational argument underlying this procedure. A simple mathematical function related events in the inclined-plane situation to events in the free-falling-body situation. In contrast, in the behavioral sciences in general and in the educational branch of these sciences in particular, such well-established relationships between the laboratory phenomenon and the out-of-the-laboratory phenomenon do not exist. Such relationships as do exist can be expressed in words that are vague in comparison to the mathematical relationships characteristically found in physics.

This means that the procedure for applying the laboratory generalizations of the behavioral sciences must involve much more caution than is necessary in the physical sciences. This does not mean that the physical scientist is never wrong in his applications, for he is, but because of the rigorous nature of his deductions he is less likely to be wrong than is the behavioral scientist. The rationale of the physical scientist can be wrong, and it often fails to take into account factors that influence large-scale phenomena but do not influence events in the test tube. For this reason, large scale manufacturing plants are sometimes failures although the small pilot plant was a success.

In spite of the risk that generalizations derived from laboratory experiments may not be applicable to real-life problems, many scientists believe that this should not deter us from experimentation with educational problems on a laboratory basis.

Apart from the obvious advantages of laboratory experimentation that have been discussed, many phenomena simply are not amenable to study under the conditions in which they are ordinarily observed. This does not mean that all educational phenomena can be studied with advantage under laboratory conditions, because many are not amenable to such investigations. For example, if the researcher were interested in the effect of neurotic behavior of the teacher on pupil behavior, he would not use a laboratory approach, because psychologists generally hold the opinion that the main effect of the teacher's neurotic behavior is observed after pupils have been subjected to it over substantial periods of time. In the laboratory, we could not and would not expose individuals to neurotic behavior over several months or years. Such matters must be studied in educational situations as they occur.

The essence of a scientific experiment, that one condition is manipulated while other conditions are equal, is easy to understand. In educational research we can only approximate that condition. If we were to undertake a study involving the exposure of students to two different learning conditions, we would assign our students at random to the one or the other learning situation. We might follow the simple procedure of assigning the first student who came to the one condition, the second student to the other condition, and so forth. This would be called a procedure of random assignment. Our hope would be that the students in the one group would be very much like the students in the other group, but that is not exactly the way it would work out. Almost certainly one would find that the one group included slightly more capable learners than the other, or perhaps one group might have slightly better motivated students. Other things would not be equal, at least not quite equal as one would want. This fact tends to cloud the results. The results would be particularly clouded if the group that was expected to do best, in terms of our hypothesis or expectations, not only performed the best but also included the ablest and best motivated students. This becomes bothersome when the actual difference in the result of the two different learning conditions is small. When we are faced with this situation, we don't have to throw up our hands and conclude that the results are uninterpretable. We can use statistical methods for the analysis of our results, which take into account the fact that other things are not strictly equal. However, the research worker should not expect statistical methods to clear up the muddy waters of poorly designed experiments. Statistical methods can help when there are unavoidable ways in which other things are not equal, but they are not a universal cure-all.

The student undertaking research should also reflect on the fact that if differences are so unclear and small that they tend to be shrouded by other effects, then they may not be of consequence. An important task of the research worker is to identify conditions of importance. A meteorologist might find that the smoke from a neighboring town increases local rainfall, but this finding is not important if the increase is less than 1 per cent. Too much educational research focuses on effects that are small, but real, yet so small that they are quite inconsequential.

The educational researcher often has to depart from the basic rules of experimental design because administrative conditions restrict what he can do. For example, the research worker may want to assign pupils at random to different groups to be exposed to different teaching materials. However, the school may say that the researcher cannot do this, because the children are already assigned to classes. The research worker cannot then do a true experiment though he may do a study that comes close to being an experimental study. Such studies are called quasi-experiment. This term has been widely used since it was first introduced by Cambell and Stanley (1963). The essential difference between a genuine experiment and a quasi-experiment lies in the fact that, in the genuine experiment, the different conditions to which the different groups are exposed are assigned at random to the groups. On the other hand, in the quasi-experiment the conditions are taken as they are found in naturally occurring situations. The difference may appear to be a small one, but it is actually immense. The genuine experiment, for logical reasons, necessarily yields more certain knowledge than the quasi-experiment and, whenever possible, should be undertaken in preference to the quasi-experiment.

Cambell and Stanley (1966) make a distinction between quasi-experiments and pseudoexperiments. They cite as examples of a pseudoexperiment the early studies in which it was shown that pupils who studied Latin knew more about English than those who did not. The fact that the pupils taking Latin differed from those who did not take Latin, perhaps even before they entered school, was not taken into account; but it inevitably biases the outcome. Even if such differences prior to the study of Latin were taken into account, this would not overcome the fact that while the one group was studying Latin it was also probably enjoying cultural advantages to which the non-Latin group was not exposed. Although we should distinguish between quasi-experimental and pseudoexperimental studies, there is a big gray area where the two overlap.

There are those who raise the cry "Artificiality!" when the proposal is made that studies be conducted under the grossly simplified conditions of the typical laboratory experiment. This criticism should be evaluated in terms of the fact that most of our knowledge of the highly complex events of the physical world has been derived from the study of simplified events that the scientist has studied in the laboratory. The study of simplified phenomena under artificial conditions has been a highly successful technique in developing useful knowledge.

Complex Variations in Experiments

We have considered the simplest form of the experiment, namely, that in which a single condition is varied and the effect of this variation is determined. More complex plans for experiments are possible in which several factors are varied. The multifactor type of design was first invented by Fisher while he was working in the field of experimental agriculture. Within such a multifactor design the effect of each factor can be sorted out from the others through the use of statistical procedures. These multifactor designs can be applied to any field, but they are most commonly encountered in research areas where already much is known, such as agriculture. In less sophisticated areas, the experimenter may have difficulty in identifying one variable that seems to be important, let alone several.

The Need for a Cautious Approach to Experimentation

Experimentation is the most powerful method for deriving knowledge that has any certainty of validity; hence, it should be vigorously pursued. Nevertheless, experimentation is one of the more difficult methods to pursue successfully. It is, therefore, necessary to consider in detail all the common difficulties that experimental studies are likely to encounter. This is likely to give the student the impression that the difficulties of experimentation are so many and so widespread that the new researcher should simply avoid experimental studies. Such an inference should not be drawn; rather, the reader should take the approach that once he is forewarned of the difficulties commonly encountered, he is well equipped to design productive experimental studies.

Even though it is commonly said that experimentation is the path by which a science advances, this should not be taken to mean that it is the only one. Most of the major figures who have advanced science in the last hundred years have not been notable as experimentalists. Einstein never carried out a major experiment, and neither did Darwin or Freud. Although experimental workers have checked many of the deductions of Einstein, these experiments followed rather than preceded major advances. To a considerable extent, experiments serve to consolidate advances already made, rather than make advances in and of themselves. Priestley's experimental studies of combustion served to demonstrate to the scientific world what he already was sure was true. Much classic experimentation serves the purpose of demonstrating to the world at large what the scientist already knows to be the case. The moral to be drawn is perhaps summarized by the statement that although thought without experimentation may be productive, experimentation without thought is futile. In other words, when the student embarks on an experiment, it is assumed that he is checking some aspect of a well-thought-out theory, which may be his own or somebody's else's.

There is also doubt (see Gadlin and Ingle, 1975) whether experimentation in the behavioral sciences is comparable to experimentation in physics or in chemistry. It is not uncommon for participants in experiments in the behavioral sciences to try to produce the results that the experimenter wants, particularly if the experimenter is a likeable person who is known to the participants. Of course, what the participants believe to be "good" results may not be at all what the experimenter expects to see happen. Experimenters are supposed to be completely objective and completely indifferent to how their experiments turn out. In fact, experimenters are human and may be prejudiced into hoping that results they obtain will come out in a particular way. Participants are sensitive to the cues in the experimenter's behavior that indicate to them that the experimenter prefers some outcomes rather than others. After the first few subjects are run the word may even be passed around among those who are to be subjects that the game in the experimental situation should be played in a particular way. In contrast, molecules do not tell one another what they believe the chemist wants, which simplifies the task of the chemist. The existence of this factor has often induced psychologists to work with animals, particularly laboratory animals, although this does not entirely eliminate experimenter expectancy effects. The breeds selected by laboratory psychologists for experimentation are those that are likely to conform to the experimenter's expectation of how an experimental animal should behave in the situation. Some psychologists, such as Kruglanski (1976), do not think that such criticisms of behavioral experiments are relevant.

Barber (1973) has made many suggestions concerning how these kinds of experimenter effects can be, to some degree, controlled. One suggestion is for there to be several experimenters, that is to say several different individuals who actually engage in the collection of data. Another proposal is to minimize contact between the experimenter and the participants in the experiment by having automated methods of giving instructions, recording data, and so forth. Barber does stress the fact that none of these proposals completely eliminates the influence of the experimenter on the outcomes.

This discussion has been on deficiencies of experiments with humans that cannot be adequately remedied at this time. Let us now turn to some of those deficiencies that can be remedied.

Some Difficulties in Undertaking Experiments

Let us now examine some of the major difficulties encountered in developing experimental studies, realizing that well-designed experiments can be carried out by the student who is aware of the common pitfalls.

A description of how to conduct experiments has to be written in a negative tone because they are numerous pitfalls to avoid and few positive rules to follow. In the behavioral sciences even well-established research workers often conduct experiments that have to be redesigned and redone later because the original version was shown to include a fundamental flaw. One can even trace the development of the design of some lines of experimentation over a period of fifty or more years and see the slow elimination of poor aspects of the design. Studies of concept learning, for example, have shown a gradual evolution of design that makes present-day procedures much more effective in providing clear answers to questions than were the early procedures of nearly half a century ago. Sometimes even prolonged effort does not eliminate all of the snags and snares in experimental procedures. For example, decades of experimental work have been involved in attempts to design an experiment to determine whether learning in a motor task can occur without reinforcement. Although some of the outstanding experimental psychologists have tackled this problem of design, it has not been solved. Whatever the design involved, some ingenious person always manages to suggest some subtle way in which reinforcement is occurring. Problems of experimental design are not readily solved, and some may be virtually insoluble.

Problems of design are studied not only by experimental scientists but also by mathematical statisticians, who view them from a rather different standpoint in terms of the logic they involve. The problems of experimental design studied by mathematical statisticians are considerably different from those considered here, for they revolve largely around the efficiency of experimental design. This concept of efficiency is related to the matter of planning experiments so that the maximum amount of information is obtained from a given number of observations. Problems of experimental design in this sense of the term are briefly considered in the following chapter, which is planned to make the student of education sensitive to such problems and to perhaps encourage him to study further.

The student should also be sensitive to certain difficulties in experimentation in the behavioral sciences that are largely a product of the type of events studied. These difficulties are rarely discussed in books on experimental design because such works are usually written by statisticians who are unfamiliar with common flaws in the mechanics of actual experimentation. It requires experimentation in the field to become aware of these difficulties, which are not necessarily a product of the logic of the design.

Flaws that have been commonly observed in experimentation in education are now discussed, although there are undoubtedly many others that occur with less frequency.

Deficiency in design as a result of failure to include a control group. This is the most elementary of all deficiencies in experimental design. A principal wished to find out how much progress his fourth-graders had made in social studies as a result of the curriculum offered. He was able to find a published test that seemed to measure the achievement of objectives of social studies stressed by the fourth-grade teachers, and he administered the test at both the beginning and the end of the school year. He was pleased to find that the group made as much progress as that shown by the norm group described in the manual for the test. What the principal did not know was that pupils who did not study material related to the content of the test made just as great a gain in score over the year as the pupils whose achievement was being evaluated. Experimental design always involves the establishment of conditions such that a comparison can be made between the effects of two or more conditions. Where the second condition is absent, the results become uninterpretable.

Deficiency produced by the experimental procedure generating the results. This deficiency is somewhat similar to that previously discussed. One should make sure that the experimental procedure itself does not introduce increments in score that can be carelessly attributed to the experimental treatment. An example is necessary in order to illustrate this error in experimental design. Ballard (1913) performed a well-known experiment in which he assigned schoolchildren the task of learning poetry. At the end of the learning period, the children were asked to write out as much as they could remember of the poem. Ballard returned to the school the next day and asked the children to write out once more all they could remember of the poem. He was surprised to find that on the second occasion, the children were able to recall more of the poem than they had on the first occasion. This apparent increment in learning, after formal learning had supposedly ceased, became known as the *phenomenon of reminiscence,* and for forty years it was described in textbooks on education and learning as a genuine phenomenon. However, information that is now available indicates that reminiscence is probably a product of faulty experimental design. The error lies in the fact that the procedure used to measure retention immediately after the learning session is itself a learning experience, which increases the scores achieved on subsequent measures of retention. Ammons and Irion (1954) performed an experiment in which groups were given poetry to learn. Some were tested immediately after learning and also after an interval of time, whereas others were tested only after an interval of time. Only those groups that were tested immediately after learning showed the apparent phenomenon of reminiscence. The groups tested only after an interval of time produced average scores no greater than the average of the groups tested immediately after learning. This study suggests strongly that the supposed phenomenon of reminiscence is a product of faulty experimental design.

Various designs that can be used routinely have been suggested to take care of this hazard. One that has been suggested makes use of four experimental and control groups and can be used generally for determining the effect of a particular learning condition. The four groups used in this design, denoted by the letters A, B, C, and D, are exposed to four different schedules as follows:

Group A	learning experience,	test,	retest
Group B		test,	retest
Group C	learning experience,		retest
Group D			retest

Only Group A is administered the entire series of tests and learning experience. The remaining groups are administered only varying portions of the schedule. In this way the experimenter can determine whether some irrelevant aspect of the experiment is producing any increment from test to retest in Group A.

A similar design can be used when the experimenter is interested in a change in performance that can be attributed to a particular learning experience. Such a design would be applicable, for example, in the case where the research worker was interested in finding out whether a formal course in rapid-reading skills actually made a change in the reading skills of, say, tenth-graders. The design would be as follows:

Group A	pretest,	reading instruction,	post-test
Group B	pretest,		post-test
Group C		reading instruction,	post-test
Group D			post-test

A gain from pretest to post-test scores might be found in Group A, and one might be tempted to jump to the conclusion that the gain could be attributed to the instruction given in reading. However, if Group B were to manifest a similar gain, then one might well suspect that it could be attributed only to the fact that the students learned from the pretest how to take such tests and this knowledge improved performance on the post-test. This conclusion would be confirmed further if Groups C and D showed lower post-test scores. Group D adds further information because it can indicate whether the post-test is particularly easy or difficult in comparison with the pretest and which, hence, may show gains in scores that are only artifacts.

Deficiency produced by contamination of data. Many experimental designs give spurious results because of spurious elements. For example, a scientist was interested in discovering the abilities related to talent in a course in creative writing. As a part of his study, he administered a battery of tests of creativity to the students at the beginning of the semester and planned to study the relationship between these test scores and measures of the characteristics of their written products during the course. The tests were scored, and the researcher discussed these scores with the instructor in the course in order to obtain cues concerning the relationship of the tests to creative talent—but this was an unfortunate mistake. What it did was to open the possibility that the instructor's evaluations of the students' writing might be influenced by his knowledge of their creativity test scores. The data provided by the instructor concerning the students and their creative product was contaminated by his knowledge of their scores on the tests of creativity.

Contamination is one of the most common errors of educational research design that render data uninterpretable. Such contamination is often difficult to identify and may pass unnoticed. One of many reasons why research plans should receive independent review is so that such factors can be identified.

The research worker's expectation of how data should appear may also contaminate the outcomes of research in many subtle ways. On one occasion, a graduate student was administering to subjects a complex perceptual task involving the use of complex equipment. After the task had been administered to two subjects, the graduate assistant looked at his data and found that they were far from what was expected. He soon noted that a switch that should have been turned on had been left in the "off" position. After he had remedied this defect in the procedure, the subjects began to behave according to expectation. The fact that he found an error in the procedure and remedied it was entirely to the good, but suppose the data from the first two subjects had been according to expectation. In the latter case the entire set of data might have been collected and interpreted as if they had been collected under the conditions that were supposed to exist in the experiment. What this means is that errors of procedure tend to be caught only when the data run contrary to expectation. The net effect of this is that experimenters tend to produce data that fit their expectations.

Deficiency that results from making unwarranted assumptions about the nature of the scales used. The most common examples in education of designs that manifest this error are those involving the use of growth scores. For example, a researcher set up the hypothesis that teachers who introduced into their classes rewarding comments (such as, "That's good, Billy") produced greater gains in pupil knowledge of social studies than those who did not. This study was to be conducted in sixth-grade classes in a large school system in which the teachers follow a rather rigidly prescribed social studies curriculum. The general plan of the study was to administer equated forms of a social studies test at the beginning and end of the sixth grade, and to correlate average gains in scores for each class with the observed frequency of rewarding comments occurring during visitation periods. If the researcher were not aware of the central defect of this design in the early stages of his work, it would probably become apparent in the later stages, when it becomes evident that some classes had greater knowledge at the beginning of the sixth grade than others had at the end. Even though some increased their average scores from, say, thirty to fifty correct items, others increased their average scores from fifty-five to seventy-five. These two increases are numerically equal and according to the design of the study should be treated as equal, but the equality of these two increments must be considered an unjustifiable assumption. As a matter of fact, there may be reasons for believing that the one increment is much more difficult to achieve than the other in terms of the time and effort required. Also, the two increments may differ qualitatively, in that the one may be achieved by bright students whereas the other is achieved by dull students. The two increments cannot be considered comparable, and studies assuming that they are should not be designed. Such studies will provide results that are uninterpretable.

Deficiency that results when relevant variables are confounded with irrelevant variables. This is one of the more obvious errors of experimental design. The meaning of the term *confounded* can perhaps be best explained by means of an illustration. A researcher wished to study the effectiveness of flash cards in the teaching of reading. In order to do this, sixty first-grade pupils were given a reading readiness test. They were divided into two matched groups such that for each pupil in one group there was a corresponding pupil in the other group who had the same reading readiness score and who was of the same age and sex. Both groups used the same readers and workbooks, but the teacher of one group devoted time to the use of flash cards each day whereas the other teacher did not. At the end of six months the reading skills of both groups were measured, and the relative achievements of the two groups were compared. However, this comparison was quite meaningless, because any advantages attained by one group over the other might as easily have been a product of differences in teachers as a product of differences in method (flash cards versus no flash cards). It could be said of this situation that differences in teachers were *confounded* with differences in method, so that any differences in the two groups could not be attributed to the one or the other. It is imperative that such confounding of the main conditions be avoided.

Various procedures could be adopted to remedy the technical defect in this experiment. One would be to use the same teacher for both groups, but this introduces another difficulty: the teacher may be in favor of using flash cards and his prejudice may influence the results in some subtle way. Another procedure is to have several different teachers use the one method in their classes and another different group of teachers use the alternative method. In this way, differences in teachers could be expected to average out. Statistical methods exist that permit one to estimate the extent to which the resulting difference between the two methods of teaching can be considered to be reliable and not just a result of differences between the teachers involved.

Deficiency resulting from sampling by groups and not by individuals. Somewhat related to the error described previously is this sampling problem. Consider the spurious design involved in a study in which the effects of two methods of teaching reading were compared. In this study, the researcher selected six second-grade classes from one school that agreed to use Method A, and six second-grade classes from another school that were to use Method B. The researcher drew the unjustified conclusion that the results showed that Method A was superior to Method B on the basis of the fact that, although both groups had closely similar initial scores on a reading test, the final scores for Group A were substantially higher than those for Group B. The conclusion was not justified because there might have been differences between the two schools other than those in teaching methods. Differences in socioeconomic level or social status of the two school populations might alone lead one to anticipate that differences in rate of learning to read would be found. In this experiment differences in treatment in which the researcher was interested were confounded with other differences. This is similar to the deficiencies previously discussed, but it can be remedied without adding additional cases.

The basic defect in the design could have been remedied by the simple procedure of dividing the six classes in each school into two groups, one of which would have been exposed to Method A and the other to Method B. In this improved design, it would be possible to estimate differences between methods within each of the schools and to estimate the differences between schools regardless of method. Assigning individuals at random to treatments rather than groups to treatments will always avoid this flaw.

Deficiency as a result of insufficient cases. One of the most elementary errors in experimental design results from failure to include a sufficient number of cases, but no simple rule can be given to guide the student in this respect. Part of the difficulty stems from the fact that when very small differences between groups exist (in relation to their internal variation), more cases are needed to demonstrate the difference rather than when relatively large differences are involved. Much also depends on the nature of the experimental design used, for some designs are much more sensitive than others in identifying small differences.

However, quantity can never make up for quality in the collection of data. The researcher is always better off with a few carefully made observations than with large quantities of observations made under varying conditions and of doubtful reproducibility.

If very large numbers of observations have to be made in order to obtain a reasonably accurate estimate of a difference, then it is doubtful whether a difference of that particular magnitude is large enough or consequential enough for the researcher to spend his time in further studies of the phenomenon. The author's own prejudice, which he follows in his work, is that if a difference between two treatments is not clearly apparent when each treatment is applied to fifty cases, then the phenomenon is one of small consequence. Certainly phenomena for investigation that provide for clear-cut results of the type sought can be found quite easily.

Deficiency in design as a result of failure to take subject bias into account. In most situations, there is a tendency for human subjects to behave in a way that they feel is expected of them. Thus, in a classic experiment in which a group was singled out for observation in a factory, it was found that any variation in the conditions of work produced an increase in output, which remained even after the original conditions were restored. Groups singled out for study in schools are likely to learn more than groups not thus identified. For this reason, in any educational experiment where there is an experimental group and a control, both groups should feel equally singled out, or better still, both groups should be unaware of the fact that they are participating in an experiment. For this reason, in experiments with drugs, one group receives the drug to be tested whereas the other receives a placebo that looks and tastes exactly like the drug. Both groups are kept in ignorance of the fact that some received the drug and some did not.

Deficiency produced through the lack of well-developed experimental techniques. A student may decide to conduct an experiment on a significant problem before establishing whether suitable experimental techniques are available. This error is very common among graduate students. Because the development of experimental techniques is a painstaking endeavor often requiring long and sustained effort, such students are likely to find themselves engaged in a project requiring much more time than the thesis or dissertation ordinarily demands. The graduate student should choose an experimental research in an area in which well-worked-out techniques already exist.

The history of experimental studies shows that the development of an experimental technique for the study of an important problem has often sparked a long train of related studies. For example, when Ebbinghaus developed a series of experimental techniques involving the use of nonsense syllables, he made it possible to study problems of memory that had never been amenable to study before. The approaches he used are still the basis for much research. Even in those sciences that have had a longer period of rapid advance than has psychology, a single important technique may have had an equally significant long-term effect.

The student who is conducting his first research and who is intrigued by experimental approaches to problems would be wise to choose an area for study in which there are already well-developed laboratory techniques. Although his time would be well spent on the development of a new technique, such an enterprise is not generally considered appropriate for a dissertation or thesis.

Deficiency as a result of planning studies in which rare events form the crucial aspects of the data. An experimental design is not likely to be feasible if it is built around a rare type of event. An example from outside the field of education provides an illustration of a type of problem familiar to the reader. During the early days of the development of antipoliomyelitis serums, experiments were carried out in an attempt to determine the value of various experimental serums. In some of the first experiments, approximately 20,000 pupils were randomly assigned to two groups. One group was given the experimental serum, whereas the other was administered a placebo. At the end of the season, when the incidence of polio in the general population had fallen to its lowest ebb, the number of cases of polio in the two groups was counted. In such an experiment, it might have been found that in the inoculated group there had occurred six cases and in the placebo group ten cases. Although this difference is numerically large, it can be accounted for in terms of the differences one might expect if many samples of 10,000 cases each had been administered the placebo. In the conduct of such research, it soon became quite obvious that what appeared to be large samples were inadequate for the purposes at hand; and it was necessary, as the reader will remember, ultimately to use samples of as many as 300,000 cases in both the experimental and the control group.

Again, suppose it were planned to introduce a safety program into the elementary schools of a small city. It might be proposed that steps be taken to evaluate the effectiveness of the program by excluding half the elementary schools from it and then by comparing the traffic-accident figures for these schools during a semester with those for the schools that had the safety program. The weakness of the design is that too few children are likely to be involved in traffic accidents for the comparison to be statistically meaningful.

Deficiency in design resulting from the experimental procedure itself affecting the conditions to be observed. A serious difficulty in educational research results from the fact that the process to be observed is often changed beyond all recognition by the mere process of observation. The description and recording of events within the classroom presents this problem in an acute form. We can no longer accept the notion, based on wishful thinking, that the introduction of an observer into the classroom does not affect events therein, for clearly it does. Indeed, some have suggested that it just may not be possible to study the events in the classroom under the conditions that ordinarily prevail. They have likened the situation to the Heisenberg principle in physics, which states that both the position and the velocity of certain particles cannot be determined at the same time. These difficulties of conducting classroom studies seem to be insuperable at the present time, but it must not be assumed that they do not exist.

Experiments That Yield Qualitative Data

Some forms of experiment yield qualitative data, that is to say, data that are not easily converted into scores. Some highly influential series of experiments have assumed this form. For example, the classic series of experiments undertaken by Wolfgang Kohler on chimpanzees were of this character. Kohler studied how chimpanzees solved problems and how the conditions of problem solving determined the kinds of solutions that were produced. The data thus derived are descriptive, but they represent a starting point from which hundreds of later studies began. Even a modern book on the psychology of problem solving would discuss Kohler's work, a fact that indicates the importance of this classic series of investigations. Another highly significant series of investigations that have yielded knowledge of lasting importance is that conducted by Jean Piaget and his associates at Geneva. The Piaget studies are focused on the conceptual development of children. In a typical series of Piaget experiments, children of a wide range of ages are exposed to a particular problem that was designed to discover the nature of the logical structures underlying behavior. The children are each questioned concerning the reason for the particular solution given. The data are then used to demonstrate a particular pattern of development in the nature of logical thought of the children. For example, in one series of studies the children were given some geometrical shapes of different colors and were asked to put together those that belonged together. The four-year-olds took some of the shapes and arranged them in a line. They had their own logic for the particular arrangement. Children about a year older interpreted the task in a different way, using the shapes to assemble an image of some object. The eight-year-olds, in contrast, were making systematic classifications that met all ten criteria used to determine whether the children did or did not understand the nature of a logical class. However, these same children had difficulty when they had to set up a classification system that had to leave a place for objects that were not present. For example, suppose the children were given a mixture of red and blue squares and triangles, and some red circles, but no blue circles. If the children were to set up a comprehensive classification system they would have to leave a place for blue circles, that is to say, for a null class. The eight-year-old does not do this since he can handle only that which is present and cannot conceptualize as a part of the system that which is absent, but by the age of eleven or twelve, the child is able to do this.

Thus, the descriptive data show a gradual progression through childhood in the ability to use a logic of classes, and this progression can be demonstrated through descriptions of how children of different ages solve problems involving classification. In the case of the Piaget data, the findings are very clear and highly reproducible. Nothing would be achieved by attempting to convert the data into a numerical form.

One suspects that the key to success in applying this kind of qualitative approach is to be a genius like Wolfgang Kohler or Jean Piaget. Few of the more ordinary research workers have had much success with this approach. The genius is able to design experiments that produce clear-cut data, which few others are able to do. The approach to research that involves measurement is generally much easier to pursue and permits the average research worker to produce interesting results, even though these results may not be as scintillating and epoch making as those produced by the great names.

Data of this kind can be moved one step toward quantification by counting the number of children at each age who use each of the different ways of "putting together those that belong together." Piaget does this, but only on rare occasions. This procedure produces nice neat tables, to which one can apply familiar tests of statistical significance, but often such a procedure adds little to knowledge, which is why Piaget rarely does this. Those who are interested in the statistical procedures for analyzing such tables, and testing hypotheses related to them, will find the article by Light (1973) useful. The article by Light is directed to those who have had minimal experience in the use of statistical tests of significance.

The Design of Transfer of Training Studies

Most areas of research have their own special experimental designs. For example, research on the study of transfer of training has evolved distinct designs to handle the investigation of the problems involved. Most transfer experiments involve two learning tasks commonly designed *Task 1* and *Task 2*. The general purpose of such an experiment is to determine the effect of learning one of the tasks on the learning or retention of the other task. Two basic experimental designs are involved, known as the *retroaction* and the *proaction* designs.

The problem of generalization of learning, or transfer of training as it has been commonly called, is—from the educational standpoint—one of the most important areas of learning and development that can be investigated. If school learning were conceived to be the accumulations of isolated items of information, the expected consequences of education would be extremely limited. Fortunately this is not the case, for school learning is conceived largely as the learning of techniques, skills, principles, and methods that can be applied to a vast range of problems outside the school. This is possible because the solutions to some problems learned in school can be generalized to certain other problems outside school.

The retroaction design involves the following experimental procedure:

Transfer Group: performs Task 1—performs Task 2—performs Task 1
Control Group: performs Task 1 rests or performs some unrelated task—
performs Task 2

This is referred to as the retroaction design since the backward effect of Task 2 on the retention of Task 1 is studied. In this design there is always a problem raised concerning what to do with the control group while the transfer group is performing Task 2. Just to allow them to rest is not satisfactory because this may give the control group some advantage over the transfer group. On the other hand, to engage the control group in some supposedly irrelevant task might conceivably raise or lower their subsequent performance on Task 2.

The proaction design is rather different and can be represented in the following way:

Transfer Group: performs Task 1—performs Task 2
Control Group: rests or engages in irrelevant activity—performs Task 2

In this design the purpose is to determine if the performance of Task 1 facilitates or interferes with the *subsequent* performance of Task 2. The task may be either a learning activity or merely a measure of performance at a particular level of learning. In most transfer experiments both tasks involve a learning activity.

Research on transfer at the beginning of this century typically involved learning situations similar to those that occur in schools, but the trend in recent times has been to use greatly simplified learning situations that bear only a remote resemblance to school learning. Although the early studies were directed toward the determination of the amount of transfer from one school subject to another, more recent research has been aimed at the development of a theory of transfer. Thorndike's theory of transfer, known as the *identical elements theory,* held sway for over a quarter of a century. The inadequacies of this theory are now apparent. The problem is that of finding a substitute theory that can be of value in the designing of curricula and training programs.

Concerning Difficulties in Manipulating Experimental Conditions

Some conditions can be successfully and easily manipulated or varied in experiments with human subjects, whereas others cannot. Most of the experimentation that has been undertaken in the field of education has involved the manipulation of learning conditions—perhaps because these are the most readily manipulated. Unfortunately, much of this work fails to meet the standards of good experimentation because in reading an account of the experiments one cannot determine just what was the nature of the variable manipulated. When one reads that one group of classes was taught by programmed methods and one group by traditional methods, one has little basis for inferring just how the two groups of classes differed in the learning conditions provided. They probably differed in numerous unspecified ways.

The first rule to follow in designing an experiment is to be sure that one knows exactly how conditions are to be varied among the experimental groups. This is much more than a matter of attaching labels such as programmed or traditional. If such categories are to be used, then a clear set of specifications must be drawn up to establish just how these two sets of learning conditions are to differ. Such a set of specifications would have to indicate the characteristic behaviors of teachers and their interactions with pupils under these two conditions and also any other teaching events that distinguish one method from the other. In addition, some provision would have to be made to collect data in the classes in order to determine whether the conditions actually differed in the way in which they were supposed to differ in terms of the experimental design. But even if all this were done, the experiment would still not be worth undertaking as a scientific endeavor for it would involve a jumble of variables and no clear-cut conclusion could be drawn concerning the relationship of particular learning to the achievement of the pupils. Experiments that make significant contributions to knowledge involve the manipulation of much simpler conditions. Let us consider some of the conditions that are commonly varied in educational experiments.

Conditions related to the presentation of information to the pupil. Some of these variables have been extensively studied in connection with the use of new educational media. For example, many studies have been undertaken that compare the relative effectiveness of visual and aural presentations of content. On the surface such studies appear to be easy, but they involve all kinds of difficulties. One can readily present information by means of movies or by lecture, but there are difficulties in ensuring that the same amount of information is presented through the two media. Furthermore, the visual medium may present the information in pictorial form or in written form. If the written form is used, the outcomes of the experiment may be determined by the fact that reading rate is generally more rapid than speech—which gives an advantage to the visual presentation. A comparison of the effectiveness of different media may not make too much sense at this time. Perhaps a more important problem is that of determining the particular techniques that can be effectively used with each medium. In addition, there are important problems to be studied concerning the value of transmitting information through more than one sensory channel. Many major projects that involve the development of movies for instructional purposes have implicitly assumed that the use of ears *and* the eyes together is better than the use of either alone and that both sensory channels should be used simultaneously. This assumption is probably unwarranted and suggests a whole area for research.

Extensive research has been undertaken in the area of audiovisual communication using both actual instructional materials and "artificial" materials developed especially for experimental purposes. When the author and some associates began to work in this area in the early 1960s, they began their work by making a review of previous studies, most of which had involved classroom materials. Their conclusion was that such studies did not seem to be leading anywhere and, indeed, the findings of some of the studies seemed to be misleading. They concluded that the only productive approach to the scientific study and design of audiovisual materials was through laboratory research and embarked on a program of such studies. Some of the results of the latter program are reported in a publication by Travers (1969). These laboratory studies did seem to be leading toward the development of a set of principles that could be used in the design of audiovisual teaching materials, although previous research outside the laboratory had not led to such an outcome. Although the student of education may become fascinated with the possibility of conducting a laboratory study of some problem in this area, he should approach the project with caution. Most such studies require the use of laboratory equipment that is not typically available in colleges of education. Indeed, it is the absence of such equipment that has limited advances in knowledge in this important aspect of education.

Conditions related to feedback. Even though Thorndike stressed the importance of knowledge of results, this is still a neglected but promising area for research that permits the manipulation of important variables and also permits experimentation within the classroom. Research already indicates that the manner in which a teacher marks and comments on the papers of the students may make a substantial difference in their learning rate, but, as yet, relatively little is known about the value of various classes of reinforcement. Insofar as the feedback of information calls for behavior on the part of the teacher, difficulty may be experienced in exerting experimental control. However, feedback provided by written comments and by various ways of enabling a student to check on his answers when workbooks are used are clearly amenable to experimental study. Perhaps such studies are more easily carried out in classrooms run along traditional lines than in those with a more modern atmosphere. In the classroom run along more modern lines, much of the feedback is provided by peers in informal ways and little control can be exerted over it.

One of the conditions related to feedback that has produced interesting and consistent results is failure—a condition that has generally been demonstrated to have a depressing effect on intellectual processes. However, most of the studies of this problem have been laboratory studies, and much more needs to be learned about the effect of failure in a classroom situation.

Conditions related to classroom management. The experimentally minded educational research worker is likely to be tempted to manipulate conditions of classroom management. Studies that attempt to compare one condition of classroom management with another are generally referred to as *studies of teaching methods.* The experimenter simply does not have the control over this class of variable needed to undertake much in the way of systematic experimentation. The same thing may be said of experiments with administrative conditions. The administrator is not able to change or modify his pattern of administration at will. One might hazard the generalization that experiments in which humans are required to produce a change in their own behavior as the variable manipulated are not likely to be very good experiments if they are undertaken in classroom settings.

Some further consideration must be given to this problem. Suppose that a researcher desires to study the effect of certain aspects of teacher behavior, such as the number of rewarding statements, on specific aspects of pupil learning. Teachers may be willing to cooperate and to provide a specified amount of praise for pupil accomplishment, but some teachers will be much more convincing than others when they praise a pupil. If an experiment has been set up involving a group of teachers who administer much praise and a group who administer little praise, the experimenter can be sure—however well he has trained and rehearsed the teachers in their respective roles—that some teachers will deviate markedly from the prescribed course of action. Whenever behavior is the condition to be manipulated, we cannot expect to conduct experiments with clear-cut results. Even more complicated and unsatisfactory are experiments in which the cooperating teachers are personally involved in the outcome and hence are likely to be influenced in their behavior by their own desires. Most experimental demonstrations of the merits of new methods in education suffer from this limitation, particularly because they usually require teachers to adopt, for experimental purposes, methods that they believe to be unsound. Under such conditions, the teaching methods with which the new methods are to be compared are presented in a way that can be described only as a caricature. The results of such studies obviously cannot demonstrate any useful principle.

A final matter to be considered in classroom experimentation is what may be called the personal bias of the pupils. To some extent, pupils will behave in the way in which they believe they are expected to behave. If they know that the class, or the teacher, is being observed, they are likely to cooperate with the teacher, because cooperative behavior is considered most desirable for children. This pupil phenomenon is most pronounced, and even teachers who have serious problems in maintaining class control may have no trouble when they are being observed.

Conditions related to motivation. Although motivation is widely considered to be a major factor in determining rates of learning, not too much success has been achieved in establishing the conditions in the classroom that raise or lower motivation. McClelland et al. (1953) based their work on the assumption that motivation can be aroused by the introduction of appropriate cues, such as telling a person that his performance on a particular task indicates his worth. Numerous studies have now been conducted in which such cues have been manipulated by the experimenter, but the results have often proven to be very difficult to reproduce. The student is cautioned against considering undertaking a study in this area because of the high probability of obtaining negative results. Heckhausen (1967) has provided a review of research in this area.

A student who reads an account of an experiment rarely realizes the laborious work that went into the design of the final experiment. The published account of the experiment omits reference to most of the false starts that were made and may, perhaps, fail to mention that the research worker initially was investigating a different problem, which he was forced to abandon because it did not prove to be amenable to study with the tools available. Also, at the start, the experimental scientist may have difficulty stating his problem in a form that permits a rigorous experiment to be undertaken. For example, Gilbert (1959) showed that in order for a printed word to be received and understood by the person who views it, a certain amount of time must be provided that is free of new stimuli. This is why reading fixations occur. Each fixation represents the time required to perceive the words around the fixation point. When the author became interested in this phenomenon, he began to ask questions about the effect of different words on the time required and whether it made a difference in the time involved if the words were familiar or relatively unfamiliar. This led to a redefinition of the problem in terms of information theory. The words carried information and, hence, the more information they carried the longer the processing time would probably have to be. But then he encountered problems in determining the amount of information transmitted by particular words or groups of words. This, in turn, led to abandoning the use of words for the purpose of studying information-processing time and individual differences in information-processing time. Other materials such as letters of the alphabet or digits were then used as experimental materials because they permitted the experimenter to estimate the quantity of information carried. Thus, a perception problem ended up as an information-transmission problem and this, in turn, required the experimenter to turn to entirely different materials from those that he had orginally intended to use.

One of the major functions of a trial run is to determine what is and what is not measurable in terms of available instruments or new instruments that it is feasible to develop. Quite commonly an experiment or investigation is planned, but attempts to execute part of it demonstrate that the suggested procedure could not possibly yield any results because of the crudeness of the available measurement procedures. The need for such preliminary trial runs to establish the meaningfulness of results as well as the feasibility of obtaining measurements of adequate accuracy has not been properly recognized by educational researchers. It is easy to point to large educational investigations that have been pursued over many years at a cost of hundreds of thousands of dollars and that have produced no results of any consequence; these investigations would never have taken place if a few preliminary studies had been conducted.

The preceding sections emphasize the negative side of experimentation —what not to do; but mere avoidance of pitfalls does not ensure that the resulting experiment will be even mediocre in value. In the literature can be found reports of study after study that are flawless in technique of design but otherwise completely inconsequential. Ingenious experimentation of the type that builds a science of behavior owes its contribution to the fact that it is built on a sound theory and that the idea could be developed experimentally under available circumstances. These two conditions need to be discussed further.

A sound idea for experimentation in the behavioral sciences must find its roots in the current tide of organized ideas that constitute the present state of the art. Many ideas that appear sound from the viewpoint of the layman may not be sound from the point of view of current knowledge. The layman will always protest this statement, as he always has, for it is inevitable that he will conceive of himself as an authority on problems of education. This conflict between lay opinion and scientific opinion is not new and has occurred in fields other than the psychological. The layman's emphatic belief that the earth was flat or that it was the center of the universe arc illustrations of common sense being wrong while the scientist was right. Today it is not uncommon for the student of education to base the ideas about which he wants to experiment on lay opinion as well as on his professional background. This is a real handicap, but it is hard indeed for a person who has spent the first twenty or thirty years of his life thinking in terms of the layman's conception of behavior to change and to think in terms of the scientist's conception. Early habits of thought are probably never entirely discarded.

Many experimentalists have pointed out that the careful surveillance of the collection of data is vital for successful scientific research. This is not just a matter of watching to see that the experimental procedure is carried out with care. Incidental observations made during the course of an experiment may often provide valuable data. One does not have to go far to find discoveries of the utmost importance that have been made as a result of incidental observation during the course of some other investigation. A classic example is the observation by Fleming that led to the discovery of penicillin. Fleming noted that staphylococci died in certain dishes that had become contaminated from outside sources. Although many research workers would have written off this phenomenon as an experimental nuisance, Fleming saw that it suggested a means of destroying staphylococci causing infections. Roentgen's discovery of X rays was also the result of an incidental observation made during the course of an inquiry into the nature of certain kinds of radiation.

One cannot tell the experimentalist what to look for, but only that he should be forever vigilant. When he sees something of particular interest he would be well advised to stop and investigate. Many scientists have said that a research worker is fully justified in dropping everything in order to explore an unusual event that has caught his attention. Even though systematic investigation is most desirable, it does not mean that the scientist should be compulsive about following his plans through to the end and shutting out all distracting phenomena.

A final word of encouragement. Finally, the student is again urged not to be overwhelmed by the difficulties of experimentation. Rather, he should feel that he is now familiar with the major difficulties commonly encountered and that he is now in a position to plan well-designed studies. Because most flaws in experiments arise simply because the novice in research is unaware of their existence, the reader at this point should feel prepared to try his hand at designing experimental studies. The great value that this approach offers to the development of a science of behavior in educational situations is a factor that should urge him to use experimental methods whenever they are feasible. The more ambitious doctoral student may well deliberately choose these most powerful of all methods of collecting information.

Summary

1. The scientific experiment is the most prestigious method of achieving scientific knowledge, although much knowledge has been acquired by other means. Although the human naturally experiments with his environment, the scientist has introduced refinements into experimental techniques.

2. The major refinement in experimental techniques must be credited to Galileo who was the first to study simplified situations in a laboratory setting. Galileo's study of balls rolling down an inclined plane is a classic example of laboratory experimentation. The scientist typically experiments in his laboratory with simplified situations, because natural phenomena are too complex for him to understand. Much important knowledge related to education has been achieved through laboratory experimentation.

3. There is no clear distinction between demonstrations and experiments. Many of the most famous experiments in the physical sciences may be described as demonstrations, and many of Piaget's experiments on child behavior are of this character. There are even some famous cases of students who have managed to demonstrate very important phenomena.

4. Conventional experiments by American research workers follow a certain pattern that persists because it has been productive of knowledge.

The typical pattern is to vary some condition and to determine how this influences the outcome of the experiment. The experimenter has to arrange conditions so that other things are equal, even though they rarely are completely so. In the laboratory the experimenter can come nearer to arranging for other things to be equal than he can in a field setting. Outside of the laboratory there may be many important conditions exercising an effect that the experimenter cannot control.

5. Galileo had a theory about how balls rolling down an inclined plane behaved like falling bodies. The results enabled him to predict the behavior of falling bodies. Experiments should be based on some kind of theory about how the events in the laboratory are related to outside events. In educational research we often have only a very vague theory about how events in the laboratory are related to events in the classroom. We should have much better theories.

6. Experiments can be conducted in natural settings, such as classrooms, as well as in the laboratory. Many difficulties are encountered in experimenting in natural settings. Some of these difficulties can be circumvented through the use of statistical techniques, but such techniques do not overcome the deficiencies of poor experiments.

7. Many experiments undertaken under natural conditions only approximate what has been referred to here as a true experiment. If the approximation to a true experiment is good, then the term *quasi-experiment* is applied to it. If the approximation is very bad, then it is called a pseudoexperiment. Such a pseudoexperiment is worthless for contributing to knowledge.

8. Although the simplest design for an experiment involves varying a single factor, more complex designs may be used in which several factors are varied.

9. There is a question whether experimentation in the behavioral sciences with human subjects is in some ways fundamentally different from experimentation in the physical sciences. Those who participate in experiments in the behavioral sciences, as subjects, may attempt to influence the outcomes in terms of their own prejudices.

10. Published experiments show many common deficiencies. These are summarized as follows:

> Deficiency in design as a result of failure to include a control group.
> Deficiency produced by the experimental procedure generating the results.
> Deficiency produced by contamination of data.
> Deficiency that results from making unwarranted assumptions about the nature of the scales used.
> Deficiency that results when relevant variables are confounded with irrelevant variables.

Deficiency resulting from sampling by groups and not by individuals.
Deficiency as a result of insufficient cases.
Deficiency as a result of failure to take subject bias into account.
Deficiency produced through the lack of well-developed experimental techniques.
Deficiency as a result of planning studies in which rare events form the crucial aspects of the data.
Deficiency in design resulting from the experimental procedure itself affecting the conditions to be observed.

11. Some experiments yield qualitative data that may be extremely significant. Such data must be handled by special methods. Some qualitative data can be converted into quantitative data.

12. Special forms of experimental design have been developed for studying particular classes of problems. The design of transfer experiments was given as an example.

13. Many conditions cannot be easily manipulated, that is to say varied, for experimental purposes, but others can be. Numerous successful experiments have been conducted on the form of educational materials and the way in which they are presented to students. Much research has been undertaken on the motion picture and on problems related to the use of audiovisual materials. A more difficult area of research is that which attempts to study the effects of varying teacher behavior. Even cooperative teachers cannot always produce the pattern of behavior that they want to produce. Motivation is another area in which experimenters have great difficulty in controlling experimental conditions.

14. Experimental techniques often require much work to develop, and good experiments are generally the outcome of many false starts.

CHAPTER 10
Problems of the
Design of Experiments

In the preceding chapter the practical problems of experimentation, with particular reference to the feasibility of undertaking various types of experimentation, were discussed. In this chapter the logic of design is discussed, but the reader should keep in mind that designs that are methodologically sound from the statistical and logical viewpoint can be applied to trivial problems and can even be based on assumptions that are inconsistent with those that the use of the particular data require.

Terminology of Experimental Research Design

In order to understand experimental research design, it is necessary to understand certain terms that are commonly used in the discussion of designs. The knowledge derived from a research is generally derived from a *sample* of a *universe*. The sample might be all the eighth-graders in Chicago whose birthday falls on the first day of any month, and the universe might be all eighth-graders in Chicago at the present time.

The researcher is sometimes interested in the effect of the presence or absence of some conditions on behavior, such as the effect of drill on spelling achievement, or the effect of knowledge of results or lack of knowledge of results on computational skill. Differences in the conditions in which the researcher is interested are referred to as differences in *treatment*. In the simplest type of educational study, differences between the presence or absence of a particular condition are studied, and this would represent a comparison between two levels (presence or absence) of a particular treatment. In more complicated experiments, many different treatments may be involved and the interaction of these treatments may be studied. For example, one might study formal drill versus no formal drill in the teaching of mathematics, and the teaching might be undertaken by either extroverted or introverted teachers. Extroverted teachers might be more successful with drill methods than with nondrill methods, and the reverse might be true of introverted teachers. Designs that permit the estimation of the effect of each treatment can be adopted within a single study.

Sometimes the research worker is concerned with the characteristics of the individuals involved in a study, especially in relation to some aspect of performance. Thus, in studies of the results of different teaching methods, the researcher may wish to take into account pupil differences in ability because he may believe that some methods are better for bright pupils and others are better for dull pupils. The characteristics of the population studied that are taken into account in a design are referred to as the *population characteristics*. These may be physical characteristics or psychological characteristics such as are measured by tests. They may also be derived from the person's background and represent the experiences to which he has been exposed.

It is not the purpose of this book to familiarize the student with the statistical problems underlying advanced designs and their merits. Such matters are well taken care of in textbooks devoted to these problems.

There is some division of opinion among those engaged in educational research concerning the utility of complex designs that take into account a large number of different variables, except in areas where much knowledge has already been acquired. Those who design studies involving numerous variables claim that this is necessary if useful results are to be achieved. The argument is that many variables are involved in most behavioral phenomena, and hence these should be taken into account in any study that is planned. On the other side of the argument it is claimed that the research worker usually does not know what these variables are, and guesswork rather than sound theory is likely to be the basis for including those that are included. Only rarely do elaborate designs give the impression of being firmly rooted in theory. Skinner (1956), who has participated in this controversy, has pointed out that most of the important facts of science were discovered long before complex designs had ever been invented. In addition, it is true that important facts in the behavioral sciences continue to be brought out by workers in educational research using the simplest type of experimental designs. Many fine studies may illustrate the use of complex designs, but it seems likely that simple designs will serve a useful purpose for many years to come.

Functions of Statistical Method

It would be inappropriate in this book to provide an extended discussion of statistical methods, because these require intensive study on the part of the student of education who is preparing himself to engage in educational research. The student will always be limited both by what he knows and by what is known in the field of statistics in the planning and execution of studies.

Statistics serve a number of different functions. First, they commonly serve the purpose of summarizing data. A mean is calculated for this kind of purpose. A state department of education will indicate the *mean* cost per pupil in elementary education in the state. The presentation of the *mean* cost in the superintendent's report saves the report from being cluttered with data from every school or from every school district. The mean is used as a descriptive statistic. Although the use of descriptive statistics seems to be a simple and straightforward procedure, there is a great amount of mathematical work on the problem of the choice of suitable statistics for summarizing data. Some statistical procedures for summarizing data are very complex. For example, factor analysis is a very elaborate procedure that sometimes permits one to summarize the information provided by a very large number of test scores on each pupil in a form that involves only a few scores. The calculation of the mean is a method of summarizing data that almost anyone can apply, but factor analysis can be applied only by those who have sufficient scientific sophistication.

Procedures that just summarize data have become progressively less and less acceptable as the core of doctoral dissertations in education and in the behavioral sciences. Part of the reason for this is that the procedures can be mechanically applied, but it is generally agreed that a thesis or dissertation should require the student to solve a problem at least partly by concentrated personal effort and reflection. There is little educational value in grinding out a study by mechanical means.

A second purpose of statistical methodology concerns the justifiability of inferences made from data, or, in other words, the confidence that can be placed in particular inferences. The testing of hypotheses involves the application of statistical devices known as tests of significance. These tests enable one to estimate the confidence that can be placed in various inferences from the data. Tests of significance vary in the degree to which they are efficient. Some tests do not make proper use of all the information provided by the data, whereas others do. Most tests of significance are based on assumptions that have to be satisfied if the application of the test of significance is to be fully justified. A test of significance may require, for example, that the events studied be distributed in the form of a particular kind of bell-shaped distribution known as the normal distribution, but very few measures show a distribution very close to this form. Usually we know only that the conditions required by most tests of significance are only partially satisfied, but some comfort can be found in the fact that, in the case of most tests of significance, studies have shown that considerable departures from the assumptions called for can be made before the statistical test becomes substantially biased.

The graduate student of education is most likely to be mainly involved in statistics that serve the second major purpose; namely, the testing of hypotheses. Through such methods a science of behavior in educational situations is likely to be produced.

General Characteristics of a Well-Designed Experiment

First, it is necessary that the data of the experiment be as free as possible from bias. This means that there must not be some condition operating, other than the experimental condition, that influences the data in one group rather than another. We have already pointed out that bias is commonly reduced by assigning cases to the experimental and control groups by random methods. Sometimes bias is reduced by matching cases in the experimental and control groups.

This would probably not have been the only source of bias in that study. The schools in which the diagnostic tests had been introduced might have had better facilities than the other group of schools, and this superiority would have reflected itself in teaching and in the resulting level of reading skill. Perhaps this discussion may not only illustrate the problem of eliminating bias but also point up the advantages of an experimental method in which treatments are assigned to cases by a bias-free method.

Second, the experiment must be designed in such a way that it is possible to determine the magnitude of the differences that might be the result of sampling alone. This can be stated in another way; namely, that the experimental data must yield an estimate of error. This condition could be overlooked in most of the experimentation conducted by the physicist or chemist, because in such experiments errors of measurement are extremely small and data tend clearly to support or reject the hypothesis under consideration. It is only when the experimenter enters fields where errors begin to be large in comparison with differences between treatments that the concept of estimating error becomes a matter of prime importance. Many experiments of great significance were performed before the statisticians' concept of estimating error was introduced, but the scientists who undertook those experiments were not oblivious to the idea. They relied on their knowledge of errors of measurement that their equipment and materials involved.

There are some excellent experiments in psychological literature where no systematic effort has been made to estimate error. The early studies of learning conducted by Ebbinghaus involved no such attempt; but here again, the results were so clear-cut that the experimenter's knowledge told him that the errors were extremely small compared with experimental effects.

Third, the experimental design must ensure that there is sufficient precision for the data to be able to provide answers to the questions that are asked. In one experiment, students of education in their sophomore year were divided into two groups. One group was given extensive opportunity to visit school classrooms, whereas the other devoted an equivalent amount of time to additional academic work. It was hypothesized that those who had the school experiences early in their course would be able to profit more from the academic work and would be able to see its implications for classroom practice more clearly. The criterion for the success of this procedure was to be found in terms of the effectiveness of the student's performance in practice teaching. The experimenter was careful to divide the twenty-four sophomores by random assignment to the classroom visitation and the academic work groups, and fortunately all twenty-four stayed with the program long enough to complete student teaching. The students were rated during student teaching by the regular classroom teachers to whom they were assigned, on the basis of their overall effectiveness as well as on more specific aspects of performance. For the purposes of this study, the overall rating of performance was used and an attempt was made to determine the significance of the difference in the rated performance of the two groups that had been exposed to different educational treatments. As one might expect, the results were negative, because the difference between treatments was small compared with the size of the error involved in making the ratings. The experiment lacked the precision to answer the question that was asked.

What can be done to increase the precision of such an experiment? One answer, but perhaps not the most satisfactory one, is to increase the number of observations. As observations are added to the original experiment, a more and more precise and stable estimate can be made of the difference as a result of treatments. In the present case, additional observations could be added by dividing the sophomores year after year into two groups and providing the differential training for each pair of groups.

But this is not the only method by which the precision of an experiment can be increased. It is the one that should be used as a last resort and only after other means of increasing precision have been exhausted. The main alternative involves the removal of known sources of error. Thus, in the study of student teaching that has been described, if one could obtain a more reliable measure of student teaching than the ratings used, a main source of error would be reduced. However, one might not be able to find a more satisfactory measure than that provided by ratings. Another source of error is the variation shown by the students in their teaching performance, for many different reasons. Some may have problems in the classroom because they feel insecure. If the two groups exposed to the two training methods before student teaching could be selected to make the groups as uniform as possible, with respect to characteristics that influence performance in student teaching, then another source of error would also be reduced.

Controls in Experimental Design

The design of research is closely associated with the use of what are called *experimental controls*. Although well-designed experiments and other forms of research have been undertaken for many hundreds of years, the use of the term by scientists goes back for only about one hundred years. Boring (1954), who has studied the history of the concept of control in experimentation, finds three common uses of the term, which have added confusion to writings on scientific methodology because they have been used interchangeably.

First, the term *control* is used to refer to a restraint on experimental conditions. Thus in the administration of a test to determine whether children who have had certain diseases suffer a hearing loss, it may be considered desirable to conduct the tests in a soundproof room so that extraneous noises do not interfere with the results obtained by some pupils and not by others. Extraneous sounds are *controlled* so that the resulting conditions will be as uniform as possible.

Second, the experimenter exercises control over the variable that he is manipulating. In determining auditory acuity, sounds are presented that vary in loudness and pitch. It is important to control the pitch of the sound because some persons may have a hearing loss only for sounds of a certain pitch. It is known, for example, that as individuals grow older they begin to manifest a hearing loss for sounds of high pitch. Thus, the experimenter *controls* the pitch as well as the loudness of the sound that is presented as a stimulus.

Third, there is a sense in which the scientist refers to *control* groups or *control* experiments. Boring introduces this meaning of the term by referring to Mill's method of experimental inquiry. Mill's first method is the Method of Agreement, which states that if A is followed by a, then presumably A is the cause of a. The word *presumably* is used advisedly, because it is obvious that A is not necessarily the cause of a even if it always has preceded it. In my home, eggs are always served after grapefruit at the breakfast table, but nobody would claim that the grapefruit causes the eggs. In Mill's second method, it is postulated that if A is always followed by a, and if the absence of A is always followed by the absence of a, then A can be asserted to be the cause of a. This method is an extension of the first, and it involves the introduction of the *control* consisting of *the absence of A*. It represents a very common method of educational experimentation. For example, it can be shown that children who have certain speech defects improve if they are given remedial speech treatment and do not improve if such remedial work is withheld. If studies of this problem had demonstrated *only* that those who had remedial work improved, it would still leave open the possibility that improvement was not the result of the treatment but of the passage of time and various unidentified influences. However, by showing that the withholding of treatment is associated with an absence of improvement, the experiment is enormously strengthened and the conclusion that the treatment produces improvement is justified. The use of control groups is of crucial importance.

The extent to which controls (in the third meaning of the term) need to be introduced is always a matter of judgment. If a teacher of calculus administers a pretest to his students to determine how much they know about the subject matter of his course and then administers a final examination, and if the content of both tests relates only to the course in calculus, it may be inferred that substantial increases in scores from the pretest to the final examination may be attributed to learning in the course. Indeed, if this mathematics professor were to introduce a control group that took both examinations but that received no training in calculus, his colleagues would probably speak of him as being unreasonably overcautious and too free in wasting the time of his students. On the other hand, the psychology professor who also gives a pretest and a final examination may well wonder whether increases in scores are a result of learning in his course. In this case, the increase may be a result of general reading, discussions with other students, and related materials learned in courses in biology, sociology, and other subjects that overlap with psychology. It would be necessary to include a control group in the latter case in order to improve the possibility of attributing above-chance scores on the final examination to the content of the course.

There is also a fourth meaning of the term *control*. Sometimes an experimenter may suspect that a particular characteristic of those experimented with may affect the results of his experiment, and that some control needs to be exercised over that variable. For example, suppose an experimenter is interested in the relative effectiveness of two sets of teaching materials. He selects two groups of students at random who are required to learn the materials as a part of their program. The experimenter suspects that an important condition related to mastering the materials is the level of intelligence as measured by tests of general intelligence. The experimenter knows this from his experience in teaching similar materials, but has an open mind concerning the reason for this relationship. In the experiment, differences in intelligence are going to cause variation from student to student in what is learned, and this is an unwanted source of variation. The experimenter can obtain a measure of the intelligence of each student in the experiment and use a statistical technique, known as analysis of covariance, to take this measure into account in calculating the results of the experiment. In such a study, the measure of intelligence would be referred to as a control variable. In doing this the experimenter is able to separate out the variation produced by this control variable. The more sources of variation that can be separated out, the better able is the experimenter to see the differences that can be attributed to differences in the materials.

Sometimes a variable that needs to be controlled is the student's initial knowledge of the area. This is important in studies that compare differently designed teaching materials. The control of this variable involves giving a pretest.

A type of experimental design has become widely used in recent years in which the experimental subject is also the control. Operant psychologists have a particular preference for this design. As an example, let us suppose that a psychologist is interested in methods of obtaining wider participation in recitation procedures in the classroom. The experimenter proposes to the teacher that an experiment be conducted to determine whether the reticent child can be slowly drawn into the class discussions. Five children are identified who are low participators, and these five are to be both the subjects of the experiment and the controls. In order to do this, the class is observed in a series of recitation situations, which are run as they have long been run and without change. A record is kept of the participation of these children in the discussions. The frequency with which each child participates is referred to as his *base rate*. The base rate would be determined for each of a series of recitation sessions until the base rate had become stable and, that is to say, did not vary substantially from one session to the next. A stable base rate has to be established as a first step in all experiments in which the individual student serves as his control.

Once the base rate is established, the teacher then begins to introduce reinforcements whenever any one of these five students attempts to participate. The teacher may do this by responding warmly and encouragingly to the child. A record is then kept of the rate of responding of the children under the reinforcement condition. One would expect that the rate of responding would slowly increase. Once a higher rate of responding is achieved, a new condition may be called for. The teacher may then slowly eliminate the reinforcements, in order to determine whether a stable new base rate of responding has been achieved, or the teacher may cut off the special reinforcing conditions. When the latter happens the behavior of the pupils may slowly deteriorate until it returns to the original base rate. However, it should be emphasized that many teachers and research workers would consider the practice unethical of letting a newly formed desirable behavior slowly extinguish itself through deliberate neglect on the part of the teacher.

If the experiment is undertaken so that the second part is not included, then there may be a question of whether the results were an artifact. Some condition might have come into play that increased the responsiveness of all children, and not only those that were being reinforced. In order to circumvent such a criticism, one could introduce the reinforcing procedure at different times for different children. One may begin by reinforcing just one of the children. Then two weeks later, one may begin reinforcing the second child, and so forth.

Selection of Subjects for an Experiment

A crucial decision in the design of an experiment is the selection of those who are to participate in an experiment. Experiments are designed to produce generalizations, that is to say to produce results that can be applied to groups other than those on whom the experiment was originally run, but the results can be applied only to those individuals who are similar to the individuals who participated in the experiment. In technical terms one might say that one wishes to conduct an experiment in such a way that the results will apply to a particular population, such as all adults or all seventh-graders in a particular region. In order to do this one must conduct the experiment on a sample of all adults, if the results are to be generalized to all adults, or a sample of seventh-graders if the results are to be generalized to a particular group of seventh-graders. All too often experimental studies are conducted on a group of college under-graduates and the results are generalized to all kinds of groups including children. In the present literature of psychology the most notorious cases of such errors of generalization are found in the case of books that carry the title of how to improve learning in the classroom but which are based on data derived from the study of emotionally and intellectually impaired children. But there are plenty of other examples from the psychological literature. Operant psychologists have few inhibitions about applying gen-eralizations derived from studies of rats, but they justify this by making the dubious assumption that the findings are so general that they apply to all living organisms. Most psychologists today have become much more wary and cautious in applying the findings of studies to new species, or to new groups within the same species. Most psychologists take the con-servative position that findings should be generalized only to similar groups, or to groups that represent a similar sample as the one studied. Sometimes research workers may wish to repeat their experiments using very different samples in order to determine whether the results can be generalized to a different population. Sometimes research workers may use complex designs that include several different samples from different sources, in order to determine initially whether the results have generality. Thus, it is clear that both the initial plan and the final description of any experiment should include information about the way in which the subjects were selected for the experiment and some indication of the groups to whom the results can be reasonably applied. Many experiments are woefully deficient in such information.

Those who work in college all too often use college students as subjects for experiments because they are available. At one time it was a common practice to require students in certain courses to participate in the experi-ments of the faculty as a course requirement. There are ethical considera-tions related to this practice. If the experiments provide experience related to the course and from which the student can benefit, then the requirement is a reasonable one. A course in psychology may require students to have such experiences, particularly if the experiment is explained to them afterward. Courses in educational research can reasonably expect students to participate as subjects in ongoing projects if these are made a part of the learning experience. However, if the experiments in which students are required to participate are irrelevant to the objectives of the course, then any requirement of the student to participate in the experiment represents exploitation of the student and should be avoided. Such exploitation is unethical.

Since one cannot usually require particular individuals or groups to participate in experiments one is left with two alternatives, either to find individuals who are willing to participate for pay or to find volunteer subjects. The payment of subjects represents a financial burden to most experimenters. The author's experience has been that one cannot obtain subjects for the minimum wage. One could perhaps make the pay given to subjects more attractive by giving each participant a ticket in a lottery, with one or more of the subjects guaranteed to win a substantial sum, but then there is the problem that the experiment would attract the risk takers who are a special group in themselves. Of course, those individuals who are willing to participate in an experiment for relatively modest pay are also a special group and probably at a lower socioeconomic level than those who do not participate for pay. Every means of obtaining subjects tends to attract one group of individuals rather than another, but the only group that has been carefully studied is that composed of volunteers.

Rosenthal and Rosnow (1975) have assembled most of the information available concerning the characteristics of volunteer subjects. Psychologists and sociologists have long been interested in this problem because of suspicions that the condition of being a volunteer influences the outcome of experiments. Some of the characteristics studied seem to have been selected more as a whim of the experimenter than for any sound reason. For example, numerous studies have explored whether firstborns are more likely to volunteer for experiments than laterborns. This is like studying whether blondes are more likely than brunettes to prefer eating beef over lamb. Fortunately most of the studies have investigated variables of greater potential consequence.

Studies of volunteering of subjects are complicated by the fact that the nature of the experiment may determine the kinds of characteristics that are manifested by the volunteers. Also, the way in which the volunteers are approached and their relationship to the experimenter may influence the type of volunteers obtained. Rosenthal and Rosnow, who have tried to sort out these situational factors, present their conclusions graded according to the confidence they believe can be placed in them.

Rosenthal and Rosnow are confident with their conclusion that volunteer subjects tend to be better educated and come from a higher social class than those who do not volunteer. This fits the data assembled on those who return questionnaires when compared with those who do not. Perhaps the volunteers, because of these characteristics, understand and appreciate the value of research, but those who lack these characteristics may view research as a silly activity. Volunteers are more sociable and have a higher need for approval.

Rosenthal and Rosnow have considerable confidence in their next group of conclusions although they are less confident of these than they are of those conclusions that were just described. They find that the volunteer subjects are more arousal seeking, which explains why they volunteer for experiments involving stress. They also volunteer more readily for experiments in sensory isolation, hypnosis, and sex. Volunteers are more unconventional. Females are more likely to volunteer than males, but they are less likely to volunteer for research involving physical stress such as that produced by shock, high temperature, or interviews about sex. Volunteers being less conforming are also less authoritarian.

Certain obvious situational factors influence volunteering. Experiments that are interesting attract volunteers and subjects are attracted to experiments in which they can participate with approval. Investigators who are viewed as being important will have more success in attracting volunteers than those investigators who are relatively unknown. Money can be used as an incentive to attract subjects but it is especially effective when it is given in advance and the person knows that he still does not have to volunteer. There are also some obvious conclusions such as that it is difficult to get volunteers for experiments that involve disagreeable characteristics.

Rosenthal and Rosnow provide a long series of suggestions concerning ways in which experimenters can attract volunteers. The reader should study their volume if he wishes to conduct an experiment in which volunteer subjects are needed.

The Function of Replication in Relation to the Problem of Estimating Error

In the behavioral sciences, a single experiment in which a measurement is made on one subject exposed to experimental treatment and the same measurement is made on a control subject cannot yield meaningful results. The design of experiments that can achieve this end and that can be used to derive useful generalizations requires the introduction of what are known as replications.

The term *replication* is frequently used with reference to experimental designs, and it refers to the making of additional observations comparing two or more treatments. Some replication is obviously necessary if there is to be any experiment at all. This can be explained by an example.

Suppose that it is desired to determine the effect of a second-grade workbook on the development of skills. A very unsophisticated experimenter might start with two beginning second-graders of the same age and with equal reading skill. One of these two pupils might be given a particular workbook to use during the semester, whereas the other would not. At the end of the semester, both pupils would be again tested, and let us say the pupil who had had the workbook made the higher score. Just what can be concluded from such an experiment?

The answer to this question is that no conclusion of any value can be drawn. If two pupils have equal scores on a reading test at the beginning of a semester, they will probably have different scores by the end of the semester—as a matter of fact, they will very probably have different scores if they are retested only a day later. The latter effect illustrates the fact that there are errors of measurement. Thus, the pupil who achieved the higher score might have achieved this score without the use of a workbook. Also the child who had the workbook might also have had certain advantages, such as a parent who worked with him on his reading difficulties. All of these uncontrolled sources of variation in final test scores are collectively referred to as *experimental errors*. In order to estimate their magnitude, it is necessary to replicate the treatments (with and without a workbook) with additional cases.

This matter can be considered from another point of view. If the score of the pupil in the one group is X_1 and the score of the pupil in the other group is X'_1, then the single difference $X_1 - X'_1$ cannot be evaluated for its significance because there is no standard with which it can be compared. If a second pair of cases is added to the data, a second comparison $X_2 - X'_2$ may be computed, but the added data also enable us to begin making an estimate of variability within each group through the comparisons of X_1 with X_2 and X'_1 with X'_2. As pairs of cases are added, it becomes more and more possible to evaluate differences between groups, because the data enable us to estimate what differences would be expected if both members of each pair were drawn from the same group.

The question is inevitably asked at this point concerning the number of replications that should be included in the design. This is not an easy question to answer. Sometimes it is possible to compute the number of replications that are needed to attain a particular level of precision. There is also a second procedure, which is particularly applicable to research in the behavioral sciences, where data are collected not at one time but in a series of separate sessions. When this is done, replications can be added until the desired precision is reached; that is to say, until conclusions can be drawn with a definite degree of risk that they are wrong. A procedure known as *sequential analysis* may be used at any given stage in the collection of data to determine how many additional replications are needed in order to obtain the desired degree of precision.

Replication is necessary in order that the variability of subjects exposed to a particular treatment may be estimated. However, the multiplication of observations may serve an additional purpose if more is done than merely adding cases randomly selected in pairs from the same populations. In the case of a study comparing two reading methods, it would be desirable to draw samples exposed to both methods from different intellectual levels, and perhaps too from schools in different socioeconomic neighborhoods. If such a plan of investigation were pursued, it might then be possible to determine whether one method was superior to the other, not only for children in general but for children at different intellectual levels and for children from different socioeconomic backgrounds. An interaction might be found between method and intellectual level—that one method was better with the brighter children and one with the duller. If the design is properly planned so that it includes other factors, much more information can be derived from a single inquiry than if all replications represent only the addition of randomly selected observations from the same population.

More information will be supplied by a single pair of observations if factors other than that which is being studied (differences in teaching method) are controlled, but control is important only insofar as it affects the variable in which we are interested; that is to say, in the example under consideration—reading achievement. The procedure of matching one member of each pair with the opposite pair on one or more relevant variables can be adopted. If pairs could be matched absolutely on all relevant variables, and if our measure of reading achievement involved no error, the remaining difference between pairs would be attributable entirely to differences in reading method. This situation is, of course, a limiting condition that can never be actually achieved. Usually we do not know what all the relevant variables for matching the pairs should be, and many variables that can be identified cannot be measured.

There is, of course, no certainty that even in an experiment where subjects are carefully paired for exposure to the two treatments there may still be differences between the groups thus selected for study. This is why it is necessary to obtain an independent measure of experimental error. All that can be done is to assign subjects to the two treatments in such a way that there is an equal probability of the subjects in the two groups being affected by these uncontrolled conditions.

Matching procedures increase the precision of experimentation, that is to say, they increase the amount of information that can be derived from a particular number of cases. Thus, experiments with matched cases can be undertaken with a smaller number of subjects than when assignment is by a random procedure. Nevertheless, there are often serious difficulties in the matching of groups. Relevant data are often not available. Often there are not a sufficient number of subjects to permit the careful matching of several groups. This is clearly shown by the fact that educational literature is remarkably devoid of studies that have involved the use of carefully matched groups.

There is also a criticism of matching procedures arising from the fact that matching has often been accomplished only after large numbers of cases have been collected in both the experimental and the control groups. When this is done, it usually results in the very uneconomic procedure of discarding subjects, which means that time and energy are lost. Such loss of data is not a necessary part of a matching technique, for if only carefully matched subjects are used in an experiment that is tedious to undertake, it may be possible to reduce materially the time spent in experimentation.

An approximation to the effects of matching can also be achieved through a number of different statistical procedures. When the latter are adopted, the two groups that have received different instruction may be considered to differ on their final performance on a reading test, partly because the two methods of instruction produce different effects and partly because the pupils in the two groups differ with respect to other important characteristics (on which they would have been matched in the methods previously discussed). If measures are available of these other variables influencing the reading scores, then statistical methods can be employed to determine the difference in the performance of the groups exposed to the two reading methods attributed to these other variables and, hence, the difference that can be attributed to instructional procedures. The use of these statistical procedures is generally preferable to the use of matching procedures because they permit the utilization of all the data available.

Sources of Error

A basic problem in the design of research is the estimation of error. Without such an estimate, the results of a study cannot be interpreted. Little has been said about the sources of such errors, so a brief consideration of this matter is now appropriate.

A convenient classification of error is provided by Lindquist (1953). He divides sources of error into three types according to whether they are associated with *subjects, groups,* or *replications.* He refers to these three types of errors as S errors, G errors, and R errors, after the first letters in the words *subjects, groups,* and *replications.* These errors can be illustrated by a simple example. Suppose that sixty first-graders were to be used in an experiment to determine the relative effectiveness of two methods of teaching reading, and that they were divided at random into six equal groups. It is possible that one of these groups might have more than its share of bright pupils, and, as a result, that group would have an advantage in learning to read regardless of the method used. This source of error, which is entirely the result of chance factors determining which pupils are to be exposed to each method, is referred to as an S-type error. However, even if the groups are perfectly matched, it is possible that one group might have advantages over the other group during the experiment itself. For example, one group might have had had a better teacher than the other. The errors introduced through such uncontrolled events are referred to as G-type errors, because they are attributable to differences in conditions to which the two groups are exposed. If the same experiment were repeated in another school, it is possible that the method of teaching reading that is found most effective in the first school might be least effective in the second school, and this phenomenon might be a genuine one. It is certainly conceivable that a method of teaching reading that is highly effective for teaching children from literary homes might be a poor method for teaching children in impoverished neighborhoods. Such differences between replications are referred to by Lindquist as R-type errors. Such an effect as that discussed could also be referred to as an interaction of socioeconomic background and teaching method. It is desirable to design studies so that errors resulting from all of these sources are reduced to a minimum.

Factorial Designs

Up to this point, our discussion has been limited to simple, classical designs that are based mainly on the concept that an experiment is performed by keeping all factors constant except one. The essential principle that Fisher introduced to revolutionize experimental design was the concept that more than one factor could be varied within the structure of a single experiment. Such an experiment involving many factors may contain all the information and provide the same precision as a series of independent experiments involving each of the factors singly, and it will provide savings in effort and work on the part of the experimenter. An additional advantage of the multifactor design is that it may permit the estimation of the effect of the interaction of the variables.

The concept of interaction is a relatively advanced one in the history of the experimental sciences, and it has become particularly useful in the biological and social sciences. It has become a key concept in the biological sciences largely through the study of chemicals in the form of fertilizers and drugs. In the use of fertilizers, the interaction phenomenon is dramatic in effect. Nitrogen alone added to a deficient soil may produce little effect on growth, and the same may be true when phosphorus alone is added. However, when both are added to the soil the effect on plant growth may be remarkable. Under these conditions, it would be said that the variance of plant growth because of nitrogen alone, or of phosphorus alone, would be negligible, but variance because of the *interaction* effect of nitrogen and phosphorus would be large. Other well-known and important interaction effects are found in pharmacology, where the combined effects of Drugs X and Y are found to be greater than what one would expect to find from the effects of the two drugs administered separately. This effect is known as the *synergistic effect,* and it is extensively illustrated by the well-known procedure of compounding several drugs into a single dose of medicine.

In the behavioral sciences, it is not possible to point to clear-cut and well-recognized phenomena that illustrate the interaction effect, possibly because such interaction phenomena are not usually studied in most experiments. One reason for this is that it is only rarely possible to provide a rationale on the basis of which these phenomena can be studied. It is easy to see why plants do not grow in a deficient soil even if either nitrogen or phosphorus is added, for plants need both of these elements in an available form, and one can well understand why both elements, when added together, produce results that are greater than would be expected from the effect of each separately. Other interactions in the biological sciences are fully in accord with expectation, but in the behavioral sciences one is much less certain of what to expect. Perhaps it may be well to pause at this point and consider some cases in educational research where one may expect to find interaction effects.

One such situation is presented by the relationship of teachers to the type of curriculum in terms of which they can most effectively work. It has been suspected for a long time that the teacher who presents what has been called an "authoritarian" personality has great difficulty in working within the framework of a school program in which pupil initiative is encouraged. It is alleged that such teachers work most effectively within a traditional type of curriculum, where nearly all activity is initiated, controlled, and directed by the teacher. Such a situation does at least call for habit systems that are consistent with those one might expect to find in the so-called authoritarian personality. On the other hand, the teacher who feels secure in a classroom situation and who does not find activity initiated by the pupils threatening, may be most effective in a situation where there was no need to control every movement of the pupils and where he could function more as a counselor and guide than as a dictator. As far as the author is aware, it has never been demonstrated that there is this type of interaction between teacher and teaching program, yet it is reasonable to suppose that such an interaction may be crucial. If such a study could be undertaken, it should provide data that would be important for the selection of teachers.

Testing of Hypotheses

All that has been said thus far is based on the assumption that the experimenter has in mind certain clear-cut hypotheses to test. The methods of experimental design that have been discussed are such that they assist the experimenter in testing his hypotheses with the minimum amount of data for a given degree of precision, and sometimes they permit the formulation of generalizations that cover a wider range of circumstances than would be possible if the classical type of experimental design were used. It is common to formulate the hypothesis in a form known as the *null hypothesis*. In this form the hypothesis states that no difference is expected. Thus, if an experiment were to be carried out involving two methods of teaching reading, and reading skill was measured by a test at the end of the training period, the null hypothesis would state that the two groups would not differ. If a difference were found between the mean scores of the two groups, the next step would be to determine by appropriate statistical methods the probability that such a difference or a larger difference would occur by chance. If the chances are found to be quite small that such a difference or a larger difference would occur by chance, the null hypothesis is rejected. Because the testing of the hypothesis from the data involves the determination of probability that such a difference or a greater difference would occur by chance, there is a certain logic in stating all hypotheses in the null form. In the sense described, it is possible to test the null hypothesis, and if the chances are extremely small that the difference (or a larger difference) would have occurred by chance, we may be willing to accept the alternative possibility that the difference was a product of differences in treatment. The latter hypothesis cannot be proven in terms of the data, but it does become more and more plausible as the null hypothesis becomes less and less plausible.

There is also a somewhat different approach to the matter of stating what we expect to find and evaluating our expectancies in terms of the data. In place of stating that we expect no difference (the null hypothesis), and of rejecting or accepting this expectancy or hypothesis in terms of the data, we may ask a question of this type: "If the data shows that there is a numerical difference between the treatments, then with what degree of confidence can we consider that difference to represent a real difference between the treatments and not just the consequence of random errors?" In asking this kind of question, we are not expecting an answer in a form where a decision is made to accept a difference as a genuine difference or to definitely reject the notion that the difference represents something other than the operation of error factors. On the contrary, we expect only to find out whether the chances are high or low that an equal or larger difference would be found if the experiment were replicated. The answer to our question indicates the confidence that can be placed in the particular difference or in statements that we may make about it. In a particular experiment, the answer to our question might be "There is one chance in a thousand that a difference as large as or larger than the one found would occur by chance." If the data provided this answer, then one would be highly confident that the difference found was not just the product of chance circumstances.

The analysis of variance and related statistical techniques that are outside the scope of this book are the techniques used for testing hypotheses, and they always provide an estimate of the probability that a particular difference could have occurred as a result of variations produced by chance circumstances. The probability value that must be reached before it is decided to reject the null hypothesis is a matter of judgment, but it will depend on the consequences of making an error. In this connection, two types of error have been distinguished and have become known as *errors of the first kind* and *errors of the second kind*.

In an experiment comparing the effect of two methods of teaching reading, the results might be presented in the form of the statement, "The probability that the observed difference or a greater difference would occur as a result of chance variations alone is 0.1." This means that if the two treatments had no differential effect, the results of sampling would produce a difference this size or greater in 10 per cent of all experiments. The experimenter might say to himself that this probability is small, and hence it is reasonable to conclude that the observed difference is generated, not by chance variations in the sample drawn, but by differences in treatment. If more thorough experiments were carried out later, substantial evidence might be collected to show that this conclusion was wrong. If this were the case, the experimenter would have made an *error of the first kind*. In this type of error, the null hypothesis stating that there is no difference between treatments is rejected when it should be accepted.

Errors of the second kind are exactly the opposite type of error. They represent the case where the experimenter accepts the null hypothesis when he should not have done so. It is not possible to say that these errors are more or less serious than errors of the first type, because everything in this respect depends on the circumstances. Fortunately, in education, the result of committing either type of error is not likely to be catastrophic, but in experimentation in other fields an error of either type may on occasion result in the loss of human life. In the interpretation of experimental results, it is important to keep in mind the consequences of each one of these types of errors. If the penalties involved in committing one of these types of error are heavy, caution must be taken in arriving at a conclusion that may make these penalties take effect.

Sampling and Problems of Generalization in the Design of Studies

The design of experimental studies and investigations in the behavioral sciences, as in the biological sciences, is intimately connected with the problem of sampling. The intention of the author cannot be to provide the student with an adequate background in the theory of sampling; it can be only that of making the student sensitive to some of the problems in the area so that he can turn to more comprehensive works to learn about the details of their solution—at least insofar as these problems have a solution.

In the testing of almost any hypothesis by statistical means, an assumption is made that the observations recorded represent a sample drawn from a defined universe by methods that do not introduce bias. A universe from which a sample is drawn consists of all those cases that might be included in the sample. Universe is a technical term and is used in a technical sense.

Suppose that the director of research in a large school system decided to survey the reading abilities of children who had passed their ninth birthday but who had not yet reached the age of nine years and six months. In this school system, the slightly less than 10,000 school children who fell within this age range were distributed among twenty-five schools. It was clear that the director of research could not test all of these children on the particular test to be used. Therefore, he decided to test a sample and to use statistical methods for making inferences concerning the total population from the scores derived from the sample. A member of the board of education immediately suggested that it would be administratively convenient to limit the testing to pupils in a single school, since these pupils could then be tested together in a single session. The director was quick to point out that it was a well-established fact that one could not justifiably make inferences from the reading performance in a particular school to the reading performance in all schools, because average scores on the particular test in earlier years had been shown to fluctuate substantially from school to school.

Thus, it is clear that the accuracy of the inference made from a sample to a universe will depend on the way in which the sample is selected. The suggestion of the member of the school board lacks merit because it introduces bias into the sample for the sake of administrative convenience. Whatever sampling procedure is used, it is absolutely essential that it not include any systematic bias. The simplest method of obtaining a sample from a population is that of obtaining a random sample, which is simply a sample in which every case in the population has an equal chance of being included. By definition, the sample deliberately derived from one school could not be considered a "random" sample because cases from other schools would have no chance of being included in it. One way of obtaining such a sample would be to obtain a list of all such children, number them consecutively, and then select from this list by means of a table of random numbers. Such tables can be obtained from libraries. In using such a table, it would be appropriate to start by taking the first four digits and selecting the child who had the number corresponding to these four digits. The investigator would then take the next four digits and select the child whose number corresponded to these digits, and so forth.

Thus, each child in the population identified would have equal opportunity for being included in the sample to be studied.

In this simple type of inquiry, it is presumed that the director of research is interested in estimating the mean reading score of the defined population from the sample. In the case of the random sample that has no systematic bias, the best estimate of the population mean is the sample mean. It is, of course, expected that there will be a difference e (e for error) between the sample mean and the universe mean, but because the method of drawing the sample introduces no systematic bias, if the inquiry were repeated with new samples one would expect e to be negative as often as positive.

In this very simple inquiry, much can be done to reduce the value of e to a minimum. If the investigation is efficiently designed, it will be possible to obtain an unbiased sample such that e is smaller than it would be with a random sample of the type discussed. In essence, what is done is to take steps to ensure that the sample is as far as possible *representative* of the universe sampled with respect to important characteristics that are related to reading. For instance, it is known that girls show a tendency to be better readers than grade-school boys of the same age. Hence, it would be desirable to ensure that the sample included the same proportion of boys and girls as was included in the universe under consideration. Because neighborhood is also related to reading skill, it would also be desirable to ensure that the schools were represented in the sample in proportion to the actual enrollment of the particular age group under study. Thus, the sample would be stratified, and by making the sample more and more closely representative of the population, the tendency would be for the error term e to be steadily reduced.

Let us now consider a slightly more complicated problem of design in order to illustrate the relationship of problems of design to problems of sampling. Suppose that the director of research had been asked to evaluate a remedial reading program. In this program, approximately one hundred children in the elementary grades were given special remedial training in reading each year. The problem may be stated in this way: "If the reading skills of the pupils are measured at the end of the year of special remedial training, what is the probability that a random sample of children, similarly selected but without training, would perform as well or better than the trained sample?" It is therefore necessary to estimate the reading characteristics (mean and standard deviation) of the universe from which the remedial reading group was a sample, for the time at which the remedial group finished its special training.

The director of research would do well to start by identifying the universe to be sampled. One way of doing this might be to administer a reading test to all grade-school children at the beginning of the year. In each grade (or possibly in each age group), the lowest 10 per cent or 5 per cent might be considered to be the population eligible for remedial training in reading. Another method of identifying the universe might be to define it in terms of the cases recommended by teachers, but this method is likely to provide a highly variable population from year to year. Therefore, let us assume that the director of research identified his universe in terms of a cutoff on a distribution of test scores. His next step would be to select a sample to be given remedial training, and, at the same time, to select a second sample that would also be followed up but would be given no remedial training. The latter sample, referred to as a *control sample,* would be used for estimating the reading skills at the end of the year of the universe of pupils who did not receive special training. The data would then permit a comparison of the reading skills of the group receiving special training with the group that was not so trained.

In all sound experimental design, it is important to start by defining the universe to be studied and then to establish methods for sampling that will maximize the information supplied. All too often the reverse procedure is undertaken. The author is aware of a book that describes the behavior of four cases of reading difficulty. These four cases are presented without any inkling of the nature of the population of which they may be considered to be a sample. The reader is thus left wondering about the inferences that can reasonably be made from the data provided by the sample of four. On the other hand, if it were known that these cases were every tenth case admitted to a reading clinic for eight- to twelve-year-old children in a large city public school system, it might have been possible to make certain inferences from the data about other children admitted to the reading clinic. One should not make inferences about typical children in classrooms from data derived from special clinic cases, and neither should inferences in the reverse direction be made. If the children sampled are drawn at random from public school classes in a particular city, then the data derived from them can be used for making inferences about children in public school classes in the same city.

Perhaps the most common single error in educational research is to study a number of cases and then seek a population of which the cases could reasonably be considered to be a sample. When such a population is believed to be found, an attempt is then made to draw inferences about that population from what is known about the cases studied. This procedure is unjustified as a basis for making inferences.

The Error of Sampling One Universe and Generalizing to Another

Although consideration has been given to the cardinal sin in experimentation of failing to identify the universe sampled, a still more grievous sin is commonly committed by those who attempt to utilize and to apply research results. This is the error involved when a specific and well-defined universe is sampled and the results are generalized to quite different universes. Writers in the area of mental health seem to specialize in this error. They find, for example, that the children who come to a particular clinic and are examined there display an inability to do schoolwork under pressure and have to be given reassurances of the teacher's support if they are to learn effectively. In numerous writings such data or similar data have been taken as a basis for inferring that optimum classroom conditions for typical schoolchildren involve warm supportive behavior on the part of the teacher. Of course, the conclusion may be right even though it is based on an invalid inference. The error is obvious but rarely pointed out. Here, the behavior of children sampled from a clinic population has been studied. The scientist may make inferences about the clinic population from the behavior of the sample, but there is no basis for making inferences about other populations of children such as normal school populations. Although this example of false inference is commonly found in the writings of clinical psychologists and psychiatrists, a similar error is made by writers on education who specialize in areas other than the clinical. It is a very easy error to make. The student of education should be particularly on his guard when he comes to writing the last chapter of his thesis—the place where he can bring out the full implications of his study for education. At that point he had better ask himself to identify carefully the population to which his results may be reasonably generalized and the assumptions that underlie that generalization.

Individual Differences and Block Design

Research designs of the block type, which originated in the work of Fisher, are unsatisfactory in the way they handle the matter of individual differences. This can be explained by means of an example. Suppose that a study were being conducted to estimate the extent to which differences in pupil satisfaction in different classes could be associated with teacher differences. In this study, four high school teachers, who were each teaching four different classes of thirty pupils, were selected. Two of these teachers were judged to be the most intelligent in the particular school, and two were judged to be the least intelligent. The pupils in each class were also divided into the fifteen more intelligent and the fifteen less intelligent in terms of a well-known intelligence test. The experimenter had in mind the hypothesis that the ablest students derived satisfaction from the ablest teachers but not from the least able teachers, and that the reverse was true in the case of the least able students. The experimenter in this case was undoubtedly thinking in terms of a continuous distribution of the intelligence of teachers, and probably assumed that what happens in the case of the two extreme groups of teachers can be used as a basis of generalization to intermediate groups.

However, such a generalization is often not justified. The relationships established with extreme groups may not represent two points on a linear continuum. The responses of pupils to the intermediate teachers may be quite different from what it might be expected to be on the basis of that assumption. This situation can be remedied to some extent by including intermediate groupings, but the inclusion of more groupings adds greatly to the complexity of the design.

Brunswick's Representative Design

Particular attention to the problem of generalizing from experimental results has been paid by Brunswick (1947). Brunswick points out that thinking in psychology is still influenced largely by classical experimental design, in which an aspect of some phenomenon is isolated and then studied under laboratory conditions. Thus in psychophysics, the aspect of the phenomenon of visual acuity that has been most closely studied is the ability to perceive two closely situated points of light as distinct points. The separation that such points must have before they are perceived as separate by a particular individual would be considered a measure of the visual acuity of that individual. In further classical types of experimentation with this problem, the relationships of numerous conditions to visual acuity, as thus defined, have been studied.

Brunswick points out that these designs have one central weakness that has been disregarded. Even though they are usually planned with the purpose of including a sample of cases representative of a particular population or subpopulation, they fail to sample the variety of conditions to which it may be desired to generalize the results. In a great number of psychological experiments, the results found under one set of conditions may not be reproducible under other conditions. Indeed, one laboratory may be unable to reproduce the results of another laboratory. Even in a simple experiment in which visual acuity is to be measured and studied by means of two points of light, it is doubtful whether the results are satisfactorily generalizable to other situations. If the purpose is to obtain results that can be generalized to other situations, the results may be disappointing. A person who has relatively low visual acuity in the laboratory situation may do surprisingly well in other situations, for it is known that visual acuity is related to the general nature of the visual field, the intensity of surrounding illumination, the wavelength of the light involved, the state of adaptation of the eye, and so forth. Brunswick suggests that we sample these conditions systematically in order to obtain results that, by and large, are applicable to these varied conditions.

Brunswick developed at least one example of a representative design that involved a problem of size constancy.[1] In this design, size constancy was measured under a great many different conditions, such as in a closed space like a room, outside the building, under different illuminations, and so on. The purpose was to derive principles that could be applied under these varied conditions. Similar types of representative design are extremely difficult to undertake on matters of educational interest. For example, it would be valuable to be able to measure the expressed attitude of white children toward black children under varied conditions in order to predict related behavior under those conditions. Although the researcher might want to do this, the probability is that he would be able to measure such an attitude only under classroom conditions, and this would provide inadequate information for predicting what expressions and other evidences of attitude would occur under other conditions. Representative designs in the attitudinal area are rarely feasible.

The acute reader at this point may well ask why it is that a "representative" design is suggested. Would it not be simpler to list the extraneous variables that might affect the outcomes of an experiment and then incorporate them in a design of the Fisherian type? When this can be done, it is, of course, the recommended procedure, but in research in the behavioral sciences the conditions that affect a particular phenomenon are usually so numerous that it is not feasible to incorporate them in a block design, for an unwieldy number of blocks would be involved. In most cases, it would also appear that these incidental conditions, though numerous, each contribute only a small effect—probably too small to produce significant results in a feasible design. In this type of situation, Brunswick suggests that a systematic effort be made to obtain representative samples of these conditions.

Brunswick's position leads one to understand why a single study, conducted in an educational setting, so often has little to offer the practitioner in other settings. School studies have to be repeated under varied circumstances and with consistent results before they can provide knowledge that has any widespread application. Sometimes the argument is put forward that a study, yielding positive findings, undertaken in one setting can be used as a basis for practice in another similar setting. This assumes that we already know what makes two settings similar or different, but the fact is that we do not. Too often an educational research has been repeated in two different locales that are judged to represent similar circumstances, and the results have been completely dissimilar. Circumstances obviously existed that produced the difference in results and yet the nature of these

[1] Size constancy is the tendency to see objects as being of a given size even though the distance between the object and the observer varies. Thus, a Cadillac appears to be a big car even though it is viewed at a distance of several hundred feet.

circumstances was not at all apparent. If a great amount of knowledge was available concerning the influence of various conditions on the outcome of education, there would not be the great need for educational research.

The concept of representative sampling that Brunswick has developed has come in for much criticism. One criticism that the reader will probably already have considered is that major advances have already been made in many areas in the behavioral sciences without resorting to the elaborate procedures that Brunswick's system demands. The psychology of learning is an example. Most of the important facts and principles of human learning that are discussed in typical textbooks were derived from laboratory experiments. For example, the principle that knowledge of results is an important condition for learning was derived from a consideration of learning as it occurs in the laboratory and was demonstrated with simple laboratory experiments. Yet it seems to have wide application in the field of teaching.

A second criticism of representative sampling is that it results in the production of probabilistic laws—that is to say, laws that state only that there is a certain probability of a certain happening as a result of a given set of conditions. Because Brunswick's system permits prediction over a wide range of situations, it is inevitably limited in the accuracy it can achieve. On the other hand, the more traditional approaches, because they aim ultimately at establishing all of the determinants of a particular event, have the aim of perfect prediction.

The Effect of the Research Worker's Intrusion on the Situation He Wishes to Observe

Sociologists and social psychologists have long recognized that when the research worker goes out to collect data, he often influences the situation he observes to an extent sufficient to produce marked changes in it. A book by Webb et al. (1966) has made an excellent summary of these *reactive effects,* as they have become called, and classifies them under the following categories:

1. *The guinea pig effect.* People who recognize that they are guinea pigs behave differently from the way they ordinarily behave. The typical response is for the guinea pig to be on his best behavior, but sometimes hostile responses may occur. Children in schools who come under observation show an undue amount of cooperation with the teacher, and the use of television or film recording in the absence of the experimenter does not overcome this effect. One may attempt to solve this problem by returning to visit the classroom, day after day, until the children cease to be inhibited by the experimenter's presence. However, this procedure introduces other problems. When the author visited a first-grade class on

repeated occasions, he found that the children began to acquire new behaviors toward him. Although on the first few visits the children kept their distance from him, after a few visits they began to interact with him. Some brought books to him and asked how to read certain words, and others began to ask him questions about why he was there. The classroom became a different place because of his presence and nothing he could do would alter that fact.

2. *Role selection.* Each person's repertoire of behavior permits him to play a number of different roles and the role he chooses depends on the social cues that are present. A superintendent, for example, may play a very different role at a school board meeting than at a meeting of his principals. In the one situation he might appear as a docile, submissive person, and in the other situation he might appear as authoritarian, controlling, and severe. The role that he might turn on when interviewing a research worker in his office might depend on such irrelevant cues as whether the research worker reminded him of a board member or of one of his principals. Again, a pupil may have to choose whether to react to the research worker as he would to his father or as he would to his teacher.

3. *Learning effects initiated by the research worker.* The encounter with the research worker may initiate learning and upset the validity of subsequent observations. Ask a student on a state university campus "Should students run their own Union without interference from the faculty?" The student may never have thought about this matter before, but your question may start him thinking. Before your encounter has developed much further, the student may be on his way toward becoming a campus activist.

4. *Response sets.* The best known of these sets is for a respondent to tend to agree with the questioner. This latter phenomenon is known as acquiscence set. Another well-established response set is for the respondent to give the more socially desirable response.

In addition, there are a number of interviewer effects that are more appropriately discussed in later pages.

The book by Webb et al. has some interesting suggestions concerning how the effect of the intrusion of the research worker may be often removed through the use of what they term *unobtrusive measures.* A simple and commonly cited unobtrusive measure is that used in determining which of the many exhibits in a museum are the most interesting to those that pass through its halls. One could, of course, ask the visitors as they leave, but such an intrusion into the life of the visitor begins to raise the problems that have just been discussed. An unobtrusive measurement of visitor interest might be derived by measuring how much the floor was worn away in front of each exhibit. At least such a measure might not be influenced by the presence of the research worker, although it might be influenced by other sources of error.

Webb et al. reviewed a number of different "erosion" measures. They suggest that the extent to which particular books in the library are actually read could be determined by measuring the wear on the corners where the pages are turned. Although the number of times that a book is withdrawn may provide some indication of the extent to which the book is read, there is always the possibility that a book may be withdrawn, but not read. Also, books may be read but not withdrawn. The erosion measure would appear to provide a much better measure of use than would those derived from circulation records. Other suggestions for erosion methods include the proposal that the activity of children be measured by the rate at which they wear away their shoes. The writing and scribbling activity could be measured by the wear on uniformly sharpened pencils.

Human behavior not only wears away selectively certain parts of the environment but it also leaves positive traces behind. Webb et al. refer to the use of these positive traces as *accretion methods* of data gathering. One example they give is that of studying the attractiveness of an advertisement by determining the number of different fingerprints found on the page. Examples of accretions nearer to educational research are the doodles and notes left by school board members, the materials in the wastebaskets of classrooms, school newspapers, and the exhibits prepared by children on display in classrooms. Inscriptions on the desks of the pupils represent another accretion that might be used as a source of data in some research. The use of accretion methods has had a long history of successful use in archeology, which has been highly dependent on the existence of trash heaps from past cultures as a source of data.

Erosion and accretion traces may have certain systematic sources of error built into them. The amount of wear on the floor in front of an exhibit may be contaminated by the fact that the exhibit is in a particularly favorable or unfavorable place, or that it is to the right of the entrance door and, hence, in the direction in which visitors tend to turn. Despite the fact that these are conditions that depress the validity of measurement, such measures are not usually disturbed by the research worker's intrusion on the situation, although sometimes such intrusion may have an impact. For example, if it became known that the doodles of school board members were being studied, the subsequent doodles would show the effect of that knowledge.

There are also many other unobtrusive measures that are not influenced by the intrusion of the observer. School records of various kinds form a rich source of data in some school systems. Even as simple a record as the absentee rate for each pupil has proved to be a very interesting variable in some studies. Where teachers are encouraged to enter anecdotal material on the cumulative record, the notes thus entered may be a rich source of information both about the pupils and about the teachers who recorded them. Some archival records suffer from having been severely and deliberately distorted. The minutes of school board meetings commonly present only selected material of which the board wishes to have a record, and the more interesting aspects of the evening's deliberations are never entered.

Summary

1. The field of experimental design has developed a vocabulary of its own with which the student should be familiar. The vocabulary includes such terms as *universe, sample, treatment,* and *population.*

2. Statistical procedures serve many different purposes. One major purpose is that of summarizing data. Another is that of helping to determine the justifiability of inferences made from the data.

3. Well-designed experiments display certain logical features that eliminate certain forms of bias in the resulting data. Assigning cases at random to treatments removes one source of personal bias. Experiments also have to be designed in such a way that it is possible to estimate the amount of variation that might be attributable to chance factors alone. When the results of experiments are very clear-cut, errors that result from sampling are very small and do not have to be estimated through complex statistical procedures. Only very few experiments in education-related areas produce such clear-cut results. A third point of design is that the experiment has to be of sufficient precision to provide the information needed. Precision can be increased by adding more observations. Another way to increase precision is to reduce the errors inherent in the design.

4. Although traditional experimentation involved the variation of only one factor in an experiment, the design methods developed by Fisher may involve the variation of many factors in a single experiment. Such multi-factor designs may be much more efficient than the single factor design.

5. Experiments involve controls, but the term *control* has many different meanings. A control may be a restraint on an experimental condition. The experimenter also exercises control over a variable or variables on which the experiment focuses. Then there may be control groups. In some experiments, a technique known as analysis of covariance is used to control certain characteristics of the experimental subjects. Operant psychologists commonly use a form of experimental design in which the individual exposed to the experimental treatment is his own control. In such experiments a first step is generally to determine a base rate of responding of the behavior to be studied. Once the base rate is established then the experimental condition is introduced, in order to determine whether this

changes the rate of responding. In operant experiments, the experimental condition introduced is generally a set of reinforcements. If the experimental condition produces a change in behavior, then the experimental condition is withdrawn, after which the rate of responding may return to the base rate.

6. The selection of those who are to participate in an experiment is a crucial factor in the design of an experiment. If the results are to apply to a particular population, then the experimental group must be derived from that population. All too often experiments are conducted with one population and the results are applied unjustifiably to another population. Experiments should ultimately be repeated with different populations in order to determine whether the results can be applied to various groups. All too often experiments are undertaken with particular groups because they are available.

7. Since nearly all experiments are undertaken with volunteer subjects, an important matter is how volunteers differ from other individuals who might have been included if they had been available. The volunteers tend to be better educated and to be of higher social class than those who are not volunteers. They also seem to be characterized by other important qualities. Experimenters can also adopt certain techniques to attract volunteers.

8. Replication is a feature of all experimental design. Replications within a design permit one to estimate experimental error.

9. Errors may be conveniently classed into those resulting from subjects, groups, and replications. This is just a convenient way of looking at sources of error and developing strategies for keeping them at a minimum. Subject errors are simply caused by the fact that one group of subjects may have an advantage over another group as a result of selection factors. Group error factors are caused by conditions that favor the performance of one group over another. The third type of error represents differences from one replication to another.

10. Factorial designs permit one to study the effect of several factors within a single experiment. The designs also permit one to study the interaction of the factors. They permit much more information to be derived than can be derived from single factor experiments.

11. Statistical methods are used for testing hypotheses. Hypotheses may be stated in the null hypothesis form. Hypotheses can also be stated in the form of whether a difference found will be one in which one has some degree of confidence because of a genuine effect and not of chance effects in the data. Errors are made in rejecting and accepting hypotheses. When one rejects the null hypothesis, and subsequent data shows that one should not have done so, then one has committed an error of the first kind. When one accepts the null hypothesis but should have rejected it, then one has made an error of the second kind.

12. Experimentation makes the assumption that the cases included in the experiment represent a sample of the population to which one wishes to generalize the results. All too often the reverse procedure is used. A group of available children is exposed to a program and then a population is sought to which one might generalize the results. Sampling one universe and generalizing to another has long been an error made by psychologists.

13. The conditions under which an experiment is undertaken may influence the results. An experimental program for teaching reading may have different outcomes when it is given as a special requirement for designated pupils than when it is a part of the regular classroom routine. If one wishes to generalize experimental results to many situations, then one should conduct the experiment under many different conditions.

14. A final point to make is that the conditions of an experiment may greatly influence the results. In particular, the fact that those participating may know that they are being observed may be crucial. Children whose work in an experimental teaching program is closely watched may behave differently from those in the control who are not subjected to such scrutiny. This difference may result in children in the experimental group achieving differently from those in the control group. Furthermore, individuals in experiments may believe that they are supposed to behave in a certain way. The use of unobtrusive measures may sometimes overcome these effects.

CHAPTER 11
Instrumentation
in Educational Research

Mechanical and Electronic Equipment as Eyes for the Educational Research Worker

Educational research workers have rarely used equipment to record classroom behavior that is not directly observable, because administrators in schools of education almost uniformly have no conception of what such equipment can accomplish. Perhaps this viewpoint reflects an undue preoccupation by educational administrators with surface phenomena that is to say phenomena that are clearly observable. Many principals are more concerned with how orderly and neat a classroom appears to be rather than with whether much learning is taking place in that classroom. Research workers have also tended to show a similar preoccupation with surface events. Thus, there has been extensive research on different methods of teaching children to read, but almost no concern with the effects of these methods on whether the children are also learning to like or dislike reading. Whether children can read or not is directly observable in test situations, but whether the children like to read is under the surface and thus more difficult to appraise.

A chapter on the development and use of measuring techniques seems to be appropriate in a section on research techniques. Whatever one's approach to the investigation of a problem may be, success in the investigation depends on the skill with which one can make observations. Let us pause here to consider what a research worker means by the term *observations*.

Although most people think of an observation as an experience involving looking, hearing, touching, smelling, or tasting, the research worker uses the term in a rather different sense. The research worker can sometimes observe directly what he wants to find out, but more often, what he is interested in observing are reactions in learners that are hidden. For example, in the study of reading and learning to read, a research worker may be interested in whether the learner shows any emotional responses, either positive or negative, to the materials; however, these responses are not very easily observed directly. Another research worker may want to find out whether pupils are challenged by particular tasks, but challenge is an inner state that cannot be seen with the naked eye. An observer may hope to be able to recognize symptoms of a child feeling challenged, but the symptoms may be subtle, fleeting, and easily confused with other forms of behavior. Much of what is important in education is not evident on the surface, for the pressures on the children to conform are such that they hide much that is going on inside of them. Yet what happens inside a child may, over the long term, be much more important than the trivia that can be observed on the surface.

Research workers, in all fields, have this problem of wanting to observe that which cannot be directly seen, and all research workers have to devote much of their effort to developing means of observing and recording that which is not directly observable. The biologist has his microscope. The biochemist uses X-ray crystalography to discover the complex structures of the chemical building blocks of the body. Physicists have used cloud chambers to enable them to observe the passage of electrons through space. The laboratory equipment of the scientist is a means of permitting him to observe indirectly that which he cannot observe directly.

Behavioral scientists have developed a range of devices for probing beneath the surface of observable behavior. In most psychology departments research workers have various forms or devices that collect information that could not easily be collected otherwise. In addition, some equipment is usually available that will automatically record directly observable behavior and which is used to eliminate the errors of human observers and sometimes to release the human observer from the tedious task of observing behavior over long periods of time. Some of the devices used by psychologists are pieces of equipment that can pick up the information needed by the research workers. Some of the probing devices are in the form of paper-and-pencil devices or interview techniques. Let us consider first the use of mechanical or electronic equipment as an aid to the educational researcher. Issues of the *American Psychologist* have provided a review of equipment that is available for psychological research (see American Psychological Association, 1976).

Equipment Used in Behavioral Research

The last quarter century has shown an enormous proliferation of equipment that is available to the behavioral research worker. This equipment has opened up new areas for the research worker to explore. Before considering some of the more commonplace pieces of equipment, such as timing devices, we consider some of the devices that are available for the recording of hidden bodily responses to the environment.

This type of equipment is designed to record very slight electrical changes in the body that occur when the individual begins to attend to an object, or is emotionally responsive to an object. Under such conditions a great number of different bodily responses occur that can be recorded. The heart and heartbeat is perhaps one of the most sensitive responsive systems. Equipment is now available that can record a change in the rhythm of even a single heartbeat. A study using this equipment is one undertaken by one of this author's students, Sharon Evans, who was interested in the responsiveness of normal and retarded children to new objects. The infant had electrodes placed upon his chest, through which the heartbeat was recorded. The electrical signal picked up from the chest wall, as the heart contracted, was picked up by the electrodes and then amplified and passed into a piece of equipment called a tachograph that functions as a computer. The tachograph led to a recorder through which the rate of the heart was recorded. If a single beat were out of rhythm, then the record would show a change in heart rate. The response of the heart is extremely sensitive to the shifting of the attention of the individual to new objects and could be used to show the response of the infant to a novel object.

Much research on infancy requires the use of such equipment. The equipment makes up for the fact that attending responses cannot be readily judged from behavior. Similar equipment can also be used in older children for recording activity in the brain by placing electrodes on the surface of the head. Visual attention to particular objects can be identified by the absence of alpha rhythm. This can easily be recorded in a person who is relaxed, not sleeping, and not attending to anything in particular. Equipment is also available for recording changes in the resistance of the hand of the skin, which also takes place as a part of an attending response. The change in the skin, known as the galvanic skin response, also takes place as a result of emotional arousal. The author has some of this equipment and has found that it has extended substantially the fields that students might want to explore. A school of education interested in early education and infant research must have equipment of this kind available, otherwise research workers and students are narrowly limited in what they can do.

There are several manufacturers of such equipment. The author has had some equipment manufactured by the Grass Manufacturing Company that has proven to be extremely good and reliable and usable by students. The equipment is sufficiently widely used so that on any campus, there will be at least one expert who knows how to use it and who can explain to new users just how it should be connected, calibrated, and used.

Simpler devices for measuring bodily changes related to emotionality are also available. The familiar sphygmomanometer, which the doctor uses to measure blood pressure, can be used in some studies to obtain a measure of response to stress. In one study the blood pressure was recorded of individuals who were engaged in their first experience as counselors in order to identify the degree of emotionality evoked by the experience. The same investigator also used a piece of paper that was sensitive to skin moisture for measuring emotionality. The same counselors pressed their fingers onto one piece of paper and the darkness of the fingerprint left behind was used to measure their emotionality in the situation. Simple procedures of this type are very easy to master and are well within the intellectual and financial capability of graduate students of education.

Apparatus designers have also produced a variety of equipment that is especially adapted for operant type experiments. This equipment provides the delivery of such reinforcements as tokens or candy or anything else in a capsular form on any schedule that the experimenter may want. This equipment is useful if one is interested in an operant approach to learning. However, most of this equipment has been designed primarily for use in animal experiments. In human experiments, where one needs to give the learner particular forms of feedback, the best piece of equipment for controlling the entire learning situation is the computer. A computer can feed information to be mastered to one or more learners, record and examine the responses for accuracy, provide whatever reinforcements are called for, give additional instruction if the learner has difficulty with whatever he is supposed to master, and so forth. The computer can be used in this way to study particular forms of instruction and without the unpredictable behavior that characterizes all human teachers to some degree. Although, as was previously stated, the computer has not yet been shown to be a particularly useful device for teaching ordinary children, in ordinary classrooms, the computer is a fine piece of scientific equipment that can be used to undertake very precisely defined teaching procedures. Of course, one may well criticize the computer for lacking perhaps all the most important human qualities that a teacher can bring to help the student. Problems, however, still remain of how to present subject matter that needs to be investigated through research involving computer-controlled learning. The computer has also been used in classical types of learning studies involving the learning of nonsense syllables since it has the capability of controlling rate of presentation and time factors that are important aspects of learning.

One can, of course, be carried away with the use of the computer as a means of controlling an experiment. The author once spoke to a psychologist conducting experiments with the rote learning of nonsense syllables who used a computer to present syllables to his learners. He explained how he programmed the computer to do this and how he had to arrange for a hook-up to the computer, as well as the other problems that were involved in using the computer. The author was also doing work with nonsense syllable learning at that time, and he explained to his colleague that he simply photographed the nonsense syllables and projected them onto a screen through a projector that had a simple timer to control the presentation. This author had much less trouble in his investigation than his colleague had. Also, every time this psychologist did an experiment, he was using time on a very expensive piece of equipment for which the university had to pay the hidden costs, whereas the author used only a few hundred dollars worth of equipment. Furthermore, it took him more time to set up an experiment than it took the author. One can overdo the use of computer equipment in controlling experimental conditions, though there are times when a computer is invaluable for that purpose.

Simple timing devices are essential for many kinds of research studies. The simplest of these is the familiar stopwatch, which now comes in electronic form. Large tabletop models are more convenient than the small pocket variety, and they are less readily stolen. Many more complex forms of timers are also available. For example, Hunter timers can be used to turn equipment on and off for particular intervals. A series of these timers can be arranged to provide a timed cyclic performance. For example, a series of these timers might be arranged to project a set of words on a screen for, say, two seconds, followed by a five-second interval, and then the timers might order the projector to show a new slide for two seconds, and so forth, until the entire series of slides have been shown. One could, of course, present such a sequence by hand, but the intervals would not be accurately timed and experimenter errors would be common. Timers are relatively inexpensive; a set of timers can be purchased for a few hundred dollars.

Some equipment in most psychological laboratories is designed for use in studies of perception. This equipment has been very valuable in research related to reading in recent years. The most common piece of this kind of equipment is the tachistoscope, which is designed to present visual displays for very short intervals, sometimes as short as 0.001 second. Why would anyone want to display material for such a short time? The answer is that one can slow up visual perception by displaying material for very short intervals of time. Thus, with a tachistoscope, one might display a sentence such as WHAT MONTH IS THIS? for perhaps 0.005 second. The person who tried to read what was displayed might say that he saw absolutely nothing. So it is shown to him again for the same short duration. This time he says that there seemed to be some words, but he could not read them. Then the sentence is displayed again, and this time he says that he sees a short word in the middle of a group of words, but he does not know what it is. After the material has been presented many times, the reader is able slowly to decipher the sentence. What the tachistoscopic technique seems to do is to slow up the process of perception. In ordinary reading, the short sentence might be read very rapidly in perhaps 0.05 second, but the process takes place so rapidly that the reader of the sentence cannot tell the experimenter what is happening and how the perceptual process operates. The tachistoscope makes it possible to study the slow emergence of a perception. The tachistoscope may be used with a great range of materials. Pictures may be presented for brief exposures in order to discover how children, or adults, extract information from pictures. Children do this in a different way than adults. Even children in nursery school can be studied with this kind of equipment and enjoy playing the game for the experimenter. Tachistoscopes are also very easy to operate and can be mastered by the graduate student in a half hour.

Eye cameras and equipment for the study of eye movement have often been the only pieces of equipment available in schools of education. The recording of eye movements is still a technique of great value for it can be used to determine what a person looks at and how long he looks at it. Some methods for doing this have been recorded by computers so that the eye movements can be later reconstructed and re-examined.

The motion-picture camera has long had an important place in behavioral research, but its major role has been in the study of infants. Much that cannot be readily seen in infant behavior becomes observable when a film is examined frame by frame. Arnold Gesell used film records extensively in developing his description of the emerging behavior of infants. Indeed, his laboratory files included thousands of hours of records of infant behavior of all ages and with all kinds of defects. The replay of these films permitted Gesell and his associates to identify typical behavior patterns in infants at particular ages. In more recent studies the camera has been used to pick up behavior of infants that has been hidden to direct observation. For example, the camera has shown evidence that when a two-week-old infant makes swiping motions at an object, he opens his hand briefly as it comes near to the object. In other words, the action is not just a random movement, but a precursor of a grasping response that seems to be innate. The replay of films also makes it possible to draw out sketches of the position of the hand and fingers at a number of points as the object is approached. The drawings show the opening and closing much more dramatically than the film. Films can also be used to record the motion of the eyes and to identify the direction of the gaze and the fixation points of the infant. The motion-picture camera has much potential for the study of play since it provides a detailed record of interactions from which measures of interaction can be derived. Speech may, of course, be recorded on the film or tape and then analyzed separately.

Speech recording in natural situations presents special problems in that the records are all too often so contaminated with other sources of noise as to be uninterpretable. Classrooms are particularly poor situations in which to make sound recordings of speech.

In all such recordings, there are two special areas of concern. First, there is the effect of the recording equipment on the behavior recorded. Although people who are used to being recorded may cease to respond to the recording equipment, children do not. The knowledge that what children do or say is being recorded may have marked effects on their behavior, even to the extent of disrupting the normal pattern. The second area of special concern is the ethical one. Although children may think that it is fun to be recorded, teachers do not. The presence of any recording equipment may make the teacher feel that the experimenter is infringing on his, the teacher's, rights of privacy, even when the teacher has given permission for the recording. A teacher may have difficulty in saying no when asked, and the giving of permission to record may not eliminate any of his underlying anger.

When videotape recording was first introduced, educators seized upon the technique as a potential tool for the training of teachers. With videotape equipment, the teacher educator and classroom supervisor thought they would be able to capture the performance of the student teacher and then discuss and critique the performance in an interview. Was not this technique used successfully by football coaches? These arguments were persuasive. An excellent review of research on the use of videotape techniques for training teachers by Fuller and Manning (1973) brings out the problems involved. The research began to show that student teachers who were exposed to images of themselves became fixated on their appearance rather than on what they were doing as teachers. Indeed, many found the experience of viewing themselves in a television picture as traumatic. Self-confrontation is a difficult situation with which to cope. Such self-confrontation does not usually add to one's self-esteem. Perhaps a person can accept only so much of reality. Too much reality is frightening, and perhaps disruptive of learning.

Home-made Equipment

The equipment used in experiments may be as complex as a computer, or as simple as a few trinkets with which a child plays, or which he uses to solve a problem. The merit of a piece of research has little to do with complexity of the equipment involved. The classical experiments of Skinner were all undertaken with simple equipment that he built himself, and the same was true of Thorndike. Piaget uses equipment that a high school student could build, given Piaget's design. Most of the important findings in the behavioral sciences have been made through the use of quite simple equipment, and the genius of those who made discoveries has been in the development of the ideas around which the equipment was built. A good idea for an experiment is a first necessary condition; the design of the equipment involved is secondary. This is a very important point because there are always research workers who seem to be more concerned with the development of equipment than with the finding of an important idea. Indeed, there is an old adage in the physical sciences to the effect that if you do not have a good idea for an experiment, then build an impressive piece of equipment for one can publish a paper on the equipment. The pursuit of such a policy may help to advance the individual even though it may not help to advance knowledge.

The simple equipment used by many great behavioral scientists may entice the graduate student into thinking that such equipment is easily developed. Such is not the case. Piaget uses such simple materials as glass funnels containing liquids of different colors and strings of beads, but a great amount of thought and care went into the selection of the materials, and many different forms of materials were tried out by Piaget before he found the materials that demonstrated exactly what he wanted to demonstrate. Even simple materials need to be tried out before they are adopted in an experiment, and the tryout invariably calls for revision of the materials. The development of simple experimental materials may require as much painstaking care and effort as would the complex use of a large computer.

Verbal Instruments for Collecting Data

The chapter on survey methods discusses some of the problems related to the collection of data through the medium of asking questions, but a great range of other devices, dependent upon the use of words, may be involved in educational research. These may be relatively simple in design, as is a form on which a person enters a record of his education and work experience, or very complex, as is a device such as the Minnesota Multiphasic Personality Inventory. The graduate student of education should realize that the building of a simple device is well within his capabilities and the time he can devote to it, but the complex instrument may take a large part of a lifetime to produce.

A first point to note about verbal instruments is that they may be used to probe into aspects of behavior that are far removed from the verbal. Thus, if one wishes to discover something about the mechanical skills of an individual, one may ask him questions about such matters as what hobbies he has, what kinds of things he can repair, what tools he is familiar with, how he spends his spare time, and so forth. One can even ask some of these questions in a form that prevents the individual from faking the test. Thus, one can ask him to identify the names of tools that are either described or shown in a photograph, or one can ask him to name a tool that would be suitable for a particular purpose. Such verbal tests can be used to probe mechanical and motor skills as well as interests, if the assumption is made that individuals acquire information about the areas in which they are interested.

The questionnaire about the individual's activities is probably the simplest of all devices to construct. Nevertheless, the simplicity of the device is likely to hide the fact that the data derived from it all too often are biased in certain directions. For example, if students are asked to enter on a simple form the grades they have achieved in courses they have completed in the past, one is likely to find that the grades they enter are a little better than their actual grades. As a general rule, any questionnaire is likely to provide data that portrays those who filled in the entries as being better, or more adequate, or more moral than they really are. The research worker should arrange the collection of data so that it is possible to check on the accuracy of reporting of those who fill in the entries. The fact that such a check is possible will not necessarily improve the accuracy with which the entries are made. Indeed, individuals often incorporate bias into their answers, not as deliberate falsification, but unknowingly. Sometimes one can check on the accuracy of the response to one item by comparing it to the response on another item. Year of graduation from high school can be used as a check on age. Such internal checks are commonly used. Some investigators have also asked individuals to fill out the information again, after an interval of time, in order to compare the two sets of responses. This provides an estimate of the consistency with which the questions were answered.

The expectation of the research worker is that in any contact with individuals who are being studied, these individuals will attempt to present themselves in the best possible light. This is as true when the data collection process involves the collection of simple facts, as when the process involves complex personality assessments through the use of lengthy personality inventories. The designer of any instrument for collecting data must keep this systematic bias in mind, and do all he can to eliminate it.

The Utility of the Single Test Item or Observation

Most inferences that can be made as a result of educational research are based on multiple observations. From observing a child's response to but a single problem assigned by the teacher, no responsible person is likely to make inferences concerning the child's educational achievement level or his scholastic aptitude. The single observation provides insufficient information for making either one of these inferences. Multiple observations can be used for making fairly accurate inferences about a child's achievement. Achievement tests are a means of providing multiple observations about a child's achievement, and the scores derived from these multiple observations have been demonstrated to measure certain achievements satisfactorily.

In other phases of educational research a similar state of affairs is found; the single observation has only the most limited value. If a socioeconomic index is desired for comparing the background of children, it is unlikely that reliance could be placed on a single observation, such as whether or not a child's home is equipped with a telephone. Although the presence or absence of a telephone is undoubtedly related to general socioeconomic conditions, it is only one of many possible criteria. A checklist of a number of items could be prepared, with each item hypothesized to be related to socioeconomic conditions. The list might include the presence or absence in the home of a telephone, a bathroom, an encyclopedia, a refrigerator, a separate bedroom for the child, and so forth. The scores on each of these items would be arrived at by counting the checks according to a key. The total information provided by all of the items might be of use, whereas the individual items considered separately might be almost useless. The small amount of information encapsulated in each single item makes the use of many items necessary.

The reader should not conclude that there are no areas of science in which single observations are of great importance. Medical science is replete with examples of instances in which a single test provides almost certain knowledge about the presence or absence of a particular disease. Chemical analysis depends on sequences of observations, each one of which is unambiguous in its interpretation. In physics, too, a single observation, such as is made in the determination of the density of a body, may provide highly valuable information to predict the behavior of the body in a multitude of situations. The contrast with educational research is marked.

Combination of Observations

Once it is recognized that observations must be combined in order to provide information that has any utility, two problems immediately arise. First, there is the problem of *what* observations are to be combined. Second, there is the matter of *how* they are to be combined. Most of the knowledge available about these two problems has been derived from studies of verbal responses to verbal problems such as appear in tests. Such knowledge, however, does have applicability to the wider range of materials used in educational research.

Consider the problem of estimating the size of a child's vocabulary or the relative size of the vocabularies of different children. One way of doing this might be to ask the child to define a series of words selected at random from a standard dictionary. If in this way we were to ask the child the meaning of ten words, and the child were to define five accurately, we might infer that the child could define 50 per cent of the words in the dictionary. However, a random sample of ten words would provide only the most limited amount of information about the child's total vocabulary. Chance may have resulted in the selection of common words, or perhaps very rare words, or words that the pupil happened to know. If any of these instances were to occur, our estimate of the pupil's vocabulary would be inaccurate. In order to avoid this eventuality, several courses of action could be taken. One of these would be to use a larger sample of words, the purpose of which would be to increase the precision with which it was possible to estimate the total vocabulary.

There is a second way in which multiple observations can be used, which can be described by returning to the problem of measuring vocabulary. If we were to draw a sample of one hundred words from the dictionary by taking the last word on each right-hand page, or every twentieth right-hand page, it is probable that our list would contain many common words with which almost everybody was familiar. The inclusion of these words in a test would provide little information since everybody taking the test would be familiar with them. Another procedure might be to select ten words that 90 per cent of the children to be tested would know, ten words that only 80 per cent of the children would know, ten words that 70 per cent would know, and so forth. This would form a rudimentary scale used to determine how difficult a level of vocabulary the individual can define. When such a scale is used, the purpose of measurement is no longer that of estimating the knowledge of the individual of all the words in the dictionary, although this can be estimated indirectly. The score of a child on such a scale would permit one to estimate how the child stood in relation to other children in vocabulary.

Dimensionality and Clustering Observations

There are unsatisfactory features in the procedures discussed for the measurement of vocabulary stemming from the fact that knowledge of vocabulary cannot be considered to be a unitary trait. Consider, for example, the case of the student confronted with a vocabulary test consisting of equal numbers of scientific and nonscientific words. Such a test might contain fifty test items in each of these two areas. Now it has been fairly clearly established that knowledge of scientific words is not very closely related to knowledge of general vocabulary, and thus the test measures two rather distinct abilities. If the student taking the test obtained a score of sixty items correct, it would be impossible to determine from the score alone whether the student had answered most of the scientific items correctly, or most of the nonscientific items correctly, or a considerable number of both types of items correctly. Two persons might obtain equally high scores, one by obtaining a high score on the scientific items, and one by knowing the nonscientific items. The score alone would not indicate whether the person was strong in the one area or in the other. This is because the test does not consist of a homogeneous group of items all measuring the same ability. If a measuring instrument is to have maximum utility, it should be designed to measure only one variable.

If a collection of items has such a mixed nature, then the score derived from it has only limited meaning. What is needed for meaningful measurement is a group of observations or items that belong together in some significant way and that can be used collectively as a measuring instrument. Such a group of items is sometimes referred to as a *homogeneous scale,* but one has to be careful about the use of the word *homogeneous.* Some writers who talk about a homogeneous group of items mean only that the items all *appear* to be measuring the same kind of variable, as would be the case with a test of scientific vocabulary or a checklist for measuring the socioeconomic status of the home. Others use the word to refer to a group of items that all belong together because it can be shown statistically that they all measure the same variable. What one really needs for meaningful measurement is a group of items or observations that not only belong together in some meaningful way but that also can be demonstrated by statistical means to measure a common property.

The research worker commonly is faced with the problem of having at his disposal numerous observations that must be grouped together into separate and distinct scales in order to provide meaningful measures. It is this problem of grouping that must now be considered.

Combining Observations in Meaningful Ways

The scientist who approaches educational problems is commonly faced with an abundance of observations and must find some way of grouping them so that they provide useful information. In the conduct of many types of school surveys, such as are undertaken by school- and college-accrediting associations, the accrediting agency may accumulate large numbers of items of information about educational institutions. Such information is not easily handled as a mass, and in some way the observations must be combined into groups if they are to be easily interpreted. If the home backgrounds of children are being studied, the social worker or research worker may collect hundreds of items of information about each child. Such data may include items indicative of socioeconomic level— home ownership, car ownership, size of home, value of home, and the number and type of appliances in the home. In addition, data might be obtained on a range of phenomena such as the number of brothers and sisters, the health of the parents, the sibling rivalries manifested by the children, the education of the parents, the number and type of books in the home, the preferences of the parents for the children, the father's occupation, the age of the parents, the number of neighborhood friends of the child, the religious affiliation, and the like. If, say, 300 items of information were collected about each of 200 children, the resulting collection of 60,000 items is not usable for most scientific purposes until it is organized in some way. Some of the ways of doing this are now given brief consideration.

The a priori method. The research worker who planned to obtain a large quantity of information about the backgrounds of the pupils probably had some theory about the characteristics of the backgrounds that were relevant for his purpose. Suppose the goal was that of predicting the pupils' levels of academic achievement. He might have started out by postulating a number of different kinds of conditions in the backgrounds that might be related to achievement. One of these conditions might be the economic status of the home; another might be the degree to which tensions and frictions were absent from the home; another might be the cultural status of the home as indicated by the number of books or the presence or absence of a piano; and so forth. The list of items of information to be collected might well have been drawn up after a set of broad categories had first been established. After the data had been collected, the items would be grouped into these broad categories and a score would be derived for each. Thus, one score would indicate the relative socioeconomic status of the home; another the degree of psychological tension in the home; and another its cultural status. Thus, the 306 items might be made to yield a dozen or fewer scores and the data would be reduced to manageable proportions. The advantage of the method is that it produces a set of measurements that are closely related to the theory on which the study was originally based.

Although this method is attractive, it has its limitations, particularly in studies in which not too much is known about how the items of information should be grouped together. The latter is true of such an area as school characteristics, in which a checklist might be used to describe a school by summarizing what are believed to be certain important facts about it. On the other hand, there are areas in which much is known about how items of information should be grouped. If the items referred to the biographical history of adults, it might be useful to group them in terms of the extent to which they reflected mechanical interests, scientific interests, clerical interests, and so forth.

The a priori method of grouping items of information rarely produces measuring devices that have particularly desirable properties. Too often the scales thus produced are too highly correlated with one another, which means that they measure characteristics that overlap. Considerable further work often has to be performed with these scales to refine them to the point where they are actually useful. A discussion of these additional steps is beyond the scope of this book.

Methods of grouping that depend on the interrelationships of the items. The student is familiar with the concept that two tests are said to measure the same variable when they are highly correlated, and that they measure different variables when they are uncorrelated. The same concept can be applied to items of information of all kinds. On the basis of this concept, it is possible to sort a pool of items into groups on the basis of whether the items are or are not correlated. Each group of items would then include all those items that were highly interrelated from a statistical point of view. Also, the items in one group would have little correlation with those in other groups—at least this would be so under ideal conditions. The actual procedure for doing this and the technical concepts involved are considerably more complex than is indicated here.

The mathematical techniques for sorting items from a pool of items into a series of scales measuring separate and distinct variables are complex and controversial. The early techniques, which are still used, are summarized in a book by Torgersen (1958). Later theoretical development of so-called nonmetric methods are described in the volumes edited by Shepard, Romney, and Nerlove (1972). These methods make it possible to take a pool of, say, 150 personality inventory items, administer them to a group of individuals, and then, on the basis of the responses to each item thus collected, apply mathematical techniques to sort the items into scales. Many of the methods can be applied by computers, but this does not mean that the complex techniques should be blindly applied. Shepard et al. point out that many pools of such items provide such fragmentary and unstable data that the results of scale analysis are meaningless, that is to say, if the study were repeated with a new group of individuals taking the same items, different scales might come of the analysis. Also, the results achieved with one pool of items might be quite different from the results achieved with another pool of items, even if the two pools were selected to provide what were believed to be comparable materials. If one starts with a poorly thought out pool of items for an inventory, sophisticated scaling techniques will not improve matters.

A second criticism of much that is done with mathematical scaling techniques is that they can be applied to only certain kinds of data. For example, data from open-ended questions are not generally suitable for the application of these techniques. Research workers have often been tempted to use data in a form that can easily be fed into a computer, even though the form of the data is unsuitable for the study, and other forms of insight might lead to much greater insight into the phenomenon under investigation.

A third criticism of these techniques is that the use of a mathematical scaling technique may force the data into a pattern that is not particularly useful. The technique imposes a structure on the data that may not be worthwhile.

These warnings are intended to prevent the student of education from obtaining a mass of data that he does not understand, and from hoping that a mathematical game played by the computer in relation to the data will bring meaning, even though there seems to be none.

The grouping of items of information in terms of the variables it is desired to predict. In a later chapter on problems of prediction, it is pointed out that items of information are often assembled in order to make predictions. There are, for example, many studies in which information about the home and cultural background of children has been collected in order to predict and anticipate difficulties in school. Let us consider such an example in order to illustrate the method of grouping items of information.

Suppose that items of information about home and cultural background were collected for the purpose of predicting (1) reading disability, (2) social difficulties in school, (3) absenteeism, and (4) degree of success in an academic curriculum. The research worker collected 150 items of information about the background of each child entering a junior high school in a large city. The school served a residential area of varied economic circumstances. The data collection was continued until a record was obtained of the backgrounds of each of 400 pupils. These pupils were followed through the school. A reading-disability group was slowly and carefully identified. Reports that enabled the research worker to identify a socially maladjusted group were obtained from teachers and added to by counselors. Records of absenteeism were available, as were records of grades. Once the research worker had obtained all this information, he selected from the pool of background-information items a group that predicted reading disability. When a total score was derived from this group of information items, the score was found to predict reading disability with considerable success in subsequent samples. A similar procedure was adopted for predicting each one of the remaining three variables that the study had been designed to predict.

This method of using multiple items of information has been used successfully for combining items for all kinds of purposes. It has been used for predicting performance in various types of training programs; for predicting success in certain occupations, such as that of salesman; for predicting delinquency; and so forth. In most studies that have used items of background information, the resulting predictions have been extremely limited in accuracy. Of course, this does not mean that the method might not provide highly accurate predictions when used to combine other types of information.

The disadvantage of the method lies in the possibility that the measures it produces, as in the example discussed, often are closely related to one another. It is possible that three of the four scales produced were measures of the extent to which the atmosphere of the home was favorable to intellectual development. The fourth scale, related to social adjustment, may have measured a different characteristic.

Although this procedure does have a certain logic in it, there are procedures considerably more complicated that could be used to provide more accurate and efficient predictions. These other methods take into account not only the relationship of the items to the variable to be predicted but also the extent to which the items provide overlapping information. This involves complicated statistical procedures requiring the use of computers to be efficiently undertaken.

Some Cautions Regarding the Fractionation of Pools of Items

The procedures discussed in this chapter are analogous to mechanical procedures for the fractionation of crude oil. The crude oil is fed in at one end of the fractionating plant, and a whole range of petroleum products, some useful and some not, comes out at the other end. Procedures for grouping and selecting test items are of this character. They can be applied and used without much knowledge of the why and the wherefore, and their application can be considered in most cases as a step in the direction of developing tools for research; but it can hardly be considered research.

This point is made because the author has frequently been faced by a graduate student coming to him with a proposal for a doctoral dissertation to consist of the application of a certain technique to a pool of items the student proposes to build. This is not an activity that should be encouraged in the graduate student. It represents a laborious and time-consuming routine. It does not encourage the type of activity that is often considered to lie at the very core of a program of doctoral studies—namely, the thinking through of an important problem to the point where ways are found to arrive at a solution. Research of any consequence requires more than the mere application of a mechanical routine. If research could be undertaken by the latter means alone, it could be produced in a factory by a relatively uneducated labor force.

Much of what is undertaken in the name of research fails to note that the mere identification of a variable is no guarantee that it is going to be of any use. New measuring instruments in the behavioral sciences can be developed very easily. The great difficulty is to discover and develop variables that have predictive value. This usually requires prolonged endeavor and what has been termed scientific insight. It does not result from any mechanical procedure, but rather from the development of a sound theory and the testing of deductions from this theory.

It thus behooves the scientist to begin all work on the development of measuring instruments with a theory concerning how the variables he is attempting to measure relate to the specific aspects of behavior that he is studying. If this is done, it will be necessary to test the instruments in order to determine whether the measures they provide permit the making of the predictions that were anticipated. If they do not do so, one should discard not only the instruments but also the theory on which they were based. Measures that have merit in terms of their internal properties do not help in building a sound theory and do not contribute to knowledge if they show no signs of operating in the way expected.

Finally, it must be reiterated that the information provided by a single observation related to education is extremely limited, and even a group of relatively homogeneous items cannot be expected to provide more than a hint about other types of events. This may be looked upon in another way in the case where the observations refer to behavior. If a group of test items occupies five minutes of time, this must be recognized as an extraordinarily small sample of a person's behavior. What a person does in a five-minute period is only the most limited basis for generalizing about what the same person will do during other five-minute periods. At the same time it should be recognized, of course, that a test situation is not *any* sample of behavior, but should be a sample of behavior that has been demonstrated to have particular significance for predicting how the person will behave in certain other situations. Nevertheless, there is a definite limit to the amount of information that can be obtained about behavior in a given period of time.

On the Advantage of Obtaining Ready-made Devices

The discussion thus far has stressed the complexity of building measuring instruments. If the reader is not discouraged with the possibility of building his own testing devices, he should be. Some theses and dissertations have called for the production of new verbal measuring devices, but the production of the device may well double or triple the amount of work called for by the study. For this reason, the majority of studies conducted today as degree requirements use instruments that have had a substantial history of use. In recent years a very large number of studies have used well-known instruments such as the Strong Vocational Interest inventory, the Minnesota Multiphasic Personality Inventory, the Edward's Personal Preference Schedule for measuring needs, and Rokeach's simple device for the assessment of values. Many other instruments could be added to this list, all of which had a long history of producing interesting findings, and that is a key point in their favor.

The instrument that has already been used has numerous advantages over the new device, just developed by the research worker. Instruments that have survived the years of trial and use, have adequate reliability. The new instrument often has to be worked and reworked in order to obtain a level of reliability that is acceptable for any purpose. The previously collected data also indicates the kinds of situations in which the instrument can be used to make predictions with an accuracy that is better than chance. The cumulative evidence also indicates the general theory of behavior that the instrument supports. If an instrument is claimed to be a device for measuring anxiety, then the history of research with the device should show whether it really does identify individuals who are identified as anxious by other means. The data available should also tell one whether the instrument indicates a general tendency to be anxious or a tendency to have one's anxiety aroused in particular classes of situations or in the test situation itself. For many available instruments there are literally thousands of studies available showing how the instrument functions. In some cases, summaries are available, but the reader should note that the summaries given in test manuals are often slanted to make the instrument appear more useful than it actually is.

Fortunately for many research workers, excellent reviews are available of most testing devices that have ever been published in the Mental Measurement Yearbooks edited by Buros. These volumes have been noted for their highly critical and sometimes devastating reviews of published tests. An instrument is usually reviewed by several different authorities in the field, and each is accompanied by an extensive bibliography of research related to the use of the device. Reviewers have tended to be overcautious rather than overenthusiastic, which is an error in the right direction. New instruments are typically reviewed with the greatest caution. The Buros volumes have provided a particularly valuable source of information to research workers over the years.

At a simpler level, textbooks on measurement commonly provide general descriptions and limited reviews of the more widely used measuring devices. Such reviews are of limited value, and they rarely emphasize the extent to which a measuring device has been built on a basis of adequate reflection, but limit their concern to whether the device has, or has not, utility.

A Caution

All the types of measuring devices considered in this section share a common disadvantage. They all exert an influence on the individuals on whom data are collected and thereby change the data. As was pointed out earlier, individuals want to appear in a good light when answering any set of questions. The situation exerts an influence on the data collected. This happens not only when a form is filled in but whenever an individual believes that he is being observed by another.

Summary

1. Educational research has been grossly deficient in the use of instruments for recording data, yet such instruments can reveal many aspects of behavior that would otherwise remain hidden. Much of what is important

in education is not evident on the surface and should be probed with suitable instrumentation. Educational research workers have used paper-and-pencil instruments to advantage, but have rarely used devices that measure physiological responses.

2. A great range of equipment is now available for undertaking behavioral research. Some of this equipment can measure physiological responses that are extremely sensitive indicators of attention, interest, and emotional states. In addition, operant psychologists have used a great variety of devices for controlling schedules of reinforcement and other aspects of the conditioning process. In some areas of research, such as research on infancy, the use of such equipment is almost essential for obtaining meaningful results. The computer is also a useful device for controlling some aspects of experiments. Studies of perception need to be instrumented since perception is such a rapid process. Eye cameras have a place in such research.

3. The motion-picture camera has been largely replaced by the video-tape recorder as a research instrument, though for slow-motion studies the camera has many advantages. However, cameras and videotape recorders may, through their presence, modify the behavior that is being recorded. Self-confrontation on a screen also produces strong emotional responses that may disrupt any learning that the procedure is designed to produce.

4. Home-made equipment also has a part to play in research. The production of such equipment is not as easy as it seems. Extensive trials are needed with preliminary forms of the equipment before a final usable form is produced.

5. Verbal instruments for the collection of data have been the rule, because such devices are readily available. A great deal is known about such devices and how to construct them, and many on the market have had fifty years of use.

6. A single observation is rarely of much utility for research purposes and little, if anything, can be predicted from it. Observations generally have to be combined before they have much utility for making predictions or for other purposes. The combination of items to produce measuring instruments is a complex art in itself. There are many different ways in which items can be combined together for the purpose of making predictions. The most common method of doing this is probably the *a priori* method. The method is justifiable in cases in which a considerable amount is known about the prediction problem. Scales developed in this way generally have to be refined by other methods before they become particularly useful. Mathematical techniques can also be used for sorting out observations, or items, into scales. These techniques are highly controversial and have not had any particular history of success, but they still have potential for research purposes. A third procedure is to group items in terms of the

variables that one may want to predict. Many useful scales have been produced through this kind of procedure. All too often, such procedures have been applied without first performing a careful intellectual analysis of what is involved in the problem. Careful thought is a prerequisite for all statistical analysis; all too often, thought follows rather than precedes such analysis.

7. There are great advantages in conducting research through the use of ready-made tests and other instruments. The years of use behind such devices provide a useful backgrounds for research.

CHAPTER 12
Research Through Surveys

Surveys are commonly conducted to establish the nature of existing conditions. That is the simplest form of survey. At a more complex level, surveys may be used to explore the causes of particular phenomena. Thus, a survey may be used to determine the attitude of parents toward schools in a particular area, but the survey may also be used to try and determine the cause of favorable or unfavorable attitudes toward the schools. Such a survey might help to establish that although the parents were well impressed with the performance of the teachers, their relationship with principals left much to be desired. Such a school district might then set up a program in public relations for training its administrators.

The literature on surveys is extensive. The reader might do well to begin his exploration of the area by perusing a review of social science research, such as that by Babbie (1975). The literature on surveys that is widely used for instruction in the area has remained surprisingly stable over the years. Many old classics in the area are still used and consulted. Parten's book (1950) is still read by students despite its age, and Backstrom and Hursh (1963) is still being used. New printings of the latter seem to come off the press at regular intervals, and with no apparent decline in demand. Among more recent books is that by Babbie (1973), and although it is an excellent book, there is little in it that was not contained in Backstrom and Hursh's earlier text. Moser and Kalton's (1972) review of research in the area has become almost a standard reference work and is of great value in determining the research that has been undertaken on specific problems. In many ways the Moser and Kalton volume must be considered the classic in the field. Another text is that by Warwick and Lininger (1975). The reader is advised to start his exploration of the area by at least skimming a text in the area of social research and then studying in greater detail one of the general books on surveys.

Much that has been written on the survey represents knowledge that has accumulated through practice rather than through research. Indeed, many of the interesting problems related to the conduct of surveys have not been studied, perhaps because most of those who conduct surveys are under pressure to produce data for clients. In most survey organizations the conduct of research is a very secondary matter. For that reason much of the research that has been conducted on the techniques of survey research

317

has been undertaken by students, though government organizations have sometimes made some contribution to research studies.

There are also books on specialized aspects of survey technology. The reader's attention is directed to Silvey's book (1975) on how to decipher data derived from social surveys. Silvey is particularly helpful both on constructing tables for use in reports and interpreting those tables. There is also an excellent literature on sampling techniques and sampling problems.

Students from outside of North America may be interested to know that works have been published on the problems and uses of survey techniques in different parts of the world. A recent perusal of the library shelves showed volumes on the survey techniques from India, Africa, and South America. Each region presents special problems in the collection of data.

A distinction must be made between a survey and a sample survey. In a sample survey, data are collected about only a portion of the population with which the survey is concerned. The design of the sample survey is such that the individual cases examined provide data from which inferences can be made about all of the possible cases. Thus, a study of teachers in 100 rural high schools within a particular state may permit the making of inferences about teachers in the other 500 schools.

The survey is an attempt to build a body of knowledge through the use of direct observation, but direct observation is probably limited in the knowledge it can produce. Chemistry and physics could not have been produced merely by observing naturally occurring chemical reactions, and even wise men were unsuccessful at understanding human nature by observing the behavior of their fellow humans. Psychology, as well as chemistry and physics, required for their advancement the development of experimental procedures to supplement observation before even limited understanding could be achieved. Direct observation, even in its more sophisticated form represented by the survey method, is limited in the knowledge it can achieve. Nevertheless, there are many situations in which experimentation is impossible or impractical, and the survey method can help us to achieve understanding under such circumstances.

The events or conditions that may be enumerated or measured during surveys include a great range of phenomena. The popularity of the public opinion survey as a newspaper feature makes one think of attitudes and opinions as the main source of data in surveys, but this is not necessarily so. Various classes of events that may form the central core of an educational survey must be given brief mention here.

Physical Conditions Related to Learning. Many characteristics of the physical environment can be measured, such as the floor space per pupil in different schools, the number of books per pupil in the library, the intensity of the natural illumination on the pupil's desk, the mean temperature or humidity, and the like. Many school surveys devote considerable effort to

the measurement and evaluation of such characteristics of a school program, and on the surface these surveys would appear to be on a solid
foundation, for it is clear that the measurement of these variables is objective and does not involve the judgment of the investigator. These measures
have satisfactory reliability, and thus their weakness is not at first apparent.
The inadequacies of the procedure result from the fact that its usefulness
depends on the choice of suitable environmental variables—that is to say,
variables that are genuinely related to the effectiveness of learning of the
pupil. But very little is known concerning the relationship of such variables
to learning processes in pupils. If the student looks back over research in
the area, he is likely to find, not only little positive evidence to help in the
selection of variables but much negative evidence indicating the apparent
lack of relevance of many variables he might choose. Such studies may
have failed to demonstrate the relevance of some of these physical variables
because any effect they may have is perhaps long term and not sufficient
in magnitude to manifest consequences over a period of a few weeks or
even a semester. Long-term studies of the effect of these physical conditions
are rarely feasible.

Behavior of Teachers and Other Behavioral Conditions Related to
Learning. Numerous studies have been conducted that attempt to determine what teachers do in the classroom or how they spend their time.
Some of these studies serve the purpose of providing data that is necessary
for rethinking and redesigning classroom procedures to make more effective
use of the time available. For example, if it is found that, say, 50 per cent
of the teacher's time is devoted to minor administrative routines, then
some steps can be taken to eliminate these routines.

Pupil Achievement. Surveys that are most likely to reveal facts of
importance for educational administration are those provided by the pupils
themselves. Such information has direct relevance to the control and study
of the learning process that the other classes of facts revealed by surveys
do not. Another chapter is devoted to observation procedures that may be
used to conduct surveys of pupil-teacher interactions in classrooms. In
addition, surveys may be made regarding the reading achievement of pupils
or their achievement in other so-called basic skills. Sometimes surveys of
the information of the pupils may be made, as when a school determines
what the pupils know or do not know about their local community, about
health practices, about contemporary affairs, or about some other matter
judged to be of significance in the educational program. Such surveys need
not be confined to matters of student knowledge but may also include
events in the attitudinal field.

A significant survey of school achievement of recent years has been the
National Assessment Program that was designed to keep track of changes

in the level of achievement in the nation's schools. John Flanagan's Talent Survey has also produced data on changes in school achievement during the 1970s. An earlier chapter discussed the National Assessment Program and the difficulties of interpreting the data. At the risk of being repetitive, it should be emphasized that overall school achievement is not just a result of what the schools do but also reflects the extent to which the culture as a whole encourages learning.

Achievement surveys of a more local character have also become widely used. These programs have been introduced under the banner that bears the word *Accountability*. Teachers are held to be in some vague way accountable to the government and taxpayers that provide funds. The tests supposedly show the degree to which the teachers in the schools are accomplishing what they are paid to accomplish. The underlying conception is like that found in Victorian England in which the teachers were paid on the basis of a formula linked to the results of tests administered once a year to children by Her Majesty's Inspectors of Schools. The children were given tests in what today would be called basics. The test papers of each pupil of each teacher were scored and the scores determined the salary of the teacher. The system had devastating results and dragged down the English school system until it became one of the worst in the Western world. As a result of massive parent protest, Parliament eventually passed legislation ending this teacher evaluation system, and thus began a new era in English education.

The accountability systems found in various state departments of education bear some resemblance to their earlier English counterpart. These systems have some potential for providing some information about trends in education, but how such trends are to be interpreted is not clear. For example, the evidence derived from surveys of achievement suggests that there has been a slight increase in reading scores over the last decade, but that scores in most academic subjects have declined. Such findings are not very helpful to anybody. The changes are extremely small and no one knows quite how they should be interpreted.

Achievement surveys, though designed around the concept of accountability, are potential sources of data for research. There is even a place for the study of how such surveys are biased by teachers.

Much more needs to be done on the work habits and living habits of pupils. The surveys of television watching by children have already produced valuable information, but there is much to be known about how children spend their out-of-school time and what they learn during that time.

Surveys of Aptitude. Considerable interest has been stirred in recent years by a large-scale survey of aptitudes conducted through the enterprise known as Project Talent. As a part of this survey, a very large and comprehensive battery of aptitude tests was administered to a cross section of high school students in the United States. A careful follow-up of a sample of these students permitted a great amount of useful information to be collected. For example, such a study permits one to find out the extent to which students with high-level talent fail to find jobs commensurate with their level of ability and hence, a determination can be made of the degree to which talent is wasted in particular groups.

The data from Project Talent are so extensive that research workers outside the staff of the study have been encouraged to make use of the material. The library of information that has thus been made available will become the basis for many doctoral dissertations for years to come. Much of the data will also increase in scientific value as time goes by for it will provide a benchmark on the national utilization of talent against which the data from future surveys can be compared.

Attitude Surveys. One of the most common types of surveys involves attitudes. In the usual attitude survey, those who are questioned are asked to express an opinion or belief. A question such as, "Which one of the following presidential candidates would you prefer to see in office at this time?" asks for an expression of attitude, as do all questions related to voting behavior. The interest of pollsters in tapping public attitudes arises from the common belief that attitudes are related to behavior. Sometimes this assumption is justified, as it is in the case of voting behavior. Positive attitudes toward a candidate are more likely to accompany voting for the candidate than are negative attitudes. Nevertheless, most pollsters recognize that a single question concerning a person's opinions or beliefs provides a rather unreliable measure of the person's attitudes. In order to remedy this basic deficiency, several questions may be asked, each one of which may probe the person's attitudes but from a different angle.

Surveys concerning attitudes may be concerned not only with whether the person's attitude is positive or negative but also the extent to which it is so. Thus, a survey of attitudes toward the schools may determine not only whether public opinion is on the positive or negative side but also how far it is negative or positive. Such studies introduce the idea that an attitude can be measured against a scale from positive to negative and that the responses to particular items in the poll can be used to indicate how positive or negative a person's attitudes are. The scaling of items is a complex problem in itself.

Surveys of attitudes involve problems related to the design of questions and sometimes involve the scaling of those questions along an attitude dimension.

An ambitious attempt to study pupil attitudes by survey methods is the Purdue Public Opinion Panel, which conducts an opinion poll in cooperating high schools, mainly at the junior and senior levels. Schools that participate pay a very small fee to help cover expenses and in return obtain a report on the responses of their own students as well as on the responses of a wider sample of pupils. Surveys conducted in this manner are usually related to matters of widespread interest, such as the attitude of pupils toward various aspects of the curriculum or toward their parents. The results serve the purpose of stimulating thought rather than that of solving specific problems.

Much of the material collected about pupils by means of surveys is collected through the medium of paper-and-pencil devices, but information about pupil behavior can sometimes be collected by other means. It is possible, for example, to obtain records of the number of books borrowed by each pupil from the library if a survey of reading is being made. The consumption of foods in the cafeteria can provide some evidence of eating habits in relation to health. Absentee rates may also be of considerable interest. Artistic products and other products of the pupils' hobbies can provide evidence of how their leisure hours are spent. A wealth of objective pupil data that are not derived from verbal responses of the pupils can be incorporated in a survey.

Delphi Techniques

A form of survey that has attracted considerable attention in recent years is based on what have been called Delphi techniques. These techniques were developed at the Rand Corporation by Olaf Helmer and his associates in the 1950s. Olaf Helmer was concerned with the problem of developing ways of forecasting future events in the area of national defense on the basis of expert opinion. The traditional way of doing this was to collect expert opinions which were then tabulated. Delphi techniques take this process a step further by attempting to achieve some degree of consensus. When such a technique is applied, expert opinions are collected, usually together with reasons why those interviewed hold the opinions they do. Then the information obtained on the first go-around is fed back to those who answered the questions. The individuals then see how their associates answered the questions and also the reasons given by those who gave different answers from their own. Individuals may then reconsider the positions they have taken and feel free to change their previous responses. The same procedure can be pursued one or more additional times, with the hope that some kind of consensus might be achieved. Weatherman and Swenson (1974) have described a number of applications of the technique, and some of these applications are in the educational field.

The ultimate worth of the technique depends upon proof that the technique does actually produce predictions that are better than those that could be produced by the simpler methods. Such proof is lacking at the present time. There is the possibility that the technique may produce predictions that are inferior to those produced by majority opinion of experts or through a careful selection of experts with good records at predicting the future. The widespread use of Delphi techniques, in various forms, seems unjustified at the present time.

The technique has some obvious weaknesses. Some forceful individuals may state their positions in a strong form that weaker individuals will feel obliged to accept. Some individuals may have a strong desire to be on the side of the majority. Some may, through habit, take a middle-of-the-road position that they have found to be safe. The Delphi technique involves a complex set of social relations that may disrupt effective decision making. Very little is known about how these social relationships operate.

It is useful to reflect at this time that those who forecast election results from early returns use an entirely different approach. They use voting groups that have had a history of showing the outcome of elections. Certain precincts have been demonstrated to be highly predictive of how the rest of the state or nation will vote, and the voting of these precincts is used to predict the outcome of the election. In other areas it may be possible to identify individuals who have had a good record of predicting the future in particular areas of activity and to use those individuals for making future predictions. Unfortunately, in government the reverse procedure is more commonly used. For example, both Presidents Johnson and Nixon continued to rely on judgments related to the Vietnam War that were made by high officials who had been consistently wrong over many years. If these presidents had selected advisors with a record of making accurate predictions, the war would have been over much sooner.

The Semantic Differential—An Approach to the Study of Affect

The typical approach in most attitude surveys is a direct one through asking those interviewed to express an opinion that reflects the attitude in question. Sometimes an attitude may be probed by asking questions that involve different aspects of the attitude. One may also provide the interviewee with a set of statements, each of which represents a different attitudinal position, and from which the interviewee must select the statement that most nearly represents his position. All of these approaches generally involve a probing of what is termed the affective aspect of attitude, that is to say, the aspect of attitude that has to do with how one feels. Psychologists don't use the term *feeling*, but prefer to use the term *affect*. That part of an attitude that has to do with the feeling elements in attitude are referred to as the affective aspects. There are, of course, other aspects of attitude. For example, attitudes have a cognitive aspect, that is to say, our attitudes are based on information or what is believed to be information.

Still another approach to the exploration of the affective aspects of attitude that has been widely used in recent years is the approach involving Charles Osgood's technique known as the Semantic Differential.

The ideas underlying the technique have been described in a book by Osgood, Suci, and Tannenbaum (1957). The technique explores some of the elements of meaning that an individual ascribes to a concept. For example, one might be interested in exploring the meaning that the concept *political leader* has for certain groups of individuals. In order to do this, those whose concepts are being explored are presented with a list of opposite terms such as:

rough   —   —   —   —   —,   —   —   smooth

young   —   —   —   —   —   —   —   old

happy   —   —   —   —   —   —   —   sad

The list might consist of fifty or more such items. The individual is asked to make a mark on one of the seven positions between each pair of opposites that best expresses how he feels about the concept. Although this is a strange task, hardly anybody ever has any difficulty in doing it. The position of the marks along the scale indicates the individual's feelings related to the concept. In the original Osgood study, twenty concepts were studied denoted by such varied words as *lady, boulder, sin, father,* and so on. Then, after extensive statistical analysis, Osgood et al. concluded that the elements of meaning indicated by the responses reflected three main constellations of meaning. The first constellation he referred to as the *evaluative factor.* This factor showed up in the responses to such items as good-bad and negative-positive, among others. The second constellation represented what they called a *potency factor,* reflected by such scales as hard-soft and severe-lenient. The third constellation represented what Osgood et al. called an *oriented activity factor* found in such scales as active-passive and excitable-calm. They also found a number of other variables of lesser importance.

The exploration of Osgood and his colleagues was at a theoretical level. In order to understand the implications of the work for conducting research in education, a practical illustration is in order. Useful applications of the work require considerable adaptation of the technique. An interesting adaptation by McKennel and Bynner (1969) is suggestive of some of the modifications that can be undertaken.

In the McKennel and Bynner study the semantic differential technique was used to explore four concepts: the boy smoker, the boy nonsmoker, the self, and the ideal self. Discussions with children were used to develop the set of scales that were used to explore the four concepts. Nineteen scales were developed such as:

neat and clean	versus	scruffy
good at school work	versus	not good at school work
usually does as told	versus	disobedient

The analysis of the data indicated that the nineteen bipolar scales seemed to consist largely of three factors that were described as educational success, toughness, and precocity. An example of the kind of findings produced by the study is that the smokers rate themselves low on educational success, but consider educational success to be an important feature of their ideal selves. The smokers do not reject the values of adult society that places a strong premium on educational success. They just do not live up to this set of values. Smokers also attribute great value to precocity and consider themselves precocious. The toughness dimension is also of interest in that it is associated by smokers with smoking and is also an incentive for non-smokers to take up smoking.

A point to note is that the dimensions used in the semantic differential type of study should rarely copy without modification the dimensions developed by Osgood et al. The kinds of bipolar scales that can be concocted are infinite in number, and the scales used for a particular study should be very carefully designed.

Surveys—Consequential or Trivial?

Surveys have all too often represented the main technique used by students of education in their theses and dissertations, partly because the survey approach seems deceptively easy to pursue. All too often these theses and dissertations have represented endeavors that could never have any impact on any part of education. For example, many of these studies carry a title such as, "A Survey of the Use of Audiovisual Materials in Ochipewa County." Such studies usually involve a survey of the use made by teachers of the materials in question, and the author of the study usually concludes that the teachers do not use the materials that are available, that they misuse the material, or that the teachers do no know what material is available. Copies of the study are sometimes sent to the district school office where they are typically filed by an orderly secretary, and there the matter rests. The study ends up serving only the purpose of permitting the student to obtain his degree, and perhaps an increment in salary, but the survey as a source of information is never retrieved from the file drawer or wastepaper basket. How does it happen that the findings of the study were not eagerly awaited by administrators and teachers?

The answer to this last question involves several factors. First, the administrators of the school district probably knew all about the uses and misuses of audiovisual materials in the school district. The study was not likely to tell them anything they did not already know. Teachers were not particularly interested because they, too, knew about their own short-comings in the use of materials. In addition, the teachers, like the administrators, had far more pressing problems on their minds than anything that the survey researcher was likely to investigate. Lastly, all of those involved might have been highly suspicious of the motives of the student in making his survey, feelings that the enterprise was an outright attempt to highlight the inadequacies of the teachers. Such suspicions might also have been accompanied by a tendency of those interviewed to fail to report truthfully the use of the materials that formed the focus of the inquiry.

If the results of a survey are to have any kind of impact, they must focus on issues with which some group has deep concern. The annual survey undertaken by the Gallup organization on how the public views the schools is an example of such a survey. Politicians, school board members, school administrators, teachers, and parents are all concerned with how the schools are viewed by the general public. The results of the survey are cited in the press and stir up much controversy, but they are also taken seriously. The results are used to pinpoint aspects of the running of the schools that need to be viewed in a different light by the public, or which need to be changed by school administrations.

Students of education do not have to confine their surveys to trivial issues as they so often do. At any time and in any place, there are issues of the greatest importance that need to be explored in terms of what people think and feel.

The Questions to Be Asked and How They are Presented

Since most surveys conducted involve the use of questionnaires and questioners, much of the rest of the chapter is limited to a discussion of surveys involving such techniques. A first step in the development of a survey is to decide just what information is to be collected. This is not as easy a matter as it may seem. Suppose that one wishes to survey a community for the level of education of adults. A first point to note is that the term *educational level* is far from being a clear one. It may mean the number of grades of schooling completed, but it may also include technical training and on-the-job training. For some it may mean the extent to which they have succeeded in becoming educated adults through their own initiative, despite limited formal schooling. Some may think of education as a lifelong program involving a continuous contact with adult community education projects. A first step in planning such a survey would be to decide just what one meant by level of education. Then decisions have to be made concerning whether one can assume that the level of education described by those interviewed can be regarded as a correct description of their actual level of education. Immediately one encounters such questions as whether those interviewed will try and present themselves as better educated than they actually are, and how many in the sample will be unwilling to discuss the matter at all.

This leads one in the planning stage to consider the matter of the kinds of interviewers to use, if the survey is to be conducted by interviewers. Moser and Kalton (1972) seem convinced that the nature of the interviewer makes a difference in the collection of survey data, but there seems to be a lack of research concerning the relationship. One suspects that affluent white interviewers should not be sent into poor black neighborhoods to collect data about nutrition, health, or similar areas of concern. The Latin American would hardly be the person to send to an affluent Anglo suburb to collect data on attitudes toward minorities. Some kind of matching of interviewer and interviewee seems desirable, but Moser and Kalton cite evidence indicating that too much rapport may not be an advantage. At least, under some circumstances, individuals questioned may be more willing to open up to a complete stranger than to a person toward whom they have a feeling of friendship.

Sudman and Bradburn (1974) have summarized the small amount that is known about interviewer effects. They conclude that the effect of the interviewer is at a maximum when the questions are threatening to the interviewer, that is to say, when the questions produce anxiety in him. Examples of questions that are threatening in this sense are those that ask about sexual behavior, honesty in dealing with others, and matters such as death, bad habits, and antisocial behavior. Sudman and Bradburn conclude that questions related to such issues should be handled through anonymous questionnaires rather than through interviews, though Kinsey dealt with sexual matters with apparent effectiveness in face-to-face interviews.

At least one study shows that the interviewers who collect survey data are not all equally successful. Hauck and Steinkamp (1964) sent out interviewers to collect economic data from a rural population and found sizable differences in the capability of different interviewers to obtain the data with accuracy. Some of the data involved the amount of money kept in savings accounts, which could be verified. Interviewers differed both in the accuracy of the data they were able to elicit from those questioned and also in the completeness of the data provided. An attempt to identify the characteristics of the successful interviewers suggested that they showed greater self-confidence, dominance, and likableness than the less successful interviewers.

The graduate student conducting a survey is usually the only interviewer, and he should be aware of his characteristics and how they will influence the responses he will obtain. He should recognize that the people he interviews are not merely sources of information that will flow from the interviewees' vocal cords to his pen. On the contrary, the interviewer will be dealing with another human being with whom he will be slowly developing a relationship. The chances are that some of his interviewees will be doing much more than just answering his questions. They will be wanting to please the interviewer and tell him what they believe he wants to hear. This social relationship may result in the distortation of the information that is sought. Other interviewees may withold information or say that they do not know the answers when they actually do. Pollsters agree that the collection of data by interview involves a complex set of social relationships that often contaminate the data collected.

The interviewer may remove himself partially or completely from the interview situation, either by conducting his interviews by telephone or by the use of a mailed questionnaire. Relatively little is known about the effectiveness of the latter techniques. The telephone technique limits the sample of cases to those who have telephones, and mailed questionnaires reach only those individuals who have permanent abodes. Moreover, both of these techniques tend to exclude the lowest socioeconomic levels. Additional research is needed on the use of these techniques. Much of what is known about these techniques is derived from the impressions of the pollsters themselves who now have had over half a century of experience. Mailed questionnaires seem to be particularly useful when the answers are short and require little thought. Apparently questionnaires tend to be filled in rather hurriedly. Also, if the questions call for the looking up of documents, as in finding out the age of the house in which the party lives, then a questionnaire will give superior results. On the other hand, interviewers can encourage the interviewee to give careful and reflective answers and can probe when an answer is uninterpretable, as it sometimes is. Good interviewers, with well-thought out questions, will have relatively few answers that have to be discarded because they cannot be coded. The mailed questionnaire also has the disadvantage that it may permit the recipient to discuss the questions with others before a response is made. Indeed, questionnaires sent to one person are sometimes filled out by another. The interview also permits the recording of spontaneous responses.

The best of both worlds may sometimes be achieved by combining the mailed questionnaire with a follow-up interview. A questionnaire may be mailed out and then an appointment may be made to discuss the responses with the individuals on the mailing list. The U.S. Census uses this kind of procedure, delivering the often very lengthy questionnaires as far as possible in person, and then picking up the completed questionnaires. When the questionnaires are picked up a check is made to ensure that all questions have been answered and that the answers are codable.

Anyone who plans to undertake a series of interviews for the collection of survey data would do well to profit from what others have learned about interviewing from experience. The Survey Research Center of the University of Michigan has published a manual for the training of its own interviewers that is well worth reading (Survey Research Center, 1974). A well-written short book about the adventures of survey interviewers has been produced by Converse and Schuman (1974), who provide a lively account of some of the odd situations that interviewers may encounter.

Both the interview and the questionnaire need some kind of introduction. Interviewers usually have a short set speech they deliver. The mailed questionnaire is accompanied by a brief cover letter. The letter should indicate why the survey is being undertaken and why the receiver has been selected as a participant. Providing a stamped envelope for the return of the completed questionnaire is more than a matter of courtesy, for the unused stamp seems to motivate the recipient to return the material. Some research workers have provided a small sum of money for filling in the questionnaire. Even as small an amount as twenty-five cents may increase returns, provided it is sent with the original materials. Individuals who see the twenty-five cents right in front of them when they are first confronted by the questionnaire seem to be better motivated to return the materials than those who read in the covering letter that they will be sent twenty-five cents when the completed questionnaire is returned. The thought of twenty-five cents in the future seems vague and unimpressive. The delivery of twenty-five cents with the materials not only seems concrete but it seems to imply that the sender of the materials trusts those who are to receive them and that there is faith that the materials will be returned. Faith and trust are hard to cast aside.

Mailed questionnaires always have to be followed by letters of reminder, which usually include another copy of the original materials. Such reminders contribute substantially to the return rate. Many receivers of questionnaires intend to provide the information, but they mislay the materials before finding time to fill them in. Sometimes several follow-up letters are needed to obtain an adequate return. Sometimes a telephone follow-up is effective. However, Moser and Kalton report data that successive follow-ups may produce a decline in the quality of the returns. The later returns may be filled out in a slipshod manner.

Returns from mailed questionnaires tend to be biased in that better educated persons are more likely to respond than those who are less educated. Undoubtedly there are other biases in the manner in which questionnaires are answered that have not yet been as well established.

This leads to a consideration of the sensitive matter of guaranteeing the anonymity of the recipient of the questionnaire. If such anonymity is not guaranteed, then those who return questionnaires may well be very different individuals from those who do not. Of course, there are many surveys in which anonymity is of no consequence. The main point is that if the research worker promises anonymity to the respondent then he must keep that promise. That has not always been done, for research workers have sometimes used hidden codes that enabled them to identify the names of individuals who return particular questionnaires. This practice lacks integrity and should not be followed. Sometimes the research worker may provide a guarantee that only he will know the names of the respondents, but many may not trust the research worker sufficiently for the promise to have any impact on them. If the author were to receive a questionnaire dealing with personal issues, he would wonder how careful the research worker would be in safeguarding the privacy of those answers to the questions, because he has seen research workers who were quite careless in the way in which the anonymity of respondents was safeguarded.

The Design of Questions

The formulation of questions is a crucial matter, but however hard one may try to formulate good questions in terms of the purposes of a study, almost any list of questions is open to criticism. Suggestions for the design of questions can be found in many sources including Cantril (1947), Parten (1950), Backstrom and Hursh (1963), and Moser and Kalton (1972). There is general agreement among these authors, whose work spans many decades, perhaps because most of what can be said about the matter reflects common sense rather than the results of research.

1. The most obvious point is that questions should be clearly stated in the simplest possible terms. This is obvious, but much less obvious is the fact that the writer of a question is rarely in a position to decide whether a question meets this standard. One finds out whether questions are clear by running a pilot study and probing the respondents to see whether they understood each question as it was supposed to be understood. One can make a check on the difficulty level of the vocabulary used in the questions by checking it against a vocabulary list such as that provided by Lorge and Thorndike (1944).

2. Questions should not evoke uniform, stereotyped responses. Questions that raise such issues as whether teachers are underpaid or overpaid are likely to evoke the stereotyped response that teachers are underpaid, particularly if the question is directed to teachers. The Gallup polls over nearly fifty years have asked the question, "Are you in favor of labor unions?" The very uniform, stereotyped response to this question is yes, even in the case of groups who are notoriously antiunion.

3. Although questions that produce stereotyped responses should be avoided, questions must nevertheless produce responses that represent a firm position of the individuals questioned. In other words, the responses to the questions should have reliability. The answer a person gives today to a particular question should be the answer he will give tomorrow. Thus, it is necessary to avoid questions that are answered impulsively and without much previous thought.

4. Avoid loaded questions. Don't ask a question such as, "The superintendent of schools has been criticized for placing too much emphasis on learning basic skills. Do you agree with this criticism of him?" The question almost begs for agreement and loads the data to put the superintendent in a bad light. Those who answer the question may feel that they want to be like a majority who are taken to be critical of the superintendent. The loading of questions is a matter of degree. An even more loaded question is one such as, "Important citizens of this community have recently criticized the superintendent through letters to the press. Do you agree with these citizens?" The respondent in this case does not even have the chance to admit that he knows nothing of the criticism that has appeared in the press, and he may not be willing to set himself off against the leading citizens.

5. Questions should not be hypothetical, that is to say, they should not refer to conditions that exist only in the imagination. Don't ask city people if they would be happier or less happy living in small towns. Most of them probably have never lived anywhere except in the big city and cannot know what it is like to live in a small town. Many surveys related to women's rights make this error by asking men how they would feel in a world in which women truly had equal rights, and by asking women how they would feel toward men in such a world. One cannot know what that world would be like until it arrives. Only then can one answer such questions in a meaningful way, but not before. Hypothetical questions are always quite fascinating for graduate students conducting surveys, because they are so interesting and fire the imagination, but the data they yield have little meaning.

6. Avoid presuming questions. This is a *don't* stressed by Moser and Kalton. A presuming question presumes that the person interviewed has had some particular experience that he would have to have had in order to answer the question. A question such as, "For whom did you vote at the last school board election?" presumes that the individual voted at the last school board election. He may not tell the interviewer he did not vote and may make up an answer. Such questions should be preceded by the question, "Did you vote at the last school board election?" If the answer is yes then the interviewer inquires about whom the interviewee voted for.

7. Be on guard lest a question have a special meaning for a particular group. Backstrom and Hursh tell a charming story about a question involving the government control of *profits*. When an uneducated population was asked this question, they were almost unanimous in stating that "prophets" should be controlled only by God. Such special interpretations can be identified only if the questions are tried out in a pilot study by sensitive interviewers who know how to probe the minds of those interviewed.

8. Avoid the use of emotionally loaded terms such as *unpatriotic, extreme right, Communist, progressive educator, permissive classroom,* and

so forth. A question such as, "Superintendent Smith says that the schools are better today than they were twenty-five years ago. Is Superintendent Smith telling the truth?" The respondent has to decide the truth of Smith's statement, but at the same time he has to decide whether or not to imply that Smith is a liar. Emotionally loaded names and prestige names used in questions can have an enormous influence on responses. A question that begins, "President Lincoln advocated the use of . . ." is likely to elicit heavy endorsement for whatever Lincoln advocated.

9. Avoid lengthy or complicated questions. A person can hold a short statement in his memory long enough to reflect upon an answer. If he is given a long statement, he may forget the first part of it before he reaches the end. If the question has to be long, there are advantages in permitting the respondent to read the material, but this gives advantages to the more literate interviewees. When the interviewer has to provide the interviewee with a list of answers from which one is to be selected, the interviewer may also have to provide a list that the interviewee can peruse at leisure.

10. Avoid introducing embarrassing or anxiety-producing questions when direct face-to-face interviews are involved. Earlier the point was made that such questions are better handled through anonymous questionnaires delivered through the mail.

11. Ask questions only about those matters with which the respondents have some familiarity. Surveys of what the public thinks about how classrooms should be conducted in their school system will produce meaningless results, because the public may have no understanding of what the alternatives are. Indeed, the public often knows little about how the school around the corner is run.

12. The question must be such that inferences can be made from the responses obtained to responses obtained in other situations. This may not seem obvious when it is first considered, but it is precisely what is wrong with the question that elicits a stereotyped response—one given in the particular situation but presumably not given in other situations. If a survey is made to determine how the electorate will vote in a certain election, it is important to be able to assume that behavior in answering the survey questions will be related to behavior in the voting booth. If these two aspects of behavior are unrelated, the survey ceases to have any purpose. All questions asked in the survey method must be such that it is reasonable to assume some generality of the response. The relationship between verbal behavior and other aspects of performance is complex, and a simple one-to-one relationship can rarely be expected.

13. Avoid double-barreled questions. Don't ask a question such as, "Do you think that drinking and smoking in public places are objectionable?" Sometimes one is tempted to ask such questions, but such questions do not permit a rational response from the person who objects to public drinking but not to public smoking. Occasionally what appear to be double-barreled

questions may be justified. For example, if one were interested in discovering attitudes toward members of the counterculture, one might describe such individuals as *typically* long-haired, dressed informally, often in blue jeans, preferring natural foods, and living informally. Although respondents might have separate attitudes toward each of these attributes, one might be interested only in an overall attitude toward the group of individuals as a subculture, but one could not use the word *counterculture* because it might have little meaning to many.

Identification of the Individuals to Be Sampled

Any survey requires that those to be questioned, observed, or studied, be identified in some way. In many educational surveys, all of the individuals in whom one is interested may be included in the survey. A study has been completed of the views of teachers in the Kalamazoo, Michigan, School System concerning the accountability system. All of the teachers were included in the study, though the study could have been conducted with only a sample of the teachers. This sample could have been identified in many different ways. A useful text on the problem of sampling is that by Sudman and Bradburn (1976). Among the techniques used for this purpose are the following:

1. Random Sampling. Suppose that there are 800 teachers in a system and that one wishes to interview 200 of them. One way to do this would be to hold something like a lottery. Each name is placed in a capsule and the capsules are then mixed in a rotating drum. Then 200 capsules are drawn from the drum. In this system, every teacher has an equal chance of being included in the sample. The drawing of the names is strictly random. Nobody would follow this procedure, exactly, because it would be inconvenient to go through the routine of typing out the names of each teacher and then packaging each name in a small capsule. An easier procedure would be to obtain a printout of the teacher's names. One could then assign a number to each teacher from 1 to 800. The next item needed is a table of random numbers, which can be found in a book on sampling statistics, of which there are many. Books are also available that provide tables of random numbers. The next step would be to read the first three digits in the table, which might be 487. This would tell us to pick teacher number 487 as the first teacher to be included in the study. Then one would read the second three digits in the table, which might be 006, and would mark teacher 006 for inclusion. Thus, one would proceed until 200 of the teachers had been identified. This procedure would provide a random sample of the teachers in the system.

Another satisfactory way of obtaining the sample of 200 teachers would be to obtain a list of the teachers and then to select every fourth teacher in the list. One should be careful *not* to select the first 200 teachers because, if the names were listed alphabetically, one might find that the sample included a particularly large group of teachers with certain national origins, because common names in some languages tend to begin with certain letters. If the teachers were ordered in the list, not alphabetically, but in terms of the school to which they were assigned, then the block of the first 200 teachers might include only those from certain schools.

There are many possible problems related to the selection of a sample from a list. For example, a graduate student who wished to obtain four comparable samples from a list of pupils went down the list marking each group of four students A, B, C, or D in order. Thus, the list was marked A, B, C, D, A, B, C, D, A, B, and so on. The students had been arranged in the list in order of their IQ scores. The reader should figure out how the sampling process would produce systematic differences among the four samples of students.

2. Nonrandom methods of sampling. One way to improve our ability to make inferences about a total population from a sample is to increase the sample size. Thus, national polling organizations may ordinarily use a sample of about 1,000 for the typical weekly poll published in the newspapers. But for very special events where greater precision is required, the sample may be increased to many times that number. Predicting close elections requires a greater precision than when the outcomes are not at all close, so close elections are predicted with large samples. Another way to improve predictions is to use what are called stratified samples. In a stratified sample, one does not select cases at random, but rather one selects cases that have characteristics that match the characteristics of the total population. Thus, in conducting a poll of adults about their attitudes toward the schools of the district, one would probably want to interview individuals who represented different socioeconomic levels, different parts of the school district, and perhaps different educational levels. One would probably select a sample that accurately represented the school district as a whole with respect to these characteristics. In most cases one would want to identify a number of interviewees in each category that would be proportional to the number in the total school district population. This is called proportionate stratified sampling. Occasionally, there is a need for disproportionate sampling.

Proportionate stratified sampling always increases the accuracy with which inferences can be made, provided appropriate variables are used for stratification. In the case of sampling adults in a school district for a survey of attitudes toward the schools, one would not stratify with respect to such variables as height and weight, because these are certainly unrelated to attitudes. One would stratify with respect to socioeconomic level because this would very likely be related to attitudes toward the school. Indeed, one would select variables for stratifying the sample that are likely to be related to the attitudes that one is interested in appraising. Sometimes previous studies can be used to find out the variables that are related to the particular attitudes to be surveyed.

In some surveys a disproportionate stratified sample may be used. Consider the case of a study undertaken in a Midwest city in which the investigator was interested in the attitudes of different religious groups. If the city were sampled at random, his final sample might include 30 per cent Catholics, 50 per cent Protestants, 8 per cent Jews, and 12 per cent in other categories. Since the investigator's main interest was in differences among the major religious groups, he would be interested in a sample that contained roughly the same number of Catholics, Protestants, and Jews, even though such a sample would be different from that of the total city population. The investigator would have to find means of identifying groups of Jews to be interviewed since these would appear only in small numbers in a random sampling. Many studies require disproportionate sampling of this kind.

A first step in sampling usually consists of identifying those people who are to be included in a sample. This may not be entirely easy. The telephone directory fails to list the poorest members of the community and also those who do not wish to be bothered by a ringing phone. Some communities have a list of residents, but such lists are not necessarily complete. Some residents do not wish to have their names listed in the register because the register is used by advertisers and others and becomes a means of distributing junk mail. One way around the problem posed by a lack of a list of residents is to identify those to be sampled by what is called an area sampling method. In this technique, highly detailed maps of the regions to be sampled are used and the area is systematically sampled. If, for example, a particular small area is to be included in the sample, then all persons living within that identified small area are included in the sampling. The sample thus selected is largely independent of the whims, likes, and dislikes of the persons collecting the data. Nevertheless, the method is not as simple as it seems, and difficulties are encountered in tracking down the persons identified. There are also definitional problems. If a person has a residence in a particular locality, it does not necessarily mean that he lives there, and decisions have to be made about such matters.

In the case of area sampling, we may identify only one person in each area, or every person, or every adult who resides there may be included. In the latter case, the term *cluster* sampling is applied. Cluster sampling has advantages in that a single interviewer can make a single trip to interview several people. This may reduce the time, effort, and money required to conduct the survey.

Sometimes a technique known as multistage sampling is used, again, for reasons of economy. Suppose that our survey of attitudes toward education were to be conducted not in a single school district but in the entire state.

As a first step in planning this survey, we might decide that we would not sample all of the 200 school districts, but would instead select a small number of representative school districts, perhaps as few as 20. Then, within each of these districts thus identified, samples would be identified for interview. The samples might also identify clusters of individuals. This form of multistage selection of samples can reduce the cost of the survey enormously. One would have to send interviewers to only 20 school districts instead of 200, and within the school districts, one would have to interview individuals in only selected localities.

Another technique occasionally used is to permit the interviewers to identify the individuals to be questioned. Some polls use this practice, but in such polls a great amount of data is also collected on those individuals who are interviewed. The additional data are then used to determine the degree to which those interviewed constitute a representative sample of the population. Pollsters also use certain corrections, derived from experience, which they believe permit them to overcome interviewer bias. For example, educated interviewers tend to select individuals for interview at the higher educational levels of the population they are to interview. Even if they are to interview laborers, they are likely to interview the more educated laborers. When interviewers conduct their own selection, they are usually given some guides to follow in doing this, such as the proportion in each of several income levels or the geographical areas in which they are to collect data.

All pollsters have had problems in ensuring that their interviewers provide honest data. In the early days of public opinion polls, pollsters discovered that some interviewers found it easier to stay at home and fill out the questionnaires from their imagination. Since they were paid on a piece rate, that is to say, so much for an interview, some of the interviewers found a simple and profitable way of fleecing the organizations for which they worked. Modern polling organizations claim that they have foolproof methods of checking up on interviewers and that cheating by interviewers is virtually impossible. If the graduate student employs others to conduct interviews, he should be very certain that the interviewers perform their tasks conscientiously.

How Large Should the Sample Be?

This question is asked by most graduate students who conduct a survey, but there is no simple answer. There are far more important issues in conducting a survey than the mere size of the sample. The classic example of a very large sample failing to make a prediction is that of the poll conducted by the Literary Digest in 1936. In this survey, a sample of 10 million respondents to a mail survey were tabulated showing that Alf Landon would win the election. When Roosevelt won by a landslide, the

Literary Digest was virtually forced out of business. Certainly the sample in this case did not lack adequate size, but it lacked other important features. The names included in the poll were derived from telephone directories, so that the sample obtained in the Depression era was much more selective of high income than it would be today. In addition, the poll obtained only about a 20 per cent return and the returns were overloaded with the better educated sections of the population. Such a poll with 10 million cases was far less accurate than a modern poll with perhaps only 1,000 well-selected cases. No competent pollster today would settle for a 20 per cent return, though many graduates undertaking research projects settle for even less.

Thus, it is evident that merely increasing the size of a sample does not necessarily lead to improved accuracy unless great care is exercised in identifying the sample to be interviewed and studied and efforts are made to obtain a high return. The total effort of the individual conducting a survey must be to arrange all factors so that the greatest accuracy of measurement can be achieved. This involves using carefully worded questions that have had a preliminary tryout, the careful identification of the individuals to be questioned, and the effort made to ensure that every person to be included in the sample is actually contacted.

Statistical methods are available that can be used to indicate some aspects of the accuracy of a poll. Such methods tell us the variation to be expected if we were to take other similarly selected samples. Two samples, drawn in exactly the same way, would not be expected to produce precisely the same results. However, the more accurate the poll is, the more nearly would successive samples agree one with another. Using this kind of technique, pollsters will commonly indicate the accuracy to be expected from a particular poll. Of course, such estimates always assume that the method of identifying the sample polled was a good one. This may not necessarily be the case. For example, a pollster may assume that the sample represents those who are going to vote, but a large section of the population polled may not vote at all. In the latter case, the error inherent in predicting from the sample to the voting population may be much larger than statistical estimations would suggest.

The Coding and Handling of Survey Data

Plans for the handling of the survey data should be made when the initial plans for the survey are made. Data will be entered on some kind of questionnaire form, regardless of whether there is an interview or a direct mail contact. The design of the questionnaire is important for the later handling of the data.

If the questionnaire is to be filled out by the respondents themselves, and not by an interviewer, then the form and appearance of the questionnaire is important. Those who conduct surveys agree that it is poor practice to squeeze as much into a single page of a questionnaire as possible. Questions should be spread out so that they are easy to read, so that the answers are easy to record, and so that the reader does not feel overwhelmed by a mass of tightly printed material. In other words, make the task as easy as possible for the person responding.

The questionnaire should also be designed so that the information derived from it can be easily used. This generally involves coding. Thus, Question 10 may have six different answers of which the respondent must choose one, and these can be coded either 0 to 5 or 1 to 6. Sometimes the respondent may perform the coding himself. For example, on one census form, the person responding has to find his occupation from among a list, and he must then read off the number of the occupation and enter it on the questionnaire. Such self-coding systems are highly attractive to those who conduct surveys on very limited budgets, but they introduce errors. Respondents have a way of misreading code numbers and sometimes of entering them in the wrong places. If coding is undertaken by the person conducting the survey, then he can check his work or have it checked by another individual. There is no easy way of checking self-coding procedures.

The main purpose of coding is to convert complicated data into a simple form that can be presented in tables and charts. Simplicity is a good thing, but one has to be careful that the process of coding does not simplify data to the point where meaning is lost. This is particularly true in the case of free answer responses that sometimes are expressed with much feeling and meaning. For example, the author recently read a report published by a teacher organization that described a study undertaken by an independent research group brought in to study the problems of administration of the local school system. The answers to the open-ended questions gave clear expressions of anger of a kind that would not have been apparent if they had been coded into categories indicating the various features of the administrative system to which the teachers objected. The report quoted every answer of every teacher, providing a clear picture of how the teachers felt toward the administration of the schools. Although each teacher expressed his anger in his own way, the message of anger ran clearly through the long list of responses. The only way in which the data might have been reduced in volume would have been to present a random sample of the responses. Such a sample was not presented because the procedure might have aroused the suspicion that the sample did not fairly represent the total picture. The effect of presenting all of the several hundred responses was overwhelming for not a single teacher had any kind words to say about the way the system was administered.

The decision to list all of the free answer responses in a report must always be based on the judgment that the responses are of sufficient interest so that people will read them. Lists of responses that no one will read are worthless.

Scales and Ratings

The typical question in a survey can be answered on a yes-or-no basis. This is the most convenient type of answer to tabulate, but it does not always provide the information needed. If one were investigating attitudes toward various places that provided higher education for those who could profit from it, one might be interested in a variety of plans that varied from completely free higher education for all who qualified, to plans that called upon the student and his parents to bear the full cost. One might prepare a list of statements that represented a range of positions on this issue and ask those interviewed to read the list and to select the position that most closely agreed with their own position. The following set of statements is of this type.

Which statement best reflects your view of how the costs of higher education should be paid in the case of students who can qualify for admission?

1. Higher education should be free for all.
2. Higher education should be free only for those who cannot afford it. For the others, the government should pay a part of the cost.
3. The cost of higher education should be borne, as far as possible, by the student and his family.
4. The cost of higher education should be paid for by the student and his family, but with the help of government-guaranteed loans.
5. The cost of higher education should be borne by the student and his parents.

These five statements form a crude scale. One end of the scale reflects the attitude that all higher education should be supported by the government. The other end reflects the position that each young person and his family should fend for themselves and raise money for college by whatever means they can. The scale is a crude one, but each person who answered the question by choosing one of the answers would indicate his rough position on the scale. One could do a much more sophisticated job of scaling by starting with a larger number of items. One way to obtain such items would be to ask adults to write short statements on how a college education should be financed. Then there are procedures that can be used to find the relative scale position of the various items. After all the items had been scaled, one could then select a small number of them that were roughly equally apart on the scale. One might also want to retain a larger number than five items, for this might help to improve the reliability of measurement.

Although this sounds as though it were a simple procedure to follow, the determination of the scale value of each item is a complex task and may be laborious. The reader may wish to consult several sources on ways to scale items. Lemon's book (1974) provides a good general review of the problem. A relatively old book by Edwards (1957) is still excellent, and Green (1972) has a technical book on the problem. Of some interest is the application of scaling methods to the scaling of products for the market. Haley (1972) has provided an interesting review of this field. He shows, for example, how foods can be scaled on such dimensions as snack versus meal-like and nondiet versus diet. On such scales, potato chips score high both on the snack end and the nondiet end of the dimensions. A similar technique could be used to scale school materials on such scales as interesting-dull and practical-theoretical. Sometimes it may be to the advantage of the person conducting the survey to undertake a scaling procedure that provides a scale of measurement that has, in a sense, a scale of equal units. Most of those who conduct surveys do not bother to develop series of suggested responses that have a set of scale positions. Those concerned with the accurate measurement of attitudes often scale their items, but pollsters are interested in data at what might be called a cruder level.

The multiple-answer question that forms a crude scale finds its most common use in rating procedures. Although rating procedures are widely used in other contexts, it is convenient to consider ratings in the present context.

Ratings

Some of the events involved in educational research must be reduced to quantitative terms by means of a rating procedure. For example, one may observe hundreds of interactions between teachers and pupils and reduce them to a single rating, indicating the hostility or warmth of the teacher toward the pupils. Social workers may have seen hundreds of families on welfare, each of which has shown through numerous behaviors how they view the welfare system. These attitudes may range from passive acceptance to active hostility against welfare and the political conditions that make welfare necessary. The social worker may want to summarize these attitudes in the form of a single rating. Ratings represent a form of summarizing data and numerous observations are condensed down into a single numerical rating. Many surveys ask those interviewed to summarize their experiences or feelings in this way.

It is extremely difficult to define for the rater just what events are to be observed, and, in fact, this is not usually done except in the vaguest terms. For example, a teacher may be asked to rate pupils for their ability to work with other children in small groups. It is probable that the researcher engaged in this enterprise would supply the teacher with a rating scale in which various positions would be described in such terms as "Works well with groups, seems to add to what the group accomplishes, contributes to the smoothness with which the group operates"; and perhaps at the other end of the scale the statement, "Generally seems to be a source of friction and irritation in a group." Such a series of statements does very little to orient the rater in the matter of what to observe, but rather it assumes that the rater knows the kinds of observations that are necessary and relevant in order to arrive at the kind of judgment that the scale demands. There is no entirely satisfactory way of remedying this situation. An obvious partial solution is to provide a preface to be read as an orientation to the use of the scale. Although such a preface may help to orient the rater on the matter of what he is to observe, it can refer to only a limited sample of the universe of behaviors to be observed, because a long list becomes tedious to read and remember. It may also draw attention to certain specific behaviors, and the rater may easily forget that the behaviors listed are supposed to represent only a sample, not the total universe, of behaviors to be observed.

An alternative procedure, which has considerable merit, is to develop a rating scale consisting of many scales, each of which is directed to a fairly specific aspect of the total domain of behavior that is to be observed. If pupils are to be rated on their ability to work in small groups, each pupil might be rated with respect to each one of several aspects of the behavior and perhaps as many as twenty aspects might be listed. When such a procedure has been adopted, it is usually desirable to perform a factor analysis of the ratings to determine whether they can be considered to contribute to a single principal factor. One major advantage of the multiple-rating approach, in addition to the assistance that it gives in defining the domain of behavior to be observed, is that it usually helps to increase the reliability of ratings.

Efforts to Control the Rating Process

Efforts to exercise control over the rating process are familiar, for the common ones are cited in every textbook in educational measurement. The reader is undoubtedly familiar with the following commonly stated rules:

1. Define several points on each scale with as much precision as possible.
2. Restrict each rating scale to a narrow range of behavior that can be well defined.
3. Change the ends of the scale so that the "good" end is not always at the top or always at the bottom of the scale.

4. Avoid words such as *average* in the middle range of the scale. The rater
   who does not wish to give too much effort to the rating procedure is
   likely to class too many as average.
5. In the directions, indicate the need for honest rating and, wherever
   possible, state that a low rating will not have any consequence for the
   person rated, either directly or indirectly.
6. Assure the rater that his anonymity will be safeguarded.

But rules such as these, which are useful tips and provide some help
in rating, do not result in the exercise of adequate control over the rating
process, at least not the type of control that an experimenter might wish
to exercise over the way in which measures are produced. The usual
suggestions are not to be disregarded, for they may convert wholly inadequate procedures into procedures that, although poor, have enough value
to make them usable to a limited degree.

The various attempts to improve the traditional type of rating scale have
not produced any instruments that represent a startling improvement over
those of several decades ago. It is also doubtful whether any of the more
novel approaches to rating have been more successful. One of these, which
has been a source of considerable controversy, is the forced-choice approach. The reader is referred to Guilford's *Psychometric Methods* (1954)
for a discussion of this technique.

In theory, if our directions concerning what is to be observed are
sufficiently exact, if the observer has been precisely informed concerning
the operations to be performed, and if the method of recording the final
product of these processes has been well defined, it should be possible
for two observers to arrive at closely similar, if not identical, ratings after
observing groups or situations in which there are a range of differences.
Interobserver reliability provides some evidence of the extent to which all
of these factors have been specified in a satisfactory way. It is possible that
good interrater agreement may be achieved even though adequate specifications for the entire procedure have not been provided. For example,
teachers may agree on rating pupils for social adjustment even though
they cannot provide an adequate definition of what is meant by this characteristic. On the other hand, if all specifications have been accurately
made and are capably followed by two observers, it is inevitable that the
resulting ratings will agree.

If ratings are to be meaningful, it must be possible to communicate the
rating process so that different individuals can achieve the same results. If
the procedure is not communicable, then it is evident that the particular
research is not replicable (reproducible) because of the lack of commu-
nicability of the operations that it involves. For this reason, in all studies
that involve ratings it is necessary to demonstrate that there is interrater
reliability, for lack of such reliability probably indicates lack of commu-
nicability of the procedures that the research involves.

There is also considerable value in determining the consistency of rating from occasion to occasion. If there is consistency among raters, but not from occasion to occasion, it indicates that the phenomenon studied is not a stable one. If teachers were to be rated for some aspect of aggressive behavior shown toward children in the classroom, it is probable that raters would agree among each other concerning the amount of aggression shown on a certain occasion, but the teacher might show little or no consistency in this trait from one occasion to another. Indeed, the amount of aggression shown might depend primarily on such factors as the time of day and the presence or absence of petty, out-of-school frustrations.

In most rating studies an effort is made to work with characteristics that have stability over time, but it is quite conceivable that studies might be run in which changeability of the characteristic rated was sought—as, for example, if the researcher were investigating changes in the behavior of the new pupil as he adapts to the school situation. Under such a condition, the researcher would want consistency from rater to rater, but not from occasion to occasion if the occasions were so spaced as to cover a period of time over which changes were hypothesized to occur. Sometimes it may be desired to collect data in such a way that the effects of certain changes in the phenomena to be observed will be eliminated. Thus, in the hypothetical study of the aggressive behavior of teachers, it might be desired to eliminate variations that occur during the course of a day, and for this reason ratings might be collected only during the first hour of each day of teaching. By means of an analogous procedure, variations during the course of the week might also be eliminated.

Some Special Types of Survey

School Surveys and Accreditation

A special kind of survey is that undertaken to determine the state of a school or a school system. It is not uncommon for a school district to employ a firm of educational consultants to make a survey of the system in order to provide information about possible deficiencies and areas of needed improvement in the system. The employment of an outside agency ensures a degree of objectivity that the staff of the school system could not be expected to have in a study of their own system. Such a survey uses some of the survey instruments that have been discussed, such as attitude questionnaires, as well as questionnaires that deal with factual matters. In addition, a school survey may deal with facts that have not been considered here. For example, the syllabi, curriculum guides, and other classroom-related materials may be examined in order to determine whether they meet such standards as being up-to-date, in keeping with modern thought, and appropriate for the students in the school. These surveys may also investigate matters such as faculty-administrative relations, and the resulting report may advise the school board of deficiencies in the way in which the school system is operated. A great amount of skill is involved in the conduct of this type of survey, though most of the knowledge is not so much derived from research as it is from the experience that each generation of makers of school surveys has managed to hand down to successive generations. Many books have been written on this topic and many fortunes have been made from the conduct of school surveys. But the art involved has made significant contribution to our society, even though it is only very indirectly based upon research. There is a need for systematic research in the whole area.

A second kind of school survey of great importance to our society that needs to be considered here is the kind of survey that takes place when a school or college is accredited. The accreditation procedure is uniquely American and is largely a product of the twentieth century. An extraordinary feature of school accreditation is that although each state has the power to license schools and to establish educational standards, the process of accreditation, which decides whether schools meet certain standards, has been taken over entirely by private organizations over which the state has no control. The process of accreditation involves a survey to determine whether an educational institution meets certain standards that are set by the accrediting association and not by the state. Although accreditation began as a system for setting and enforcing certain standards in educational institutions, accrediting organizations have slowly moved into the role of helping educational institutions to be accredited to meet the standards. A feature of the way in which the survey is conducted places emphasis on a diagnosis of the ills of the institution through a period of self-study. The accreditation survey is also undertaken in a way that is unique on the educational scene. The accrediting survey is produced by the faculty of the institution being accredited and is usually conducted over a period of a year prior to the visit from the accrediting organization.

The period of self-study engaged in by the staff of an institution to be accredited is designed to make the staff aware of where they stand in relation to the standards that are used. Then, when the accrediting team visits the institution, a comparison is made between the standards of the accrediting organization and the standards of the institution as they are reflected in the self-study.

The accreditation movement, which first began in relation to schools and then extended to colleges, has slowly expanded its scope to include the accreditation of professional schools. At the present time, over twenty-five organizations are concerned with the accreditation of professional schools (see National Education Association, 1975). Each of these organizations encounters numerous problems that need to be investigated by research workers, but the process of accreditation has become more of an art than a science.

Accreditation activity of half a century ago soon raised problems that called for research, and during the 1930s a substantial number of studies were undertaken of accreditation problems. Studies by Zook and Haggerty (1935, 1936) remain as classics. These studies dealt with such questions as how one should evaluate the overall faculty competence of an institution, but also raised important issues such as to whether one can, in fact, evaluate an institution in terms of quantitative data alone.

The accreditation movement began through the initiative of associations that embraced both schools and colleges. Much of the emphasis of the accreditation movement early in the century came from the colleges that sought to identify those high schools from which they would accept students for admission. The University of Michigan began to identify high schools in this way as early as 1871. The North Central Association of Schools and Colleges, founded in 1895 and housed at the University of Michigan, was the prime mover in the accreditation movement, and early in the century began to accredit high schools using the staff of the University of Michigan. Other associations of schools and colleges, which were either already in existence or were to be created later, followed the lead of the Association and performed similar roles. The Southern Association of Colleges and Schools expanded its activities into the area of accrediting elementary schools. For a review of these early activities consult Robb (1971). The accrediting associations slowly expanded their activities into the area of college accreditation. Since accreditation was undertaken by major institutions, these institutions were concerned with the quality of education of their transfer students, and accrediting organizations seemed to be the natural avenue through which the problem of evaluating transfer credit could be studied.

Work on the accreditation of colleges, and the resulting realization that each institution had its own characteristics, led academicians to explore the dimensions along which colleges differed. This new line of research is commonly described as research on the characteristics of college environments. These instruments attempt to measure such varied characteristics of a college environment as the extent to which the students have independence, the emphasis of the college on the sciences or the humanities or arts, the degree in which programs are vocationally oriented, and so forth. A great number of different researches may be undertaken with such devices. A common form of research explores the extent to which students with different characteristics can profit from these programs. A brief review of these instruments and the lines of research based on them is provided by Trent and Cohen (1973).

By the end of the 1930s the conclusion of those with expertise in the field seemed to be that the standard of excellence of an educational institution could not be measured along a simple scale or a system of scales. Each institution had to be appraised in terms of the extent to which it had a program that was appropriate for achieving goals that could be defended.

The argument is persuasive that the program of a high school serving rural areas in northern Minnesota could not be appraised in the same terms as a high school serving a heavily industrialized urban area. This conclusion was derived not only from extensive experience with accreditation but also found its roots in the large body of research conducted by the North Central Association of Schools and Colleges.

The conclusion of the work undertaken with accreditation has been cast aside by contemporaries who have embraced the accountability concept in education, which uses the simplest and most naïve methods of evaluating schools and their staffs. In some states, testing programs have been instituted for the purpose of appraising school programs, and the assumption is made that there are common objectives that all children should achieve and that these common objectives should constitute the essence of a school program.

New studies are needed, beginning with accreditation studies, to explore the process whereby school personnel can both show the fact that they consider themselves accountable and can, at the same time, render the system they serve more effective. The accreditation movement did this in a way that the accountability movement did not, perhaps because the leaders of the accreditation movement were not punitive in the way manifested by some of the leadership of the accountability movement. The accreditation movement is also concerned with the continuing study of the accreditation process through the National Study of Secondary School Evaluation that produces a report on the state of the art every ten years (see the 1970 report). There is also a need for studies comparing the threatening effect of the accountability movement with the positive emphasis on institutional development seen in the accreditation movement. The entire area of how to intervene in educational institutions with positive results needs to be investigated, and the fact that several forms of intervention are presently in use is worth exploring.

Accountability programs and accrediting agency programs are not the only forms of intervention that are viable on the educational scene. New management systems are also being tried out. The introduction of these systems into education reflects the power that wealthy businessmen and women exercise over education and the belief of such individuals that whatever is good for business must be good for education. The Rand Corporation of Santa Monica, California, has produced a series of studies on various management interventions in educational institutions, but these studies are extraordinarily lacking in research involving the collection of data. Now that many institutions, and particularly colleges, are attempting to introduce program planning and budgeting systems, studies need to be undertaken that will investigate the effect of such systems on the institution in such areas as faculty-administration relations, curriculum, student participation in setting policies, and so forth.

The effect on overall school programs of collective bargaining is also a field of inquiry of considerable interest. A considerable body of research already exists that any would-be investigator should review. One would suspect that the self-surveys involved in accreditation will assume a rather different character when there is an adversary relationship between labor and management than when the traditional relationships exists. The term *adversary relationship* is not used here in any derogatory sense, but is the term usually applied to the labor-management bargaining situation. There is obviously a social difference between the situation in which faculty and administration move together on a policy that is then presented to the school board, and the situation in which the administration represents the school board and bargains with the faculty. The full consequences of collective bargaining in educational settings is not yet fully understood. Some view it as a movement from which the students and the schools, as well as the teachers, will benefit, but others see it as only a means of protecting the interests of teachers.

Surveys of Behavior in Simulated Situations

An unusual approach to the problem of conducting surveys of behavior is found in a large-scale research by Hemphill ct al. (1962). The basic purpose of this study was to discover some of the dimensions of administrative behavior in elementary schools and also to obtain assessments of how teachers and superintendents regarded and evaluated each aspect of administrative behavior. It is not a study of administrative effectiveness as such, but rather is a study of what administrative behaviors occur and who considers them desirable or undersirable.

Although there would be merit in studying principals in the actual job situation and in finding out how they handled the many situations that arise during the course of a typical school day, such an approach is not feasible. An observer would hardly be permitted to sit with the principal, listen to conversations that are often of a confidential nature, record the statements made by visitors, review the daily correspondence and the replies to it, and so forth. In the Hemphill study this problem was avoided by bringing principals from the schools into artificially constructed administrative situations. The principals were invited in groups of twenty to the centers conducting the research. There they were told that their name was "Marion Smith" and that each was the principal of the Whitman Elementary School in the town of Jefferson. They were then given an orientation to the community and school by means of a sound movie, filmstrip, personnel files, handbook, a school survey, a school census, test scores of pupils, and other information. After the fairly lengthy orientation session, each principal was then taken to what was to be considered the school office. They were told to imagine that this was the office on Labor

Day and that they were to prepare for the first day of school. The in-basket on the desk was filled with items that needed their immediate attention. One of the tasks was to go through the in-basket and take appropriate action on each of the documents it contained. Another task involved the observation of three teachers, who were still on a probationary status. This observation was undertaken by viewing kinescopes of teachers in classrooms. In addition, an attempt was made to assess the speaking abilities of the principals who were required to prepare and deliver a speech to the Whitman Parent-Teachers Association. In a second social situation a group of the principals were brought together by a mythical "Mr. Davies," the business manager for the district, with the object of selecting a new principal. The situation permitted observers to record relevant aspects of the participants' behavior.

A major outcome of a study of this kind is a set of variables that can be used in subsequent research. Before studies can be undertaken that attempt to find means of predicting administrative behavior, a set of measurable characteristics of administrative behavior must be established. The study of the principals served this purpose and fifteen major characteristics of administrative behavior were identified. These are described in general terms as follows:

1. General ability to reason and understand.
2. Superiors' overall impression.
3. Concern for human problems versus conventionality.
4. Gregarious friendliness versus independent initiative.
5. Involvement with others in in-basket work.
6. Effective participation in group interaction.
7. Anxiety versus emotional maturity.
8. Analyzing the situation.
9. Directing the work of others.
10. Job-performance values.
11. Complying with suggestions.
12. Teachers' impressions.
13. Age and experience.
14. Preparing for decision versus taking final action.
15. Instructional awareness.

This list of variables does not include many characteristics that one would expect to appear. For example, there is nothing included in it that covers such behavior as "improves working conditions" or "backs up staff." Another category that is notably absent is "delegates authority." These absences do not represent deficiencies in the appraisal procedure but simply reflect the fact that the principals studied showed an almost complete absence of these behaviors. The same is true of other categories that authorities on educational administration agree to be important but which do not emerge from the study.

The point just made brings out one of the major values of the survey. It can serve to identify characteristics that show a sufficiently wide range of values so that individual differences can be reliably assessed; but it also serves to identify those characteristics that have not been developed and to which training programs should give specific attention.

The identification of variables that can be measured provides a basis for future research. In a sense, the kind of survey under consideration provides a foundation on which future research on the prediction of administrative performance and on the training of administrations can be built. Too many studies are undertaken without the grounds having been thoroughly explored and cleared by a study such as this one. A too hasty attack on problems of training and prediction of success leads only to failure.

Summary

1. Surveys are commonly conducted to determine a particular state of affairs. At a more complex level, surveys may investigate the causes of particular conditions or attitudes. Much of what is known about how to conduct surveys comes from the accumulated experience of those who conduct surveys. Surveys must be distinguished from sample surveys.

2. Surveys are limited in the knowledge they can produce. Experimentation produces sounder information but there are many fields in which one cannot experiment. One cannot generally conduct experiments on the conditions that make voters vote the way they do, but one can conduct surveys of voting behavior and related beliefs and attitudes.

3. Some surveys are designed to discover existing conditions related to learning. School surveys do this. However, little is known about the relationship of these conditions to the amounts that pupils learn. Other surveys of school systems may involve the experience, training, and behavior of teachers. Surveys of pupil achievement are becoming common. The National Assessment Program is the most ambitious of this type of survey. Surveys of aptitudes have also been undertaken.

4. Achievement surveys have often been linked to the problem of accountability. Achievement tests have been given for the purposes of determining the extent to which schools are achieving particular objectives. Although the idea of using achievement tests to measure the efficiency of schools seems attractive, the data that are produced are rarely interpretable.

5. Surveys are more often concerned with attitudes and beliefs than with any other topic. Public opinion polls represent one form of such survey. There have even been attempts to survey the attitudes and beliefs of students in high school.

6. Delphi techniques have enjoyed popularity in recent years among students working on theses and dissertations. These techniques are designed

to produce some degree of agreement among individuals engaged in making policy decisions. The opinions of the individuals are first surveyed and the information is then fed back to the group. Opinions are then assessed a second time, and the cycle is repeated until stability is achieved. Delphi techniques may assume many different forms. Delphi techniques have obvious weaknesses, and there is very little evidence to support their use.

7. An interesting approach to surveying attitudes is found in the technique known as the semantic differential. This device is designed to measure components of feeling in relation to particular concepts. The developers of the device discovered that, in their particular studies, certain aspects of the feeling elements could be isolated, but these might not be the factors that would come out in other studies. Each investigator should find a set of factors that is appropriate for his purpose.

8. One can too easily undertake a survey that is not only trivial but that will also never make a difference anywhere. The topic for a survey should be significant and potentially capable of changing what some people do.

9. Since most surveys ask questions, the surveyor should know something about how to ask questions and what constitutes a good question. Who asks the questions may be as important as what the questions are. There seem to be interviewer effects that influence the outcome of every survey. Interviewer effects are at a maximum when the questions are threatening or embarrassing to the person interviewed. Interviewers differ in their ability to extract information from those interviewed and in the accuracy of the information extracted. Some characteristics of good interviewers have been identified. One must note that the interview is a social relationship involving complex motivations on the part of both the interviewer and the interviewee.

10. Mailed questionnaires remove the effect of the interviewer but introduce other factors. Such mailed materials seem to be particularly useful when they call for quick answers requiring little thought. Some believe that the mailed questionnaire has advantages when the questions are sensitive and the answers might embarrass the interviewee in a face-to-face encounter. The interview and the mailed questionnaire require some kind of introduction that should be carefully planned. The interviewee or the person filling out a form should be given an understanding why he is being asked to do this. Mailed questionnaires should always be followed with letters of reminder, which should include a second copy of the material. The better educated members of the sample tend to return the mailed questionnaire. If anonymity is guaranteed, then the person conducting the research must stand behind that guarantee. There should be no hidden devices through which the identity of the individuals can be surreptitiously discovered.

11. Numerous rules have been developed for the writing of questions. Questions must be clearly stated and should avoid clichés that evoke

stereotyped responses. Questions should be neither loaded nor involve hypothetical issues. One should not use presuming questions or questions involving emotionally loaded terms. A trial run with the questions will identify those that convey special meanings to particular groups. Questions should be simple and deal with matters that those confronted with them can answer in simple terms.

12. Individuals to be included in a sample survey must be identified in some way. Great care must be exercised in this matter. The selection may be by strictly random methods. One method is to use a table of random numbers. Nonrandom methods of sampling are more commonly used. If a sample is stratified, then it must be stratified with respect to variables related to those that are being studied. Such sampling may be proportionate or nonproportionate. Area sampling is commonly used and cluster techniques are introduced to cut down on cost. Samples may also be drawn for specific purposes, as when a sample is drawn that has had a history of predicting a particular election. If the interviewer is allowed to identify the individuals to be included in the sample, then the interviewer's prejudices are likely to play a significant role and bias the results. Honesty of interviewers is also a problem that polling organizations have managed to handle with some success.

13. There is no simple formula for determining the size of a sample needed for particular purposes. Much depends upon how the sample is selected. A carefully selected small sample is likely to provide much better results than a large sample that has not been carefully selected.

14. Questionnaires and forms on which answers are recorded should be designed so that the data can be easily extracted from the material. Answers may be coded. Although respondents may perform the coding themselves, this practice introduces sizable errors.

15. Many forms of attitude survey call for the simplest responses, but sometimes the surveyor is interested in determining a person's attitude with respect to a scale. The scaling of responses is a complex statistical matter. Ratings may also be used as a part of a survey. Rating scales present problems of defining just what is to be rated. A few general rules may be followed to obtain the maximum precision from the rating process. The research worker must determine the reliability of the rating procedure and do what he can to maximize it.

16. The area of school accreditation has long attracted research workers, though not so many in recent years. Problems of accountability are related to problems of accreditation and offer a great variety of problems for research.

17. A new but very costly approach to surveys is that of conducting studies of samples of practitioners in simulated situations.

CHAPTER 13
Prediction Studies

In the typical prediction study in education, the research worker is concerned with such matters as estimating the probability that a student will succeed in a particular program; the probability that a graduate will succeed in a particular job; whether there will be an increase or decrease in enrollment in the elementary grades five years from now; whether the supply of teachers will be greater than, or smaller than, the demand during next year or in later years; and so forth. Some prediction studies are concerned with economic matters, as when the future trends in the tax base of a school district are explored. Sociological forecasts have to do with trends in the structure of the family and where individuals will choose to live and how they will earn their livings. Economic and social trends are closely intertwined. In the typical prediction study in education, sources of information can be used to predict some future state of affairs. The problem of prediction then becomes that of using the available data to make the best possible prediction that the data permit. The techniques used are primarily statistical. This approach is to be contrasted with those who describe themselves as futurologists, whose approach is now briefly considered.

Futurology

Much of the literature in the area that has come to be known as futurology describes techniques whereby, through some kind of group process or reflective thinking on the part of the individual, judgments concerning the future are made with supposedly minimum error. Some of the literature of futurology presents romantic speculation concerning the future, but some is of a more sober and reflective nature. A book by Hencley and Yates (1974) describes some issues related to making judgments concerning the future of education. This book includes the use of Delphi techniques as efforts to use judgments to predict the future. This, and most other works, in the area of futurology assume that the future in every respect can be predicted if only appropriate techniques can be found. A very sophisticated literature deals with the problem of the conditions under which the future can, or cannot, be predicted. Perhaps the most notable thinker in this field is the controversial economist G. L. S. Shackle.

Shackle (1961) takes the radical position that the future can be pre-

dicted only with respect to aspects that are quite trivial. Conditions that
are stable over the years, such as the general climate of the earth, can be
predicted over the next twenty-five years at least. That is to say, one can
expect weather in the next twenty-five years to be quite like the weather
during the last twenty-five years. One can also predict the number of
blue-eyed children who will be born in Sweden in the next decade, as well
as other fairly stable features of life on earth. The more interesting things
probably cannot be predicted. Who could have predicted in 1930 that by
1975 atomic energy would be a major potential source of energy, that a
man would have landed on the moon, or that poliomyelitis would have
been conquered? Great events and great changes in our way of life are
unpredictable, according to Shackle, because they are produced by the
chance confluence of events. We do not know, and cannot know, what
will be the great events of the next twenty-five years. Some of these events
of the future will depend upon great discoveries, and great discoveries are
unpredictable. Some events will require the emergence of a genius who
feels a great urge to explore a particular problem. Sometimes an important
innovation may occur because a member of Congress was able to persuade
his colleagues that a particular line of research needed support. Innovation
requires that a leader emerge through, not so much his own efforts,
as the occurrence of many fortuitous chance events. Napoleon is said to
have once remarked that the sequence of fortuitous circumstances that
brought him to power would not happen to another person in 100 years.

There is an interesting relationship between our ability to predict the
future and our capacity to create a future to our own liking. If the future
really is actually completely predictable, then it is obvious that we cannot
create a future for ourselves. For example, if we could predict with
precision and certainty that an atomic catastrophe would destroy the world
in the year 2075, then there would be no way of preventing that catastrophe. If the event was predicted *with certainty,* then it is obviously going
to occur, and whatever must occur is going to occur. On the other hand,
if the future presents many different alternatives, all of which are possible,
then one may be able to intervene to make one event more likely than
another. We can see ourselves as having the opportunity of intervening
and influencing the future only if the future is not completely fixed for us.
The prediction that a student will probably succeed in college is within the
reasonable limits of prediction, but the prediction that the student will
make a great discovery in the field of atomic physics before the age of fifty
is not a prediction that one can reasonably expect to make. The author
takes the position that most events in the future that are important for all
humanity cannot be predicted, though perhaps a few events of importance
may be predicted. Predictions at the individual level, over the short range,
are much more feasible. This means that humans have some limited
capacity for creating their future.

Futures can either be created, or they can just happen. For much of humanity the future just happens; for others the future may be created by the individual setting up goals that he ultimately accomplishes. In a complex industrial economy the individual may feel so much a part of a giant machine that he may be resigned to accepting whatever comes his way and may make no effort to create a future for himself.

There are two kinds of ways in which an individual may create a future for himself. One way is to view various current trends, and then decide which trend he will follow. Thus, a worker may decide that employment in the future is going to be most stable in the plastics industry, and seek a future in that area. A graduate student of psychology may guess that a particular type of psychological theory has the best future, and decide to embark on a research career that embodies that theory. A dean of a school of education may believe that he can carve out a future for the college by pursuing certain approaches to education, rather than others, and may persuade the faculty to sponsor those approaches. These are all examples of what one may call the bandwagon approach to the creation of a future. The simple rule followed is to find a good bandwagon and then jump on it.

The second way of creating a future is to have a useful or important idea and to use it as a basis for one's life's work. The bandwagon approach exploit's somebody else's approach. This other approach involves creating an idea for oneself. Ford created a future when he conceived of the idea of an automobile for the common man. Einstein created a future for all humanity when he wrote his basic papers on relativity. Others who are living today are working with ideas that will create new futures even within this century. How futures are created needs to be studied and explored as a complement to the exploration of how one can predict certain, very limited aspects of the future.

The Pseudoscience of Predicting Something from Anything

There is a type of educational study that involves predicting *something* from *anything*. Usually both the *something* and the *anything* are rather vague. Many such studies begin with the graduate student's dissatisfaction with current procedures for predicting scholastic success in some field of study in which he is interested. This student may have been a high school teacher of accounting. Greatly concerned with the fact that a large fraction of students who begin accounting courses fail to achieve satisfactory grades, the graduate student may feel that there is a need for building a test that will eliminate those applicants who are almost certain to fail. Because various tests have been tried, but none has proved to be useful, he decides to collect a number of new tests and administer them to students of accounting in the hope that one of the tests will turn out to be a good predictor of grades. This might be called a shotgun approach, and it has disadvantages with which the graduate student should be familiar.

First, it is a departure from the type of scientific procedure that has yielded so much in the past and represents a return to a primitive method of achieving knowledge. It is a return to the kind of prescientific technique practiced by the medieval physician, who tried whatever herbs and techniques he had at his disposal in the hope that something would be found to help the patient. Occasionally this approach worked and the patient was cured, and a considerable amount of unconnected items of information was accumulated that were used in the primitive practice of medicine. Such scraps of lore did not make medicine a science. Neither will large numbers of correlations between test scores and measures of performance in handling life's daily problems of work and play constitute a science of behavior. Only when these apparently disconnected facts are integrated into a system is there any hope that they may form the rudiments of a science.

Second, even if a correlation existed between a test and the *something* it is desired to predict, there is always a real possibility that the correlation may be the result of some irrelevant aspect of the *something*. For example, one might find that ratings of personal attractiveness of female college students correlated with their grades in college. One might certainly suspect that this correlation was generated by the fact that male college professors might have a tendency to overestimate the academic achievement of outstandingly attractive college women. Such a hypothesis would be much more reasonable than to suppose that personal attractiveness has a genuine relationship to academic achievement.

Third, because the shotgun approach is a hit-or-miss procedure, it is necessary to include a great many potential predictors—unless, of course, a theory is available that permits predictors to be selected in advance. Many studies of the predictive value of brief biographical items of information have been carried out by administering several hundred such items to groups whose behavior it was desired to predict and then selecting the items that had the greatest predictive value. Such procedures are laborious, require extensive statistical treatment of the data, and are costly. They are most appropriate where useful results must be achieved rapidly regardless of cost, and where new areas are being explored.

John Dewey (1910) elegantly compared the relative merits of the shotgun and the scientific methods of prediction in the following statement:

While many empirical conclusions are, roughly speaking, correct; while they are exact enough to be of great help in practical life; while the presages of a weather-wise sailor or hunter may be more accurate, within a restricted range, than those of the scientist who relies solely on scientific observations; while, indeed, empirical observations and records furnish the raw or crude material of scientific knowledge, yet the empirical method affords no way of discriminating between right and wrong conclusions.

A few might take the position that the end product of all prediction studies should be a kind of cookbook giving recipes for making particular predictions. One can imagine such a cookbook at this time although the knowledge available would not make a very impressive set of recipes if it were all assembled. Such an imaginary cookbook might tell one how to predict who is most likely to pass or fail each of a dozen different courses in algebra, or it might provide a recipe for selecting those students who are most likely to profit from 400 hours of instruction in Cantonese. Such a cookbook has some appeal in our present stage of ignorance, but it does not represent a worthwhile research goal. One can understand this point best by considering the limitations of such a cookbook in another field where prediction is a central problem.

Consider, for example, the problem of weather forecasting. At one time, weather forecasts for a particular locality were made by keeping records of *what followed what* in the sequence of weather conditions. Thus, a high southeast wind in a particular locality might be taken to indicate rain, because rain followed more frequently than anything else on the tail of such a wind. Nobody knew why this was so. The probability of the occurrence was well established, but so long as nobody knew, there was no way of improving the accuracy of weather predictions. However, such a system of forecasting has been abandoned, because its accuracy could never be improved beyond that permitted by the data previously collected. The present system, which has replaced the old statistical system, is based on a knowledge of how weather conditions are produced. This new system is based largely on air-mass analysis and thermodynamics, and permits much more accurate predictions than the older statistical method. This does not mean, of course, that mathematical methods are not used for making predictions today, for they are. However, the function of mathematical methods is to use data in accordance with some complex theory of weather prediction. Modern weather forecasting has, in fact, become highly mathematical and introduces the help of electronic computers in order that complex mathematical functions may be computed at a relatively rapid speed.

The example from meteorology illustrates the difference between predictions based on the accumulation of odd bits of information and predictions based on a well-organized body of knowledge. Predictions made within the context of educational research should stem from the knowledge that is available about the phenomena as well as from knowledge in organized disciplines such as psychology and sociology. However, sometimes the knowledge available is so meager that the research worker has no alternative except to try anything that, on a common-sense basis, offers some hope of providing predictions. This represents a kind of prescientific activity that sometimes has to be undertaken as a prerequisite of later scientific research.

Empiricism and Research on Problems of Educational Prediction

Research on problems of predicting educational achievement has not usually been scientific in the sense in which the term has been used in this volume. Inevitably this has been so, for the urgent need for making accurate educational predictions has prompted those concerned with the problem to grasp whatever facts were available. In addition, in the partial solution of urgent problems that are complex in character, it is often much more feasible to try out a large number of possible solutions and see which will work rather than to develop a program of research along systematic and scientific lines. At least three types of empirical procedures have been adopted in this setting, and the merits of each need to be considered.

Method I. The Miniature-Situation Approach. This is a procedure for developing methods of prediction that really involves no research at all, but simply requires the educator to reproduce a miniature and abbreviated situation in which a subject can be given, so to speak, a trial run. The experimenter hypothesizes that performance in the miniature situation will reflect quality of performance in the larger situation in which it is desired to predict behavior. Thus, in the development of algebra-prognosis tests, an attempt has been made to introduce into the test situation some of the learning activities that pupils will have to face in his first course in algebra. Foreign language learning prognosis tests use a similar technique. One such test measures the ability of the student to learn a small amount of Esperanto. It has been shown that the ability to learn small amounts of this artificial tongue is related to the ability to learn large amounts of other languages.

This technique is generally a successful one. The major condition that may lessen the extent to which it is used is that which occurs when learning in the early stages of an activity involves abilities that are different from those involved in learning in a later stage. Such changes in the determinants of behavior as learning progresses have been shown to occur in certain instances, but these changes have not been particularly striking and probably are not sufficient to prevent the use of a miniature learning situation for selecting pupils who are most likely to succeed. However this may be, activity directed toward the development of such a technique for a particular purpose cannot be said to make a contribution to scientific knowledge. The product is a technique that in no way adds to available organized knowledge.

From the point of view of developing guidance practices, the miniature learning situation does not result in a product that fits well into current procedures. It is clearly quite impractical for the guidance counselor to administer as many miniature learning situations as there are situations in which one may desire to predict behavior. The guidance worker needs a short and comprehensive battery of tests that overlap as little as possible. Guidance batteries that are currently widely used do not include the miniature learning situation type of test.

Method II. The Hit-or-Miss Approach. This method has already been discussed, and it is briefly mentioned here in order to contrast it with other methods. This approach to the problem of prediction involves the administration of a wide range of instruments in the hope that one will be found that predicts successfully. This statement is a little exaggerated, in that the investigator is unlikely to try out just *any* instrument; rather, he will select those that appear to have at least some connection with the phenomenon to be predicted. The technique finds support in the fact that it has had a long and fairly successful history of application. A strong point in its favor is that an unpromising variable has often turned out to be the best predictor. Once this has occurred, it is nearly always possible to find a good reason why it should be so. On the negative side, several points are to be noted.

The method involves a great amount of work on the part of those administering the tests and on the part of those taking them. *Careful thinking through of the problem might result in the tryout of a much more limited battery of instruments, with less time lost by all.* This gain must be balanced against any loss that may result from unlikely variables turning out to be good predictors.

In addition, the variables that are likely to be selected are those that have some superficial relationship to the phenomenon that is to be predicted. If an analysis of the prediction problem is made in terms of current psychological knowledge, it is probable that only a few likely predictor variables will appear, but these may not have any relationship to the predicted variable obvious to the layman.

Method III. The Scientist's Approach to the Problem of Prediction. A third method involves the development of a theory concerning the nature of the phenomena to be predicted, and, on the basis of that theory, the derivation of methods hypothesized to predict.

A good example of the systematic development of a device for making predictions is found in Carroll's Modern Language Aptitude tests. The development of the Carroll tests is to be contrasted with the development of the language-aptitude tests that were previously discussed in which the student was given the task of learning a small sample of an unfamiliar language. Carroll developed his test by first making an analysis of the skills required to learn a foreign language and came to the conclusion that such a learning task involved five distinct skills. For each of these skills he developed a test. The first test in the series involves what may be called auditory alertness; the second measures the ability to learn written symbols corresponding to particular sounds; the third involves spelling ability and, to some extent, the ability to associate sounds and symbols; the fourth measures sensitivity to grammatical construction; and the fifth measures the ability to associate one word with another, an ability presumed to be related to vocabulary acquisition. The soundness of Carroll's analysis is shown by the fact that the test has been successful in predicting performance in foreign-language courses. The division of the test into a number of separate components is also of value in that the acquisition of a particular foreign language may be much more dependent on one component than on another.

The Carroll Modern Language test is an excellent example of the development of a device to be used for prediction through a systematic scientific analysis of the behavior to be predicted. So little has been done to develop prediction studies on the basis of this method that it is difficult to discuss the problems that it presents. The primary difficulty most certainly lies in the theory-construction phase itself.

Reliability: An Essential Condition for Prediction

A necessary, but not a sufficient, condition for prediction is reliability. If the predictors have zero reliability, there can be no prediction. If the measure to be predicted has no reliability, there can also be no prediction. Consider, for example, a highly unreliable predictor such as my judgment of how a new employee is going to work out. In my particular case, such judgments depend on the whim of the hour. One minute the new employee does something well and I have high expectations for him, but a minute later he flounders and I reverse my judgment. If forced to make a prediction immediately after the employee reported to work, such a forecast would show no relationship to the performance of the employee over a year. In this case, the predictor variable could not predict any more accurately than could the throw of dice. Both the fall of the dice and my judgment depend on numerous trivial and inconsequential circumstances that make them useless for prediction purposes.

Prediction is also not possible when the variable to be predicted has negligible reliability. Grades on a ten-minute test in a particular course have low reliability and may be almost unpredictable for this reason. The grade of the student on the test may depend on such factors as whether he had been sick or well on the previous day, whether he interpreted the question correctly or incorrectly, whether he attended or did not attend the lecture of a guest speaker who discussed a related topic, whether the instructor who grades the papers is tired or fresh when he comes to this particular student's paper, and an endless number of other factors. The grade on the particular test is, almost certainly, unreliable. Indeed, if the same quiz were given unexpectedly again a week later and if the papers were to be graded by a different instructor, there would, almost certainly, be only a very small correlation between the two sets of grades.

Such a measure would be virtually unpredictable. The reader may argue at this point that the illustration is trivial because nobody would ever want to predict a grade in a particular course; but many conditions that are not trivial and that one might want to predict have similar characteristics. For example, in a slum population, it may be virtually impossible to predict which of the youths will be convicted for minor or major crimes, because delinquency is widespread and chance factors determine which ones get caught. The condition to be predicted—conviction or nonconviction during a particular period of time—has virtually zero reliability and, hence, is unpredictable. In such a case, the selection of highly reliable measures as the potential predictors does not help the situation, for there is nothing sufficiently solid to predict to make a forecast possible.

The more commonly occurring problem is where both the variables selected as predictors and the measure, or measures, that one seeks to predict are of limited reliability. In such a case some degree of prediction is *possible* even though, of course, what we have selected as potential predictors may not predict at all under the circumstances involved. The reliability of both the predictors and the variable predicted sets a ceiling on the value of the correlation that could be found.

Efforts are always made in prediction studies to select variables that have as high reliability as can be found. Sometimes, however, the only measures available may have low reliability, and little can be done either to improve the measures or to obtain others with more desirable characteristics. Under such circumstances one has to accept the fact that limitations have been placed on the accuracy of any prediction that can be made.

Validity and the Design of Prediction Studies

In most modern prediction studies, the variables selected as potential predictors are those that have had a history of predicting well in related situations. Because there is hardly an aspect of human activity in which prediction studies have not already been undertaken in considerable numbers, no study need be carried out on a blind hit-or-miss basis. Generally, some kind of analysis such as Carroll and Sapon undertook in preparing the Modern Language test will provide a basis for the selection of appropriate measuring devices; but from the several that are likely to be available, the ones with the best history of prediction should be chosen. Thus, consideration must be given to the selection of instruments for which there is data showing that they can be expected to make valid predictions.

The research worker has to be extremely careful to avoid using measures merely because they have names that make them attractive for the purpose at hand. Numerous prediction studies have involved the use of measures described as providing assessments of *achievement motivation*. This term suggests that the measures should predict, for example, scores on achievement tests. What the users have often failed to note is that measures of achievement motivation, built on the basis of theory of motivation, can be expected to predict achievement only when the persons involved feel challenged by the task they are to perform. Measures of achievement motivation have construct validity, that is to say, they fit into a system of ideas of how certain predictions can be made. If they are used within that system, then they will provide limited predictions. Whenever there is information available, the research worker should attempt to determine whether a particular instrument is based on a logic that permits one to infer that a particular prediction can be made. An instrument based on such a logic is said to have construct validity.

Conditions Necessary for Effective Prediction

In predicting performance in a college algebra course from, say, the college admissions battery taken six months earlier, much may happen between the time of the taking of the tests and the taking of the course. Some students during this interval may take additional work in mathematics to prepare them for college work in the same field, whereas others, who also need the additional work, do not. Such events will seriously upset the possibility of predicting performance in the college algebra course from the admissions test battery. The longer the interval between the prediction and the event to be predicted, the smaller are the chances of making a successful prediction.

Many prediction studies end in failure that could have been avoided if the researcher had considered the problem carefully in advance. In many such cases, a careful consideration of the problem in the first place would have led to the realization that the prediction was not a feasible one.

Consider the problem of predicting the number of teachers who will resign from a large school system during each year for the next ten years. This is no trivial problem, because the long-term training of teachers requires that candidates be trained to replace those resigning from the system as well as to take other positions that will have to be filled over the course of the years. Large numbers of resignations may leave gaps that cannot easily be filled unless there has been long-term planning.

The time when it is necessary to make the prediction of whether a given group of teachers will or will not resign is four or five years before the resignations actually take place, because this is the time required for recruiting and training new teachers. This is a considerable span of years over which to make predictions, but many educational forecasts are made with a useful degree of accuracy over this period.

An immediate suggestion about how the prediction should be made is that data be obtained from the past and applied to the future. It certainly would be possible to obtain data on resignations over a long previous period, say twenty years, and to work out an average resignation rate. On the surface, this may appear to be a good method, until the data are closely examined and the discovery is made that most of the resignations occurred during a short period during the boom of the early 1960s. The reason for this was that teachers then were offered wages in industry far above those that could be obtained within the educational system. However, even if such a period of high wages for former teachers did recur, school districts in the future might be willing to offer teachers a bonus or other financial incentive to stay on in the system—in which case the resignation rate might be held at a low and constant level. Insofar as the resignation rate depends on unpredictable economic conditions and international tensions, it is not predictable by any technique that is now available. At least, economists and political scientists have not yet succeeded in predicting such events and conditions.

An alternative approach can be taken if the problem is redefined. In place of stating the problem as that of predicting the percentage of teachers likely to resign in a given year, it can be redefined as that of identifying those who are most likely to resist the temptation to resign. Stability could be given to a teaching body if it included only those who are likely to stay with the system indefinitely. It seems reasonable to assume that the personal characteristics of those who remain might be different from those who resign. One might suspect that those would stay who have a deeper interest in teaching and a more favorable attitude toward the activities it involves than those who would leave for economic reasons. (One might perhaps hypothesize that those who stay might tend to be less ambitious, and perhaps less intelligent, than those who leave.) Conceivably, a study could be designed to discover ways of identifying teachers who would not resign for economic reasons. At least some of the necessary conditions for practical predictions exist when the problem is stated in this way. However, it must be pointed out that the usefulness of a study of this kind might well be questioned. It would be hard to imagine an acceptable teacher-selection procedure that would permit the rejection of those who did not present characteristics making for long years of service. Indeed, such a procedure might well eliminate some of the ablest teachers—those who might come to provide leadership for the system. However, it must be pointed out that the problem of creating a stable body of teachers should be attacked realistically by making economic adjustments, for economic conditions are clearly a major determinant of resignations, and attempts to solve the problem by selection would not attack it at its roots.

From what has been said, it is clear that, for a phenomenon to be predictable, the determinants must exist in some well-identified and measurable form at the time when the prediction is made. If partial predictions are to be accepted, and they must be because perfect predictions cannot be made, then only partial determinants need exist in an identifiable form.

Another condition that should be established before a prediction study is undertaken is that the phenomenon to be predicted is relatively uniform in its causes; that is to say, that it generally has the same causes. An example of a condition that it has not been possible to predict with much success because of the multiplicity of possible causes is delinquency. It is obviously most desirable to predict which children are most likely to become delinquent, so that the clinical psychologist and social worker can begin to work to prevent this from happening. The difficulty is that there are many major determinants of delinquency. Some delinquency is a product of a lack of intellectual insight into what is happening. Other causes include the effects of associates, the home background, and various pathological psychological conditions, to mention but a few. Under these conditions there is no single effective way of identifying the potential delinquent, although some measures have been developed that provide rough overall predictions.

An additional important condition for prediction is that whatever is to be predicted must represent a well-defined phenomenon, and, if possible, a measurable variable. A much discussed variable, such as teacher effectiveness, does not meet these standards. On the other hand, if specific and well-defined aspects of teacher effectiveness are used in prediction studies, then there is a danger that the researcher may be able to predict only the trivial. The discovery of a significant and well-defined variable to forecast is often the major difficulty in the development of a prediction study.

Research that is designed to evaluate the effectiveness of counseling frequently suffers from the fact that the condition to be predicted cannot be described in terms of a single variable. Although we may talk in generalities and point to, say, *adjustment* as the condition to be predicted, there are many ways in which a person may adjust, and these cannot be compared to one another easily, if at all. In the face of this difficulty, many ridiculous criteria of the success of counseling have been developed. For example, in one study the success of the counseling procedure was evaluated in terms of whether the counselee returned for more counseling. A somewhat better solution might be to classify those who come for counseling into a number of different categories in terms of the type of adjustment to be made or the problem to be solved. Within any one group, it may be possible to distribute success at making the desired adjustment along a single scale.

Finally, consideration must be given to the problem of using biographical data provided by the individual about his own past for the making of predictions. The use of such data is based mainly on the assumption that the exposure of the child to certain environmental conditions results in the development of particular attributes that later become determinants of behavior, such as job success. Difficulties in the use of such data arise because of the problem of identifying just what happened in the individual's past. There is little difficulty in determining *what he himself thinks happened,* but this may be quite different from what actually happened. Also, what *he thinks happened* will probably change from time to time, whereas what actually happened will not change. For this reason, among others, the predictive value of biographical events as they are reported has been found to be low.

Fractionating Populations to Increase Accuracy of Predictions

A number of interesting cases have been found in which it was not possible to make predictions for an entire group, but in which predictions could be made within a section of that group. For example, it has been found in studies of achievement motivation that in some situations this variable shows little relationship to performance when an entire group is involved. On the other hand, when it is possible to separate those who see the task to be performed as a challenge from the total group, a marked relationship exists between achievement motivation and performance within this small group. This is not surprising, because achievement motivation can hardly be expected to operate in situations in which the individual does not feel a need to do his best.

In almost every area of educational research, one can think of situations in which it is necessary to partition a population of events in order to establish relationships. Where relationships are to be found between the qualifications of teachers and the characteristics of the curriculum, one would expect different relationships in urban schools than in rural schools. Sometimes it may be necessary to separate boys from girls in order to make a meaningful prediction. Sometimes it may be necessary to separate cultural groups. In other cases, relationships may apply to only certain types of economic conditions. A careful thinking through of most studies is likely to reveal the possibility that some of the relationships expected are more likely to occur in certain sections of the population than in others. It is of considerable interest to determine whether such hypotheses are sound.

Some tests are designed to separate into distinct categories those for whom the test provides a valid score and those for whom the score is not valid. This separation is accomplished by means of a validating score that is generally derived by scoring certain special items in the test. Such scores are referred to as validating scores and these are generally designed to indicate whether the individual tested showed reasonable cooperation. These scores may also reflect other attributes that may invalidate a test score, such as a tendency to respond to personality inventory items with an excessive number of positive or negative responses. Some persons have a tendency to answer yes to inventory types of items, and others have a tendency to answer no to these items. Such tendencies are referred to as response sets. The identification of persons who are excessively influenced by such sets is important in prediction studies. The elimination of such persons from the population studied will often show that an instrument can be used for predicting the behavior of the remaining individuals.

Clustering of Variables to Increase Accuracy of Predictions

In educational research numerous variables are frequently included as potential predictors of a particular phenomenon. These predictors may show irregular but low correlations with the variable that is to be predicted. It would be possible, of course, to compute a combination of the variables that will *best* predict the particular independent variable. If this procedure were followed, a combination that maximized the prediction would provide what appeared to be an accurate prediction, but when the same combination of best predictors was applied to a new sample, the prediction would shrink substantially. This is the well-known phenomenon of shrinkage.

In order to understand shrinkage, let us consider an imaginary study in which a research worker is concerned with finding a means of predicting that high school seniors will be arrested for violations of the law other than traffic offenses. The research worker assembled a number of personality inventories that seemed to have potential for making a prediction and spent the year collecting his data. The inventories consisted of 800 items and the relationship between each item and whether students were or were not arrested was carefully evaluated. The research worker found forty-five items that appeared to be significantly related to being arrested. A score derived from these forty-five items predicted the arrest records very well. Next year, he gave the same inventories to the next group of seniors and used the score from the forty-five items to determine which students would be most likely to be arrested. Much to his chagrin there seemed to be no relationship between performance on the items and the record of arrests. What went wrong in making the prediction the second year?

When the original set of data were collected, the research worker failed to realize that, by chance alone, certain of the items were bound to be correlated with record of arrest. One can show statistically that one would expect that 5 per cent of the items would show such a relationship by chance as a consequence of the criterion of "significance" that was used. The research worker found forty-five items that seemed to have predictive value, barely more than would show such a relationship by chance. Thus, his "good" items were just those that happened on that particular occasion to show a relationship to arrest record. When the study was repeated the next year, other items showed such chance relationships. These chance relationships would disappear when the study is repeated and produce the phenomenon of shrinkage.

Precautions have to be taken to make sure that we are not deceived by apparent predictions that later shrink to nothing. The usual way to do this is to divide the population to be studied into two groups. All measures are applied to the first group in order to identify those measures that are most likely to be effective in making the desired prediction. The most promising measures are then applied to the second group to find out how far they can be relied on to make the same prediction in a new population. This procedure is called crossvalidation. All prediction studies should have built into them a crossvalidation procedure.

A second approach to the problem of building up predictions does not suffer from this hazard. It involves, first, the clustering of those predictor variables that belong together in terms of their intercorrelations. This can be accomplished by means of factor analysis or by the related method of cluster analysis. Variables that cluster are then combined in some way. Such composite variables can generally be expected to have the merit of having higher reliability than the relatively low-reliability elements of which they are composed. Thus, in place of having six different measures of the cultural level of the student's home—such as educational level of the father and the mother, number of books, intellectual level of the magazines purchased, and so on—a single measure can be derived by combining these variables.

In the clustering of such variables, a cluster is constituted of elements that belong together, not only statistically but also according to a rationale. Unless this is done, any prediction made from the cluster is unlikely to contribute systematically to knowledge; rather it is likely to represent only an odd but perhaps useful relationship.

Just as variables within the predictor group may be clustered and then combined in the hope of improving the accuracy with which predictions may be made, so too may groups of independent variables be clustered. For example, an investigator concerned with the prediction of teacher behavior might have observed a group of teachers for the frequency with which they perform various acts, such as raising their voices, threatening to punish, offering rewards, asking for suggestions, encouraging a pupil to pursue a matter further, offering help, and so on. The investigator would probably find that only the poorest predictions could be made of the extent to which a teacher manifested any of these categories of behavior. However, it is quite likely that a correlational analysis would show that some of these behaviors tended to cluster together. It would certainly be expected that all behaviors representing expressions of hostility would represent a cluster of correlated measures of behavior. When measures of all of these behaviors are added to form a measure that might be described as the tendency to manifest hostility—from what has been learned about such a variable from other sources—one might expect this characteristic of teacher behavior to be reasonably predictable from test scores.

Clinical Versus Statistical Prediction—A Problem in the Validity of the Direct Observation of Behavior

There has long been considerable controversy concerning the relative merits of clinical predictions and so-called actuarial predictions. What is meant here by a *clinical prediction* is a judgment arrived at by a psychologist after considering a certain body of data. An *actuarial prediction* is made by combining quantitative data to derive a score, which is then used to make a prediction. Clinical psychologists have generally maintained that it is possible to make more accurate predictions through the exercise of clinical judgment than could be made by the statistical treatment of data alone—at least insofar as it is treated by the methods in common use. The problem is an important one in the current connection, because it implies that the data-processing method of the researcher is inferior to that of the machine.

Various approaches have been taken to the study of this problem. One has been to compare the actuarial prediction with the prediction of the clinician made on the basis of the same test scores.

Meehl (1954) has reviewed studies in which the accuracy of predictions made by clinicians using test scores are compared with the results achieved by statisticians using objective methods. The results seem to vary considerably from one study to another, depending on the nature of the condition to be predicted. In no clear-cut case did the clinicians predict more accurately than the psychometricians. One suspects that the psychometrician who has a well-developed procedure for predicting a particular type of event or condition will do better than the clinician, but if he does not have such a procedure, the clinician may possibly do better.

Meehl's article did not end the controversy concerning this issue. Indeed, the controversy tended to increase with a flood of articles appearing in the ten-year period that followed its publication. Meehl's work was summarized by Sawyer (1966) who attempted to redefine the problem as a comparison between clinical and mechanical prediction. Sawyer found forty-five studies that made this comparison and found that mechanical prediction was the superior method. Nevertheless the controversy still continued. Robert Holt, who had long been a critic of the kinds of the conclusions drawn from the studies reviewed by Meehl and later Sawyer, wrote a strong criticism of work in the field (1975) claiming that the conclusions were "overgeneralized, misleading and irresponsible." Holt's position cannot be neglected because the studies that have been made have had enough deficiencies for one to question the value of what has been learned to date.

Holt is right in suggesting that the studies have been selected with a certain bias to them. The typical study begins with a test that has had a good history of making a prediction, and clinicians are then asked to make a similar prediction. Of course, the predictions made by the test are more accurate. Studies have not been undertaken, which begin with a situation in which clinicians can make good predictions. Let us consider a situation in which a clinician might be expected to make a good prediction of my behavior. The clinician is assumed to have spent twenty-five hours with me previously on various occasions. He would certainly be able to predict with considerable accuracy what I would be most likely to do next Sunday or how I would spend my summer vacation. He could do this because he would know my habits and idiosyncracies. One can hardly imagine a test that would do this. In such a case one might argue that the comparison was unfair, yet it is just this kind of unfairness that has characterized studies of the past except that the unfairness has prejudiced the results in favor of statistical or mechanical prediction. The clinician can learn about well-established regularities of a person's behavior and use these regularities for prediction in a way that a test cannot. Sometimes these regularities may be dramatic and produce very important results. For example, a clinician may establish the fact that a particular individual has an extraordinary capacity for becoming involved in very serious accidents. The trend may be so marked that the clinician may be able to predict with considerable assurance that the individual will become involved in other similar accidents, and that one of these is likely to cause him grievous bodily harm. The clinician may be able to predict the ways in which other individuals will relate to work associates, or to authority figures, or to members of the opposite sex, because the clinician has been able to observe a well-established trend in these individuals' behavior.

There is little point in studying whether clinical prediction is better than mechanical or statistical prediction. A more worthwhile problem is that of discovering the areas in which the clinician can make the best predictions and the areas in which other sources of prediction are best.

Nonlinear Relationships

Most prediction problems that are investigated by educational researchers are based on the assumption that the relationships between the variables involved are linear. A *linear relationship* is simply one in which equal increases in the predictor variable are accompanied by equal increases in the variable to be predicted. It is generally acceptable to assume that any relationships that may exist are linear, for nonlinear relationships are rarely found in the educational field, even when they have been actively sought. This is hardly surprising, because most measuring instruments are constructed in the first place to have a linear relationship with certain criterion variables. Thus, the approach usually taken to instrument construction results in the lack of curvilinear relationships between the instrument and other variables. In addition, those engaged in the study of individual differences have developed a wide range of statistical techniques based on the assumption that relationships are linear.

Some examples of curvilinear relationships are found in the study of the characteristics of those who belong to extremist political groups. The political position of individuals can be measured on a scale extending from the extreme political left to the extreme right. If one studies the relationship between political position on this scale and some personality characteristics, he will find that those individuals occupying the opposite extreme positions are very similar, but that they differ from those in the middle of the scale. For example, those at either extreme tend to be rigid, but those who occupy the political middle tend to be more flexible. A curve showing the relationship between political position and rigidity is high to the political left, low in the middle, and then high again to the right. This is a curvilinear relationship.

Some Problems of Predicting Rare Events

Meehl and Rosen (1955) have pointed out that even though a measure may have predictive value for a given purpose, fewer errors may be made by *not* using this measure than by using it. Until it is understood, this appears to present a situation filled with contradictions. Consider the problem of identifying persons who will become involved in delinquencies during a given year. Suppose that a test has been developed, which, it has been demonstrated, has value in identifying future delinquents. Let us also suppose that this test was given to 10,000 high school children, and that 200 were identified as likely to become delinquent. At the end of several years, it would be possible to determine which of those identified as probably delinquent actually were delinquent. A table similar to Table 1 could then be drawn up.

One additional statement must be made in order to interpret these data, namely that the delinquency rate for this group is ten per 1,000. This is referred to as the *base rate*. With this fact in mind, the table indicates that the test does have some success in identifying those who become involved in delinquencies. However, by using the test on the group of 10,000, altogether 240 incorrect decisions were made (170 + 70). If no test had

Table 1 Hypothetical Data on the Identification of Those Expected to Be Involved in Delinquencies.

	Number Actually Involved in Delinquency	Number Not Involved in Delinquency
Those predicted to be involved in delinquencies	30	170
Those predicted not to be involved in delinquencies	70	9,730

been given and if all the group had been classified as nondelinquent, one would have expected only 100 incorrect decisions to have been made, namely, all the cases that became delinquent. Thus, fewer incorrect predictions are made by avoiding the use of the valid test than by using the test. Is it desirable to avoid the use of predictors where similar circumstances exist?

The answer to this is not a simple matter. Note that in Table 1 the test does identify correctly 30 of those who were later involved in deliquencies; but problems are created by the fact that it has erroneously identified as delinquent 170 cases who were not so. What has to be determined is whether the advantages gained by identifying the 30 delinquents outweigh the disadvantages of incorrectly identifying 170 as delinquent. If the testing requires an elaborate procedure and the help of many technicians, the losses may outweigh the gains. Also, financial and social problems may be introduced by identifying as potential delinquents those who are not.

The problem that has been discussed in this section becomes particularly acute as the base rate of the characteristic to be identified becomes very small. Attempts to identify rare talents, rare diseases, or any rare phenomena present situations such that selection devices are likely to provide a very much larger number of misclassifications than are provided by failure to use the instrument. This problem is most easily avoided when the base rate is near the 50 per cent mark. In addition, as the usefulness of the test for selection purposes is improved, the number of misclassifications is also reduced.

Summary

1. Most prediction studies undertaken by educational research workers are concerned with practical matters. A new form of prediction study is found in futurology, which has attempted broad predictions of the future.

There are serious doubts about whether futurologists can do what they have set out to do. Important events in the future may occur because of the occurrence of chance events that cannot be predicted. The emergence of a genius, for example, may produce changes that cannot be predicted.

2. Individuals may create futures for themselves in two ways. They may choose a bandwagon on which to jump, an approach that requires little initiative. An alternative is to create a future out of important ideas that the individuals themselves have generated. Individuals have potential for creating the future only insofar as there are no generally valid techniques for predicting what will happen.

3. Much research on problems of prediction has involved a hit-or-miss technique. Various attempts are made to predict a future state of affairs from whatever data happen to be available. Such an approach has little to recommend it, except in areas where there is virtually no knowledge with which one can begin. The approach also tends to be extremely costly. The method sometimes produces techniques for making predictions that have practical applications, but it contributes nothing to a scientific knowledge of the problem.

4. An essential condition for making a prediction is that the variable to be predicted, and whatever is used to make the prediction, have reliability. The reliability of the variables limits the accuracy of the prediction that can be made. Grades in college are predictable only insofar as they represent reliable measures.

5. Three different approaches can be taken to the problem of predicting educational achievement, a problem that has been extensively studied. These are as follows:

   a. The development of test situations that are miniatures of the learning situation in which it is desired to predict behavior.
   b. The administration of a wide range of instruments in the hope that one will predict.
   c. The development of a theory of prediction and the development of methods on the basis of that theory.

6. An event can be predicted if all of the conditions that ultimately lead up to that event can be observed and measured at the time when the prediction is made. The event to be predicted must also be a well-defined phenomenon.

7. Sometimes the prediction problem can be simplified by attempting predictions with only certain groups of individuals. The behavior of some individuals is much more predictable than is the behavior of others. Clustering of variables may also improve the possibility of making a useful prediction.

8. Prediction studies commonly show the phenomenon of shrinkage. After items have been selected that predict well in the particular situation,

new data are then used to check the prediction process. The original prediction capability of the items is then found to shrink. The original selection procedure selected some items which, by chance, showed predictive capacity. Various procedures can be used to eliminate or reduce the shrinkage effect.

9. The issue of the relative merit of statistical prediction and clinical prediction has long been argued. There seem to be no simple answers to the questions raised. Studies of the problem have generally shown bias by setting up tests that favor one procedure.

10. Rare events present difficult prediction problems and generally cannot be satisfactorily predicted.

CHAPTER 14
Some Problems of Conducting Historical Research

Historical Research and Case History Research

Research conducted by historians has differed from research conducted by the majority of scientists in so many fundamental ways that a chapter on the subject almost seems out of place in this volume. Nevertheless, its inclusion is justified on three grounds. First, many theses written by students in schools of education are historical in character. Second, a review of research literature is in itself an historical study, for the reviewer is attempting to reconstruct what was done and what happened in the past. Third, the last few decades have seen a rapprochement between historical research and research in such areas as anthropology, sociology, and psychology. The Social Science Research Council has made persistent efforts to bring together scholars in history, anthropology, sociology, and related disciplines so that each can profit from the knowledge of technique and method acquired by the others.

An example of this rapprochement is found in a Social Science Research Council Report by Gottschalk et al. (1945) in which the knowledge of a historian, a sociologist, and an anthropologist is pooled to provide a more complete understanding of the use of the personal document in research. Psychologists have also conducted inquiries on the fringe of historical research. For example, the writings of Allport (1942) on the use of personal documents in research has had some impact on students of historical method.

Historical research is concerned with man's past, and although it has as its aim the reconstruction of the past, such a reconstruction can never be fully achieved. The problem of the historian is similar to that of psychologists working with case history material who seek to reconstruct from such material the nature of the person to whom it pertains. The information is always fragmentary and the reconstruction provides a sketch rather than a finished portrait. Different students of a case history may arrive at different reconstructions from the same evidence, but the student of personal case histories sometimes has an advantage over the historian in that he may go out and study his case further and validate through the collection of additional evidence the reconstruction he has built. The clinical psychologist typically does this. From the evidence he collects about a case, he attempts to reconstruct the person. Then he validates his reconstruction by further observing the person. The historian cannot look to the future to validate his reconstructions of the past.

But history is not just any reconstruction of the past as Nevins (1963) reminds us. In order to be designated as history, it must reflect the spirit of critical inquiry that aims to achieve a faithful representation of past events. The historian aims to write history that is in some sense true, but much that is written about the past is notorious for deliberate distortions. Nevins points out that presidential campaign speeches reviewing events of the past four years are not examples of the writing of history, for they do not reflect the historian's dedication to the spirit of scholarly inquiry. A commissioner of education, appearing before a congressional committee to support a request for funds, may "review the progress" of the last year, but with no stretch of the imagination could his report be construed as being a history of educational progress during the year. Both the commissioner and the members of the congressional committee know that the report is biased and selective in the presentation of content. The report of the commissioner can be considered a document for the historian to examine to extract from it whatever truth is there, but it is not history.

Those who would wish to conduct historical studies in education should begin by reading material, written by historians, on the conduct of historical research. Gottschalk's book on historical method (1950) is a classic. Barzun and Graff's (1970) more recent work is also highly regarded. Both of these books handle basic problems of how to treat historical information. The student should also realize that history is written for many purposes including those of producing literature, for attempting to predict the future, as a source of inspiration, as an explanation of the human condition, and so forth. Daniels (1972) discusses the how and why of writing history. The well-known historian Allan Nevins has also discussed such issues during a lifetime of writing, and some of those writings have been assembled by Billington (1975). A lighter and more racy volume by Marston (1976) provides suggestions for the writing of history including the writing of history as fiction.

The Historian's Use of Documents

Reconstruction of the past, which is called history, is based on inferences made from documents. The term *document* is used here in a broader sense than it is used in daily living. A document is an impression left by a human being on a physical object. The impression may be made with ink on a piece of paper, with a sculptor's chisel on a piece of stone, with an artist's brush on canvas, with the potter's hand on soft clay, and in any other way in which a human may leave a trace of his activity. This conception of a document is derived from the writings of Gottschalk (1950), who makes no distinction between written impressions and other impressions. In any case, this distinction is not easily made, for primitive written communications are pictorial, and every object on which the human hand has left an impression tells a story.

Documents are derived from *sources*. A particular observer is an example of a source; he may be the source of many documents. A newspaper is another example of a source. However, the word *source* also has another meaning in that a document is commonly referred to as a source of information.

That sound inferences about a culture can be made from objects is so obvious that the point hardly needs to be pressed further. If a visitor from another planet were able to procure some of the common objects used by modern civilization but died on the return trip home, the objects themselves would permit the inhabitants of the other planet to go far toward reconstructing a picture of our civilization. Take, for example, a good quality kitchen knife. The fact that it contained high-grade steel would indicate that the civilization from which it was derived had an advanced technology in the processing of metals and had probably made substantial scientific discoveries. The name of the manufacturer on the knife would indicate a knowledge of writing and the widespread use of writing and printing in daily life. The plastic handle would provide further cues concerning the scientific and technical development of the culture. Additional inferences from other objects in the collection would not only provide some verification of the inferences made from the knife but would also add to the reconstruction.

The reconstruction of the past is undertaken in terms of a set of written symbols. The assumption is that the words of history bear a well-defined relationship to past events, much as an equation of a physicist bears a relation to the processes occurring in an experiment. One important difference is that the physicist can always reproduce the process in order to check whether his formula actually corresponds to real events. The historian has much greater difficulty in doing this. In an earlier chapter the use of models in the development of science was discussed. In a sense, history is a model of certain events of the past.

The thinking habits of most people are such that they have difficulty in thinking of written history as merely an attempt to build a verbal model of past events. One can understand why this is so. To read a chapter by a great historian of high literary talent is to have a vivid experience of living in the past with a feeling for the reality of the past much as one has a sense of the reality of the present. The compelling reality of the image of history imparted to us is an illusion conjured up through the literary and research skills of the historian. The reality of history is illusory, for one cannot know the past in the way in which one can know the present. One cannot know it in the way in which it was known to those that lived it. Written history is only an attempt to provide, through the use of words and symbols, some representation of what are inferred to be events that actually took place. How close a relationship exists between the written symbols and the actual events is always a matter for conjecture. Language itself, with its many limitations, probably has only limited capacity for representing the events as they actually happened.

The problem of selecting, examining, and making inferences from documents are the problems of historical method. They present essentially the same difficulties that are encountered in making inferences from psychological tests and other materials, but they have the added difficulty that there is often no direct way of validating the inference. When one considers that trained psychologists have been relatively unsuccessful in making predictions about individuals even from very extensive case histories, one may well wonder whether the historian is likely to be more successful in reconstructing history from the documents available.

Choice of a Subject

Every historical study begins with the choice of a subject. This may seem to be an easy decision to make, but the fact is that it is not and there is considerable controversy among historians concerning the criteria to use in the selection of a topic. Gottschalk (1951) suggests that four questions should be asked in identifying a topic:

1. Where do the events take place?
2. Who are the persons involved?
3. When do the events occur?
4. What kinds of human activity are involved?

Other prescriptions exist for defining historical topics. One of these is to define the topic in terms of some important idea or set of beliefs. One school of historians has taken the position that history is the history of important ideas and if it is not this, then it lacks significance. Thomas Carlyle thought that history was simply a collection of biographies.

The scope of a topic can be varied by varying the scope of any one of the four categories: the geographical area involved can be increased or decreased; more or fewer persons can be included in the topic; the time span involved can be increased or decreased; and the human activity category can be broadened or narrowed.

In a sense, historical studies can only begin with a very rough determination of what topic is to be involved. Since the research worker, in the beginning stage, does not yet know the scope his topic may acquire after all the facts have been assembled, he can only indicate in a rough way the scope of the projected research. As he studies the sources available to him, he may find that the proposed topic involves so many and complex events that he must limit its scope. He may also find that the area is an impoverished one and that a broadening of the scope of the study is desirable.

Historical dissertations and theses in the area of education are commonly biographical studies, perhaps because these are more readily undertaken than other forms of historical inquiry. Yet there seems to be a particular need, in education, for the historical study of important ideas that have influenced both the schools and public policies related to them. Education has so often moved through cycles of ideas only to return, ultimately, to the starting point. A better understanding of the history of ideas in education would prevent much activity that has been called "rediscovering the wheel." A great new educational program is often little more than one that had been in vogue thirty years previously. For example, the new emphasis on developing creativity through education is really a revival of a similar emphasis displayed during the 1930s when the Progressive Education Association attempted to encourage creative activity on the part of pupils. The activities involved in such creativity training today are essentially the same as those that were advocated forty or more years ago. The numerous individualized teaching programs that are claimed, by some, to represent a new great advance are extraordinarily like those developed at Winnetka many decades ago. The present vogue for Initial Teaching Alphabets (ITA) is a revival of an unsuccessful movement of a century ago; and it is highly doubtful whether the present special reading alphabets are any better than those that were tried out in school systems in the 1800s. Those who play leadership roles in education need to be far more sensitive to the history of education than they have been in the past. Research on the history of ideas in education has a very valuable function to perform.

Selection of Sources

Historical studies usually begin with a delimitation of the general category of events that is to be reconstructed. The next step is the establishment of sources from which inferences can be made concerning the nature of the events. A common classification of sources is into *primary* and *secondary*. A primary source is one which has had some direct physical relationship to the events that are being reconstructed. A person who directly observes an event would be classified as a primary source, and so, too, would a photograph or sound recording of the event. A reproduction of such a photograph would also be considered as a primary source. The writings of a person whose life is being reconstructed as a history would be considered a primary source even if he wrote about himself in the third person, as certain writers have done. Secondary sources are those that do not bear a direct physical relationship to the event that is the object of study. They are related to the event through some intermediate process. Thus, if the historian is interested in the life of a character whom we will designate X, he may have to use documents produced by Z who never knew X personally. Z may have derived his information about X through an interview with Y, a close personal friend of X. In such a case, both Y and Z introduce distortions; hence Z as a secondary source is necessarily a poorer source of information than Y. If the chain involved in the transmittal of information is lengthened from X—Y—Z to a chain of four elements, the adequacy of the information is again decreased. Psychologists have conducted experiments on the transmittal of information by this kind of human chain and have found that substantial distortions may occur in very short chains, even to the extent that the information transmitted loses all its original characteristics.

Many sources include both primary and secondary elements that the person conducting historical research, or research involving the use of personal documents, may have to sort out. Many biographies have been written by close personal friends of the principal character involved. The biography will be a mixture of information derived by direct observation and material obtained by the writer from other sources. Often there is no way of determining which parts of a source are primary and which are secondary, although this may be a vital issue in determining the inferences to be made from the material.

Criteria of the Validity of Inferences and Reconstructions

The scientist uses many different criteria to determine the validity of the ideas he develops. One criterion may be called an *internal* criterion— whether the idea fits with other ideas derived from different sources. The wave theory of light derived from a study of lens phenomena and inter-ference phenomena does not fit with the quantum theory of light derived from such phenomena as the photoelectric effect. Both conceptions of light must be inadequate—they are incompatible with one another, although each is compatible with the evidence on which it is based. Inferences made from different sources about the same historical event must be compatible and fit together if they are to be considered valid. This type of validation procedure used by the historian closely resembles that used by the scientist. But the scientist has another method of validating his inferences; namely, by making predictions on the basis of the inferences and determining whether such predictions are correct. The historian is not able to use the latter approach to validate his inferences.

A difficulty that the historian faces when he attempts to validate his inferences is that this process always involves a considerable degree of personal judgment and subjectivity. The scientist attempts to overcome this difficulty by using measuring devices and laboratory procedures that eliminate, as much as possible, the factor of judgment. For example, by inference from data, Einstein developed an equation relating mass to energy. This inference could be validated by finding situations in which there was a conversion of mass to energy and *measuring* the amount of energy produced by a given loss of mass. There is very little guesswork involved in this kind of validation. There is much greater difficulty in validating the inference that a Supreme Court justice held a particular personal view with respect to a particular issue, although to hold such a view was in conflict with a decision he had endorsed. Indirect information may *indicate* that his personal views were in conflict with the position, but how much evidence does one have to have, in this case, to substantiate the hypothesis? The answer is strictly a matter of opinion, a matter that makes the task of the historian a particularly difficult one.

Although agreement among sources and the criterion of internal consistency is commonly used, it cannot always be justifiably applied. The psychologist is, in this respect, in a much better position than the historian, for very rarely in psychological work can the criterion of internal consistency not be applied. In contrast, the historian often encounters instances in which much evidence appears on the surface to point in one direction, but the inference is wrong. Consider, for example, the documents left in Germany after the end of the Nazi regime. Document upon document takes the position that the difficulties of Germany were manufactured by the Jews. Clearly, the position is nonsense and although the documents show consistency, the criterion of consistency cannot be applied.

Evaluation of Written Documents

Before a written document can be used as a basis for making inferences, its worth for the purpose must be evaluated. This is generally done from two distinct points of view. First, an appraisal must be made of the authenticity of the source. Second, if the authorship can be established, the characteristics of the author must be weighed in order to determine whether the document he produced can be considered a sound source of information. Each of these presents problems in evaluation that must be considered separately.

The Evaluation of Authenticity. Sometimes a problem of authenticity will arise in the research that students of education are likely to undertake, although less often than in other kinds of historical research. For example, if a student were to make an analysis of the content of speeches made by superintendents during a given period of time in order to study the educational policies of the period, he would be faced with the problem of determining how many of the superintendents used ghostwriters. The same problem arises in the case of correspondence, for it is very common for an official letter to be composed by a person other than the signer. Autobiographies are also commonly written by ghostwriters and throughout history persons have earned their livings by such writing.

The historian is plagued by the fact that the details of many documents are incorrect and, unless checked, may give rise to incorrect inferences. Barzun and Graff (1970) give an interesting example of how an incorrect date on a letter might lead to incorrect inferences. They cite the case of a letter written by Berlioz to his publisher about the preparation of an index for a book. According to the letter, it was written from Paris on Thursday, June 23. No year was indicated. Establishing the date of the letter presents an interesting problem. Barzun and Graff point out that other sources indicate that Berlioz lived in Paris from July 1849 until April 1856 and hence a reference to the calendar should indicate in which one of these years June 23 fell on a Thursday. The calendar indicates that the year would have been 1853, but Barzun and Graff then point out that the year could not have been 1853 for at that time Berlioz did not have any manuscript in the final stages of completion. The year must have been 1852 and the day Wednesday rather than Thursday, June 23. The evidence indicates that Berlioz made an error in noting the day of the week.

The Evaluation of the Writer as a Transmitter of Information. The authors of documents may represent excellent sources of information or worthless sources. A number of characteristics are commonly considered in making evaluations of writers.

1. Was the writer a trained or untrained observer of the particular event? If a biologist recorded that he observed the Loch Ness monster, greater credibility would be given the report if it were made by a biologist than if a person not trained in biological observation had reported it. Related to this is the matter of the expertness of the observer. The biologist in this case is not only a trained observer but also an expert on animal life. More credence is given to the observations of experts than those of amateurs.

2. What was the relationship of the observer to the event? The closer the writer was to the event recorded, the greater, is the value of the source. Persons who arrive *after* an event has taken place or who were some distance from it are not in a position to provide reports to which great significance can be attached. An accident report of a principal who arrived on the scene after the incident occurred is likely to be worth less than that of a teacher who saw it happen.

3. To what extent was the writer under pressure to distort? There are many cases in which educational documents must be considered as almost certainly representing a distorted picture of what happened. A school board

that meets behind closed doors and then releases for publication a report of the deliberations is likely to produce a distorted statement of what occurred. The statement is likely to be designed to please the public and the personnel of the school system. Again, in a public session of a school board, a newspaper reporter is likely to give greater stress to those aspects of the proceedings that might be of political interest to his particular newspaper.

4. What was the intent of the writer of the document? This is related to the previous item, but covers a greater range of circumstances. Documents may be written for many different purposes: to inform, to remind the writer (as in the case of a personal memorandum), to command (as in the case of a directive), to produce a particular effect on a particular reader or on a group of readers (like propaganda or advertising), or sometimes even to unburden the mind of the writer (as is sometimes the case with personal correspondence). The intent of the writer of the document, if it can be determined, should have a powerful influence on the evaluation of a document as historical evidence.

5. To what extent was the writer an expert at recording the particular events? The well-trained newspaper reporter is much more likely to provide an accurate report than the casual tourist who happened to observe the same event. Untrained observers in schools may report entirely erroneous impressions. Many critics of the public schools have not been inside one since they left school and base their criticism on anecdotes brought back by their own children. Such children would be considered to lack expertness in recording events that occurred.

6. Were the habits of the author of the document such that they might interfere with the accurate recording of events? This is an interesting problem. A good writer is not necessarily a good reporter. The writer with literary talent may be unable to control the temptation to embellish. The opportunity to display a clever turn of phrase or an apt analogy may interfere with precise reporting. The talented writer is also often imaginative and creative and experiences difficulty in discriminating between what actually happened and what he imagines happened.

7. Was the author of the document of such a nature that he might omit important materials or distort others in order to avoid being sued for libel? Every writer will yield to some extent to this, but the bold writer will still report more than the timid one and with less distortion. Even though this point is an important one, advice cannot be offered that will help the historian distinguish the bold writer from the timid one.

A source of considerable controversy has long been whether historians should approach the study of a document with ideas of what they are looking for, or whether the approach should be with an open mind. To approach a document with an hypothesis concerning what the document can show has, in the past, been regarded by the majority of historians as leading to a biasing of the process of observation. However, Johnson (1965), a noted historian, has pointed out that, if scientists had restricted their activities to observing without hypothesizing, the sciences would have never developed. He goes on to argue that historians typically have hypotheses, hidden vaguely at the back of their minds, whenever they scan a document. Were this not so, most historical documents would be sterile and perhaps even trivial documents. Imagine a social worker reviewing a case history, a common form of historical document, without any hypotheses concerning the kind of person that the case history described. The reviewer of such a case history would, almost certainly, begin to attempt to visualize the person involved after reading only the first few sentences, checking this mental reconstruction with the material that followed. Such a mental image of the person involved represents, in its early stages of development, a set of hypotheses. The historian, dealing not with case histories but with other forms of documents, can hardly be expected to review all of the material without ever forming hypotheses concerning the nature of that which is being described. He must also be extremely careful to avoid allowing his hypotheses to color the appearance of the facts.

Cause and Effect Relationships

Just as the behavioral scientist generally avoids referring to Event A as being caused by Event B, so too is the historian very cautious in his use of the concept of cause. No historian would want to discuss the *cause* of war or the *cause* of depressions. Both are highly complex events with complex relationships to other events. Only the physicist dealing with very simple isolated laboratory phenomena can use the word *cause* without running into difficulties. A physicist can appropriately say that a given force causes a given acceleration in a given mass. He can make such statements because he is dealing with an isolated phenomenon. The historian is never in such an enviable position.

The historical research worker must accept the fact that he is not dealing with clear-cut cases of cause and effect and must avoid such notions in his writing. It is very easy to make such a statement as "John Dewey's experiences with the experimental school he founded in Chicago caused him to recast his views on education." Such a statement is quite inaccurate because, although Dewey's experiences in connection with the Chicago school were extremely important to him in the development of his ideas, they were only one set of circumstances among many others from which his later conception of education finally emerged. The historian generally deals with chains of related events, but he cannot say that one event in the chain was caused by the previous event in the chain. A student might undertake an historical study of the changing role of the school faculty in establishing educational policies during the last twenty-five years. In undertaking such a project, the research worker would realize that many conditions and circumstances have been responsible for the changing role of the school faculty in this respect, but he cannot identify clear-cut cause-and-effect relationships. The change that has taken place is a result of many factors and the influence of a particular factor cannot be accurately assessed. In addition, there are events and conditions that have had some influence but that have not been identified. For a discussion of this problem, the reader is referred to Barzun and Graff (1970).

Synthesis of Information

If the preparation of a history were merely the digging out of facts, the task would be a simple one. But we have already seen that the study of documents often raises puzzling problems of what is fact, and that judgment is always involved in determining the extent to which the inferences made have a high probability of being correct. These processes present difficulties enough, but even more difficult is the step involved in using the facts and inferences to build an organized account of the events that the history is to cover. This process of putting together a history after the basic research on sources is completed is referred to as the *process of synthesis*. How this should be done is a matter of controversy.

One cannot clearly separate the search for documents and their examination and study from their synthesis into a coherent work. The synthesis of historical material is closely related to the whole problem of making inferences from historical data. Consider, for example, a history focused on the life of a central character. If it included only the objective facts— what the person had been observed to do or had left some record of having done—it would be a dull and lifeless history, lacking any unifying ideas. In order to avoid producing such a cold, lifeless, and objective history, the writer may infer from the data that the person was motivated throughout life by certain powerful and enduring motives. What would be a life of Thomas Jefferson if one could not see in it dedication to the achievement of certain values? What would be a life of Galileo if one could not see in it his devotion to the pursuit of truth and his imperviousness to the social pressures of his times? The historian generally infers from his data that there are underlying characteristics that give unity to the personality he is studying. But, as every psychologist knows, there are substantial hazards involved in making such inferences, and two persons studying the same historical character may not infer the same underlying motives or other basic characteristics.

Because psychologists cannot agree on a list of fundamental motives or underlying personality traits, the historian must choose a system he prefers for the description of behavior. Typically, he chooses a popular conception of personality organization rather than a technical one. One is unlikely to find a biography of Napoleon written in terms of how he was *conditioned* to manifest power-seeking behavior; neither is one likely to find one written in terms of psychoanalytic concepts. True, a few historians have attempted to describe their human subjects in terms of psychoanalytic concepts, but these are notable exceptions and are regarded as bold experiments rather than as orthodox treatments. Perhaps the two major reasons why interpretations of behavior undertaken by historians follow popular conceptions of personality structure are that historians are most familiar with this conception of personality and that history is written for a consumer and the popular conception of personality is the only one that the consumer is likely to understand. Synthesis of conceptions of historical characters in terms of popular conceptions of behavior will continue to be made.

The point emphasized here is that the historical reconstruction of human behavior can be undertaken in many different ways. Historians aim to reconstruct real persons with motives, values, fears, inner conflicts, struggles with their consciences, hates, loves, and the wealth of internal processes that make man more than a mere empty frame. This procedure involves many assumptions about human nature that research may ultimately show to be unsound.

Although the historian is limited in his interpretation of historical characters by his own conceptions of psychology and behavior, he is also limited by the inevitable fact that he must interpret the past in the light of contemporary thought. He may attempt to build a verbal model of the past, but the model is always a product of contemporary thought. A history written today reflects events of today as well as events of the past. The mind of man can mirror the past, but the image may be distorted by the very shape of the surface. Our picture of the schoolrooms of the Middle Ages is colored by what we know about our schools today.

Even at a much simpler level of synthesis than the one just considered are the difficulties involved in putting together what are ordinarily considered to be the facts of history. Consider, for example, two items about the French revolutionary Georges Jacques Danton: (1) Danton said, "I always act in accordance with the eternal laws of Justice," and (2) Danton was a man of violent and extreme views. The two items differ in their derivation: One has been reproduced from a document whereas the other has been inferred from many separate documents. Consider the problem of putting these two "facts" together. One might write any of the following statements:

Although Danton was a man of extreme and violent views, he said, "I always act in accordance with the eternal laws of Justice."

Danton said, "I always act in accordance with the eternal laws of Justice," but he was a man of violent and extreme views.

Although Danton said, "I always act in accordance with the eternal laws of Justice," he was a man of violent and extreme views.

Even though Danton was a man of violent and extreme views, he said, "I always act in accordance with the eternal laws of Justice."

Words such as *although* and *but* can introduce meanings that may take history beyond the realm of reasonable inference.

Written history may, in several different ways, go beyond the facts. There is some agreement among professional historians concerning what can be legitimately added and what cannot be added to fact, but there is far from complete agreement. For example, historians would object to including in a written history a dialogue that, almost certainly, never took place, even though the dialogue might bring out and describe precisely some political issues that played a leading role in the political events under consideration. Even though the reported conversation might not distort history and might provide literary color, it would not represent an acceptable product of historical inquiry. Yet history that is written strictly in terms of established facts is an uninteresting and drab affair. Nevins (1963) discusses this problem by citing a vivid account of General Braddock's advance upon the French and Indian forces over the rugged terrain of Pennsylvania. The account provides a vivid picture of the ruggedness of the mountain wilderness and the problems of moving heavy equipment over bolders and tree stumps and rivulets and gorges; and yet the description also gives a picture of the beauty, as well as the inhospitability of this desolate region. Nevins points out that none of the documents on which the account is based mentions any of these specific details about the landscape, but an account of Braddock's march that omitted any mention of them would be lifeless. These details were all an inherent part of the trek of Braddock's army, and a faithful reconstruction of history requires that the historian resurrect in his imagination the setting that made it what it was.

A third sense in which the historian adds to the facts is through an attempt to derive lessons, or generalizations, from the past. Gottschalk (1963) points out that historians cannot help using generalizations. Any sentence beginning with the words, "The Romans . . ." inevitably involves a generalization about Romans. The issue among historians is not whether generalizations should be used, but whether generalizations of history drawn from the study of one civilization can be applied to an understanding of other civilizations. Are there broad lessons to be learned from history? Can the broad lessons of history, if there are such lessons, be applied to the solution of contemporary human problems? These are questions of the greatest importance, but historians have not agreed on their answers.

Quantitative Methods in Historical Studies

Research in the area of history has traditionally been considered to be a qualitative inquiry into the past. Although many historians have compared historical research to that in anthropology and sociology, the methods of the historian have remained quite distinct from those used in the social sciences. Some change in this respect has taken place in recent years and some historians have begun to explore quantitative approaches to history. These approaches are interesting and novel and, even though they produce interesting new historical findings, they are unlikely to displace the traditional approaches to historical research. A volume edited by Aydelotte, Bogue, and Fogel (1972) has brought together some historical studies that are based on measurement.

The majority of the studies that have involved quantitative methods have involved the history of the last 150 years because during that period material has been stored in archives that permit the historian to measure certain trends. The studies reviewed in this volume cover a great number of different themes. For example, one study deals with the reasons for the disintegration of the conservative party during the 1840s in the United States. In this study, voting records in Congress of the conservative party members are studied and the data show a substantial splitting of the vote of party members on major issues, as well as the existence of different factions and a lack of unity within the party. A very different quantitative study investigates the distribution of houses with more than twenty hearths in the English county of Herefordshire. The data show that the houses tended to be concentrated nearer London suggesting that their distribution reflected the influence of the London culture.

Some of the earliest efforts to apply quantitative methods involve the use of word counts. Writers typically use particular words at their own frequency rates. A word that has a high usage rate by one writer may have a low usage rate by another. The usage rates of different words can be studied to throw light on the authenticity of the source of a document. Word-usage rates can also be used as a basis for inferring inner emotional states, such as anxiety.

Another related type of analysis has been developed by McClelland (1961) in an attempt to illuminate the motives operating in individuals in different cultures at particular times in history. McClelland argues that, if the writing appearing in a culture reflects strivings after excellence and provides what he terms "achievement need imagery," the culture may be considered as one with high achievement need. If such an inference can be made, it opens the way to the study of the social conditions that lead to high achievement need in the population. It also opens the way to the study of history in terms of a modern psychological theory of personality. McClelland's approach involves a very careful quantitative analysis of written documents in order to obtain measures of the extent to which a particular culture at a particular time manifests achievement need. The approach to history is a novel one, but it has been met with considerable skepticism by professional historians who claim that the same understanding of history can be achieved by much simpler means and without a quantitative analysis of written materials. (See, for example, Gottschalk et al. (1963).)

During World War II, elaborate and careful attempts were made to make analyses of the public speeches made by Nazi officials for the purpose of identifying possible underlying conflicts within the Nazi party. In addition, some attempt was also made to use such content analyses for the purpose of inferring the probable next moves on the part of the enemy.

This brief discussion of the introduction of quantitative methods into historical research may stimulate some readers to explore the possibility of applying such methods to the analysis of educational documents. For example, what motives have been stressed in elementary school readers over the last century? How have these motives changed, and how are the changes related to cultural change during this period? These are but a few of the problems that might be worth investigation.

History as the Study of Nomothetic or Ideographic Phenomena

The distinction has been made between nomothetic laws, which apply to all persons, and ideographic laws, which reflect the individual's unique history and which, hence, do not apply to others who have had different life histories. Allport (1961) has stressed this distinction in his writings and a parallel distinction is made by historians. Just as some psychologists emphasize the unique characteristics of each individual person, so too do some historians stress the uniqueness of each historical sequence of events.

The issue is as unsettled in the study of history as it is in the study of psychology. In both disciplines there are those who emphasize the nomothetic qualities of their subject matter and those who emphasize the ideographic. Arnold Toynbee, for example, has taken a nomethetic approach to history. He has attempted to show that within a group of twenty distinct cultures common trends are found, much as there are, to some degree, common trends in the psychological development of all children, even though each child has unique characteristics that distinguish him from other children. Certain historians emphasize the unique development of each and every culture.

The issue is one mainly of theoretical interest and has relevance to the issue of the extent to which the historian can predict the future turn of events, or may be able to do so one day. Contemporary historians, good scholars that they are, make few claims that historical trends are so well established that the future of a civilization can be predicted. Hopes of being able to make such predictions go far beyond expectations reasonable at this time, but there is another important relation that historical research has to future events.

Although historians may not be able to predict the future of a civilization, the study of history does affect the future by influencing the decisions of those who participate in government. Such persons as Roosevelt and Churchill have had a deep and scholarly interest in history, and their knowledge must influence their decisions. At least, some of the grossest follies of mankind may not be repeated, although perhaps this is setting our hopes too high. In the same spirit, those responsible for the establishment of educational policy are influenced by their knowledge of the history of education. The amateur reformers in the field of education would probably drop most of their plans for the remodeling of public education if they had a better understanding of the failures of the past.

Use of Case Histories: A Special Problem in Historical Research

The teacher, the counselor, the social worker, the research worker using biographical data, and the historian share in common the task of reconstructing case histories in the course of their professional work. Although the historian writing a biography of some famous contemporary and the social worker writing a case history for presentation to a court are not likely to think of themselves as being engaged in the same activity, both are attempting to reconstruct what happened in the life of a particular individual. In addition, both are trying to be objective; both are attempting to collect information on what actually happened and to distinguish this from what was rumored to have happened; and both are attempting to fit together fragmentary pieces of evidence into a total picture. Even though the style of the product of the historian and the social worker differ substantially, both encounter similar problems of method in going about their respective tasks. The research worker who uses biographical data comes perhaps closer to the historian, not only in how he goes about his task but also in the product that emerges from the research.

In the traditional type of biographical study, biographies are examined on an intuitive basis much as the clinician examines a patient. An example of this type of approach is manifested by Anne Roe in her studies of creative talent. The purpose of the examination of the biographies in this case is to determine whether the group of creative individuals show any common characteristics running through their lives. In the case of Roe's studies the attempt seems to have had some success, and the results have been confirmed by other sources of evidence. Nevertheless, the success of this method in the case of some studies does not mean that it is always successful. The truth seems to be that the method has many dangers, and unsuccessful applications tend to be overlooked.

A major danger is illustrated by the early biographical studies of neurotic patients, which repeatedly showed that such individuals often had been exposed to traumatic experiences. The conclusion was erroneously drawn that traumatic incidents in childhood produce neurotic behavior in adult life. This conclusion is not justified, for when the background of well-adjusted individuals is also examined, it is found that this group, too, shows a similar incidence of traumatic events. A related error was made at one time as a result of investigations on the family background of psychotic patients. It was found that such patients had a large number of relatives who were "queer" in some way. It is not reasonable to conclude on this basis that psychoses are inherited, because further investigation shows that so-called normal individuals also have numerous relatives who are commonly described as "queer." The reader will recognize that the way to prevent such erroneous conclusions is to introduce a group of "normals," whose background is also examined. The introduction of a control group is really necessary in order that any conclusions at all may be reached.

The collection of biographical data involves the same care and rigorous controls that have to be introduced in the collection of any historical data. Biographical data, collected through an interview with the person whose life history is being reconstructed, provides only the most limited data and often data of rather doubtful validity. The fact is that individuals are often brought into contact with a case worker because they cannot see themselves objectively and because they grossly misinterpret the actions of others toward themselves. These conditions that bring them into contact with the case worker are just the conditions that make them poor sources of historical data. Other sources of evidence have to be introduced in order to be able to select out those facts that dovetail together and separate them from those that display inconsistencies across different sources of information. However, biographical data about living persons is not readily obtained from their contemporaries. One cannot ask questions about another person easily unless one has some good reason such as obtaining an employment record. Society does not bestow on the research worker any particular right to collect information about a person from those who have known him. Yet without such information a case history is a document of very limited value.

The information presented by autobiographies or derived from interviews is difficult to treat in any scientific study because of its diffuse nature and because of the multiplicity and variety of the events that it may cover. These characteristics force on the investigator the intuitive approach that must be taken in examining such material. The intuitive approach involves the interpretation of the material, but an interpretative process invariably introduces error. In order to avoid such errors, inventories have been developed for recording biographical information.

In the typical biographical inventory, a standard series of questions is asked about a person's background. The questions are answered by choosing one of a number of alternatives. Typical questions are the following:

In what type of community did you spend most of your time before entering school?
1. In the country.
2. In a town with less than 5,000 inhabitants.
3. In a town with 5,000 to 10,000 inhabitants.
4. In a town with 10,000 to 50,000 inhabitants.
5. In a town with more than 50,000 inhabitants.

Which group of school subjects did you prefer when you were in high school?
1. English, speech.
2. Social studies, history, geography.
3. Science, mathematics.
4. Music, art.
5. Athletics.

Biographical information collected in the form illustrated here has had a long history of practical use and also some history of having played a useful part in research. Many have regarded it with skepticism, but the fact that it has had a long history of practical utility in the selection of various classes of employees has forced researchers to give it serious consideration. It is of interest to note that the first really successful use of the biographical inventory was in connection with the selection of salesmen, particularly life insurance salesmen. Such devices remain, even today, the main instruments that are used for this purpose. Of course, such devices were not developed on the basis of any particularly sophisticated psychological theory of selling. The point stressed here is that this work of practical importance demonstrated that biographical information collected in this form could be used for making predictions, and probably with more success than biographical information collected in narrative form. Of particular significance is the fact that biographical items related to factual material had considerable predictive significance, whereas those related to opinions and attitudes tended to be of doubtful value.

During World War II, some success was achieved in the use of biographical information blanks for the prediction of performance in flying training, and there were even indications that such devices could be used for predicting aerial combat leadership. These inventories were much more sophisticated than earlier devices in the theory on which they were based, and this sophistication has been shown in work that has been undertaken since that time. A major development incorporated into more recent biographical information blanks has been an attempt to group items in such a way that they measure a number of distinct and separate influences in a person's background, or even a series of relatively independent traits that may emerge from such backgrounds. There has also been considerable interest in attempts to predict variables other than occupational success. For example, there have been many studies in which biographical information has been used to predict reaction to stress, and predictions of sufficient accuracy to be used have been achieved.

The clinician has never been particularly in sympathy with this approach to the matter of using biographical information. He has tended to believe that the very uniformity of the material included in a biographical information blank is a disadvantage. He points out that the unique event is often a crucial factor in the life of an individual, and the unique event would be missed by any standard inventory. The clinician has not proved his case in this matter, and the success achieved with biographical inventories may perhaps make him stop and ponder.

Summary

1. Historical research resembles scientific research in certain basic ways. Both involve the collection of evidence and the drawing of inferences, but the goals are different. The historian attempts to make a reconstruction of the past. History may also be viewed as a verbal model of the past.

2. Historians make inferences from documents, but the term *document* refers to any trace of what happened in the past. Documents are derived from sources. The problems involved in making inferences from documents, and in selecting and examining the documents, are the problems of historical method.

3. An historical study has to have a subject limited by the place, the circumstances, and the persons involved. Historical subjects may be broad or narrow. Some historical studies are biographical studies.

4. Historical studies require that there be sources of information available. Sources should be primary rather than secondary.

5. The inferences made as a part of any historical study should be validated against whatever other information can be obtained.

6. Written documents used in historical studies must be evaluated in terms of their authenticity. Many documents are produced by persons other than those who sign them, and the documents may not have been written at the time when they were alleged to have been written. In addition, a document has to be evaluated in terms of whether the writer actually had access to the information contained in the document and was motivated to provide an objective account of what happened.

7. Historians have to be even more cautious than scientists in attributing cause and effect relationships.

8. The synthesis of historical information is a particularly difficult task. Changing the emphasis given to particular facts may change the meaning.

9. Some historians have attempted to introduce quantitative methods into history. Perhaps the most widely used quantitative method is that involving word counts.

10. A special case of the writing of history is that of the clinician attempting to construct a biographical history of a patient. Systematic ways of doing this have been developed involving the use of biographical inventories.

CHAPTER 15
Data Processing
and Reporting

Mechanics of Data Handling

Data Processing

The plan for the processing of data should be made at the time when the study is designed. By this is meant the time when the final plan is evolved. Of course, some preliminary studies have to be undertaken to ensure that the enterprise is feasible. This is a more important matter than it may seem to be on the surface, and perhaps its importance may be brought home by citing an example.

A student once approached the author with a proposed study of the effectiveness of two methods of teaching typing. The design of the experiment, was a familiar one, with several pairs of matched groups being assigned to the two methods. At regular intervals throughout the training program tests were to be taken by the students. These tests would require rather prolonged periods of typing, lasting for as much as an hour each. The experiment was to be conducted over two semesters. During the conference with the student on this matter, a rapid computation was made of the volume of data to be collected and the time it would take to derive the scores that would be subjected to analysis. As nearly as could be determined, the work would have taken about six months of the student's full-time attention. Also, the data would have consisted of sheets of typing and were such that it hardly seemed possible to design a device that could quickly score the material. It would have been an unreasonable use of the student's time to spend six months in clerical work, since this period could be much better spent in training related to his professional goals.

Various devices may be used to facilitate the derivation of scores from the raw data. One of these is a stencil scoring device. Unless it is absolutely essential, research should never be conducted in such a way that the answers to a test are marked in a booklet. A separate answer sheet is a compact method of recording raw data. If the scores are to be converted to standard scores, then it is sometimes convenient to print the conversion table right on the answer sheet. If possible, the researcher should avoid having scores recorded on both sides of the answer sheet, because it is inconvenient to transcribe these scores onto rosters. Sometimes the separate answer sheet should not be used. Whenever speeded tasks of simple functions are involved, the task of finding the appropriate place on the answer sheet and marking it may contribute more to the variability of the score than the function it is desired to measure. In such cases, it is obviously desirable to avoid the use of a separate recording system. In such a case the problem should be printed right on the answer sheet above or beside the place where the answer is to be recorded.

An alternative to the answer sheet is a version of the IBM punched card. Such cards are familiar to the reader through their several common uses—as checks, as bills, and so forth. They can be printed so that they have spaces on them similar to those found on answer sheets. The cards are then marked with a soft pencil, just as would be answer sheets, but, of course, they cannot be scored with the usual test-scoring machine. Instead, they are run through a machine that converts the marks to punched holes. A computer can then be used to derive scores for each card.

Test scoring machines can be adapted to analyze many kinds of data. Such machines not only score but also are fitted with item counter devices, which permit the counting of the number of answer sheets that are marked in a particular position. It is thus possible to run answer sheets through the machine and to determine the number of respondents that chose the first answer on the first problem, and the second answer, and so forth.

Test scoring machines have been constructed for special purposes. Test-cor, a Minneapolis organization, was one of the first to develop a special machine for the high-speed scoring of the *Strong Vocational Interest Blank*. This company then branched out into machines that were especially adapted for the scoring of other instruments. Many other organizations now offer special scoring services. The graduate student who is interested in obtaining the services of one of these organizations would do well to consult the university counseling center in order to obtain advice on which service to use.

Some ingenious investigators have used a plan to reduce the clerical work involved in the handling of data, but one that is not endorsed here. The procedure is simply that of requiring the subjects to undertake the clerical work. Where responses are to be coded, the subjects perform the coding; where the tests are to be scored, the subjects score the tests. This is an undesirable practice, for two reasons. First, it introduces sources of error variance over which the researcher may have no control. This is to some extent true even when a simplifying device such as an answer sheet is used. At least some error is introduced through errors in marking the answer sheet, but this becomes particularly pronounced when a speeded function is involved. If a complicated recording procedure is used, substantial errors may be introduced by the process. Second, a problem of ethics is involved. The researcher may have some justification in asking for the time of persons for the purpose of advancing knowledge, but he must respect their time and ask them to do only what is essential. The researcher should not be guilty of exploitation. Of course, the issue does not arise if the subjects are paid, except that it may be much more efficient to employ a few well-supervised, trained clerks than a large number of untrained persons.

What to do about missing values is a particularly perplexing problem to which there is no completely satisfactory solution. In studies involving the analysis of correlation coefficients, a missing value in a table of raw data is of little concern. It does not matter much whether the coefficients in a table are based on slightly different numbers of cases. In factor analysis and in many other mathematical methods that are used for structuring data, slight variations in the number of cases from coefficient to coefficient are of little consequence.

On the other hand, when block designs are being used as the basis for an experiment or as a basis of any other type of research, the problem of missing values becomes acute, because the computational methods that have been developed and that form the basis of tests of significance require the use of all cell entries. If certain cells are disregarded, the net result is to introduce an unknown amount of bias into the test of significance. There is no point in applying a test under these conditions, since it will not yield any kind of answer to the question posed.

At one time it was commonly suggested that mean values be substituted for the values of missing observations. The argument was that the measures were presumed to be normally distributed, and in such a case the class interval that includes the mean includes also the most frequently occurring values. Thus, the insertion of the mean is an attempt to substitute the most probable value for the missing one.

Another approach is to compute expected values for those missing from the other values provided by the data. Through the computation of regression equations, it may be possible to provide a solution to this problem. However, this procedure is likely to produce more internal consistency in the resulting data than they would otherwise have. It will also bias tests of significance to an unknown degree. This problem has been worked on, and solutions that attempt to eliminate bias in tests of significance have been developed for many of the more common block designs.

Another problem that sometimes arises is whether to discard certain observations that for one reason or another fall far outside the range of the other observations. Such discards must not be made after a preliminary inspection of the data has shown that the discarding of certain observations would make the data more in accordance with expectation. Discarding *must* take place before the significance of the data has been examined, for if this rule is not rigorously observed, the tests of significance that are applied will probably be biased. On the other hand, if this practice is observed, there is no reason why the researcher should not set up rules for discarding observations. These rules must apply to all observations, never only to certain groups. An example may illustrate this point.

An example of the effective discarding of data is found in a recent study involving four different methods of teaching the principle of refraction from physics. Four methods of instruction were used, one involved in actual demonstration, two involved the use of diagrams, and another provided a lecture without a demonstration or diagrams. Each of several classes in three schools were divided into four groups and each group was exposed to one of the teaching methods. A cursory examination of the data revealed that the children in one of the schools were showing no learning on the task regardless of the instructional method used. In addition, evidence showed that the children in this particular school did not perform significantly better on a test of their ability to apply the principle of refraction than a control group of children who took the test but who were given no instruction. On this basis, *all* the data from the school where the children did not learn were discarded. This involved discarding equal numbers of cases from each method of instruction. This procedure reduced the experimental error and made the relative effectiveness of the different methods of instruction more apparent.

It is important to note that the data could be discarded without biasing the results; in this case data were dropped from all four experimental instructional procedures. One could not discard data involving only one method of instruction in one school without biasing the results. For example, discarding one small group of students exposed to the demonstration of the phenomenon of refraction, because that particular group did not do very well, would have had the effect of making that method appear more effective than it really was.

The researcher should always be on guard lest the procedure established for discarding observations by some means affect tests of significance that are later applied. This can happen in many ways, but the basic effect is always produced by there being a greater number of discards in one group than in another.

Observations can be recorded on rosters or on cards with numbered spaces. The author's preference is for the latter system, because it provides greater flexibility and facilitates certain operations with data, such as the separation of groups of cases on which it is desired to conduct special studies. The roster method of recording is highly inflexible, and even the correction of errors on rosters may present difficulties.

It is particularly important to check the accuracy with which all entries are made. The procedure is such a simple one that it often gives the false impression that it is not possible to make errors on such a straightforward copying task. One very common type of error is the transposition of digits, such as occurs when a number is correctly read as 51 but incorrectly recorded as 15. Another source of error is the recording of digits in incorrect boxes on the cards or on the roster. All recordings must be checked with the most scrupulous care in order to catch such errors, for they may seriously affect the conclusions drawn from the data.

The processing of data presents certain problems that are now considered. The scientist should *know* his own data. Unless there is a close personal contact between the researcher and his data, many important findings will never be made. Limitations may remain unnoticed unless close contact with the data is maintained throughout the processing procedure. For these reasons, it is good practice to perform a part of the data-processing by hand.

The student should be warned against the incorrect use of information derived from data. An example of incorrect use of information is the researcher who gets to know his data well in order that he may derive from them hypotheses to be tested later by means of statistical tests. It should be remembered that statistical tests of hypotheses are not designed to test hypotheses derived from the data themselves. If such tests are applied to these hypotheses, they will produce answers that are biased.

The problem is perhaps better understood by considering an actual example. A research worker studying the differences between delinquents and nondelinquents finds negligible differences between the two groups in all of the variables where he had planned to test the difference. A close scrutiny of the data did reveal that the blue-eyed children who were unusually tall for their age showed a high incidence of delinquency; this was advanced as one of the major conclusions of the study. The error made by the research worker in this case is that if one were to compare the two groups on a large number of characteristics, some combination of characteristics would be found that just happened to differentiate the two groups. There would be no reason for believing that these results would be repeated in a new sample.

The student should list, during the planning stages of the study, all of the *reasonable* hypotheses that he proposes to study. His data should be collected for the purpose of testing these hypotheses and no others. All subsequently developed hypotheses squeezed out of the data would be subject to the criticism that they are not firmly rooted in the theory on which the study was based, and any apparent positive results would probably be the result of chance peculiarities of the particular sample.

Processing Qualitative Data

Much of the data collected in educational research is qualitative and presents special difficulties when it is to be processed. In the early stages of acquiring information about a phenomenon, no attempt can be made to process carefully the facts that are collected. Freud's classic observations on the behavior of disturbed patients are examples of qualitative data collected and examined for the purpose of developing hypotheses, and the conclusions that he drew guided the research work of subsequent generations of psychologists. Early explorations are usually made in this way, but ultimately such observations must be analyzed systematically. The mere inspection of data without the aid of systematic analysis is a hazardous process, and there is always the danger that the researcher will dream into his data elements he wishes to see there but that do not really exist. For this reason every effort must be made to reduce such data to a form in which they can be analyzed by appropriate methods. In this way, personal prejudice can be eliminated from the interpretation of the material.

As a first step in the analysis of qualitative data, it is necessary to code the facts that are involved. This means simply that a number must be assigned to each class of fact. Thus, if the cumulative records of children are to be studied, it may have been determined that perhaps eighty items of information are to be coded. Those concerned with the coding operation might be asked to code all items of information on a sheet, a section of which might be as follows:

42. Progress through school   0 = never held back a grade
                                              1 = held back one grade
                                              2 = held back two or more grades

43. Speech   1 = no speech difficulties reported
                                              2 = speech difficulties but no action taken
                                              3 = speech difficulties and remedial work started

Through such a code sheet the qualitative information obtained in the cumulative record is converted into a set of numbers, which are then used for the analysis. Sometimes the numbers are entered directly onto the code sheet, if it is short. If the code sheet is long, the code numbers are often entered on a separate sheet or card.

Any set of rules established for the purpose of quantifying qualitative material should be tried out by submitting the material to different coders in order to determine whether the rules can be applied with consistency by different workers. This tryout helps to establish the error resulting from differences in the judgment of different persons. The tryout may also result in the development of methods that eliminate these discrepancies. The reliability of such procedures should always be given in the report of the study, unless the procedures are such that it is clearly evident that *careful* independent workers can produce independent results. This might be true where the entire process of quantification required only the counting of the number of words written in documents produced by subjects.

Errors are commonly made in clerical procedures that involve the coding of data. These are usually referred to as errors of carelessness, but in actual fact they are probably caused not so much by the failure of the clerk to be conscientious as by the immensely boring nature of much of this work. It is thus essential for all clerical work of this kind to be rechecked independently by another clerk. It may not be necessary to lay down the standard that only perfect agreement is to be accepted, because this may be unrealistic; but some standard should be established. Scores that do not agree within one point, or two, or three—or whatever is considered reasonable—must be redetermined, preferably by another person. Clerks must work independently, otherwise this check would be quite meaningless.

Statistical Analysis of the Data

The previous sections of this chapter were concerned with the mechanics of handling data and converting it to a form that will permit meaningful analysis. The data yielded by the coding and recoding process may be so clear that there is no doubt what it means, but this only occurs under ideal conditions. More generally, data present a complex and unclear picture and the research worker has to turn to statistical analyses to find out just what the data mean, if they mean anything at all.

A first step in the analysis of data is to compute a few simple statistics, such as means. These statistics can usually be easily computed by hand on a pocket calculator. Indeed, they should be computed by hand if the research worker is to gain an intimate knowledge of his data.

In this modern age of computers the research worker may be tempted to turn his data over to a computer with only a cursory study of it. This is a poor policy because an intimate knowledge of the data is always important. Often the most important features of data can be found only by direct inspection, and these interesting features may be quite unexpected. In the case of a previously cited study in which the pupils in one school showed no learning on the experimental task, this feature of the data was apparent from a preliminary inspection, but might not have been so apparent from the subsequent complicated analysis. Some analysis should always be made by hand by the research worker himself before he embarks on the overall analysis undertaken by other means.

The research worker should not arrange for statistical analyses that he does not understand. If he does this, he is likely to get into difficulties. The author was recently brought such an analysis by a graduate student who had arranged for a factor analysis of his data on a computer. The student understood neither the nature of factor analysis nor the procedure by which it was accomplished. The analysis was meaningless to him, and he wanted me to find meaning in it. However, the analysis was also meaningless to me because the data were not appropriate for factor analysis. The student did not know enough about statistical procedures to select an appropriate form of statistical analysis. He should have sought advice before feeding his data into the computer center.

If the student is to use computers for the analysis of his data then he should have some understanding of what computers do and how they do it. Most computer centers in universities provide brief courses in the use of computers, and the pages that follow will prepare the student for such a course.

A Brief History of Computers

Every educational research worker today must have some knowledge of computers in order to plan his work effectively. A general knowledge of what computers can do is important because many research approaches to problems have been made feasible through the availability of these devices. The educational-research worker also needs to know something about computers because he will often be called upon to advise on the installation of computers in school systems.

The conception of a modern computer was first developed by Charles Babbage (1792–1871) who was able to persuade the British government to support an effort to develop a computing machine over a ten-year period. Babbage's machine, which he referred to as his analytic machine, was a tremendously ambitious venture, but it ended in failure largely because the art of machine construction in his day was not sufficiently advanced to perform the functions that he wished it to perform. He did manage to produce a small "differencing" machine that could solve some simple problems in the application of calculus, but this device was far short of the highly elaborate machine of which he had dreamed. Indeed, the "analytic" machine that Babbage planned to produce would have had a storage capacity not far short of that of a modern computer and an extraordinary capability for performing complex numerical operations. Parts of his machine, exhibited in the London Science Museum, are reminders of the great dream that Babbage had. His failure was a product of his excessive ambition. Had he been willing to settle for more modest goals, the modern computer might have been developed much earlier than it was.

Babbage's dream was for a digital computer; that is to say, a machine that would deal with numbers and perform arithmetical operations with them. Many computers were subsequently built that handled quantities rather than numbers. These computers are referred to as *analog* computers. A digital computer adds one number to another and finds the sum, but an analog computer adds, say, one voltage to another voltage, and finds the sum of the two voltages. The difference between the two kinds of computers is that between a counter, which can register only whole numbers, and a voltmeter, from which a voltage can be read within certain limits of accuracy. Analog computers are typically built for specific purposes such as solving particular kinds of equations. For example, many analog computers were built prior to World War II and were designed specifically for solving systems of simultaneous equations. Problems that can be solved on analog computers can also be solved on digital computers.

The digital computer can be adapted to handle symbols other than digits and thus has the potential for becoming a general-symbol manipulator and, ultimately, a universal problem-solving machine. For example, Euclidean geometry can be so coded that the axioms, and rules for making deductions from them, can be stored in a digital computer. The computer can then be programmed to produce the proofs of certain propositions; that is to say, it can originate proofs of Euclidean theorems. The fact that such manipulations of symbols can be performed has encouraged some to believe that the computer will ultimately become the universal problem solver.

Thus, the emerging modern conception of a computer is of a machine that manipulates symbols, much as man manipulates symbols in his thinking, rather than a machine that is limited to arithmetical operations. A machine conceived in this way has the potential for making decisions on the basis of data in accordance with the rules in terms of which it is designed to operate.

Description of Computers

All computers involve five essential systems: (1) the input system, (2) the output system, (3) storage systems, (4) the processing system, and (5) the control system.

Input systems are quite diverse. Anyone who has traveled by air is familiar with the input system used by the airline clerk to check your reservation. The essential information, such as your name and flight and the date, are typed by the clerk on what looks like a typewriter keyboard. Then there is a short delay of a few seconds followed by the information about your reservation that appears on a cathode ray tube, which is the same as a television screen. The airline clerk is operating a computer terminal similar to that available to students in many universities. Such a terminal is a simple input and output system. Communication with the central computer is undertaken through the use of a language similar to ordinary speech, but the terminal will accept and understand only certain terms in that language. A very large number of terminals may be connected to a single computer. When input is made through one of these terminals, the information will be held in storage until the time when the computer is free to handle it. That is why the airline clerk has to wait a few seconds before receiving back an answer.

In the case of the typical computer terminal, the data is placed in the computer through the use of a set of keys that are depressed. Sometimes other forms of input are more desirable. Very large volumes of data may be recorded on tape that can be fed into the computer system at the central operating station. Such systems permit the verification of the data thus recorded before it is processed by the computer.

Outputs may also appear in various forms. A common form of output at a terminal is a display on a cathode ray tube. Outputs may sometimes be printed through the use of high-speed printers that write hundreds of characters per second. Such printers may produce material at a much more rapid rate than it can be read. A fast reader may read at perhaps a line a second, but a high-speed printer may type out material at a rate of ten or more lines per second.

Computers may also produce outputs in the form of graphs. Points may be plotted from the data stored in a computer. Such outputs are particularly important in fields in which a graph is used to project future trends.

Storage systems are developing so rapidly that one is hesitant to write about them lest the descriptions become obsolete before the book is in print. The early computers of the late 1940s and 1950s were very limited in the storage capacity of the central processing unit. This meant that large problems often had to be handled piecemeal by the computer. This limited storage capacity was made up for, to some extent, by the use of storage facilities outside of the central unit. Thus, some computations could be stored on tapes, while additional computations were being made. Much time was occupied in these early computers in taking information out of their central storage units and placing it in temporary storage outside the computer and then later putting the information back into the computer again. In the modern computer, storage systems for holding data and other information are a part of the total mechanism, and time in the processing system is not tied up in putting information into external systems of storage and taking it out again. A great variety of memory units are used in different pieces of equipment including magnetic disks, drums, data cells, photo disks, and so forth. Storage systems may store information in the form of numbers or letters of the alphabet and words. The smallest amount of information that can be stored is referred to as a bit. Some of the storage units, that is to say memories, that are now being built have enormous capacities. A laser memory system has been built that offers storage capacity of a million million bits in sixty square feet of floor space. That would be enough storage capacity to store the information in perhaps a quarter of a million college textbooks. Such a system also permits the computer to gain access to any piece of information in less than nine seconds. Time of access to information is a very important matter. Large-capacity storage systems are of little use if a long time is required to gain access to the information. Although the capacity of the laser beam memory is overwhelming, even larger capacity systems are being developed holding millions of items of information per square inch.

These figures are of very general interest, but most users of computers at the graduate level do not have to be concerned much today with the problem of whether the computer has sufficient storage space to handle their problem. Each item of information is stored in a particular location in the storage system, and each location has an *address*. The addresses are simply numbers that indicate particular storage locations. Thus, the address represented by the number 292 represents a particular location where information is stored. A program might direct the machine to go to location 292 and read the information stored there before performing some operation on it. When the computer reads information from a storage location, the information is not erased. Only when new information is placed in a storage location is the original information stored there erased.

The processing unit generally consists of one or more registers in which information is placed and in which operations are performed on the information. For example, the machine may be directed to take whatever number is stored in 292 and place it in the register of the processing unit. A second command to the machine may call for the removal of the number stored in memory location 396 and to add to it the number from location 292, which has already been entered in the register. The register now contains the sum of the two numbers. A third command may call for the removal of the sum in the register and the storage of the sum in memory location 896. The register in which such operations are performed is commonly referred to as the *accumulator*.

Finally, every computer has a control unit that interprets the program of instructions and arranges for their execution. The control unit takes commands from the stored program in numerical order and keeps track of which command is being worked on at a particular time. As soon as one command is executed, the machine moves to the next appropriate command. Hence the control unit goes through the cycle of obtaining a command, interpreting it, executing it, and then reading a new command.

A program may also require a machine to make certain decisions and to undertake work in terms of the results of those decisions. At a certain point, the machine may be instructed to apply a test of significance, such as a test for the significance of the difference between two means. If the difference between the means is significant beyond a certain level, then certain additional tests are applied; but if the difference does not surpass the particular level, then the work is terminated. In order for a computer to make such decisions and to take appropriate actions, the details of how the decisions are made have to be spelled out precisely and in detail in the program.

Communication with the Computer

Computers are devices that do exactly what they are instructed to do with great rapidity and high precision. Computers can give answers to problems only when they are given precise instructions in a form they can understand. Computers are generally used in educational research to perform complex mathematical operations of the kind that most graduate students of education learn to undertake in courses in statistics. The computer itself uses a highly detailed set of instructions that are far more detailed than the user ever need understand. A user gives instructions through the keyboard of a typewriter, in a simplified English calling for the application of a particular program to his data. He might, for example, call for the computation of a Pearson product moment correlation coefficient from the data he provides. The computer presumably would have access to that program from its available store of programs. The program would originally have been written in a language developed for the purpose that is completely precise and unambiguous. The simplified English used by the user at the terminal is likely to be a language called BASIC. In this language, programs are called for, from storage, which are written in sophisticated computer language. Computer languages generally involve the common mathematical symbols, such as plus and equals, and also many common English words such as, SUM, DO, GO TO, READ INPUT, WRITE OUTPUT, and END. An example of a program is shown in Figure 1.

In order to function, a computer requires a sequence of commands referred to as a program. This set of commands is written in a programming language but, from the point of view of the machine (with no apologies for the implied anthropomorphism), this is a shorthand kind of language that has to be translated into detailed directions before it can be actually used for controlling the operation of the machine. For example, in a program language one might write a simple arithmetic statement of the form $R = A/B$. In order for the machine to find R from the quotient of A divided by B, a series of more detailed directions must be written. The machine must be instructed to take the quantity A from storage; then take the quantity B from storage and divide it into A; and then store the quotient in the storage location assigned for R. If the program writer had to write out all the details implied in his statement $R = A/B$ a great amount of time would be occupied in preparing a program for the calculation of even a simple function. He is saved this time by having a program language that permits him to write a brief statement. There is then a simple way of converting his brief shorthand statement into the detailed instructions required by the computer. The conversion of the shorthand statement to computer longhand is undertaken by means of a device known as a *compiler*. The statements written in the programming language are expanded

```
          DIMENSION SX(23),SXQ(23),VAR(23),XM(23),T(23,23),X(23)
   C      N IS THE NUMBER OF VARIABLES
   11 READ 7,N
    7 FORMAT (I2)
          DO 2 I=1,N
          SX(I)=0
    2 SXQ(I)= 0
          TX=0
   C      X(I) THE VARIABLES THAT ARE READ IN
    5 READ 1,(X(I),I=1,N)
    1     FORMAT(3F2.0)
  998     IF(X(1)-99.)3,10,3
    3 DO 4 I=1,N
   C      SX(I) IS THE SUMMATION OF X
          SX(I)=SX(I)+X(I)
   C      SXQ(I) THE SUMMATION OF X SQUARED
    4 SXQ(I)=SXQ(I)+X(I)*X(I)
   C      TX IS THE SIZE OF SAMPLE
          TX=TX+1.
          GO TO 5
   10 DO 6 I=1,N
   C      VAR(I) IS THE VARIANCE DIVIDED BY THE SIZE OF THE SAMPLE
          VAR(I)= (TX*SXQ(I)-SX(I)*SX(I))/(TX*TX*(TX-1.))
    6 XM(I)= SX(I)/TX
   C      MEAN OF X(I)
          DO 16 I=1,N
          DO 16 J=1,N
   C      T(I,J)=(X(I) MEAN-X(J) MEAN) DIV BY SQ RT OF (VAR(I)/N+VAR(J)/N)
   16 T(I,J)=(XM(I)-XM(J))/SQRT (VAR(I)+VAR(J))
          PUNCH 8,TX
   C      NO. OF DATA CARDS
    8 FORMAT (F8.2,2X,5HCARDS)
          PUNCH 19
   19 FORMAT (5HMEANS)
   C      HEADING CARD-MEANS
          PUNCH 18, (XM(I),I=1,N)
   18 FORMAT (F7.2,15F5.2)
          PUNCH 20
   C      HEADING CARD SIG. DIFF. BETWEEN MEAN
   20 FORMAT(24HSIG. DIFF. BETWEEN MEANS)
          PUNCH 88, ((T(I,J),J=1,N),I=1,N)
   88     FORMAT(8F10.5)
          GO TO 11
          END
```

Figure 1 Illustration of a program written in FORTRAN.

by this device into detailed instructions. Sometimes this may involve a very large expansion. A statement calling for a square root, or a sine, or a logarithm can easily be expanded into a set of more than fifty steps.

A program may contain a number of what are referred to as subroutines. For example, a routine for the extraction of square roots can be stored to be available whenever needed. The existence of such subroutines can greatly simplify the preparation of instructions because, in place of a long set of instructions needed for calculating square roots each time a square root is needed, a single command can be used calling for the subroutine.

Many different program languages have been invented for special purposes. For example, Cobol is a language that is particularly well suited for handling many kinds of business problems. The letters in Cobol stand for *Common Business Oriented Language*. Many other languages have been developed for special purposes. Fortran (Formula Translator), one of the first programming languages to be developed, has particular advantages in handling mathematical quantities and is probably the most widely used computer language at the present time. An attempt has been made to establish, through an international committee, a uniform international programming language; however, although the specifications for such a language have been drawn up, there are few signs that such a language is likely to be adopted very soon. The student who takes a short course in a programming language in America today is more likely to be trained in Fortran than in any other language, perhaps because equipment using that language is widely available.

The programming languages suitable for handling numerical data and the solution of algebraic problems are not generally suitable, without modification, for handling other forms of symbols such as those that are used in logic. When a programmer wishes to have a computer undertake logical derivations or manipulate symbols according to some set of rules other than those involved in arithmetic, he must use language that has been specifically built or adapted for that purpose. An adaptation of Fortran for this purpose has the exotic name of Lisp (signifying *List Processor*). This language is useful for instructing computers to play games such as bridge and chess and has important applications in the study of certain problems in the behavioral sciences.

The reader is referred to elementary texts on computers and to the manuals published by computer manufacturers if he wishes to gain further familiarity with computer languages. Specific references of the latter kind are not given here because the manuals are revised so frequently that the references would be obsolete before they appeared in print. Such manuals provide an introduction to the syntax of the language and a classification of the statements that can be made in it. The reader should realize that syntactical rules of a programming language are far more rigid than those governing the use of common language. In a programming language the omission of a comma might jeopardize the utility of the entire program. For this reason, new programs invariably contain "bugs," and the procedure universally called debugging typically takes more time than the writing of the program itself. A check system is commonly introduced into a new program in order to facilitate the debugging procedure. Learning to write programs is an incomparably good exercise in the precise use of language. New programs do not have to be written for most applications of computers since a large number of programs have been written in the past and most of these have been stored in libraries. Major computer centers not only have such program libraries but they also have program catalogs covering programs available in other centers. Programs are typically written in a general form that permit them to be applied to a range of problems, rather than just to the specific problem for which they were originally written. Thus, a program for computing correlations might have been originally written for computing all the correlations between, say, 25 variables; but the program could also be applied to problems involving the intercorrelations of 100 variables or more, the limit being set by the storage capacity of the computer. A program for analysis of variance will not specify that it was designed for, say, a two-way classification problem; it will indicate that it is for an N-way classification problem. The program is a general procedure for solving a class of problems.

New programs can often be readily adapted for new purposes. Indeed, when a program is not available, a first step taken by a programmer is likely to be that of searching for a program that can be readily adapted to the purpose at hand. The doctoral student in a college of education is very unlikely to have new programs prepared or have old programs adapted for his purpose, because programs are available for almost every statistical manipulation he is likely to encounter.

Some Points for Graduate Students Using Computer Services

The enormous speed of computers, in comparison with desk calculators, makes them highly economical for performing statistical analyses. For example, a statistical analysis that might require six weeks of the work of a person operating a desk calculator might well be executed on a computer in less than one minute. High-speed computers will perform as many as 15,000,000 operations in a minute. Under such circumstances, a computer, for which the charge time is $300 per hour, may still perform extraordinarily large amounts of work for less than $25. With such facilities now almost universally available, doctoral students can embark on studies they could not have undertaken at all only a few years ago, simply because of the prohibitive cost of analyzing the data. Also, if computers are available, one can also include in the analysis procedures that have little likelihood of yielding results, yet which are of interest and useful for providing cues for further studies.

The research worker should not be tempted to ask for computer help merely because he would not know how to undertake the analysis himself. He must also be cautious in handing over data to a computer without examining it carefully himself. There is much to be said for a researcher knowing his data well. Sometimes an examination of the data will indicate that a proposed analysis cannot be appropriately undertaken. A simple analysis involving means and standard deviations is often profitably undertaken before the data is sent away for more sophisticated analyses.

A check should be undertaken of the statistical analysis that is returned from the computer because, although computers virtually never make mistakes, programmers sometimes do. The author can recall an occasion when a large table of correlations appeared to be providing results that were inconsistent with all expectations. The hand calculation of a few of the correlations indicated that those produced by the computer were incorrect. What had happened was that the program used to arrange them for the printout had an error in it and they had been printed in an incorrect order. In such operations, there is always the possibility of human error. Some kind of independent spot-check is mandatory.

Writing the Report

Even though the author imagines Heaven as a place where one can do research without ever having to write a report, the requirements of this world are that research has to be described in writing. For many research workers, the preparation of the report is a particularly burdensome task. The following points should be kept in mind in understanding this task.

First, the report should be written in a uniform style throughout. Table headings, footnotes, and appendix material should follow a consistent format. Editorial assistance is very helpful in producing such consistency. Many graduate schools recommend manuals to follow in the writing of theses and the student should familiarize himself with the style requirements of his school. He will probably have to set himself a few rules to follow. For example, some use the word *data* as a plural noun as it is in the Latin from which it is derived, but some newer writers prefer to consider *data* as a singular noun. A number of rules to follow in such respects should be noted.

Second, a scientific report must be written in clear and concise terms; there is little place in it for personal animosities, anecdotes, displays of wit, and the like. A report of a very interesting research project was ruined by the overwhelming intrusion of the research scientist's personal whims, his hostilities toward colleagues, stories of personal experiences that had no relevance to the topic, and other inconsequential material. The reader of such a report reacts much like a teacher who has read through a pupil's term paper that would have been outstanding were it not for an inexcusable boner in the last paragraph. His first impulse is to give the student a failing grade, but later, after his emotional reaction has subsided, he may change the grade to a C or even a B. Much the same is likely to be true of a reader of a research report who finds it spoiled by a display of personal prejudice and irrelevant humor. This does not mean that the report has to be written in a dull pedantic style. Enthusiasm can still appear between the lines while the report as a whole is conveying the spirit of adventure. But the report should be a presentation of research, not a presentation of the personality of the author, although the latter inevitably shows through.

Third, the tone of the report should be one of appropriate modesty. The scientist is a humble person who realizes that even the labor of a lifetime is likely to add but a small increment to man's knowledge of his environment. In writing a research report it is easy to let one's enthusiasm lead to an overemphasis of the importance of the findings. The scientist is rarely in a position to evaluate the significance of his findings in the total picture of knowledge. Only through subsequent history can such an evaluation be made.

It is common for a dissertation to be written in at least two forms. The initial form presents the material to an examining committee. The second form is a condensed version that presents the material for publication. The initial version, like any other piece of writing, must be written with the nature of the specific audience in mind. It is to the student's advantage that he know personally those who constitute this audience and be able to write specifically for them. To some extent, he should write with their expectations in mind. If one of them is likely to ask the student to relate his findings to some particular theory, then he should be sure to do this.

In the case of writing for formal publication, the problem is much more difficult. The student would do well to start by reading articles in the journal that is being considered as a place of publication. From this overview, he should arrive at judgments concerning the nature, length, and organization of the articles that the editors favor. Editors, like any other people, have personal preferences, and these must be taken into account because they may be the deciding factors in determining acceptance or rejection of the student's product.

Overall Format of the Report

The research report is a record of what the researcher did. Like all good records of history, it should permit the reader to reconstruct what happened without distortion. The research report typically follows a time sequence, beginning with an account of previous work, followed by a description of the research undertaken, and ending with ideas for future studies. There are many ways of providing a documentary record concerning what happened in a particular study, but the following outline represents a plan of presentation that is commonly found in research literature:

1. *Introduction*
   A. The problem
   B. Previous research
   C. Theoretical implications of previous research
   D. Relation of present research to the theoretical position stated in C
   E. Specific hypotheses to be tested
2. *Procedures*
   A. General procedure adopted in the research

    B. Equipment and other types of instruments used
    C. Directions given to subjects
    D. Selection of subjects and their characteristics
3. *Results*
    A. A summary of the data
    B. Tests of significance
    C. The testing of the hypotheses outlined in 1E
    D. Conclusions
4. *Implications*
    A. Implications of the research in relation to the theoretical position previously taken
    B. Implications for further research
    C. Practical implications (if any)

Introductory Sections of the Report

The introductory sections usually begin with a statement of the problem. In the reporting of most research studies, at least the general nature of the problem to be investigated should be outlined in the first paragraph of the report. The statement may not be in a full and precise form at this stage, because it may first be necessary to introduce the reader to a number of terms and concepts before the problem can be accurately set forth; nevertheless, there should be a statement of the problem, even if only in a general form.

The introduction must also provide an appropriate theoretical orientation for the reader. This may involve a history of the problem and a review of related studies. In some cases, the theoretical framework of the problem may be so familiar to those who are likely to read the article that it may be unnecessary to state it except in general terms. For example, a student working on the problem of reinforced learning would obviously not review reinforcement theory, which has been described fully in so many other sources. On the other hand, if the research is concerned with a theory with which the reader is unlikely to be familiar, it is essential that the theory and its background be outlined in the introductory section. If the theory is the researcher's own, it is desirable that it be fully presented in terms of the procedures described in earlier chapters of this book.

In the preparation and execution of a research, extensive work is often undertaken on the review of previous studies in the area. If the review is done by a senior research worker with broad experience in the field, this may constitute a major contribution in itself. When substantial effort has been devoted to this phase of the undertaking, it is possible that a separate article may ultimately be prepared and published to cover the outcomes of this activity. Such publications may form an immensely valuable contribution to the professional literature.

The review of the literature should lead up to the full and complete statement of the problem. If the introduction gives or implies the statement of a theory, as it should, the problem should be stated as a deduction or consequence of the theory. Earlier in the introduction, the student should have defined all the terms needed for understanding both the theory and the statement of the problem. By the end of the introductory section, the reader should be fully prepared for understanding the explanation in subsequent sections of how the problem was solved.

Description of the Procedure

The vital importance of the section that describes the procedure or method is often not appreciated by the novice in scientific research. The criterion of a well-written description of the procedure or method used is whether it provides sufficient detail for another researcher to reproduce the study. Too often the experimenter writes up his work only to find that insufficient detail is given for another even to begin to reproduce it. In the behavioral sciences, the writer faces real difficulties in deciding what are and what are not the important details to report in describing his procedure. It is clearly impossible to detail all of the conditions related to the undertaking of a study. For example, in describing an experiment is it relevant to report that the experimenter was a woman, or that she was a blonde, or that she was born in Germany? The author knows of one study in which it was relevant that the experimenter was a woman, and the results probably could not be reproduced without a control over that factor. However, he does not know whether any experiment has been reported in which it was relevant that the experimenter was blonde or was born in Germany. In any event, if a factor is important in one study it does not mean that it would necessarily be important in another study. The decision has to be made in each case concerning what is to be reported and what is to be omitted. That this decision must be based largely on judgment reflects our lack of knowledge about behavioral phenomena.

The description of procedures should include a reproduction of verbal directions given to the subjects. If these are lengthy, they can be relegated to an appendix, or a footnote can indicate where a complete set of directions can be obtained. Minor differences in wording may have substantial effects on the outcomes of a study. Unfortunately, matters of intonation and emphasis cannot be accurately described, although these may have substantial effects on the results.

The description of apparatus is likely to be unsatisfactory unless great care is taken. Because it is not usually possible to publish a blueprint, it is necessary to specify the essential details of the apparatus. However, the experimenter sometimes may not know what are the essential details. This statement may need some explanation.

The author was concerned some time ago with the replication of an experiment that involved apparatus. The piece of equipment specified was the Harvard tachistoscope, which is widely used in psychological laboratories and is readily available. The object to be viewed through the tachistoscope was illustrated in the original article, and this was easily reproduced by a draftsman. However, after some work with the equipment, it became evident that a crucial feature of the entire arrangement was the size of the object presented. This had not been specified in the original article, but the results could be reproduced only when the object was a certain size. The original experimenter had been unaware that this was an essential aspect of his experiment and had failed to report it. Unless there is a great deal of replication with variation, the experimenter is likely to be unaware of the essential characteristics of his apparatus.

One advantage of using standard apparatus can be seen when the problem of description arises. It simplifies matters greatly to be able to report that a Hunter Timer or a Brush Model 392 amplifier was used, because this equipment can be duplicated by other experimenters. The use of homegrown type of equipment requires careful description.

Sometimes the research worker calibrates apparatus, in which case it is necessary to describe the method and technique used in calibration. Sometimes the equipment used in calibration is as complicated as the apparatus itself.

A common omission in studies of educational behavior is a failure to indicate just who was included and who was excluded from the study. This is the matter of specifying the sample that was included, or perhaps one should say what universe was sampled in selecting subjects for study. There is the same need for specifying the universe that is sampled when the objects are inanimate as when they are living. The student will realize that unless the researcher knows how his sample is drawn, he will not know to what his results can be generalized.

Reporting the Results and Stating the Conclusions

The results of a scientific study should usually be presented in a table for which there is some explanatory material; but, since many studies in education do not approach ideal standards, this method of reporting cannot always be attained. A distinction should be made between the results of the study and the interpretation of the results. By "results" is usually meant the summarized data and the test that is applied to determine whether they are or are not consistent with the hypothesis they were designed to test. In educational research some test of significance must usually be applied to the data in order to test the hypothesis. It is usual to describe this test in the results section of the report. The results section should also describe any special and unexpected events that occurred during experimentation, as when subjects were unable to complete the schedule because of illness or other causes. The treatment of missing values should also be discussed in the results section.

As far as possible, the table or tables presenting the results of a study should be self-explanatory and should not require extended reading of the text in order to understand them. On the other hand, the material in the text should point out the important aspects of the data and draw attention to the relevance of the results.

Just how much tabular data should be presented is always a matter of judgment. As a general rule, only those statistics that are crucial to the testing of a hypothesis should be presented. Detailed raw data rarely can find a place in a research report, except where they are of such unusual interest that their reproduction is definitely in the interest of science.

A common error in the presentation of results is the division of the results into too many separate tables. Many research reports can be improved by the consolidation of tables into larger units.

Some comment should be made on the problem of what to do with experiments that do not yield anything that can ordinarily be reported as results. Reference is made here not to experiments that yield negative results, which can usually be reported by the procedures discussed, but to experiments that are prevented, by some technical hitch, from being carried through to their proper conclusion. These abortive efforts are not entirely useless in the information they provide. Indeed, if the problems they raise are never discussed in the literature, others will attempt similar experiments and end in similar difficulties. The difficulty of reporting such effort stems from the understandable unwillingness of editors to accept articles about them. The way out of this dilemma is to report the results of abortive experiments in the introductory section of a report of a further experiment that was successful. One may preface a successful experiment with an account of the various avenues and approaches that were explored before it could be undertaken. Such an account can be brief, but it should be sufficient to warn others about the limitations of the alternatives that were explored.

This does not mean, of course, that weaknesses in the approach revealed during the course of the study should not be noted. Sometimes it is necessary and desirable to admit that the main knowledge derived from an experiment is how to design a more conclusive study. A study designed as a crucial and conclusive experiment frequently turns out to be, on further examination, ambiguous in its results because of the various ways in which they can be interpreted.

A common error is made in drawing conclusions from research results. This error is seen in cases where an investigator collects data that reject a hypothesis. Under such circumstances, some investigators are inclined to turn around and seek reasons why the experiment was really not a crucial test of the issue it was designed to settle. The situation indicates either that the investigator had become too attached personally to his own ideas or that the test of their validity was inadequate in the first place. If the latter were the case, the question can be raised as to why the experiment was ever conducted. If the experimenter changed his mind during the research and began to question its utility, then he should have stopped his work and certainly not published his results.

Writing the Implications and Discussion Section

The creative research worker will inevitably speculate on the implications of his study that extend beyond his immediate purposes. He will also want to communicate his thoughts on such matters to a wider public. True, nobody is ever likely to treasure these thoughts as much as their creator; nevertheless, some of these thoughts may be useful to other research workers, and a few may even be real gems. The section of the report dealing with implications can be used appropriately for setting forth these thoughts.

It is important that the section on implications be more than a splurge of personal notions. Whatever ideas are presented must be set forth in a well-organized form. Sometimes it is convenient to organize them around a few areas for which the implications have special importance. For example, in one study of mechanical problem solving, the implications were organized around two topics; namely, the selection of mechanical troubleshooters and the training of troubleshooters. Good organization will develop in the reader of the report a better appreciation of the importance of the writer's ideas than will a poorly organized section.

Brevity in the implications section is also a very desirable characteristic. Most readers have only limited appetite for the speculations of others. A lengthy section may produce boredom and lead to the rejection of even the good ideas that are presented. Even though a discursive style can, at times, be extremely useful for driving home a point, a certain degree of crisp conciseness should be aimed for here, as in other parts of the written report.

The section on implications is also the section in which it is appropriate to give some indication of the future direction of the program of research of which the report represents a part. Perhaps it is a good idea to remind the reader again that if research is to be profitable, it must be programmatic. A research report should end, therefore, not with a note of finality, but with some indications of the unfinished business that should be the next preoccupation of the researcher.

If the report has been introduced with the presentation of a theory that the research is designed to extend or modify, then the final section may well restate the theory in the light of the findings. This process may involve such radical changes in the original formulation that what is virtually a new theory has to be stated. Whenever the research results in the restatement of a theory, it follows that the research report should indicate how changes in the theory should modify current practices.

Use of Diagrams, Tables, and Figures

A common error in the writing of technical reports is the failure to use diagrams effectively. In many reports, the reader has to wade through ten or more pages describing a complicated piece of apparatus when a simple diagram and a page of description would have sufficed. Some readers are very likely unable to translate verbal descriptions into visualizations of the equipment described. The medium used for communicating should be appropriate to the material to be communicated.

If diagrams of apparatus are given, and they are necessary if any apparatus has been used in the study, it is most desirable that they be prepared by an artist. This is not necessarily as expensive a procedure as it sounds. If an artist is provided with a good sketch, he is likely to produce a finished diagram with considerable speed. Many apparatus drawings can be made for approximately $10 each.

The artist or draftsman will have to be informed of the size to which a diagram will be reduced on publication. Usually, he will draw it on a larger scale and his drawing will be reduced photographically.

Figures and graphs should be presented in such a way that they are self-explanatory. The headings and captions to figures and graphs should provide all the explanation needed. Discussion of what the table or graph demonstrates in relation to the hypotheses can be appropriately included in the text.

Other Points on Organizing the Research Report

When a research report is of such a length that it requires organization into chapters, the reader should be provided with certain devices that will enable him to keep track of the argument and to find his way around in the mass of material. This can be done in several ways.

1. Chapter summaries should be provided. These should help the reader to organize his thoughts by going over the highlights of what he has read and the conclusions and arguments presented. The summary should be strictly that; it should not include new material that happened to occur to the researcher after the report was written. It can be organized into a series of numbered paragraphs, and these should be written in a concise form.

2. A system of paragraph and section headings should be adopted. Indeed, some writers like to begin by preparing a list of headings and then writing the sections and paragraphs in any order, working at any one time on those where they feel that their thinking has reached the point of maturity and where an organized statement can be put down on paper.

Some writers prefer to use a system of major headings and minor headings, in addition to chapter headings, but this can be done only where the material lends itself to this type of organization.

3. A good table of contents is a most desirable guide for the reader. Where paragraph and section headings are used, these should be listed in the table of contents.

4. Brief mention must be made of style of writing in the report. Anyone who tries to advise another on questions of style is treading on uncertain ground. When one sees how often literary critics have been wrong in predicting the acceptability of the works of writers, one realizes how unreasonably prejudiced one may be in one's preferences for style. Also, a person's style is dear to his heart, and suggestions that it be changed or even that it be criticized may arouse ire. Therefore, with a certain sense of self-preservation, at this time only certain common features of technical writing are pointed out that detract from its value in communication.

There is the error of using too difficult a vocabulary level. A writer should not select a word just because it is appropriate and because *he* knows the meaning of it. A necessary condition for the use of the word is that the reader also know its meaning. When unfamiliar words are introduced, the writer must remember that the reader will have to learn them. It is not sufficient that they be formally defined once and then used. This is like asking a person to learn a word by exposing him to it once. What one has to do in writing is to give the reader as much opportunity as is feasible to learn new terms. These terms must be not only defined but also used in contexts where their sense can be inferred from the general meaning of the sentence. The writer who introduces several unfamiliar terms and then fails to provide the reader with a learning experience is likely to find that most of his public does not read beyond the introduction.

A few technical writers have acquired the reputation of writing in a language that is familiar only to themselves. Such writers may have been careful to define their terms, but because these terms have not acquired general usage, readers have never learned them and much of the writing that uses this language is never carefully read. Hence, much of it is lost. For this reason, the reader should realize that new terms should be coined only when it is absolutely necessary to do so.

Although abbreviations are widely used in contemporary technical writing, the opening paragraphs of an article should not overwhelm the reader with a flood of new symbols he must master to comprehend the rest of the article.

Just as unfamiliar words should not be used except where they are essential, so too is it desirable to avoid passing references to obscure theories with which the reader may not be familiar. If such a little-known theory must be mentioned, it is desirable to introduce it by presenting its main features. Such brief descriptions can be appropriately introduced as a part of the text. The nineteenth-century practice of using lengthy and elaborate footnotes to explain any obscure point in the text is one that has become much less frequently used in scientific literature.

Some repetition is necessary in most writing, and the old adage applies that the teacher should start by telling his audience what he is going to say, then he should say it, and finally he should say what he has said. A report, as much as a lecture, is a learning experience for the audience and a teaching experience for the writer. Thus, systematic repetition of the type described by the adage is a desirable feature of written presentation.

A frequent error of style, which is particularly common in the literature of educational research, is writing out in extended detail facts that have been presented in a table in concise form. The following is such an example from a mythical report:

> The table under consideration shows the percentage of correct answers to the arithmetic problems given by various categories of college students. It can be seen that freshmen, sophomores, juniors, and seniors obtained on the average 32, 34, 43, and 44 per cent of the problems correct. When the same group of freshmen is divided according to whether they came from Type A, Type B, or Type C schools, the percentages are 29, 31, and 33. The corresponding figures for the sophomore group are 31, 32, 36; for the junior group, 41, 42, 45; and for the senior group, 43, 44, 45.

Drivel of this kind fulfills only the purpose of confusing the reader, who would have understood the data perfectly well had he been left to examine a well-constructed table. By contrast, a writer does well to point out the highlights of a table, as well as any important features that might otherwise escape notice.

A similar stylistic fault is seen when a writer is attempting to explain a mathematical operation that he has performed on data and does this by giving an extended account of the arithmetic involved instead of providing a brief account of the algebra or of the general purpose of the operation. An example of this kind of error of presentation is the following:

> The totals for each one of the horizontal rows were squared and from the sum of these values was subtracted the square of the grand total divided by 500. The result of this operation was then divided by 6 and the dividend was entered in Table X. A similar arithmetical operation was then performed with the totals of the vertical rows, etc.

The writer should have stated that he performed an analysis of variance according to customary procedures. If he wanted to explain further what he was doing, a brief algebraic explanation would have sufficed.

Final Publication

Most theses and dissertations do not achieve publication beyond that provided by microfilm services or the reproduction of a summary in *Dissertation Abstracts*. This is usually not because the findings do not merit publication, but because the author does not take the necessary steps to incorporate his findings in the professional literature. Most doctoral dissertations from a well-established graduate school contain enough of consequence to provide at least one publication, and some may yield several. They would not have been accepted in partial fulfillment of the requirements for a degree if this had not been so. A dissertation of no consequence occasionally may slip by through some misunderstanding, as when everybody involved had become committed to accepting the dissertation before its worth had been properly evaluated, but such cases are exceptions. Failure to publish the results of a doctoral project is almost always the result of the student's not taking the steps necessary to achieve this goal. Often it is because of lack of motivation: the achievement of the doctoral degree represents the achievement of a personal goal, and publication has little to offer to the student. In addition, he may have already revised his product so many times that any further revision is seen as a most distasteful and repulsive task. However, the doctoral student, although aware of these impediments, should recognize that he has to consider more than personal gain in deciding whether or not to publish. He also must consider that in the preparation of his dissertation he has occupied much professional time on the part of a faculty, and that he can repay this debt to society by making his findings part of the body of professional knowledge represented by published literature. If he does not do this, much of his time and the time of others will be lost, and later students may repeat his work without ever knowing that they are merely repeating what has already been done. Master's degree students have lesser responsibility in this respect.

The most desirable place of publication is the professional journal that specializes in the field in which the student has worked. Many such journals publish without charge except for special materials such as tables and cuts. Less desirable as places of publication are those journals that require the authors to defray the publication cost. The free-publication journals should be able to select the best contributions.

Most journal editors will provide considerable help in shaping an article so that it presents its material in the most effective way. Suggestions by editors concerning the revision of manuscripts should be given careful consideration. In such matters, the editor's experience is likely to provide a sounder basis of action than that of the neophyte in the field. Editors are deeply concerned with making their journals into the best publications they can possibly produce. They can achieve this goal only with the cooperation of authors.

New Methods of Distributing Technical Information

Thirty years ago it was a relatively simple matter to publish long articles that included substantial quantities of tabular material, but today lengthy scientific documents are extremely difficult to publish. This change is partly the result of the large increase in publication costs that has taken place over the period. However, an additional factor is the expansion of research in the behavioral and educational sciences, with the result that most journals receive many times as much material as they ever have space to publish. One partial solution for this problem is for journals to provide additional sections in which material can be published at the expense of the author. A few writers have been attracted by this proposition, and especially by the fact that it results in immediate publication and the usual long delay is eliminated. Nevertheless, the expenses of such early publication are high and beyond the economic circumstances of most young research workers, even if they are fortunate enough to have their article accepted.

Those who have thought about the problem of providing publication facilities, and hence of the problem of distributing scientific information, agree that traditional journal sources will become progressively even less adequate than they are at present. New methods of distributing scientific information must be found, and some are in the process of being developed.

One approach has been to provide locations where materials supplementary to short publications can be deposited and remain available to interested users. Another approach is to publish only abstracts for general distribution, but provide a copy of the complete paper to a limited group of interested specialists who purchase the papers on a subscription basis. Still another approach is the development of government sponsored depositories of information that provide catalogs of the information available and copies of the documents at a nominal charge.

The rapidly developing information sciences are likely to evolve many new and highly original methods of information distribution during the next few years. These will influence the way in which the graduate student goes about reviewing the literature that he finds to be relevant to a problem, the format of the thesis or dissertation, and the way in which the knowledge that he discovers is disseminated.

Summary

1. The plan for the processing of data should be drawn up at the time when the study is designed. Data should be collected in a form convenient to processing. IBM answer sheets and cards can often be used in the data collection process. Various scoring services provide means for scoring complex tests.

2. In the processing of data, missing values often present a problem, and there are various techniques for estimating values for the missing entries. Observations should not be discarded except under very special circumstances, and then only under conditions that will not bias the results.

3. Data can be recorded on cards or on rosters. Great care must be taken to ensure that the data are handled accurately. Data should not be copied until it is absolutely necessary. Some of the data should be processed by hand so that the research worker can become thoroughly familiar with his data.

4. The hypotheses to be tested should be listed before the data are examined. Hypotheses derived from the data cannot be tested validly with ordinary statistical techniques.

5. Much data collected has to be coded before it can be analyzed. The reliability of the coding procedure should be tested. Two coders, working with the same material, should show high agreement in their work.

6. A first step in the statistical analysis of data is to compute a few simple statistics. The research worker should arrange for statistical analyses that he understands. The student should take a brief course on the use of computers before he feeds his data to a computer.

7. Computers have had a history of over a hundred years, although the general purpose digital is a relatively recent invention. The computer has emerged as a manipulator of symbols that functions as an artificial intelligence. Computers all involve certain basic components such as an input system and an output system, storage systems, processing systems, and control systems. Communication with the computer takes place through the use of a language designed for the purpose. Many different computer languages have been developed. Most computer terminals can be operated through the use of a language that is very much like ordinary English. The input at the terminal is through a keyboard. The output may be from a printer or from a cathode ray tube. Information is stored in units of the storage system, each of which has an address.

8. Programs for the computer are written in sophisticated computer languages such as Fortran. Such languages provide very precise directions to the computer since they are never ambiguous. Through the use of the relatively simple language of the computer terminal, programs written in more sophisticated languages are called for from storage.

9. The introductory sections of a research report should always contain a clear and concise statement of the purposes of the research. These sections should also outline the background of the problem and the theory on which it is based. They may sometimes form the basis of an article for journal publication. The section of the report that describes the procedure should be sufficiently detailed to permit reproduction of the study. This is not the easy matter that it may appear to be on the surface.

10. The results section of the report should contain statistical summaries

and reductions of the data rather than the raw data. The conclusions drawn from the study should be clearly related to the hypotheses that were stated in the introductory sections.

11. The final section on implications should discuss the problem, "Where do we go from here?" The writer of such a section should avoid the temptation to throw in many wild ideas. The section should be a well-organized presentation of thoughts and concepts that emerge from the study.

12. Diagrams and tables should as far as possible be self-explanatory. Often they are appropriate substitutes for lengthy discussion.

13. The student should seek to publish at least an abbreviated account of his study so that the results are made available to the profession.

14. Many new methods of information storage and distribution are appearing. These will undoubtedly influence the way in which information contained in theses and dissertations is distributed.

References

Ableson, R. P. *et al.* (Eds.) *Theories of cognitive consistency: A sourcebook.* Chicago: Rand McNally, 1968.

Allport, G. W. *Pattern and growth in personality.* New York: Holt, Rinehart and Winston, 1961.

Allport, G. W. *The use of personal documents in psychological science.* Social Science Research Council Bulletin No. 49. New York: Social Science Research Council, 1942.

American Association of School Administrators. *Administrative problems in search of researchers.* Washington, D.C.: American Association of School Administrators, 1966.

American Psychological Association. *Technical recommendations for psychological tests and diagnostic techniques.* Washington, D.C.: American Psychological Association, 1954, revised 1966.

American Psychological Association. *Standards for educational and psychological tests.* Washington, D.C.: American Psychological Association, 1974.

American Psychological Association. Instrumentation in psychology. *American Psychologist,* 1975, *30,* 191–468.

Ammons, H., and Iron, A. L. A note on the Ballard reminiscence phenomenon. *Journal of Experimental Psychology,* 1954, *47,* 184–186.

Aronfreed, J. *Conduct and conscience: The socialization of internal control.* New York: Academic Press, 1968.

Aydelotte, W. O., Bogue, A. G., and Fogel, R. W. *The dimensions of quantitative research in history.* Princeton, N.J.: Princeton University Press, 1972.

Babbie, E. R. *Survey research methods.* Belmont, Calif.: Wadsworth, 1973.

Babbie, E. R. *The practice of social research.* Belmont, Calif.: Wadsworth, 1975.

Backstrom, C. H., and Hursh, G. D. *Survey research.* Evanston, Ill.: Northwestern University Press, 1963.

Ballard, P. B. Oblivescence and reminiscence. *British Journal of Educational Psychology Monograph Supplement,* 1913, *1,* No. 2.

Barber, T. X. Pitfalls in research: Nine investigator and experimenter effects. In R. M. W. Travers (Ed.) *Second Handbook of Research on Teaching.* Chicago: Rand McNally, 1973. Pp. 382–404.

Barzun, J., and Graff, H. F. *Modern Researcher.* New York: Harcourt Brace, 1970.

Bellack, A. A. *The language of the classroom.* New York: Columbia University, Teachers College Press, 1966.

Beller, E. K. Research on organized programs of early education. In R. M. W. Travers (Ed.) *Second Handbook of Research on Teaching.* Chicago: Rand McNally, 1973.

Benjamin, H. R. W. *Sabre tooth curriculum.* New York: McGraw-Hill, 1939.

Bidwell, C. E. The social psychology of teaching. In R. M. W. Travers (Ed.) *Second Handbook of Research on Teaching.* Chicago: Rand McNally, 1973.

Billington, R. A. (Compiler and introducer.) *Allan Nevins on history.* New York: Scribner, 1975.

Bloom, B. S. (Ed.) Taxonomy of educational objectives. Handbook 1, *Cognitive Domain.* New York: David McKay, 1956.

Bloom, B. S., Hastings, J. T., and Madaus, G. F. *Handbook on affirmative and summative evaluation.* New York: McGraw-Hill, 1971.

Boles, H. W., and Davenport, J. A. *Introduction to educational leadership.* New York: Harper & Row, 1975.

Boring, E. G. The nature and history of experimental control. *American Journal of Psychology,* 1954, *68,* 573–589.

Bower, T. G. R. *Development in infancy.* San Francisco: Freeman, 1974.

Bronfenbrenner, U. *Two worlds of childhood, U.S. and U.S.S.R.* New York: Simon and Schuster, 1970.

Brookover, W. B., and Erickson, E. L. *Sociology of education.* Homewood, Ill.: Dorsey Press, 1975.

Broudy, H. S. *A critique of performance based teacher education.* Washington, D.C.: American Association of Colleges of Teacher Education (PBTE Series No. 4), 1972.

Brunswick, E. *Systematic and representative design of psychological experiments.* Berkeley, Calif.: University of California Syllabus Series, No. 304, 1947.

Buros, O. *Mental measurement yearbooks.* 1st 1938, 2nd 1941, 3rd 1949, 4th 1953, 5th 1959, 6th 1965, 7th 1972 (2 vols.) Highland Park, N.J.: Gryphon Press, 1938–1972.

Cantril, H. *Gauging public opinion.* Princeton, N.J.: Princeton University Press, 1947.

Carroll, J. B., and Sapon, S. M. *Modern language aptitude test.* New York: Psychological Corporation, 1959.

CEDaR. *Catalog of selected educational development and research programs, projects, and products.* Washington, D.C.: Council for Educational Development and Research, 1974.

Chapanis, A. Men, machines, and models. *American Psychologist,* 1961, *16,* 113–131.

Coats, W. D. *Investigation and simulation of the relationship among selected classroom variables.* Cooperative Research Project No. 6–8330, U.S. Office of Education, 1966.

Coleman, J. S. et al. Equality of educational opportunity. Washington, D.C.: U.S. Office of Education, Department of Health, Education, and Welfare, 1966.

Coleman, J. S. *An evaluation of educational opportunity.* Santa Monica, Calif.: Rand Corporation, 1968.

Converse, J. M., and Schuman, H. *Conversations at random: Survey research as interviewers see it.* New York: Wiley, 1974.

Cook, H., and Stingle, S. Cooperative behavior in children. *Psychological Bulletin,* 1974, *81,* 918–933.

Cronbach, L. J. The coefficient alpha and the internal structure of tests. *Psychometrika,* 1951, *16,* 297–334.

Dale, E. Audiovisual methods in teaching. New York: Dryden, 1946.

Dale, E., and Eichholz, G. *Children's knowledge of words.* Columbus, Ohio: Bureau of Educational Research, Ohio State University, 1960.

Daniels, R. V. *Studying history: How and why.* Englewood Cliffs, N.J.: Prentice-Hall, 1972.

Della Piana, G. M. Reading research. In R. M. W. Travers (Ed.) *Second Handbook of Research on Teaching.* Chicago: Rand McNally, 1973. Pp. 883–925.

Dewey, J. *How we think.* Boston: Heath, 1910.

Domas, S. J., and Tiedeman, D. V. Teacher competance: An annotated bibliography. *Journal of Experimental Education,* 1950, *19,* 101–218.

Downing, J. A. Initial teaching alphabet. In *Encyclopedia of Education,* vol. 5, pp. 89–95. New York: Macmillan, 1971.

Eccles, J. C. *The understanding of the brain.* New York: McGraw-Hill, 1973.

Edwards, A. L. Techniques of attitude scale construction. New York: Appleton-Century-Crofts, 1957.

Edwards, A. L. *Edwards personal preference schedule.* New York: Psychological Corporation, 1953.

Edwards, A. L. *The measurement of personality traits by scales and inventories.* New York: Holt, Rinehart and Winston, 1970.

Edwards, W., Guttentag, M., and Snapper, K. *A decision-theoretic approach to evaluation research.* In E. L. Struening and M. Guttentag (Eds.) *Handbook of Evaluation Research.* Beverly Hills, Calif: Sage Publications, 1972.

Eisner, E. *Educating artistic vision.* New York: Macmillan, 1972.

Ennis, R. H. Children's ability to handle Piaget's propositional logic: A conceptual critique. *Review of Educational Research,* 1975, *45,* 1–41.

Fantz, R. L. Pattern vision in young infants. *Psychological Record,* 1958, *8,* 43–47.

Flanagan, J. C. *An empirical study to aid in formulating educational goals.* Palo Alto, Calif.: American Institutes for Research, 1976.

Freides, D. Human information processing and sensory modality: Cross modal functions, information complexity, memory and deficit. *Psychological Bulletin,* 1974, *81,* 284–310.

Fuller, F. F., and Manning, B. A. Self-confrontation reviewed: A conceptualization for video playback in teacher education. *Review of Educational Research,* 1973, *43,* 469–528.

Gadlin, H., and Ingle, G. Through the one-way mirror. The limits of experimental reflection. *American Psychologist,* 1975, *30,* 1003–1010.

Gagné, R. M. *The conditions of learning.* New York: Holt, Rinehart and Winston, 1st ed. 1965, 2nd ed. 1970.

Gallup, G. H. Sixth annual Gallup poll of public attitudes towards education. *Phi Delta Kappan,* 1974, *56,* 20–32.

Gibson, E. J. *Principles of perceptual development and learning.* New York: Appleton-Century-Crofts, 1969.

Gibson, E. J., and Levin, H. The psychology of reading. Cambridge, Mass.: MIT Press, 1975.

Gilbert, L. C. Speed of processing visual stimuli and its relation to reading. *Journal of Educational Psychology,* 1959, *55,* 8–14.

Glass, G. V. Primary, secondary, and meta-analysis of research. *Educational*

Researcher, 1976, *5,* No. 10, 3–8.

Gordon, I. *Child learning through child play: Learning activities for two- and three-year-olds.* Haddenfield, N.J.: Griffin, 1972.

Gordon, I. J. An early intervention program: A longitudinal look. Gainesville, Fla.: University of Florida, Institute for Development of Human Resources, 1973.

Gordon, I. J. *The infant experience.* Columbus, Ohio: Merrill, 1975.

Gottschalk, L. *Understanding history: A primer of method.* New York: Alfred Knopf, 1950.

Gottschalk, L., Kluckhohn, C., and Angell, R. The use of personal documents in history, anthropology, and sociology. *Social Science Research Council Bulletin* No. 53. New York: Social Science Research Council, 1945.

Green, P. E. Applied and multidimensional scaling: A comparison of approaches and algorithms, New York: Holt, Rinehart and Winston, 1972.

Guilford, J. P. *Psychometric methods.* New York: McGraw-Hill, 1954.

Guilford, J. P. *The nature of human intellect.* New York: McGraw-Hill, 1967.

Haley, R. I. Attitude research in transition. New York: American Marketing Association, 1972.

Halpin, A. W. *Theory and research in administration.* New York: Macmillan, 1966.

Halpin, A. W., and Croft, D. B. *The organization of climate of schools.* Contract No. SAE # 543 (8639). U.S. Office of Education, Department of Health, Education and Welfare, 1962.

Hamilton, P. D. *Competency based teacher education.* SRI Project 2158, Contract Office of Education C—0—72—5016. Washington, D.C.: Office of Planning, Budgeting, and Evaluation, U.S. Office of Education, 1972.

Hartshorne, H., and May, M. A. *Studies in the nature of character. Vol.* 1, *Studies in deceit; Vol.* 2, *Studies in service and control.* New York: Shuttleworth, 1928 and 1929.

Hauck, M. and Steinkamp, S. *Survey reliability and interviewer competence.* Urbana, Ill.: University of Illinois Press, 1964.

Hazlett, J. The National Assessment Program: A study in misunderstanding and suspicion. *Society of Professors of Education Newsletter,* 1976, 12–17.

Heckhausen, H. *The anatomy of achievement motivation.* New York: Academic Press, 1967.

Hemphill, T. K., Griffiths, D. E., and Frederickson, N. *Administrative performance and personality.* New York: Teachers College Bureau of Publications, 1962.

Hencley, S. P., and Yates, J. R. (Eds.) *Futurism in education.* Berkeley, Calif.: McCutchan, 1974.

Hogben, L. *Mathematics for the million.* London, England: Allen & Unwin, 1936.

Holt, R. R. Clinical and statistical measurement and prediction. *Catalog of Selected Documents in Psychology,* 1975, *5,* 178–179.

Hull, C. L. *Principles of behavior.* New York: Appleton-Century-Crofts, 1943.

Husén, T. *The learning society.* London, England: Methuen, 1974.

Illich, I. D. *Deschooling society.* New York: Harper & Row, 1970.

Insko, C. A. *Theories of attitude change.* New York: Appleton-Century-Crofts, 1973.

Jensen, A. R. *Educability and group differences.* New York: Harper & Row, 1973.

Johnson, A. *The historian and historical evidence.* Port Washington, N.Y.: Kennikat Press, 1965.

Johnson, D. W., and Johnson, R. T. *Learning together and alone.* Englewood Cliffs, N.J.: Prentice-Hall, 1976.

Jones, B. and Alexander, R. Developmental trends in auditory-visual cross modal matching of spatio-temporal patterns. *Developmental Psychology,* 1974, *10,* 354–356.

Kay, W. *Moral education.* London, England: Linnet Books, 1975.

Kennedy, J. M. *A psychology of picture perception.* New York: Jossey-Bass, 1974.

Kohlberg, L. *The development of modes of moral thinking and choice in years ten to sixteen.* Unpublished doctoral dissertation. University of Chicago, 1958.

Kohlberg, L. The cognitive developmental approach to moral education. *Phi Delta Kappan,* 1975, *56, 670–677.*

Kohlberg, L., and Turiel, E. Moral development and moral education. In G. Lesser (Ed.) *Psychology and educational practice.* Chicago: Scott Foresman, 1971. Pp. 410–465.

Kruglanski, A. W. On the paradigmatic objections to experimental psychology. *American Psychologist,* 1976, *31,* 655–663.

Kuhn, S. The structure of scientific revolutions. 2nd ed. Chicago: University of Chicago Press, 1970.

Learned, W. S., and Wood, B. D. *The student and his knowledge.* New York: Carnegie Foundation for the Advancement of Teaching, 1938.

Lemon, N. *Attitudes and their measurement.* New York: Wiley, 1974.

Light, R. J. Issues in the analysis of qualitative data. In R. M. W. Travers (Ed.) *Second Handbook of Research on Teaching.* Chicago, Ill.: Rand McNally, 1973. Pp. 318–381.

Lindquist, E. F. *Design and analysis of experiments in psychology and education.* Boston: Houghton Mifflin, 1953.

London, I. D. Research on sensory interaction in the Soviet Union. *Psychological Bulletin,* 1954, *51,* 531–568.

Lorge, I., and Thorndike, E. L. The teachers word book of 30,000 words. New York: Teachers College, Columbia University, 1944.

Loveless, N. E., Brebner, J., and Hamilton, P. Bisensory presentation of information. *Psychological Bulletin,* 1970, *73,* 161–199.

Makarenko, A. S. *The road to life.* 2 vols. Moscow, Russia: Progress Publishers, 1951.

Marston, D. *A guide to writing history.* Cincinnati, Ohio: Writers Digest, 1976.

McClelland, D. C., Atkinson, J. W., Clark, R. A., and Lowell, E. L. *The achievement motive.* New York: Appleton-Century-Crofts, 1953.

McClelland, D. C. *The achieving society.* Princeton, N.J.: Van Nostrand, 1961.

McClelland, D. C. *Power: An inner experience.* New York: Irvington, 1975.

McKennel, A. C., and Bynner, J. M. Self image and smoking behavior among school boys. *British Journal of Educational Psychology,* 1969, *39,* 27–39.

Meehl, P. E. *Clinical versus statistical prediction: A theoretical analysis and a review of evidence.* Minneapolis: University of Minnesota Press, 1954.

Meehl, P. E., and Rosen, A. Antecedent probability and efficiency of psychometric signs, patterns, or cutting scores. *Psychological Bulletin,* 1955, *52,* 194–216.

Morsh, J. E. *Systematic observation of instructor behavior.* San Antonio, Texas: Air Force Personnel and Training Research Center, Lackland Air Force Base, 1955.

Moser, C. A., and Kalton, G. *Survey methods in social investigations,* 2nd ed. New York: Basic Books, 1972.

Murray, H. A. *Explorations in personality.* Oxford, England: Oxford University Press, 1938.

National Education Association. *National professional accrediting agencies: How they function.* Washington, D.C.: National Education Association, 1975.

National Study of Secondary School Evaluation. *Evaluative criteria.* Washington D.C.: National Study of Secondary School Evaluation, 1970.

Nevins, A. *The gateway to history.* Chicago: Quadrangle Books, 1963.

Nunnally, J. C. The study of change in evaluation research: Principles concerning measurement, experimental design, and analysis. In E. L. Struening and M. Guttentag (Eds.) *Handbook of Evaluation Research.* Beverly Hills, Calif.: Sage Publications, 1972.

Nuttin, J. M. *The illusion of attitude change.* New York: Academic Press, 1975.

Office of Economic Opportunity. *An experiment in performance contracting: Summary of preliminary results.* Washington, D.C.: Office of Economic Opportunity, 1972a.

Office of Economic Opportunity. *A demonstration of incentives in education.* OEO Pamphlet 3400–7. Washington, D.C.: Office of Economic Opportunity, 1972b.

Osgood, C. E., Suci, G. J., and Tannenbaum, P. H. *The measurement of meaning.* Urbana, Ill.: University of Illinois Press, 1957.

Parten, M. B. *Surveys, polls, and samples.* New York: Harper, 1950.

Peddiwell, J. A. Sabre-tooth curriculum. New York: McGraw-Hill, 1939.

Peters, R. S. A reply to Kohlberg. *Phi Delta Kappan,* 1975, *56,* 678.

Piaget, J. *The moral judgment of the child.* Glencoe, Ill.: Free Press, 1932.

Piaget, J. *Origins of intelligence.* New York: Freeman, 1969.

Piaget, J. (tr. Arnold Rosin.) *Psychology and epistemology.* New York: Viking Press, 1972.

Popham, W. J. (Ed.) *Evaluation in education.* Berkeley, Calif.: McCutchan, 1974.

Robb, F. C. Accreditation—schools. *Encyclopedia of Education,* vol. 1. Pp. 49–54. New York: Crowell-Collier, 1971.

Rokeach, M. *The nature of human values.* New York: Free Press, 1973.

Rosenshine, B. *Interpretive study of teaching behavior related to student achievement.* Final Report, U.S. Office of Education Project No. 9–B–010. Philadelphia: Temple University, 1970.

Rosenshine, B., and Furst, N. The use of direct observation to study teaching. In R. M. W. Travers (Ed.) *Second Handbook of Research on Teaching.* Chicago: Rand McNally, 1973. Pp. 122–183.

Rosenthal, R., and Jacobson, L. *Pygmalion in the classroom: Teacher expectation and pupils' intellectual development.* New York: Holt, Rinehart and Winston, 1968.

Rosenthal, R., and Rosnow, R. L. *The volunteer subject.* New York: Wiley, 1975.

Sawyer, J. Measurement and prediction, clinical and statistical. *Psychological Bulletin,* 1966, *66,* 178–200.

Schalock, H. D., Kersh, B. Y., and Garrison, J. H. From commitment to practice. The Oregon College of Education elementary teacher education program. *Performance Based Teacher Education Series No. 20.* Washington, D.C.: American Association of Colleges of Teacher Education, 1976.

Seay, M. F., and Meece, L. E. *The Sloan experiment in Kentucky.* Lexington, Ky.: University of Kentucky Bureau of School Services, 1944.

Shackle, G. L. S. *Decision, order, and time, in human affairs.* Cambridge, England: Cambridge University Press, 1961.

Shepard, R. N., Romney, A. K., and Nerlove, S. B. *Multidimensional scaling: Theory and applications in the behavioral sciences.* Vols. 1 & 2. New York: Seminar Press, 1972.

Silvey, J. *Deciphering data: The analysis of social surveys.* London, England: Longman, 1975.

Simon, A., and Boyer, E. G. *Mirrors of behavior III: An anthology of observation instruments.* Wyncote, Penna.: Communications Center, 1974.

Skinner, B. F. *Behavior of organisms.* New York: Appleton-Century-Crofts, 1938.

Skinner, B. F. A case history in scientific method. *American Psychologist,* 1956, *11,* 221–233.

Skinner, B. F. *Verbal behavior.* New York: Appleton-Century-Crofts, 1958.

Skinner, B. F. A case history in scientific method. In S. Koch (Ed.) *Psychology: A study of a science.* Vol. 2. New York: McGraw-Hill, 1959. Pp. 359–379.

Smith, B. O. et al. *A study of the logic of teaching.* Urbana, Ill.: University of Illinois Press, 1962.

Smith, B. O. et al. A study of the strategies of teaching. Urbana, Ill.: University of Illinois Press, 1967.

Smith, E. R., Tyler, R. W., and the Evaluation Staff. *Appraising and recording student progress.* New York: Harper, 1942.

Smith, N. B. *American reading instruction.* (Reprint of 1934 edition.) Newark, Del.: International Reading Association, 1965.

Smith, P. B. Controlled studies of the outcome of sensitivity training. *Psychological Bulletin,* 1975, *82,* 597–622.

Snow, R. E. Theory construction for research on teaching. In R. M. W. Travers (Ed.) *Second Handbook of Research on Teaching.* Chicago: Rand McNally, 1973.

Special Communication. Many are unable to comprehend instructions in grocery store packages. *New York Times,* 1976, 17 March, p. 49.

Stanley, J. C. Analysis of variance principles applied to the grading of essay tests. *Journal of Experimental Education,* 1962, *30,* 279–283.

Stogdill, R. M. (Ed.) *The process of model building.* New York: W. W. Norton, 1970.

Stogdill, R. M. *Handbook of leadership: A survey of theory and research.* New York: Free Press, 1974.

Stone, L. J., Smith, H. T., and Murphy, L. B. *The competent infant.* New York: Basic Books, 1973.

Struening, E. L., and Guttentag, M. *Handbook of evaluation research.* Beverly Hills, Calif.: Sage Publications, 1975.

Stuffelbeam, D. L. *The CIPP model of evaluation.* Kalamazoo, Mich.: Evaluation Center, College of Education, Western Michigan University, 1975.

Sudman, S., and Bradburn, N. M. *Applied sampling.* New York: Academic Press, 1976.

Suppes, P. C. *Computer assisted instruction: Stanford's 1965–66 arithmetic program.* New York: Academic Press, 1968.

Survey Research Center. *Interviewer's manual.* Ann Arbor, Mich.: Institute of Social Research, University of Michigan, 1969.

Terman, L. M. *The gifted child.* In C. Murchison (Ed.) *A Handbook of Child Psychology.* Worcester, Mass.: Clark University Press, 1931. Pp. 568–584.

Thorndike, E. L. *An introduction to the theory of mental and social measurement.* New York: Science Press, 1904.

Thorndike, E. L. *The Thorndike-Century Junior Dictionary.* Chicago: Scott Foresman, 1935.

Tolman, E. C. *Purposive behavior in men and animals.* New York: Appleton-Century-Crofts, 1932.

Torgerson, W. S. *Theory and methods of scaling.* New York: Wiley, 1958.

Travers, R. M. W. *Studies related to the design of audiovisual teaching materials.* Final Report, U.S. Department of Health, Education, and Welfare, Office of Education Contract No. 3–20–003, 1966.

Travers, R. M. W. *A study of the advantages and disadvantages of using simplified visual presentations in instructional materials.* Final Report of Grant No. OEG–1–7–070144–5235. U.S. Office of Education, Department of Health, Education, and Welfare, 1969.

Travers, R. M. W. *Essentials of learning.* 4th ed. New York: Macmillan, 1977.

Travers, R. M. W., and Alvarado, V. The design of pictures for teaching children in elementary school. *Audiovisual Communications Review,* 1970, *18,* 47–63.

Travers, R. M. W., and Dillon, J. *The making of a teacher.* New York: Macmillan, 1975.

Trent, J. W., and Cohen, A. M. Research on teaching in higher education. In R. M. W. Travers (Ed.) *Second Handbook of Research on Teaching.* Chicago: Rand McNally, 1973. Pp. 997–1071.

Triandis, H. C. Attitudes and attitude change. New York: Wiley, 1971.

Turiel, E. Stage transition in moral development. In R. M. W. Travers (Ed.)

Second Handbook of Research on Teaching. Chicago: Rand McNally, 1973. Pp. 689–731.

Tyler, R. W. *Constructing achievement tests.* Columbus, Ohio: Bureau of Educational Research, Ohio State University, 1934.

Tyler, R. W. *Basic principles of curriculum and instruction.* Chicago: University of Chicago Press, 1950.

Warwick, D. P., and Lininger, C. A. *The sample survey: Theory and practice.* New York: McGraw-Hill, 1975.

Watson, J. B. *Behaviorism.* New York: The People's Institute Publishing Company, 1924.

Weatherman, R., and Swenson, K. Delphi technique. In S. P. Hencley and J. R. Yates (Eds.) *Futurism in Education.* Berkeley, Calif.: McCutchan, 1974. Pp. 97–114.

Webb, E. J., Campbell, D. T., Schwartz, R. D., and Sechrest, L. *Unobtrusive measures: Nonreactive research in the social sciences.* Chicago: Rand McNally, 1966.

Woody, T. *Education*—1. *History of education. Encyclopedia Americana,* 1964.

Yarbus, A. L. *Eye movements and vision.* New York: Plenum Press, 1967.

Zook, G. F., and Haggerty, M. E. *Principles of accrediting higher institutions.* Chicago: University of Chicago Press, 1935.

Zook, G. F., and Haggerty, M. E. *The evaluation of higher institutions.* Chicago: University of Chicago Press, 1936.

Index of Names

Index of Subjects